EVANGELICALS

EVANGELICALS

Who They Have Been, Are Now, and Could Be

Mark A. Noll
David W. Bebbington
George M. Marsden

WILLIAM B. EERDMANS PUBLISHING COMPANY
GRAND RAPIDS, MICHIGAN

Wm. B. Eerdmans Publishing Co.
4035 Park East Court SE, Grand Rapids, Michigan 49546
www.eerdmans.com

Published 2019
Printed in the United States of America

25 24 23 22 21 20 19   1 2 3 4 5 6 7

ISBN 978-0-8028-7695-9

Library of Congress Cataloging-in-Publication Data

Names: Noll, Mark A., 1946- author. | Bebbington, David, 1949- author. |
  Marsden, George M., 1939- author.
Title: Evangelicals : who they have been, are now, and could be / Mark A.
  Noll, David W. Bebbington, George M. Marsden.
Description: Grand Rapids, Michigan : William B. Eerdmans Publishing
  Company, 2019. | Includes bibliographical references and index. |
  Summary: "This books draws together significant considerations of
  evangelicalism from three of the historians who have contributed a great
  deal to putting the subject on the map, along with selected commentary
  from others who have benefited from, or sometimes questioned, their
  work"— Provided by publisher.
Identifiers: LCCN 2019026125 | ISBN 9780802876959 (paperback)
Subjects: LCSH: Evangelicalism.
Classification: LCC BR1640 .N645 2019 | DDC 270.8/2—dc23
LC record available at https://lccn.loc.gov/2019026125

*To the many historians from many parts of the world
who have made evangelical history, however defined,
such a lively and edifying enterprise*

Contents

Acknowledgments

The editors would like to thank the publishers and periodicals that permitted us to reprint materials concerning the writing of evangelical history, as well as the writers who allowed us to reprint their essays or who wrote new essays on contemporary American controversies. Specific acknowledgment is provided with the individual contributions. We also offer our thanks to David Bratt and other editors at William B. Eerdmans Publishing Company who affirmed the value of such a book.

Because we have long enjoyed the great privilege of working cooperatively with many individuals from many parts of the world, the editors count it a humbling honor to acknowledge how much we have learned from the historians who for more than a generation have provided so much enlightenment for so many readers on so many subjects related to the general history of evangelicalism, however defined. This book is dedicated with deep gratitude to those historians.

INTRODUCTION

One Word but Three Crises

MARK A. NOLL

The word "evangelical" is in trouble—but for different and competing reasons. Toward the end of this book, we address at considerable length the contemporary American controversies posing the greatest difficulties for a coherent, factual, and responsible understanding of "evangelicalism." But before reaching that point, the book charts efforts by historians who since the 1960s have been writing general histories of Protestant evangelical Christianity—first for the United States and Great Britain, but then for Christian movements throughout the world as a whole. These two matters—contemporary controversy and the development of a historiographical tradition—stand in tight, intimate, but also perplexing relationship to each other.

Before it turns to contested questions of the present day, the book reprints some of the most important book chapters and journal articles that defined, clarified, or contested the historical development of the evangelical movement. From that work two conclusions are evident. First, when considered conceptually as a particular type of Protestant Christianity with a number of interconnected and recurring characteristics, "evangelicalism" has constituted a clearly defined historical reality. But, second, if consideration shifts to movements, networks, individuals, groups, activities, theological convictions, denominations, and memorable publications that might reasonably be included in histories of evangelicalism, there has been a great deal more complexity and not a little ambiguity. From these two conclusions it is possible to draw one more: because landmark statements concerning the history of evangelicalism reveal a remarkable combination of clarity and complexity, they provide an excellent vantage point for assessing confusion surrounding that term in the present day. In short, for understanding the *present crisis* of evangelicalism,

1

there may be no better path than to reconsider how *modern histories* of evangelicalism came to be written.

The Obvious

The first trouble for contemporary evangelicalism is the most obvious. Ever since Donald Trump emerged as a major player in American political life, pollsters and pundits have fixated on the overwhelming support he has received from a constituency often called simply "evangelicals"—or, if there is a pause for breath, "white evangelicals." Various polls tracking the presidential election of 2016 announced that Trump won 81 percent of "the evangelical vote"; subsequent polls show that this same constituency has approved President Trump's deeds in office with just about that same stratospheric majority.

Spokesmen and spokeswomen for the 81 percent have called Donald Trump "Cyrus," the ancient Persian king who, though not of the Hebrew chosen people himself, was nevertheless enlisted by Yahweh to protect Israel and its interests. Their voices have been magnified many times over, not least because of Trump's frequent appearances on the Trinity Broadcast Network, the nation's largest Christian television network.[1]

Yet huzzahs of affirmation from evangelicals who back Trump have been matched in fervor, though not in quantity, by cries of anguish from a different corner of the evangelical world. From that corner, some who once were entirely content to be known as evangelicals have published a wave of books, articles, and blog posts with titles like *Still Evangelical? Insiders Reconsider Political, Social, and Theological Meaning*;[2] "Why I Can No Longer Call Myself an Evangelical Republican";[3] "The Unlikely Crackup of Evangelicalism";[4]

1. Ruth Graham, "Church of the Donald," *Politico*, May/June 2018, https://www .politico.com/magazine/story/2018/04/22/trump-christian-evangelical-conservatives -television-tbn-cbn-218008.

2. Mark Labberton, ed., *Still Evangelical? Insiders Reconsider Political, Social, and Theological Meaning* (Downers Grove, IL: InterVarsity Press, 2018).

3. Peter Wehner, "Why I Can No Longer Call Myself an Evangelical Republican," *New York Times*, December 9, 2017, https://www.nytimes.com/2017/12/09/opinion /sunday/wehner-evangelical-republicans.html.

4. Richard Mouw, "The Unlikely Crackup of Evangelicalism," *Christianity Today*, January 3, 2018, https://www.christianitytoday.com/ct/2018/january-web-only/unlikely -crack-up-of-evangelicalism.html.

and "Polls Show Evangelicals Support Trump: But the Term 'Evangelical' Has Become Meaningless."[5]

In this recent flurry, some noteworthy authorities have reinforced impressions left by the popular media that Donald Trump's nationalist and populist backers are simply writing the last chapter of the American evangelical story in its entirety. A major recent book by Pulitzer Prize–winning author Frances Fitzgerald presents such a narrative in extensively researched detail. Entitled *The Evangelicals: The Struggle to Shape America*, it implies that the book's plot line—with three-fourths of its over six hundred pages devoted to the white Christian Right since World War II—captures the essence of evangelicalism.[6]

Yet not entirely lost in the superheated ideological cauldron of American political punditry has been another salient fact. That important fact raises the types of questions this book wants to address. This is the fact: the very high level of evangelical support for Donald Trump is like nothing seen in America's recent religious-political history—except for the even higher percentage that since the 1960s Democrats have received from Bible-believing, born-again African Americans.

To mention this other exceedingly strong religious-political connection immediately spotlights why the word "evangelical" is in trouble. For much of postwar American polling, George Gallup identified "evangelicals" as those who said they were born again or who had undergone a born-again experience. Yet if significant numbers of African Americans have been born again and have been voting for Democrats—in even higher proportions and over a longer period of time than white evangelicals have voted for Republicans— how can anyone speak responsibly about "evangelical support" for Donald Trump without serious qualifications?

The supposedly tight bond between evangelicalism and Donald Trump becomes even more mysterious if analysts take account of work done by histo-

5. Thomas S. Kidd, "Polls Show Evangelicals Support Trump: But the Term 'Evangelical' Has Become Meaningless," *Washington Post*, July 22, 2016, https://www .washingtonpost.com/news/acts-of-faith/wp/2016/07/22/polls-show-evangelicals -support-trump-but-the-term-evangelical-has-become-meaningless/?noredirect =on&utm_term=.ef9420fce2d1.

6. Frances Fitzgerald, *The Evangelicals: The Struggle to Shape America* (New York: Simon & Schuster, 2017). A perceptive review of this book that accepts Fitzgerald's basic narrative was provided by Garry Wills, "Where Evangelicals Came From," *New York Review*, April 20, 2017, 26–29. A review that challenged Fitzgerald by documenting the political pluralism of evangelical history was offered by Randall Balmer, *Christian Century*, April 12, 2017, 37–38.

rians committed to careful examination of developments over time. Indicating how those efforts should influence contemporary punditry also makes a bridge for introducing the contents of this book.

We begin below with two of the pathbreaking historical statements that have been most widely cited as conceptual frameworks for recording the history of modern evangelicalism. Attempts at defining evangelicalism as a subject of historical analysis in its own right and then writing specifically "evangelical histories" gradually increased after World War II. As several of the contributions below detail, the "neo-evangelical" movement in the postwar United States coincided with, even as it drew considerable inspiration from, self-conscious evangelical renewal in Britain that reached across the long-standing divide between evangelicals in the Church of England and Dissenting Protestants holding evangelical convictions. Although one of the results on both sides of the Atlantic was an intensification of scholarship, historians in those constituencies trailed biblical scholars and theologians in mobilizing for serious intellectual effort. Once those efforts began, however, they expanded rapidly. The Historians' Study Group of Inter-Varsity Fellowship in Britain and the American Conference on Faith and History, both founded in the 1960s, drew together individuals eager to promote deeper historical insight while still maintaining firm Christian convictions. The number of important historical works attempting to communicate a generally evangelical story also grew steadily. Most observers award pride of place to Timothy L. Smith's *Revivalism and Social Reform: American Protestantism on the Eve of the Civil War*, published by Abingdon in 1957, and George Marsden's *Fundamentalism and American Culture: The Shaping of Twentieth-Century Evangelicalism*, published in 1980 by Oxford University Press, but the number of others was also expanding rapidly.[7]

In 1984, when George Marsden described "the evangelical denomination" in the introduction to a book on modern American evangelicalism, and in 1989,

---

7. Others included William G. McLoughlin Jr., *Modern Revivalism: Charles Grandison Finney to Billy Graham* (New York: Ronald, 1959); Haddon Willmer, "Evangelicalism, 1785–1835," Hulsean Prize Essay (Cambridge University, 1962); Richard Allen, *The Social Passion: Religion and Social Reform in Canada* (Toronto: University of Toronto Press, 1971); Bernard L. Ramm, *The Evangelical Heritage* (Waco, TX: Word, 1973); Donald C. Bloesch, *The Evangelical Renaissance* (Grand Rapids: Eerdmans, 1973); David F. Wells and John D. Woodbridge, eds., *The Evangelicals: What They Believe, Who They Are, Where They Are Changing* (Nashville: Abingdon, 1975); Donald W. Dayton, *Discovering an Evangelical Heritage* (New York: Harper & Row, 1976); and Nathan O. Hatch, Mark A. Noll, and John D. Woodbridge, *The Gospel in America: Themes in the Story of America's Evangelicals* (Grand Rapids: Zondervan, 1979).

when David Bebbington brought out *Evangelicalism in Modern Britain*, this earlier momentum led to the publication of definitive conceptual statements.[8] When he published that introduction, Marsden was a history professor at Calvin College; he would later go on to train graduate students at Duke and Notre Dame. When Bebbington published a refined framework for conceptualizing evangelicalism as the first chapter of the substantial history that followed, he was in the early years of what became a distinguished career as teacher and supervisor of doctoral students at the University of Stirling in Scotland.

(It is a pertinent detour to notice a common, though never uniform, difference in transatlantic conventions of capitalization. In Britain, "Evangelicalism" and "Evangelical" have usually been capitalized, in large part because these terms have been used to describe a party in the Church of England, alongside Anglo-Catholic and Broad Church parties, before being used as a transdenominational adjective for all who embraced more general evangelical convictions. In the United States, the terms usually appear as lowercase, in large part because they were first used as general designations for most Protestant denominations before, from the mid-twentieth century, becoming more specifically applied to narrower interdenominational movements. In the United States, the lowercase convention also usually applies to "fundamentalists," "modernists," and "liberals." The second essay by David Bebbington in this book, "The Evangelical Discovery of History," explains in rewarding detail the development of what became a shared historical enterprise differentiated, if only slightly, by a common language!)[9]

The 1984 and 1989 contributions of these two historians rode the crest of a publishing wave, which these works measurably strengthened.[10] Yet their care

---

8. George Marsden, "Introduction: The Evangelical Denomination," in *Evangelicalism in Modern America*, ed. George Marsden (Grand Rapids: Eerdmans, 1984), vii–xix; D. W. Bebbington, *Evangelicalism in Modern Britain: A History from the 1730s to the 1980s* (London: Unwin Hyman, 1989).

9. Other detailed efforts to write the history of evangelical history-writing are provided by Mark Noll, "Timothy L. Smith, George Marsden, David Bebbington, and Anglo-American Evangelicalism," and David Bebbington, "Andrew Walls, Brian Stanley, Dana Robert, Mark Noll, and Global Evangelicalism," in *Making Evangelical History: Faith, Scholarship, and the Evangelical Past*, ed. Andrew Atherstone and David Ceri Jones (Abingdon, UK: Routledge, 2019), 235–56, 257–74.

10. For recent examples of such work produced by students and friends of the editors of this volume, see Darren Dochuk, Thomas S. Kidd, and Kurt W. Peterson, eds., *American Evangelicalism: George Marsden and the State of American Religious History* (Notre Dame: University of Notre Dame Press, 2014); A. R. Cross, P. J. Morden, and I. M. Randall, eds., *Pathways and Patterns in History: Essays on Baptists, Evangelicals,*

in defining "evangelicalism" is also relevant for contemporary questions. Marsden drew a distinction between evangelicalism as a set of self-consciously integrated movements and evangelicalism as a "conceptual unity" that identifies a broader set of groups possessing common traits. For defining the latter, he specified five salient beliefs: "1) the Reformation doctrine of the final authority of Scripture; 2) the real, historical character of God's saving work recorded in Scripture; 3) eternal salvation only through personal trust in Christ; 4) the importance of evangelism and missions; and 5) the importance of a spiritually transformed life."[11]

David Bebbington's characterization, which resembled Marsden's in some but not all particulars, enumerated four distinctive evangelical emphases. These four characteristics were presented as often held in common with other Christians, but as being *stressed* by those who were known as evangelicals. This "quadrilateral" rapidly became, as it were, the industry standard put to use fruitfully by many other writers in many other studies. Bebbington's account of the four characteristics contains much important detail, but they can be summarized succinctly:

- conversion, or "the belief that lives need to be changed";
- the Bible, or "the belief that all spiritual truth is to be found in its pages";
- activism, or the dedication of all believers, especially the laity, to lives of service for God, especially in sharing the Christian message and taking that message far and near; and
- crucicentrism, or the conviction that Christ's death on the cross provided atonement for sin and reconciliation between sinful humanity and a holy God.[12]

So how does Marsden's and Bebbington's careful work of definition from a generation ago relate to current political controversies? In 2015, LifeWay Research, in collaboration with the National Association of Evangelicals, carried out an extensive American survey that operationalized four statements similar to Bebbington's quadrilateral.[13] It was not a surprise, given earlier polls

---

and the Modern World in Honour of David Bebbington (Didcot, UK: Baptist Historical Society, 2015); and Heath W. Carter and Laura Rominger Porter, eds., *Turning Points in the History of American Evangelicalism* (Grand Rapids: Eerdmans, 2017).

11. See below, 23.

12. For full elaboration of those characteristics, see below, 31–55.

13. The four statements to which it sought responses were as follows: "The Bible

trying to identify the evangelical component of the national population, that this survey found 29 percent of Caucasian Americans affirming all four evangelical markers.

Everything else from the survey, however, could be considered a surprise, at least to those mesmerized by "evangelicals for Trump." This 29 percent certainly did include "white evangelicals," many of whom were members of largely white evangelical churches and doubtless voted for Donald Trump. *But* numbered among the 29 percent were also many Protestants from so-called mainline or liberal denominations, more than a few Roman Catholics, and a number of Mormons and others. *And* quite a few in white evangelical denominations did not affirm all the evangelical markers. *And* 44 percent of the nation's African Americans did affirm all four. *And* so did 30 percent of Hispanic Americans. *And* 17 percent of Americans of other ethnicities as well. Needless to say, the evangelicals identified by affirming evangelical beliefs included a large number who did not support Donald Trump.

Here's the point: the careful conceptual definitions that historians have used to write histories of evangelicalism relate only partially to the evangelicalism so casually evoked in much contemporary punditry. What Marsden described in trying to write about evangelicals in modern America and Bebbington described from his research into more than two hundred years of British history did overlap to some degree with that popular usage of "evangelicalism." But not comprehensively, not coherently, and far from completely.

Not So Obvious: The Past

Two other relationships, which are not as obvious as those fueling contemporary political debate, make for different kinds of crises. One concerns academic pushback to the canonical work of George Marsden and David Bebbington. The other concerns the viability of the term "evangelical," with its Anglo-American origins, in a contemporary world where there is now much

---

is the highest authority for what I believe. It is very important for me personally to encourage non-Christians to trust Jesus Christ as their Savior. Jesus Christ's death on the cross is the only sacrifice that could remove the penalty of sin. Only those who trust in Jesus Christ alone as their Savior receive God's free gift of eternal salvation." For the questions and a report of the survey results, see Ed Stetzer, "Defining Evangelicals in Research," *Evangelicals* (National Association of Evangelicals) 3, no. 3 (Winter 2017/18): 12–13.

more evangelical-like Christian religion outside the Atlantic region than in the United States and Great Britain.

A 1991 article by Douglas Sweeney, which is reprinted below, explored an early objection to the way George Marsden had recounted the history of American evangelicalism. To some observers, especially those concentrating on the extensive influence of Wesleyan, Arminian, Holiness, and Pentecostal movements, Marsden had overemphasized the influence of Reformed and Presbyterian traditions in the general evangelical story. Sweeney's discerning parsing of that challenge offered particularly wise words concerning how a historian's own standpoint might affect the shape of the historian's work.

Other similar efforts followed. In 1991 Donald W. Dayton and Robert Johnston edited a book, *The Variety of American Evangelicalism*, in which contributors were asked if enough commonalities linked their particular group (fundamentalists, Pentecostals, Adventists, Holiness advocates, Restorationists [Disciples and Churches of Christ], African Americans, Baptists, pietists, Mennonites, the confessionally Reformed, and Lutherans) to an entity that could legitimately be called "American evangelicalism." They were, in effect, probing George Marsden's 1984 attempt to explain both differences and commonalities within the broader stream of American Protestantism. As an anticipation of later debates among historians, but also later commenters on contemporary American religion, many of the authors equivocated. Editor Johnston defended the notion of evangelicalism as "an extended family," while editor Dayton expressed doubts about the usefulness of the category.[14]

This introduction has already touched upon the most obvious fact supporting Dayton's skepticism, a fact that will be examined several times throughout the book. It has long been obvious that America's black Protestant churches contain a higher percentage of members marked by the four Bebbington characteristics (or affirming Marsden's five salient beliefs) than do white Protestant churches. Yet the American embrace of slavery, followed by culturally enforced segregation, means that whites and blacks who share these religious emphases have shared very little else. An evangelicalism that includes both blacks and whites makes sense from an angle focused on nar-

14. Donald W. Dayton, "Some Doubts about the Usefulness of the Category 'Evangelical,'" 245–51, and Robert K. Johnston, "American Evangelicalism: An Extended Family," 252–72, in *The Variety of American Evangelicalism*, ed. Donald W. Dayton and Robert K. Johnston (Knoxville: University of Tennessee Press; Downers Grove, IL: InterVarsity Press, 1991).

rowly religious characteristics, but far less sense in the actual outworking of American history.

My book chapter reprinted below, "Evangelical Constituencies in North America and the World," explores a development that has gained considerable force only in recent decades but now also complicates the picture. The extensive survey of Canadian and American citizens described in that chapter shows that quite a few Roman Catholics in both countries look an awful lot like evangelicals in their beliefs and practices. Not that long ago, to be an evangelical simply meant to be anti-Catholic. The differences between Roman Catholics and Protestants, especially evangelical Protestants, were as clear-cut as possible. But no longer. Many more surveys than the one I examine now turn up numerous Catholics, though never a majority of that communion, who are marked by the four Bebbington characteristics and who affirm the five Marsden beliefs (apart from reference to the Reformation). As this once unbridgeable chasm is bridged, clarity in defining evangelicalism becomes more complicated.

David Bebbington's fourfold definition has been put to use positively far more than it has been questioned. But questions nevertheless have arisen. For instance, against Bebbington's depiction of British evangelicalism as a new tradition arising in the eighteenth century when Puritan, revivalistic, and Enlightenment trajectories flowed together, some have argued that eighteenth-century developments must be viewed as only the latest chapter in a much longer evangelical history stretching back to the Reformation.[15]

A new guide to general evangelical history, edited by Andrew Atherstone and David Ceri Jones, begins with a wide-ranging chapter by the editors that broadens understanding of both evangelical cohesion and evangelical contention.[16] Among other revealing insights, it shows that while "Evangelicalism" did appear as a general description from the early nineteenth century, that common coinage also showed up much less often than words and categories used to describe clashes among those who might be called evangelicals.

A broader historical challenge has recently come from Linford Fisher of Brown University, in a substantial article contending that "evangelical" has

15. This criticism is made by some of the contributors to Michael A. G. Haykin and Kenneth J. Stewart, eds., *The Advent of Evangelicalism: Exploring Historical Continuities* (Nashville: B&H, 2008), which concludes with Bebbington's "Response," 417–32.

16. Andrew Atherstone and David Ceri Jones, "Evangelicals and Evangelicalisms: Contested Identities," in *The Routledge Research Companion to the History of Evangelicalism*, ed. Andrew Atherstone and David Ceri Jones (Abingdon, UK: Routledge, 2018), 1–21.

often meant less, and sometimes more, than the Bebbington characteriza-tion.[17] It is reprinted below in abridged form. Fisher shows that from the time of the Reformation and for several centuries afterward, "evangelical" usually meant simply "Protestant" or, almost as frequently, "anti-Catholic." During the eighteenth-century revivals George Whitefield, Jonathan Edwards, John Wes-ley, and "awakened" believers in Britain and America spoke much more often of "true" or "real" religion (as opposed to nominal or only formal adherence) than they did of "evangelical" faith.[18] Fisher argues that the word took on its recent connotations only after the Second World War, when former funda-mentalists in the United States sought a less combative, more irenic term to describe their orthodox theology and their desire to reengage with society. In the process some Pentecostals, Lutherans, Mennonites, Christian Reformed, and others who had not been associated with the main body of America's earlier "evangelical Protestants" were now glad to join in using the word to describe themselves. At the same time, other Protestants who had thought of themselves as evangelicals began to avoid the word as designating something too close to fundamentalism.

A different approach to assessing the Bebbington quadrilateral came from symposia convened by the Conference on Faith and History to mark the twenty-fifth anniversary of the publication of *Evangelicals in Modern Britain*; that is also reprinted in this book. The seven contributors to that venture, in-cluding myself, expressed general appreciation for the clarity with which Beb-bington had highlighted an international and transgenerational understanding of evangelicalism. But they also probed the definition for what it might have left open conceptually or historically for further examination. The breadth of that symposium testifies at once to the significance but also the open-ended nature of evangelical history writing in the modern period.

As the documents in the book's first section indicate, uncertainties, chal-lenges, omissions, and controversies have always surrounded the question of who is and who is not an evangelical. Yet these difficulties—as David Bebbing-ton's article "The Evangelical Discovery of History" also shows clearly—have not prevented the emergence of a vigorous tradition of "evangelical history."

17. Linford Fisher, "Evangelicals and Unevangelicals: The Contested History of a Word, 1500–1950," *Religion and American Culture: A Journal of Interpretation* 26 (Summer 2016): 184–226.

18. That usage has recently received noteworthy exposition in a book by D. Bruce Hindmarsh, *The Spirit of Early Evangelicalism: True Religion in a Modern World* (New York: Oxford University Press, 2018).

Attention to this history of history writing becomes potentially relevant as background for current political considerations, especially for underscoring the possibility that contention over the meaning of a word and fruitful exposition of what it designates may exist together.

Not So Obvious: The World

A third complication for "evangelicalism" is the striking, though often neglected, fact that the United States does not equal the world. The changing shape of world Christianity deserves full consideration when thinking about contemporary American debates. The 2001 edition of David Barrett's *World Christian Encyclopedia*, for example, identified 210 million Christian believers as "evangelicals" worldwide. He counted another 510 million as Pentecostal, neo-Pentecostal, and "charismatic," most of whom should also be considered evangelicals. Of those numbers, only 64 million evangelicals lived in Europe and North America, while only 116 million of the Pentecostal-charismatic total lived on those continents. Throughout the world, in other words, an increasingly diverse array of loosely connected movements, churches, voluntary organizations, and educational institutions shares broadly evangelical commitments. Many of them also trace their origin to missionary efforts sponsored by Western evangelicals. But their shape, their chief concerns, their preoccupations, and their goals often lie very far from the politics and preoccupations of the contemporary American media.

The rapid expansion of evangelical-like movements around the world presents a different challenge to any coherent understanding of evangelicalism. Not political or ideological standoffs, but sheer, mind-boggling diversity is the crux. Yet, as several contributions to this book suggest, though the proliferation of such newer spiritual forces makes it more difficult to speak responsibly about a single evangelicalism, it may still be possible. However that question is answered, from a global perspective the clearest conclusion must be that the fate of evangelicalism depends on more than the ebb and flow of parochial American concerns.

The Book

What follows is divided into four parts. First come seven documents reflecting on the meaning of evangelicalism, problems involved in defining that meaning, and debates generated by the definitive accounts of George Marsden and

David Bebbington—but all concerned with the effort to write general histories of evangelicalism. They are presented chronologically according to the order in which they were published. A small amount of repetition is found in these accounts, but even that repetition illustrates important landmarks in the development of evangelical history. Each contribution is introduced briefly, with George Marsden explaining at greater length how his 1984 essay came to be written.

1984. George Marsden, "The Evangelical Denomination."

1989. David Bebbington, "The Nature of Evangelical Religion."

1991. Douglas A. Sweeney, "The Essential Evangelicalism Dialectic: The Historiography of the Early Neo-Evangelical Movement and the Observer-Participant Dilemma."

2001. Mark Noll, "Evangelical Constituencies in North America and the World."

2013. David Bebbington, "The Evangelical Discovery of History."

2015. Charlie Phillips, Kelly Cross Elliott, Amanda Porterfield, Thomas Kidd, Mark Noll, Darren Dochuk, Molly Worthen, and David Bebbington, "Roundtable: Re-examining David Bebbington's 'Quadrilateral Thesis.'"

2016. Linford D. Fisher, "Evangelicals and Unevangelicals: The Contested History of a Word."

The next two parts offer nine, mostly shorter comments concerning the recent American treatment of evangelicals as the prime religious constituency supporting the policies of Donald Trump. Brief introductions identify the authors and position their comments in the unfolding of recent developments. The first four, in part 2, look back in order to explain where evangelical support for Trump came from: "A Strange Love? Or: How White Evangelicals Learned to Stop Worrying and Love the Donald" (Michael S. Hamilton); "Live by the Polls, Die by the Polls" (D. G. Hart); "Donald Trump and Militant Evangelical Masculinity" (Kristin Kobes Du Mez); and "The 'Weird' Fringe Is the Biggest Part of White Evangelicalism" (Fred Clark). The next five, in part 3, attempt assessments of what occurred: "Is the Term 'Evangelical' Redeemable?" (Thomas S. Kidd); "Can Evangelicalism Survive Donald Trump?" (Timothy Keller); "Idols of the Trump Era" (Molly Worthen); "Are Black Christians Evangelicals?" (Jemar Tisby); and "To Be or Not to Be an Evangelical" (Brian C. Stiller).

In the book's final brief section, George Marsden, David Bebbington, and I offer short essays prompted by this effort at drawing together the history of evangelical histories and the upsets of contemporary American politics. Marsden returns to the question that occupied his attention in 1984—how to account for the mingled chaos and coherence surrounding the notion of "evangelicalism." This time he uses the analogy of biological taxonomy to describe evangelicalism as a *class* that includes numerous *species*. For Bebbington, it is particularly pertinent to explore the relationship of evangelicals and politics in recent British history. His essay is a timely reminder that "the Bebbington quadrilateral," which has generated such unusually fruitful application along with such unusually contentious debate when applied to American history, began as an account of British history. It also underscores the reality that the contemporary relation of evangelicals and politics is quite different in Britain than in the United States. My contribution expands comparative perspectives by asking how the recent American history of evangelicalism relates to the development of evangelical forms of Christianity throughout the world. Thick connections link evangelical history in the United States to evangelical developments in the world, but the two should never be mistaken as identical.

The object of this book is to illuminate trajectories from the past in relationship to recent debates about evangelicalism, especially in the United States. Its concerns, regarded from a global perspective, are admittedly parochial. Yet George Marsden and David Bebbington join me in knowing that the word "evangelical" comes from the New Testament term for "gospel" ("good news"). Affirming the relevance of the Christian gospel to the contemporary United States, as well as to the world, is the most basic reason why historians of evangelicalism who are also evangelicals (with whatever burden of ambiguity that term now entails) have undertaken their work.

PART I

The History of "Evangelical History"

Before the 1960s, many histories had been written about evangelical move-ments, denominations, institutions, publications, and more. But general his-tories of evangelicalism, understood as a transdenominational movement or series of connected movements, had not yet emerged. The documents in part 1 contain some of the most important reflections on how a kind of history that did not exist two generations ago became such a dynamic, but also contested, arena of productive historical inquiry.

CHAPTER 1

The Evangelical Denomination

GEORGE MARSDEN

The following reflections on how to conceptualize evangelicalism are taken from an introduction to a book, *Evangelicalism and Modern America* (Eerdmans, 1984), and are reprinted here by permission of Eerdmans. The book grew out of a conference organized by Mark Noll and Nathan Hatch and held at Wheaton College in 1983. In the part of the introduction reprinted here, I addressed an essential issue that remains very relevant for trying to define evangelicalism today. If we are to talk about "evangelicalism" as any sort of entity, what are the various ways in which we may think about the degree of unity involved? The answers to that question bear directly on an issue central to the current perceptions of crisis: What are the relationships of the parts of evangelicalism to the whole?

A bit of background may be helpful. Through the first half of the 1970s, "evangelicalism" was not a widely used term in American parlance.[1] The "new evangelicals" associated with the founding of the National Association of Evangelicals in 1942 had succeeded in reviving the term to a degree, especially among conservative Protestant leaders in various denominations and parachurch movements who were becoming uncomfortable with the term "fundamentalist." The rise of Billy Graham to national prominence after 1949 gave wide visibility to this movement. By the 1960s, it was common for insiders in a large network of loosely connected revivalist-oriented Protestants to call themselves "evangelical" if they favored Graham's more open approach to sympathetic mainline Christians. "Fundamentalist," which had been the most common term for conservative conversion-oriented American Christians in the 1920s and 1930s, now became the term for a smaller group of more militant conservatives who

1. For confirmation, see the Ngram search on Google Books for "evangelicalism," for both the United States and the United Kingdom. Usage increased steadily thereafter; "evangelical" shows up much more consistently for the entire history covered by Google Books.

typically demanded separation from churches and organizations that tolerated any degree of theological liberalism.

By the early 1970s, "evangelicals" were gaining increasing visibility in the United States. Mainline Protestants were beginning to decline in numbers and influence. Meanwhile, conservative churches were growing. Revivalist parachurch organizations, such as Campus Crusade for Christ, were flourishing, while mainline Protestant campus ministries were hauling in their sails. Conspicuous "young evangelicals" were pushing for more progressive stances on issues such as social justice, racism, and war.[2] Those moves contrasted with the stance of *Christianity Today*, the flagship journal for "evangelicals" who used that name for themselves, where an old guard under the editorship of Harold Lindsell held the line for social and doctrinal conservatism. Meanwhile Billy Graham, who had as much success as a revivalist abroad as he did in the United States, was the catalyst for building self-conscious international alliances, most notably in the Lausanne movement growing out of the International Congress on World Evangelization held in 1974. At the same time, Pentecostal and charismatic groups, which were flourishing in America and around the world, had become the fastest-growing parts of world Christianity. Anyone who was paying attention could see a vast explosion of "evangelical" religion. Still, there were not that many people paying careful attention.

One of the characteristics of those who thought of themselves self-consciously as part of an evangelical movement was their deep concern for boundary maintenance. Who was in and who was out? Where were the lines to be drawn? Was the standard going to be "biblical inerrancy," as Harold Lindsell and his allies argued? Were the radical "young evangelicals" moving beyond the bounds? What about Pentecostals?

In the early 1970s, I had the privilege of contributing to a volume that was designed to explain evangelicalism to the world, *The Evangelicals: What They Believe, Who They Are, Where They Are Changing* (Nashville: Abingdon, 1975). It was edited by two young evangelical church historians at Trinity Evangelical Divinity School, David F. Wells and John D. Woodbridge. Given the widespread concern to define the movement, it made sense for the editors, who brought together a diverse range of insiders and outsiders as contributors, to commission the lead essay, "Theological Boundaries of the Evangelical Faith." Its author was John Gerstner, a theologian of a distinctly conservative Reformed bent who regarded any departure from the teachings of Jonathan Edwards as decline. But this treatment also left the volume with a conspicuous problem since evangelicalism obviously included many varieties

---

2. See Richard Quebedeux, *The Young Evangelicals: Revolution in Orthodoxy* (New York: Harper & Row, 1974).

beyond the Reformed, a point that Gerstner allowed, but only somewhat grudgingly. To the credit of the editors, they found an opportunity to correct this unfortunate one-sidedness by producing a second revised edition in 1977 (Grand Rapids: Baker Books). In this version Gerstner's lead article was entitled "Theological Boundaries: The Reformed Perspective," but it was followed by a new essay from a notable author of books on Pentecostalism, Vinson Synon, "Theological Boundaries: The Arminian Perspective." This article included attention to Methodist, Holiness, and Pentecostal movements. The presence of these articles, despite their differences, showed that evangelical insiders tended to think of themselves as a sort of club or perhaps even a denomination with contested rules for membership. A few years later, Lewis B. Smedes fantasized in the *Reformed Journal* about a group of grim theologians gathering as a sort of evangelical College of Cardinals near Wheaton, Illinois, and voting regarding each of that year's theologically suspect evangelical leaders, "tolerated" or "*Non est tolerandus.*"[3]

But even over the course of a very few years, the visibility of "evangelicalism" on the American scene changed dramatically—especially with Jimmy Carter's declaration that he was "born again," with *Newsweek* announcing 1976 as "the Year of the Evangelical," and with Carter's election as president. Suddenly evangelicals were in the news because they were seen as having political potential. The estimates of the numbers of American evangelicals were often something like forty million or more. Clearly this number of "born-again" Americans was vastly larger and more diverse than were the numbers of those I called in my article "card-carrying evangelicals," that is, the ones who identified with the networks of self-consciously evangelical movements and institutions.

With good reason, some American evangelicals not connected with the broadly Reformed types who dominated the self-consciously "evangelical" movement came to argue that their sorts of pietistic or revivalist Christians were being largely left out of the rising number of histories and interpretations of evangelicalism. My *Fundamentalism and American Culture* (Oxford University Press, 1980) had focused on the Reformed and on dispensationalists in the fundamentalist controversies mostly in the northern United States. It nonetheless carried the expansive subtitle *The Shaping of Twentieth-Century Evangelicalism, 1870–1925*. Timothy L. Smith, the Nazarene pastor and leading historian of evangelicalism who is featured several times in this book, was particularly effective in making the point that a great number of genuine evangelicals did not identify with evangelicals shaped by the movements I described. Donald Dayton subsequently elaborated on this point, leading to very fruitful mul-

---

3. Smedes, "Evangelicalism—a Fantasy," in *The Best of the Reformed Journal*, ed. James D. Bratt and Ronald A. Wells (Grand Rapids: Eerdmans, 2011), 218–19.

tisided discussions of the issue, some of which are treated in the article by Douglas Sweeney that is reprinted below.[4]

It was particularly with Timothy Smith's concerns in mind that in the essay reprinted here I tried to sort out how evangelicalism, despite its bewildering diversities—and at the time I was thinking mostly of the American situation—might still be considered something of a unity. Smith had suggested that evangelical diversity might be thought of as a kaleidoscope or a mosaic. I thought then that mosaic was the preferable image, since it suggested some overall pattern seen among the separate pieces rather than just a jumble thrown up on a screen.

My principal point was to concede that "evangelicalism" applied to a much larger and more diverse population than to only those who identified as "card-carrying evangelicals"—that is, who used the term to think of themselves as part of a movement with clear boundaries. Yet I also wanted to point out the many historical connections among the various evangelical movements, even if only some of them saw themselves as closely linked to the "card-carrying evangelicals." And that common background did point to some common identifying traits—as David Bebbington summarized more definitively in his later and now canonical quadrilateral.

*   *   *

The greatest conceptual challenge in a discussion of this sort is to say what evangelicalism is. The issue can be clarified by asking whether evangelicalism is not a kind of denomination. Evangelicalism is certainly not a denomination in the usual sense of an organized religious structure. It is, however, a denomination in the sense of a name by which a religious grouping is denominated. This ambiguity leads to endless confusions in talking about evangelicalism. Because evangelicalism is a name for a religious grouping—and sometimes a name people use to describe themselves—everyone has a tendency to talk

4. See, in addition, Donald Dayton, George Marsden, Joel Carpenter, Daniel Fuller, Clark Pinnock, and Douglas Sweeney in a symposium on my book *Reforming Fundamentalism: Fuller Seminary and the New Evangelicalism, Christian Scholars' Review* 23 (September 1993): 12–89. Earlier, Dayton had himself offered an alternative history, *Rediscovering an Evangelical Heritage* (New York: Harper & Row, 1976). As another indication of concern over definition, Southern Baptists also carried on a lively debate as to whether they were "evangelicals" or if that designation should be regarded as a "Yankee term." See James Leo Garrett Jr., E. Glenn Hinson, and James E. Tull, *Are Southern Baptists Evangelicals?* (Macon, GA: Mercer University Press, 1983).

about it at times as though it were a single, more or less unified phenomenon. The outstanding evangelical historian Timothy L. Smith has been most effective at pointing out the dangers of this usage. Smith and his students have repeatedly remarked on how misleading it is to speak of evangelicalism as a whole, especially when one prominent aspect of evangelicalism is then usually taken to typify the whole. Evangelicalism, says Smith, is more like a mosaic or, suggesting even less of an overall pattern, a kaleidoscope.[5] Most of the parts are not only disconnected, they are strikingly diverse.

So on one side of evangelicalism are black Pentecostals and on another are strict separatist fundamentalists, such as at Bob Jones University, who condemn Pentecostals and shun blacks. Peace churches, especially those in the Anabaptist-Mennonite tradition, make up another discrete group of evangelicals. And their ethos differs sharply from that of the Southern Baptist Convention, some fourteen million strong and America's largest Protestant body. Southern Baptists, in turn, have had experiences quite different from those of the evangelicals who have kept the traditional faith within the more liberal "mainline" northern churches. Each of these predominantly Anglo groups is, again, very different from basically immigrant church bodies like the Missouri Synod Lutheran or the Christian Reformed, who have carefully preserved Reformation confessional heritages. Other groups have held on to heritages less old but just as distinctive: German Pietists and several evangelical varieties among Methodists preserve traditions of eighteenth-century Pietism. The spiritual descendants of Alexander Campbell, especially in the Churches of Christ, continue to proclaim the nineteenth-century American ideal of restoring the practices of the New Testament church. Holiness and Pentecostal groups of many varieties stress similar emphases that developed slightly later and in somewhat differing contexts. Black Christians, responding to a cultural experience dominated by oppression, have developed their own varieties of most of the major American traditions especially the Baptist, Methodist, and Pentecostal. Not only do these and other evangelical denominations vary widely, but almost every one has carefully guarded its distinctiveness, usually avoiding deep contact with many other groups.[6] Viewed in this light, evangel-

5. Smith and his students have been working on a major collective historical study with the working title "The Evangelical Mosaic."

6. Cf. Cullen Murphy, "Protestantism and the Evangelicals," *The Wilson Quarterly* V,4 (Autumn 1981): 105–16, an essay written in consultation with Timothy Smith which presents an admirable summary of this approach. Murphy describes evangelicalism as a "12-ring show" (p. 108). Robert E. Webber, *Common Roots: A Call to Evangelical*

icalism indeed appears as disorganized as a kaleidoscope. One might wonder why evangelicalism is ever regarded as a unified entity at all.

Nonetheless, once we recognize the wide diversity within evangelicalism and the dangers of generalization, we may properly speak of evangelicalism as a single phenomenon. The meaningfulness of evangelicalism as such a "denomination" is suggested by the fact that today among Protestants the lines between evangelical and nonevangelical often seem more significant than do traditional denominational distinctions.

We can avoid many of the pitfalls in speaking about this single "evangelicalism" if we simply distinguish among three distinct, though overlapping, senses in which evangelicalism may be thought of as a unity. The first two are broad and inclusive, the third more narrow and specific. First, evangelicalism is a conceptual unity that designates a grouping of Christians who fit a certain definition. Second, evangelicalism can designate a more organic movement. Religious groups with some common traditions and experiences, despite wide diversities and only meager institutional interconnections, may constitute a movement in the sense of moving or tending in some common directions. Third, within evangelicalism in these broader senses is a more narrow, consciously "evangelical" transdenominational community with complicated infrastructures of institutions and persons who identify with "evangelicalism."

Since these three senses of "evangelicalism" are not usually clearly distinguished, the word is surrounded by a haze of vagueness and confusion. In part, this haze is an inescapable characteristic of just such a loosely organized and diverse phenomenon. Much of the confusion however, arises from the widespread tendency to confuse evangelicalism in one of the first two broad senses with the more self-conscious community of the third sense, whose leaders often aspire to speak for the broader grouping. In this volume the writers sometimes look at the broader movement and sometimes at that self-conscious community. Once the reader has the distinction clearly in mind, he should not find it difficult to tell whether one or the other or both of the subjects is in view. So it may be helpful for clarifying this and future discussion to look at the broad and the narrow usages in detail.

First is the broad usage in which "evangelicalism" designates simply a conceptual unity. Evangelicals in this sense are Christians who typically emphasize 1) the Reformation doctrine of the final authority of Scripture; 2) the real, historical character of God's saving work recorded in Scripture; 3) eternal

---

Maturity (Grand Rapids: Zondervan, 1978), 32, lists fourteen varieties of evangelicalism based on distinctive emphases rather than just on denominational differences.

salvation only through personal trust in Christ; 4) the importance of evangelism and missions; and 5) the importance of a spiritually transformed life.[7] Evangelicals will differ, sometimes sharply, over the details of these doctrines; and some persons or groups may emphasize one or more of these points at the expense of the others. But a definition such as this can identify a distinct religious grouping. Because evangelicalism in this sense is basically an abstract concept, the diversities of the grouping may be more apparent than is the organic unity.

One way of looking at evangelicalism that has depended heavily on this definitional approach is the opinion survey. Pollsters deal best with abstractions and must reduce their topic to operational definitions. Whether or not one is an evangelical is thus tested by whether one professes a combination of beliefs and practices that fit a certain definition. Evangelicalism delineated in this way will, of course, come out to be somewhat different than if it is considered a movement—either in the broad or the narrow sense. For instance, the 1978–79 *Christianity Today*–Gallup survey classified between forty and fifty million Americans as "evangelicals," a number that accords with other estimates. However, even if the definition used to make such a determination is cleverly formulated and qualified, it will inevitably be inflexible, excluding some who would be "evangelicals" by more intuitive standards and including some whose evangelicalism is marginal. For example, such surveys have no very adequate way of dealing with American folk piety. Also, a fair number of Americans seem ready to profess traditional religious beliefs even though these beliefs for them have little substance.[8] Thus, though definitions of evan-

---

7. Among Lutherans, "evangelical" has a more general meaning, roughly equivalent to "Protestant," and some neo-orthodox theologians have used it in its broad sense of "gospel-believer." The definition offered here, however, reflects the dominant Anglo-American usage.

8. For instance, of Americans who do not belong to, attend, or contribute to churches 64% say they believe Jesus is God or the Son of God, 68% believe in Jesus' resurrection, 40% say they have made a personal commitment to Jesus, 27% say the Bible is the actual word of God and "is to be taken literally, word for word," 25% claim to have been "born again." George Gallup, Jr. and David Poling, *The Search for America's Faith* (Nashville: Abingdon, 1980), 90-92. Also, 84% of Americans say the ten commandments are still valid for today, but only 42% know at least five of them. For those classed as "evangelicals," only 58% could name five of the commandments. James W. Reapsome, "Religious Values: Reflection of Age and Education," *Christianity Today*, 7 May 1980, 23-25.

gelicalism are necessary and helpful, they provide only limited ways of grasping the broad phenomenon.[9]

The other major way to perceive evangelicalism broadly is to view it not so much as a category but as a dynamic movement, with common heritages, common tendencies, an identity, and an organic character. Even though some evangelical subgroups have few connections with other groups and support few common causes, they may still be part of the same historical movement. There may indeed be an "evangelical mosaic"; though it is made up of separate and strikingly diverse pieces, it nevertheless displays an overall pattern. Thus, many American evangelicals participate in a larger historical pattern, having substantial historical experiences in common. All reflect the sixteenth-century Reformation effort to get back to the pure Word of Scripture as the only ultimate authority and to confine salvation to a faith in Christ, unencumbered by presumptuous human authority. During the next centuries these emphases were renewed and modified in a variety of ways, often parallel or interconnected, by groups such as the Puritans, Pietists, Methodists, Baptists, nineteenth-century restorationists, revivalists, black Christians, holiness groups, Pentecostals, and others. Many evangelical groups, now separate, have common roots and hence similar emphases. Widely common hymnody, techniques of evangelism, styles of prayer and Bible study, worship, and behavioral mores demonstrate these connected origins.

Moreover, common cultural experiences have moved this broad evangelical movement in discernible directions. For instance, American evangelicals have all been shaped to some extent by the experience of living in a democratic society that favors optimistic views of human nature, the importance of choosing for oneself, lay participation, and simple popular approaches. American materialism has also provided a common environment for most evangelicals. And they have been shaped by cultural and intellectual fashions. Nineteenth-century evangelical hymnody of almost all denominations, for instance, tended to be sentimental-romantic and individualistic, following the larger culture. In addition, as a number of essays in this volume suggest, twentieth-century evangelicals have often incorporated current cultural values into their messages.

On the other hand, the common or parallel experiences in the movement may involve resisting cultural trends. Most notably, twentieth-century evan-

---

9. James Hunter's *American Evangelicalism* presents some valuable analysis of the polling data but also illustrates the problem of conflating evangelicalism in its broad definitional sense with its other senses. For discussion of this point, see George Marsden, "Evangelicalism in the Sociological Laboratory," *The Reformed Journal* (June 1984).

gelicals all have in common a belief that faithfulness to Scripture demands resistance to many prevalent intellectual and religious currents. While many in mainline American denominations and their educational institutions abandoned their evangelical heritages during the first half of this century, today's evangelicals all hold firmly to traditional supernaturalist understandings of the Bible message. Simple love for the traditional gospel has no doubt been the chief force in this stance. But many secondary reasons also account for that resistance: because they were immigrants, because they were culturally or intellectually isolated, because they were strongly committed to evangelism and missions, because of traditions of biblical interpretation, or perhaps because of sheer cussedness. Nonetheless, the experiences were parallel, and the resulting willingness to assert the authority of the Bible against some dominant cultural values was similar. So, alongside the striking diversities in heritages, emphases, and cultural experiences are extensive commonalities that make evangelicalism discernible as a larger movement.

Evangelicalism, however, is also a movement in a more narrow sense. Not only is it a grouping with some common heritages and tendencies, it is also for many, self-consciously, a community. In this respect evangelicalism is most like a denomination. It is a religious fellowship or coalition of which people feel a part. This sense of an informal evangelical community or coalition goes back to the international Pietism of the eighteenth century. Common zeal for spreading the gospel transcended party lines. By the first half of the nineteenth century this movement had assumed something like its present shape. Evangelicalism in this more specific sense is essentially a transdenominational assemblage of independent agencies and their supporters, plus some denominationally sponsored seminaries and colleges which support such parachurch institutions. During the first half of the nineteenth century, evangelicals from Great Britain and America founded scores of "voluntary societies" for revivals, missions, Bible and tract publication, education, charity, and social and moral reforms. These voluntary agencies constituted an informal "evangelical united front." In America the expenditures of these independent evangelical agencies at times rivaled those of the federal government.[10] International revivalism, particularly that of Charles Finney in the first half of the century and Dwight L. Moody in the second, as well as efforts in world missions, especially helped foster a unity of purpose among evangelicals from a variety of denominations.

10. Charles I. Foster, *An Errand of Mercy: The Evangelical United Front, 1790–1837* (Chapel Hill: University of North Carolina Press, 1960), 121.

Successful techniques developed in one revival group or mission field quickly spread to others. The Evangelical Alliance, founded in 1846, was the most formal expression of this international evangelical community. Evangelically oriented denominations often encouraged or directly supported some of the independent evangelical agencies on an ad hoc basis. For a few independents, such as Dwight L. Moody, evangelicalism was, in effect, their denomination. For most evangelical leaders, however, the relationship was a bit weaker. Evangelicalism was a fellowship with which they identified while they also participated in a body such as the Methodists, Baptists, Presbyterians, or Congregationalists. Many constituents at the grass-roots level, such as those who supported a Moody revival or an African mission, might be only dimly aware of their connection with a wider evangelical coalition. They would know, however, that their Christian allegiance was wider than simply loyalty to their formal denomination.

During the nineteenth century this trans-Atlantic, transdenominational evangelical fellowship or coalition, although often strained by rivalries and controversies, was unified primarily by shared positive evangelical aspirations to win the world for Christ. In the early decades of the twentieth century the basis for unity was modified, although never abandoned, in response to a deep crisis centered around conflicts between "fundamentalists" and "modernists" in formerly evangelical bodies. Fundamentalists were especially militant evangelicals who battled against the modernists' accommodations of the gospel message to modern intellectual and cultural trends. Modernists, on the other hand, allowed little room for an authoritative Bible, traditional supernaturalism, or a gospel of faith in Christ's atoning work. In short, they had abandoned the essentials of evangelicalism. To make matters worse, the leadership in the major northern denominations tolerated or encouraged this revolution. In reaction, the new fundamentalist coalition emerged at the forefront of the conservative evangelical fellowship. In the face of the modernist threat to undermine the fundamentals of evangelical faith, a threat magnified by the accompanying cultural revolution, much of surviving evangelicalism took on a fundamentalist tone. The perennially upbeat mood of the nineteenth-century movement was now tempered by accents of fear and negativism.

The situation was complicated by the prominence of dispensationalist premillennialists in the leadership of interdenominational fundamentalism. Dispensationalists, whose prophetic interpretations predicted the apostasy of old-line churches, made a virtue out of working independent of the denominations. Accordingly, they had already built a formidable network of evangelistic organizations, missions agencies, and Bible schools. Their transdenominational orientation and their evangelistic aggressiveness, together with a hard-line militance against any concessions to modernism, put them in a position to marshall, or at least to influence, many of the conservative evangelical forces. During the 1920s leaders of this movement presumed to speak for all fundamentalists and did coordinate many fundamentalist efforts. They thus developed a disproportionate influence among conservatives in the old interdenominational evangelical movement, which during the next three decades was generally known as "fundamentalist." As Joel Carpenter shows in the first essay in this volume, heirs of this dispensationalist-fundamentalist movement, especially after 1940, reorganized and revitalized the broader and more open branches of fundamentalism. This "neo-evangelicalism," as it was known for a time, preserved many of the positive emphases of the old nineteenth-century coalition as well as some of the negativism of fundamentalism.[11]

Close connections with Billy Graham gave this new leadership national impact and attention. For the two decades after 1950, the most prominent parts of this more narrowly self-conscious evangelicalism focused around Graham. Graham's prominence and the commanding position of former fundamentalists in organizing this neo-evangelical effort, however, partially obscured for a time the fact that the movement, even as a conscious community, had many other foci and included many other traditions. Since the 1960s, and especially with the successes and growing self-awareness of "evangelicalism" in the 1970s, the diversities that had always been present in the old evangelical fellowship have become more apparent. In the 1980s the movement in fact faces a crisis of identity, evidenced by debates over "who is an evangelical?"

With this background we can see more clearly how our third meaning of "evangelical" refers to a consciously organized community or movement. Since mid-century there have been something like "card-carrying" evangelicals. These people, like their nineteenth-century forebears, have some sense of belonging to a complicated fellowship and infrastructure of transdenominational evangelical organizations for evangelism, missions, social services, publications, and education. Typically, those who have the strongest sense of being "evangelicals" are persons with directly fundamentalist background, although persons from other traditions—Pentecostal, holiness, Reformed, Anabaptist, and others—often are deeply involved as well. Sometimes the people, groups,

---

11. Richard Lovelace aptly characterizes Jerry Falwell's activist fundamentalism as "really a sort of southern neo-evangelical reform movement." "Future Shock and Christian Hope," *Christianity Today*, 5 August 1983, 16.

and organizations that make up "evangelicalism" in this sense are rivals; but even in rivalry they manifest the connectedness of a family grouping that is quite concerned about its immediate relatives.

To look at evangelicals this way does require some adjustment to account for those who still call themselves "fundamentalists." By the end of the 1950s the term "fundamentalism" had come to be applied most often to strict separatists, mostly dispensationalists, who were unhappy with the compromises of the new "evangelical" coalition of Billy Graham. Fundamentalists were also adamant in condemning Pentecostal evangelicalism, while the former fundamentalist neo-evangelicals, despite some reservations, saw Pentecostals as basically allies in their preeminent task of leading people to Christ.

Since the 1970s some fundamentalists, centering around Jerry Falwell and the Moral Majority, have begun to build broader coalitions, much like the neo-evangelicals of the 1940s and 1950s. Yet even the hard-line fundamentalists, such as those at Bob Jones University, who condemn all such compromises, remain a part of the consciously evangelical movement, at least in the sense of paying the closest attention to it and often addressing it. In another sense, however, hard-line fundamentalists have formed a distinct submovement with its own exclusive network of organizations.

So with the possible exception of this extreme position, evangelicalism is a transdenominational movement in which many people, in various ways, feel at home. It is a movement as diverse as the politically radical Sojourners community in Washington, D.C., and the conservative Moral Majority. The leaders of these groups undoubtedly read many of the same evangelical periodicals and books and are familiar with much the same set of evangelical organizations and names. Institutionally, this transdenominational evangelicalism is built around networks of para-church agencies. The structure is somewhat like that of the feudal system of the Middle Ages. It is made up of superficially friendly, somewhat competitive empires built up by evangelical leaders competing for the same audience, but all professing allegiance to the same king. So we find empires surrounding Billy Graham, Jerry Falwell, Oral Roberts, Pat Robertson, Jim Bakker, Jimmy Swaggart, and other television ministers. Card-carrying evangelicals are just as familiar with Campus Crusade for Christ, Youth for Christ, Young Life, Navigators, Inter-Varsity Christian Fellowship, Francis Schaeffer's L'Abri Fellowship, and other evangelistic organizations. Other agencies for missions or social work have similarly broad interdenominational support. Educational institutions also long have provided institutional strength for evangelicals, especially in hundreds of Bible institutes. Christian colleges, sometimes still under denominational control, help provide stability and continuity of leadership for the transde-nominational movement. Wheaton College graduates, for instance, long have stood at the center of one of the most influential networks of organized evan-gelical leadership. A similarly central role has been played by independent theological seminaries such as Gordon-Conwell, Fuller, Dallas, and West-minster. Some more clearly denominational schools, like Trinity Evangelical, Covenant, Asbury, or Eastern Baptist, have also played direct roles in shaping the card-carrying evangelical fellowship. Evangelical publishers also contrib-ute importantly to the sense of community, both in major periodicals such as *Christianity Today, Eternity,* and *Moody Monthly* and in the flood of books that keeps the community current with the same trends.

We can see, then, that a decisive factor in distinguishing evangelicals in the more narrow sense from evangelicals in broader senses is a degree of transdenominational orientation. So, for instance, many Missouri Synod Lutherans, Southern Baptists, Wesleyan Methodists, Church of the Brethren, or Mennonites whose religious outlook is channeled almost exclusively by the programs and concerns of their own denomination, are hardly part of the card-carrying evangelical fellowship, even though they may certainly be evangelicals in the broader senses. A few denominations, such as the Evan-gelical Free Church or the Evangelical Mennonites, have been so entirely shaped by twentieth-century contacts with organized transdenominational evangelicalism as to be virtual products of that movement. Most ecclesias-tical bodies, however, offer more distinctively denominational orientation, and "evangelical" would not be a primary term which members would use to describe themselves. Yet still others in these same bodies are clearly evan-gelicals in the narrow sense that they orient themselves substantially to the transdenominational movement. Thus Billy Graham and Harold Lindsell, for instance, are more "evangelical" than they are Southern Baptist. Similarly, John Perkins and Tom Skinner are black evangelicals because they identify in part with the general evangelical community. The vast majority of black Bible-believers, however, although evangelicals in the broader senses, are only distantly part of evangelicalism as a narrower movement. Nor do they *think* of themselves as "evangelicals."

Evangelicalism, then, despite its diversities, is properly spoken of as a single movement in at least two different ways. It is a broader movement some-what unified by common heritages, influences, problems, and tendencies. It is also a conscious fellowship, coalition, community family, or feudal system of friends and rivals who have some stronger sense of belonging together. These "evangelicals" constitute something like a denomination, although a most informal one. Some from the tradition of the original fundamentalists and their neo-evangelical heirs, who indeed have been the strongest party in this coalition, have attempted to speak or to set standards for evangelicals generally. To perceive the difficulties in such artificial efforts to unify the diverse movement by fiat should not, however, obscure the actual unities of the movement, whether broadly or narrowly conceived.

CHAPTER 2

The Nature of Evangelical Religion

DAVID W. BEBBINGTON

The following is the substance of the first chapter (pp. 1–17) of David W. Bebbington's book *Evangelicalism in Modern Britain: A History from the 1730s to the 1980s* (London: Unwin Hyman, 1989)—reprinted here by permission of the publisher and Academic Books Permissions. It spells out in considerable detail a characterization of evangelicalism that has come to be widely used. Although this study is confined to a country outside the United States, it does include coverage of Jonathan Edwards, who in the eighteenth century was an inhabitant of an English colony, and so it implicitly treats its depiction as applying to America as well. This way of understanding the essence of the movement is not intrinsically theological but phenomenological. Hence it identifies the salient features of evangelicalism over time, whether they are theological or not. The cross is primarily a matter of doctrine, but activism is not. No particular version of the four resulting characteristics is privileged, so that, for example, conversion may be gradual as well as sudden. All that is required is an emphasis on each of the four points of conversion, activism, Bible, and cross.

*   *   *

. . . woe is unto me, if I preach not the gospel! (1 Cor. 9:16)

Evangelical religion is a popular Protestant movement that has existed in Britain since the 1730s. It is not to be equated with any single Christian denomination, for it influenced the existing churches during the eighteenth century and generated many more in subsequent years. It has found expression in a variety of institutional forms, a wine that has been poured into many bottles. Historians regularly apply the term 'evangelical' to the churches arising from the Reformation in the sixteenth and seventeenth centuries.[1] The usage of the period justifies them. Sir Thomas More in 1531 referred to advocates of the Reformation as 'Evaungelicalles'.[2] Yet the normal meaning of the word, as late as the eighteenth century, was 'of the gospel' in a non-partisan sense. Isaac Watts, for example, writes of an 'Evangelical Turn of Thought' in 1723.[3] There was a reluctance, most marked in Scotland, to apply the word to a particular group, since by implication those outside the group would be branded as not 'of the gospel'.[4] Other terms were used, especially by critics. In 1789 Joseph Milner wrote of 'Evangelical religion, or what is often called Calvinism or Methodism'.[5] Steadily, however, the word 'Evangelical' supplanted the others as the standard description of the doctrines or ministers of the revival movement, whether inside or outside the Church of England.[6] In 1793 *The Evangelical Magazine* was founded to cater for members of any denomination dedicated to spreading the gospel. That is the sense in which the word is employed here. Although 'evangelical', with a lower-case initial, is occasionally used to mean 'of the gospel', the term 'Evangelical', with a capital letter, is applied to any

1. R. T. Jones, *The Great Reformation* (Leicester, 1985); G. Rupp, *Religion in England, 1688–1791* (Oxford, 1986), pp. 121, 125. [Abbreviations in this chapter include the following: *BW = British Weekly*; *C = Christian*; *CEN = Church of England Newspaper*; *CO = Christian Observer*; *R = Record*; *WV = Wesley's Veterans: Lives of Early Methodist Preachers told by Themselves*, ed. John Telford, 7 vols. (London, 1912–1914)—eds.]

2. G. R. Balleine, *A History of the Evangelical Party in the Church of England* (London, 1951 edn), p. 40 n. Other general studies of Anglican Evangelicalism are: G. W. E. Russell, *A Short History of the Evangelical Movement* (London, 1915); L. Elliott-Binns, *The Evangelical Movement in the English Church* (London, 1928); and D. N. Samuel (ed.), *The Evangelical Succession in the Church of England* (Cambridge, 1979). On the broader movement there is E. J. Poole-Connor, *Evangelicalism in England* (Worthing, 1966 edn).

3. Watts, preface to J. Jennings, *Two Discourses* (1723), quoted by G. F. Nuttall, 'Continental Pietism and the Evangelical Movement in Britain', in J. van den Berg and J. P. van Dooren (eds), *Pietismus und Reveil* (Leiden, 1978), p. 226.

4. The term is studiously avoided in Sir H. M. Wellwood, *Account of the Life and Writings of John Erskine, D.D.* (Edinburgh, 1818).

5. J. Milner, 'On Evangelical religion', *The Works of Joseph Milner*, ed. I. Milner, Vol. 8 (London, 1810), p. 199.

6. For example, T. Haweis to S. Walker, 16 July 1759, in G. C. B. Davies, *The Early Cornish Evangelicals, 1735–60: A Study of Walker of Truro and Others* (London, 1951), p. 174; cf. J. D. Walsh, 'The Yorkshire Evangelicals in the eighteenth century: with especial reference to Methodism', PhD thesis, University of Cambridge, 1956, appendix D.

aspect of the movement beginning in the 1730s.[7] There was much continuity with earlier Protestant traditions, but, as Chapter 2 contends, Evangelicalism was a new phenomenon of the eighteenth century.

Who was an Evangelical? Sometimes adherents of the movement were in doubt themselves. 'I know what constituted an Evangelical in former times', wrote Lord Shaftesbury in his later life; 'I have no clear notion what constitutes one now'.[8] Part of the problem was that, as Shaftesbury implies, Evangelicalism changed greatly over time. To analyse and explain the changes is the main purpose of this book. Yet there are common features that have lasted from the first half of the eighteenth century to the second half of the twentieth. It is this continuing set of characteristics that reveals the existence of an Evangelical tradition. They need to be examined, for no other criterion for defining Evangelicalism is satisfactory. An alternative way would be to appeal to contemporary opinion about who was included within the movement. That approach, however, risks being ensnared in the narrow perspective of a particular period. For polemical purposes the right of others to call themselves Evangelicals has often been denied, particularly in the twentieth century. The danger is that the historian may be drawn into the battles of the past. It is therefore preferable to identify adherents of the movement by certain hallmarks. Evangelicals were those who displayed all the common features that have persisted over time.

Evangelical apologists sometimes explained their distinctiveness by laying claim to particular emphases. The Evangelical clergy differed from others, according to Henry Venn (later Clerical Secretary of the Church Missionary Society) in 1835, 'not so much in their systematic statement of doctrines, as in the relative importance which they assign to the particular parts of the Christian System, and in the vital operation of Christian Doctrines upon the heart and conduct'.[9] Likewise Bishop Ryle of Liverpool asserted that it was

---

7. The alternative usage of applying 'Evangelical' to the Anglican party and 'evangelical' to others of like mind outside the Church of England can be misleading. It has been adopted by E. Jay (*The Religion of the Heart: Anglican Evangelicalism and the Nineteenth-Century Novel* (Oxford, 1979), ch. 1, sect. 1, esp. p. 17) in order to deny the 'common spiritual parentage' of Anglicans and non-Anglicans in the movement. In reality, for all their divergences, their common inheritance was far more significant than this usage suggests.

8. E. Hodder, *The Life and Work of the Seventh Earl of Shaftesbury, K.G.* (London, 1888), p. 738.

9. H. Venn (ed.), *The Life and a Selection from the Letters of the late Rev. Henry Venn, M.A.* (London, 1835), pp. vii f.

not the substance of certain doctrines but the prominent position assigned to only a few of them that marked out Evangelical Churchmen from others.[10] By that criterion, Ryle was able to distinguish his position from that of the great number of late nineteenth-century High Churchmen whose message was similar to his own, whose zeal was equal to his own and who preached as much for conversions.[11] They elevated certain doctrines surrounding the church and the sacraments to a standard of importance that he believed to be untenable. The tone of Evangelicalism permeated nearly the whole of later Victorian religion outside the Roman Catholic Church, and yet the Evangelical tradition remained distinct. It gave exclusive pride of place to a small number of leading principles.

Evangelical Characteristics

The main characteristics emerge clearly. The High Churchman G. W. E. Russell remembered that the Evangelicals of his childhood in the mid-nineteenth century divided humanity into two categories: 'a converted character' differed totally from all others. Russell had also been taught to be active in charity, to read the Bible and to maintain 'the doctrine of the Cross'.[12] There are the four qualities that have been the special marks of Evangelical religion: *conversionism,* the belief that lives need to be changed; *activism,* the expression of the gospel in effort; *biblicism,* a particular regard for the Bible; and what may be called *crucicentrism,* a stress on the sacrifice of Christ on the cross. Together they form a quadrilateral of priorities that is the basis of Evangelicalism.

In the early days of the revival there was normally a stress in Evangelical apologetic on the first and the last. John Wesley was willing to describe two doctrines as fundamental: justification, the forgiving of our sins through the atoning death of Christ; and the new birth, the renewing of our fallen human nature at the time of conversion.[13] Similarly a group at Cambridge received the 'three capital and distinguishing doctrines of the Methodists, viz. Original

10. J. C. Ryle, *Knots Untied* (London, 1896 edn), p. 9.

11. D. Voll, *Catholic Evangelicalism: The Acceptance of Evangelical Traditions by the Oxford Movement during the Second Half of the Nineteenth Century* (London, 1963).

12. G. W. E. Russell, 'Recollections of the Evangelicals', *The Household of Faith* (London, 1902), pp. 240 f., 245.

13. Wesley, 'The new birth', *The Works of John Wesley*, Vol. 2, ed. A. C. Outler (Nashville, Tenn., 1985), p. 187.

Sin, Justification by Faith and the New Birth.[14] Original sin, the condition from which we are rescued by the other two, was also on Joseph Milner's checklist of four doctrines absolutely necessary to salvation: the 'divine light, inspiration, or illumination' of conversion; original sin; justification by faith in the merits of Christ by which 'the great transaction of the Cross is appropriated'; and spiritual renovation, the consequent working out of duty from the motive of gratitude.[15] This final factor implies activism, but in the eighteenth century Evangelicals rarely spelt out its importance in doctrinal terms. They nevertheless threw themselves into vigorous attempts to spread the faith. Likewise they did not normally put the Bible among the most important features of their religion. The Bible, after all, was professedly held in high esteem by all Protestants. Yet they were notably devoted in their searching of the scriptures. The centrality of the Bible could still be taken as read in the mid-nineteenth century, even when activism was mentioned explicitly. 'An Evangelical believer', according to William Marsh in 1850, 'is a man who believes in the fall and its consequences, in the recovery and its fruits, in the personal application of the recovery by the power of the Spirit of God, and then the Christian will aim, desire, endeavour, by example, by exertion, by influence, and by prayer to promote the great salvation of which he himself is a happy partaker . . .'[16] Thus the earlier phase of Evangelical history concurred with the late Puritan divine Matthew Henry in dwelling on three Rs: ruin, redemption and regeneration.[17] In practice, however, from its commencement the movement showed immense energy and a steady devotion to the Bible also.

Later generations, while still displaying the four main characteristics, tended to present them rather differently. The first leading principle of Evangelical religion, according to Bishop Ryle, is 'the absolute supremacy it assigns to Holy Scripture'. There followed, as other leading principles, the doctrines of human sinfulness, the work of Christ in salvation, the inward work of the Holy Spirit in regeneration and his outward work in sanctification. The primacy of scripture was directed against those who exalted the authority of either church or reason.[18] Other late nineteenth-century writers adopted a similar defensive posture, particularly against High Church doctrine on the priesthood and the sacraments.

---

14. *Life of Ann Okely*, quoted by J. Walsh, 'The Cambridge Methodists', in P. Brooks (ed.), *Christian Spirituality: Essays in Honour of Gordon Rupp* (London, 1975), p. 258.

15. Milner, 'On Evangelical religion', pp. 201–5.

16. *R*, 2 May 1850.

17. R. W. Dale, *The Old Evangelicalism and the New* (London, 1889), p. 13.

18. Ryle, *Knots Untied*, pp. 4–9.

Edward Garbett claimed in 1875 that the three cardinal Evangelical principles are the direct contact of the individual soul with God the Father, the freedom and sovereignty of the Holy Ghost and the sole High Priesthood of God the Son. His intent is to repudiate High Church teaching about the role of the priest in mediating the grace of God to the people.[19] Likewise the ministers of the London Baptist Association set about defining Evangelicalism negatively. 'In our view', they announced in 1888, 'the word "evangelical" has been adopted by those who have held the Deity of our Lord, in opposition to Socinianism; the substitutionary death of the cross, in opposition to Sacramentarianism; the simplicity of the communion of the Lord's Supper, in opposition to the doctrine of the Real Presence. It certainly has also further references . . . in opposition to those who deny the infallibility of Scripture on the one hand, and who assert another probation for the impenitent dead on the other.'[20] One eye is constantly being cast over the shoulder at the ritualists and the rationalists. Instead of the joy of new discovery that pervades eighteenth-century lists of distinctives, there is a resolve to resist an incoming tide of error.

Twentieth-century formulations again put the stress elsewhere. In asking 'What is an Evangelical?', in 1944, Max Warren, General Secretary of the Church Missionary Society, gave priority to evangelism over everything else, even worship. The need for conversion, trusting the Holy Spirit to sustain the believer's new life and the priesthood of all believers were his other three cardinal principles. Thus activism now comes first, with the centrality of the cross and the study of the Bible, though both are mentioned, relegated to a lower place in the scheme of things.[21] Warren, however, was not among the more conservative Evangelicals, whose strength was to grow later in the century. Conservatives usually attributed most importance to the authority of the Bible. Once that was granted, they believed, all other features would be assured. Thus John Stott, in asking Warren's question, 'What is an Evangelical?', in 1977, replied that two convictions cannot be surrendered. First, he claimed, 'We evangelicals are Bible people'. It followed, secondly, that Evangelicals possessed a gospel to proclaim. The cross, conversion and effort for its spread were all placed under that comprehensive heading.[22] Similarly J. I. Packer put the supremacy of scripture first in a list of six Evangelical fundamentals in 1979. To the familiar categories of the work of Christ, the necessity of conversion

---

19. Garbett (ed.), *Evangelical Principles* (London, 1875), p. xiv.

20. *C*, 5 October 1888, p, 5.

21. Warren, *What is an Evangelical? An Enquiry* (London, [1944]), pp. 18–39.

22. J. R. W. Stott, *What is an Evangelical?* (London, 1977), pp. 5–14.

and the priority of evangelism he added the lordship of the Holy Spirit (in deference to charismatics) and the importance of fellowship (in deference to Catholics).[23] Variations there have certainly been in statements by Evangelicals about what they regard as basic. There is nevertheless a common core that has remained remarkably constant down the centuries. Conversionism, activism, biblicism and crucicentrism form the defining attributes of Evangelical religion. Each characteristic can usefully be examined in turn.

Conversionism

The call to conversion has been the content of the gospel. Preachers urged their hearers to turn away from their sins in repentance and to Christ in faith. G. W. McCree, 'a London Baptist minister of the mid-nineteenth century', was typical in holding 'that conversion was far above, and of greater importance than, any denominational differences of whatever kind'.[24] A vivid account of conversion, pinpointed by Matthew Arnold as a classic, is given in the autobiography of Sampson Staniforth, then a soldier on active service and later one of the Wesleys' early preachers:

> As soon as I was alone, I kneeled down, and determined not to rise, but to continue crying and wrestling with God, till He had mercy on me. How long I was in that agony I cannot tell; but as I looked up to heaven I saw the clouds open exceeding bright, and I saw Jesus hanging on the cross. At the same moment these words were applied to my heart, 'Thy sins are forgiven thee'. My chains fell off; my heart was free. All guilt was gone, and my soul was filled with unutterable peace.[25]

Staniforth's narrative is a classic not only because of its patent sincerity but also because of its inclusion of agony, guilt and immense relief. The great crisis of life could stir deep emotion. The experience was often ardently sought, for others as well as for oneself. Prayer requests for conversion appeared in the Evangelical press: 'For a gentleman on the road to destruction, who fancies he is saved.—For an unconverted brother who is addicted to excessive drink-

---

23. Packer, *The Evangelical Anglican Identity Problem*, Latimer House Studies, 1 (Oxford, 1978), pp. 20 ff.

24. G. W. McCree, *George Wilson McCree* (London, 1893), p. 20.

25. *WV*, Vol. 1, pp. 74 f.

ing—. . . For my late foreign governess, an avowed Unitarian'.[26] Conversions were the goal of personal effort, the collective aim of churches, the theme of Evangelical literature. They could seem a panacea. 'Conversions not only bring prosperity to the Church', declared the Wesleyan Samuel Chadwick at about the start of the twentieth century; 'they solve the social problem'.[27] A converted character would work hard, save money and assist his neighbour. The line between those who had undergone the experience and those who had not was the sharpest in the world. It marked the boundary between a Christian and a pagan.

Preaching the gospel was the chief method of winning converts. Robert Bickersteth, Bishop of Ripon from 1857 to 1884, held that 'no sermon was worthy of the name which did not contain the message of the Gospel, urging the sinner to be reconciled to God'.[28] There was a danger, Evangelical preachers believed, of offering only comfort from the pulpit. Hearers needed to be aroused to concern for their spiritual welfare. If the delights of heaven were described, so were the terrors of hell. Jonathan Edwards, the American theologian who stands at the headwaters of Evangelicalism, believed in insisting on the reality of hell; Joseph Milner, an erudite early Anglican Evangelical, would preach sermons on topics like 'The sudden destruction of obdurate offenders'; and a Methodist preacher assured a backslider 'that the devil would soon toss [him] about in the flames of hell with a pitchfork'.[29] Normally, however, there was more circumspection. The minister, according to an article of 1852 'On the method of preaching the doctrine of eternal death', should remember 'that he is sent to be a preacher of the Gospel of the grace of God, and not to be a preacher of death and ruin'.[30] Fear was not neglected as a motive for conversion, but more emphasis was generally laid on the forgiving love of God. It was essential, however, that the preacher himself should be converted. How could he speak of what he had not known? Some ministers underwent conversion experiences when already in the ministry. Thomas Chalmers, the Evangelical leader in the early nineteenth-century Church of

26. C, 15 July 1875, p. 19.

27. N. G. Dunning, *Samuel Chadwick* (London, 1933), p. 54.

28. M. C. Bickersteth, *A Sketch of the Life and Episcopate of the Right Reverend Robert Bickersteth, D.D., Bishop of Ripon, 1857–1887* (London, 1887), pp. 27 f.

29. Edwards, 'The distinguishing marks of a work of the true Spirit', *Select Works*, Vol. 1 (London, 1965), p. 106. Walsh, 'Yorkshire Evangelicals', p. 290. J. Lackington, *Memoirs of the Forty-Five First Years of the Life of James Lackington* (London, 1795), p. 161.

30. T.D.B. in CO, January 1852, p. 3.

Scotland, was among them.[31] One clergyman was even converted by his own sermon. Preaching on the Pharisees in his Cornish parish, William Haslam realised that he was no better than they, but then felt light and joy coming into his soul. The cry went up, 'The parson is converted!'[32] The experience turned him into an Evangelical.

Conversion was bound up with major theological convictions. At that point, Evangelicals believed, a person is justified by faith. Because human beings are estranged from God by their sinfulness, there is nothing they can do by themselves to win salvation. All human actions, even good works, are tainted by sin, and so there is no possibility of gaining merit in the sight of God. Hence salvation has to be received, not achieved. Jesus Christ has to be trusted as Saviour. Acceptance by God, as Luther had insisted, comes through faith, not works. Justification by faith, as we have seen, was one of the distinguishing doctrines of Evangelicalism in the eighteenth century. Critics declared it to be subversive of all morality. To the typical mind of the period it seemed to destroy the obligation to observe the divine law. If salvation was available without good works, the door was opened for any form of profligacy. Gratitude, replied the Evangelicals, was the strongest motive for moral behaviour. Henry Venn, the Evangelical Vicar of Huddersfield, declared that 'faith is not understood, much less possessed, if it produce not more holiness, than could possibly be any other way attained'.[33] Consequently it was dwelt on. To the growing son of an Evangelical Anglican home in the mid-nineteenth century it seemed that the clergy taught nothing else but justification by faith.[34] Although the doctrine was sometimes watered down in the later nineteenth century,[35] it was championed so vigorously by Evangelicals in the Church of England in the 1980s that it became a central topic of theological dialogue with the Roman Catholic Church.[36] Justification by faith embodied much that was most precious to them.

Assurance was another doctrine closely connected with conversion. Once a person has received salvation as a gift of God, he may be assured, according to Evangelicals, that he possesses it. Not only is he a Christian; he knows he is a Christian. John Wesley laid great emphasis on this teaching. 'I never yet

31. W. Hanna, *Memoirs of the Life and Writings of Thomas Chalmers, D.D., LL.D.*, Vol. 1 (Edinburgh, 1851), ch. 8.

32. Haslam, *From Death into Life* (London, n.d.), p. 48.

33. Venn, *The Complete Duty of Man*, 3rd edn (London, 1779), p. xi.

34. Russell, 'Recollections of the Evangelicals', p. 238.

35. Dale, *Old Evangelicalism and the New*, pp. 51–7.

36. *Evangel*, Summer 1987.

knew', he told an enquirer in 1740, 'one soul thus saved, without what you call "the faith of assurance": I mean a sure confidence, that by the merits of Christ he was reconciled to the favour of God.'[37] The idea was not distinctive to Wesley and his followers, for those affected by Evangelicalism in the Calvinist tradition were equally attached to it. Assurance had been an important theme of pre-Evangelical Protestant spirituality, but the experience had never been regarded as the standard possession of all believers. The novelty of Evangelical religion, as Chapter 2 will show, lay precisely in claiming that assurance normally accompanies conversion. Other Christians, especially those of more Catholic traditions, found the expectation of assurance among Evangelicals eccentric, presumptuous or even pathological.[38] Yet it remained characteristic of them. Max Warren defended the doctrine in 1944 as 'the here and now certainty that "I am 'in Grace' because I have been converted"'.[39] The confidence of Evangelicals had its roots in the inward persuasion that God was on their side.

Since conversion was the one gateway to vital Christianity, parents looked anxiously for signs of it in their growing children. The Scots Evangelical mother of W. E. Gladstone, the future Prime Minister, wrote in a letter when he was about ten years old that she believed her son to be 'truly converted to God.'[40] Conversion was most common among teenagers, but the average age at the experience seems to have fallen during the nineteenth century. In the first half of the century, a higher proportion of conversions took place in adulthood. Later on, as churches drew more on Christian homes, the stage of decisive commitment tended to occur earlier. The mean age at conversion among future Methodist ministers in the period 1780–1840 was 16.9 years; the mean age in the period 1841–1900 was 15.8 years.[41] Home background clearly remained an influential factor in the 1960s. An Evangelical Alliance survey of about 5,000 Christians established that one in six had been converted before the age of twelve and three in four before the age of twenty.[42] Conversion was statistically less

---

37. *The Journal of the Rev. John Wesley, A.M.*, ed. N. Curnock, Vol. 2 (London, 1911), pp. 333 f. (25 January 1740).

38. R. A. Knox, *Enthusiasm* (Oxford, 1950), ch. 21.

39. Warren, *What is an Evangelical?*, p. 26.

40. G. W. E. Russell, *Mr Gladstone's Religious Development* (London, 1899), p. 7.

41. C. D. Field, 'Methodism in Metropolitan London, 1850–1920: a social and sociological study', DPhil thesis, University of Oxford, 1975, p. 232.

42. *On the Other Side: The Report of the Evangelical Alliance's Commission on Evangelism* (London, 1968), p. 184.

likely the older a person was.[43] Among the exceptions, conviction usually went deep. Sir Wilfrid Lawson, a Cumberland baronet, for example, underwent a decisive experience while suffering from a dangerous illness in middle age. Though retaining the sporting interests of his class, he became a generous patron of local religious services, temperance work and the whole Evangelical Union denomination.[44] For the adult there could be a drastic reappraisal of life's priorities.

'Conversion is a great and glorious work of God's power', wrote Jonathan Edwards, 'at once changing the heart, and infusing life into the dead soul . . . But as to fixing on the *precise time* when they put forth the very first act of grace, there is a great deal of difference in different persons; in some it seems to be very discernible when the very time was; but others are more at a loss.'[45] The question of timing was perplexing to subsequent generations. Could conversion sometimes be gradual rather than sudden? Anglican Evangelicals, commonly more educated, sober and respectable than their brethren in other denominations, never had qualms about accepting the validity of gradual conversions. Charles Simeon, their leading spokesman in the early nineteenth century, was emphatic: 'we require nothing *sudden*'.[46] Likewise William Jay of Bath, an Independent minister with a fashionable congregation, could testify to no 'distinct and unique experience'.[47] Methodists, on the other hand, usually looked for a datable crisis, though equally they expected it to be preceded by a long period of 'awakening'.[48] Revivalists in the mid-nineteenth century stressed the change of a particular moment. Thus, Reginald Radcliffe sought to impress on Sunday School teachers in 1860 that 'conversion is an instantaneous work'.[49] James Caughey, a vigorous American revivalist in Methodism, asserted that 'the work of conversion is so momentous, that no man can pass through it, and not know it'.[50] There was

43. A. T. Pierson, *Forward Movements of the Last Half Century* (New York, 1900), p. 207.

44. G. W. E. Russell, *Sir Wilfrid Lawson* (London, 1909), pp. 3 f. J. Burgess, *The Lake Counties and Christianity: The Religious History of Cumbria, 1780–1920* (Carlisle, 1984), pp. 88–95.

45. Edwards, 'A narrative of surprising conversions', *Select Works*, Vol. 1, p. 40.

46. Simeon, 'On the new birth', in A. Pollard (ed.), *Let Wisdom Judge: University Addresses and Sermon Outlines by Charles Simeon* (London, 1959), p. 51.

47. G. Redford and J. A. James (eds), *The Autobiography of William Jay*, 2nd edn (London, 1855), p. 22.

48. For example, *WV*, Vol. 4, p. 19 (J. Pawson).

49. *Revival*, 21 January 1860, p. 21.

50. R. Carwardine, *Transatlantic Revivalism: Popular Evangelicalism in Britain and America, 1790–1865* (Westport, Conn., 1978), p. 125.

nevertheless an undoubted drift towards the standard Anglican position as the nineteenth century wore on. Alexander Raleigh, a distinguished Independent preacher between the 1840s and the 1870s, made a conscious change of heart central in his earlier sermons, but later accepted that conversion could be gradual and unconscious.[51] By 1905 only the Baptist contributors to an interdenominational symposium on *The Child and Religion* expected a crisis of personal religious decision.[52] Conservative and sectarian Evangelicals often continued to think in these terms, but gradualism was stronger among the more open-minded. Differences of emphasis remained unresolved in the twentieth century.

Another issue revolved round the means of conversion. The orthodox teaching was that true conversion is the work of the Holy Spirit.[53] Challenges to trust Christ were thought legitimate human means for bringing about conversions, but the Spirit was still held to be responsible. In the nineteenth century, however, some of the more enthusiastic Evangelicals, eager to maximise conversions, began to teach that the crucial factor is a person's *will* to be saved. Carefully planned methods, such as meetings designed for anxious enquirers, could encourage the desire to believe. In *Lectures on Revivals of Religion* (1835), Charles Finney, the leading American exponent of this line of thinking, presented revivalism as a science, a powerful technique for securing mass conversions. It was an immensely popular work, selling 80,000 copies by 1850 and making a great impact in Britain, not least because it was adapted for the British market by removing, for example, strictures on drinking tea. Finney came close to denying the need for the intervention of the Holy Spirit. Some did draw that inference. J. H. Hinton, later a leading Baptist minister, wrote in 1830 that 'a sinner has power to repent without the Spirit'. He subsequently declared that he had been misunderstood, explaining that he did believe that the Spirit acts in conversion overall. But others did not retract. Nine students at Glasgow Congregational Theological Academy were expelled in 1844 for 'self-conversionism'. They went on to form part of the new Evangelical Union, a largely Scottish denomination committed to revivalism.[54] Eagerness for converts had the effect of modifying the theology of a section of Evangelicalism. The same motive operated later in the century on the mind of R. F. Horton, an eminent Congregationalist who

51. M. Raleigh (ed.), *Alexander Raleigh: Records of his Life* (Edinburgh, 1881), p. 15.

52. J. Cox, *The English Churches in a Secular Society: Lambeth, 1870–1930* (New York, 1982), pp. 248 f.

53. J. Milner, 'The nature of the Spirit's influence on the understanding', *Works*, ed. I. Milner, Vol. 8.

54. Carwardine, *Transatlantic Revivalism*, pp, xiv, 63, 99.

reached the identical conclusion that a person may exercise his will in order to be converted.[55] Such thinkers were trying to reduce the mysterious element in conversion for the sake of making the experience more widely known.

The most celebrated issue raised by conversion was its relation to baptism. This was the substance of what probably qualified as the chief theological controversy of the early and mid-nineteenth century. The problem was one of reconciling the conviction of Evangelicals that conversion is the time when a person becomes a Christian with two statements in the Book of Common Prayer of the Church of England. According to the order for baptism, an infant is declared regenerate at the end of the ceremony; and according to the catechism, baptism is the occasion of our new birth. Evangelicals who were also Anglicans had a tangled knot to untie. Furthermore, Anglicans of other schools were able to claim that Evangelicals were disloyal to the formularies of their church. The best known incident, remembered as what provoked Henry Manning's secession to Rome, was the Gorham case of 1847–51. Bishop Philpotts of Exeter, a punctilious High Churchman, refused to institute George Gorham, an Evangelical clergyman, to a living in Devon because he did not accept the Prayer Book teaching that baptism is the time when a person is born again. On appeal to the Judicial Committee of the Privy Council, Gorham's right to reject the doctrine of baptismal regeneration was upheld.[56] But this affair was only the tip of an iceberg. Controversy had begun as early as 1812, when Richard Mant, a traditional High Churchman, had criticised Evangelicals for rejecting the Prayer Book doctrine of baptismal regeneration.[57] Evangelicals made a variety of replies. The order of infant baptism, some held, expresses a charitable hope about the future regeneration of the child; or, according to others, the service is designed for believers who could pray with confidence for the salvation of the child.[58] Others again felt that they had to embrace a doctrine of baptismal regeneration, going on to redefine regeneration to mean not 'becoming a Christian', but something less decisive. This was the course taken, for instance, by J. B. Sumner, later Archbishop of Canterbury.[59]

---

55. Horton, *An Autobiography* (London, 1917), p. 37.

56. O. Chadwick, *The Victorian Church*, Vol. 1, 2nd edn (London, 1970), pp. 250–62.

57. D. M. Thompson, 'Baptism, Church and Society in Britain since 1800', Hulsean Lectures, University of Cambridge, 1984, pp. 12–17.

58. G. Bugg, *Spiritual Regeneration Not Necessarily Connected with Baptism* (Kettering, 1816). [C. Marsh], *The Life of the Rev. William Marsh, D.D.* (London, 1867), p. 131.

59. Sumner, *Apostolical Preaching Considered, in an Examination of St Paul's Epistles* (London, 1815), p. 137 n.

It is a shaky answer, a sign that Evangelicals found this apparent discrepancy between their doctrine and their liturgy embarrassing.

It is not surprising that the question was aired repeatedly. In Scotland, for example, a leading Episcopalian and later Primus, James Walker, insisted in 1825 that baptismal regeneration was the teaching of his church.[60] His arguments were met by a number of Evangelical clergy, and a spirited pamphlet war ensued. In England, C. H. Spurgeon, the great Baptist preacher of the Metropolitan Tabernacle, censured the Evangelical Anglican clergy in a sermon of 1864 for failing to repudiate the principle of baptismal regeneration. A storm of indignation burst about him.[61] A Prayer Book Revision Society, guided by Lord Ebury from 1859 to 1889, wished to remove 'everything which can be held to imply that Regeneration by the Holy Spirit is *inseparably connected with the Rite*'.[62] But the anomaly remained to trouble twentieth-century Evangelical Anglicans. In 1965 *The Church of England Newspaper* asked its largely Evangelical readership whether the church should cease baptising infants altogether. Of the clergy, 289 replied no, but 47 replied yes. Of the laity, 455 said no, but a remarkable 268 said yes.[63] Clearly a high proportion of the respondents were worried about what infant baptism was supposed to signify. The problem was perennial because the idea that infants are regenerate through baptism does appear in the Book of Common Prayer, whereas Evangelicals have believed that only through conversion does a person become a Christian. The recurring difficulties on this subject are a corollary of the centrality of conversion in Evangelical religion.

Activism

A second leading characteristic of Evangelicals has been their activism. It flows from the first, as Jonathan Edwards remarked. 'Persons', he wrote, 'after their own conversion, have commonly expressed an exceeding great desire for the conversion of others. Some have thought that they should be willing to die for the conversion of any soul . . .'[64] Henry Venn, by his own computation, was

60. Walker, *The Gospel Commission* (Edinburgh, 1826).
61. W. Y. Fullerton, *C. H. Spurgeon* (London, 1920), pp. 305 ff.
62. *Auricular Confession and Priestly Absolution; Lord Ebury's Prayer-Book Amendment Bill* (London, 1880), p. 2.
63. *CEN*, 5 February 1965, p. 7.
64. Edwards, 'Narrative', p. 47.

instrumental in the conversion of some 900 people during three years at Huddersfield.[65] A Methodist missioner of the later nineteenth century claimed to have seen nearly 90,000 led to Christ at his meetings.[66] Wesley's early preachers threw themselves into efforts to spread the gospel. A typical one attended class and band meetings, visited the sick and preached five or six times a week; another, when stationed at York in 1760, rode a circuit of 300 miles every six weeks, visiting some sixty societies; a third frequently managed no more than eight hours of sleep a week.[67] Preaching services at 5 a.m. were common.[68] Sunday could be immensely demanding, as the resolutions of a Methodist and his wife in 1774 reveal: 'We will attend the preaching at five o'clock in the morning; at eight, go to the prayer meeting; at ten, to the public worship at the Foundery; hear Mr. Perry at Cripplegate, at two; be at the preaching at the Foundery, at five; meet with the general society, at six; meet in the united bands at seven, and again be at the prayer meeting at eight; and then come home, to read and pray by ourselves'.[69] The dedication of laypeople that was so marked a feature of Methodism was imitated in the Church of England. Paid full-time and voluntary part-time workers became general in Evangelical parishes. There was a similar development in the Church of Scotland, where Thomas Chalmers appointed deacons for parochial visitation.[70] 'The Evangelical saint of to-day', declared the Congregationalist R. W. Dale in 1879, 'is not a man who spends his nights and days in fasting and prayer, but a man who is a zealous Sunday-school teacher, holds mission services among the poor, and attends innumerable committee meetings. "Work" has taken its place side by side with prayer . . .'[71]

The result was a transformation in the role of a minister of religion. The English parish clergyman of the later eighteenth century was very like a member of the gentry in how he spent his time. Duty consisted almost exclusively in taking services.[72] For the Evangelical, however, pastoral work was labori-

65. J. Bull, *Memorials of the Rev. William Bull* (London, 1864), p. 248.

66. T. Waugh, *Twenty-Three Years a Missioner* (London, n.d.), p. 62.

67. *WV*, Vol. 1, pp. 99, 233; Vol. 2, p. 91.

68. J. Lawson, 'The people called Methodists: 2; "Our discipline"', in R. Davies and G. Rupp (eds), *A History of the Methodist Church in Great Britain*, Vol. 1 (London, 1965), pp. 189, 198.

69. Lackington, *Memoirs*, pp. 128 f.

70. S. Mechie, *The Church and Scottish Social Development, 1780–1870* (London, 1960), pp. 52 ff.

71. Dale, 'The Evangelical Revival', *The Evangelical Revival and other Sermons* (London, 1880), p. 35.

72. A. Russell, *The Clerical Profession* (London, 1980), chs 3 and 4.

ous. 'To acquaint ourselves', ran a clerical manual of 1830, 'with the various wants of our people; to win their affections; to give a seasonable warning, encouragement, instruction, or consolidation; to identify ourselves with their spiritual interests, in the temper of Christian sympathy, and under a sense of Ministerial obligation; to do this with the constancy, seriousness, and fervid energy which the matter requires, is indeed a work of industry, patience, and self-denial.'[73] In the 1840s Spencer Thornton, Rector of Wendover, each week delivered seven evening lectures, gave two afternoon readings and conducted four Bible classes; he also held five monthly and three quarterly meetings.[74] At a higher level, Bishop C. R. Sumner of Winchester wrote more than 3,500 business letters in his last year of office and Bishop Bickersteth of Ripon excited surprise by choosing to preach three times each Sunday on his arrival in the diocese.[75] At the 1851 census of religion, whereas Anglican churches overall provided an average of 2.06 services a Sunday, a sample of churches belonging to the Evangelical Simeon Trust provided 2.52. An unsympathetic commentator was forced to conclude in 1860 that 'the evangelical clergy as a body are indefatigable in ministerial duties'.[76]

The Methodists were equally exemplary. Wesley was a typhoon of energy, preaching more than 40,000 sermons and issuing more than 400 publications.[77] John Fletcher of Madeley, a clergyman who was Wesley's designated successor, was described by his wife as 'always on the stretch for God'.[78] Adam Clarke gave up tea and coffee on Wesley's advice in 1782, and consequently saved several whole years of time over the rest of his life for devotion to Christian scholarship. 'For a short time after he left off the use of those *exotics*', according to his biographer, 'he took in the evenings, a cup of *milk and water*, or a cup of *weak infusion of camomile*; but as he found that he gained no time by this means, and the gaining of time was his great object, he gave that totally up . . .'[79]

73. C. Bridges, *The Christian Ministry*, 3rd edn (London, 1830), p. 477.

74. *CO*, March 1850, p. 213.

75. G. H. Sumner, *Life of Charles Richard Sumner, D.D.* (London, 1876), p. 212. Bickersteth, *Bickersteth*, p. 153.

76. 'English Evangelical clergy', *Macmillan's Magazine*, 1860, pp. 119 f., quoted by W. D. Balda, '"Spheres of Influence": Simeon's Trust and its implications for Evangelical patronage', PhD thesis, University of Cambridge, 1981, pp. 196 f., 199.

77. R. P. Heitzenrater, *The Elusive Mr. Wesley: 1: John Wesley his Own Biographer* (Nashville, Tenn., 1984), p. 21.

78. H. Moore, *The Life of Mrs Mary Fletcher*, 11th edn (London, 1844), p. 150.

79. J. B. B. Clarke (ed.), *An Account of the Infancy, Religious and Literary Life of Adam Clarke, LL.D., F. A. S., &c., &c., &c.*, Vol. 1 (London, 1833), p. 191.

Time was scarce. A working week of between 90 and 100 hours was expected of men in the nineteenth-century Wesleyan ministry.[80] It is hardly surprising that the connexion maintained a 'Worn-Out Ministers' Fund'. An identical shift to a new dynamism is apparent in the life of the Scot, Thomas Chalmers. In his early ministry he was not an Evangelical. After the satisfactory discharge of his duties, Chalmers commented at the time, 'a minister may enjoy five days in the week of uninterrupted leisure'. After his conversion, by contrast, Chalmers was reputed to have visited 11,000 homes in his Glasgow parish during a single year.[81] Evangelicalism brought about a striking change of attitude.

There were other effects of the imperative to be up and doing. Learning, for example, could be regarded as a dispensable luxury. At the beginning of the nineteenth century Independent ministers were trained not in theology or Greek, but simply in preaching. It would have been 'highly improper', according to a contributor to their magazine, 'to spend, in literary acquisitions, the time and talents which were so imperiously demanded in the harvest field'.[82] The same factor could inhibit scholarship even at the universities. It was said of James Scholefield, Regius Professor of Greek at Cambridge from 1825, that 'had his other numerous and important duties allowed sufficient leisure, his Editions of the ancients would doubtless have exhibited more of original research'.[83] As it was, the quest for souls generally drove Evangelicals out from centres of learning to the parishes and to the foreign mission field. The missionary movement of the nineteenth and twentieth centuries was the fruit of the Evangelical Revival. That is not to claim sole credit for the Evangelicals. On the contrary, Roman Catholic missions had for long put Protestants to shame. Yet a direct result of the revival was the creation of new missionary societies, beginning with that of the Baptists in 1792, that did so much to make the Christian faith a worldwide religion.[84] The dedication of the Cambridge Seven, a set of promising young graduates who entered the China Inland Mission in

80. Field, 'Methodism in Metropolitan London', p. 46.

81. [Chalmers,] *Observations on a Passage in Mr Playfair's Letter* (Cupar, Fife, 1805), p. 10. I. H. Murray, 'Thomas Chalmers and the revival of the church', *Banner of Truth*, March 1980, p. 16.

82. *Evangelical Magazine*, 1803, p. 203, quoted by G. F. Nuttall, *The Significance of Trevecca College, 1768–91* (London, 1969), p. 7.

83. W. Selwyn, in H. Scholefield, *Memoir of the late Rev. James Scholefield, M.A.* (London, 1855), p. 335.

84. S. Neill, *A History of Christian Missions*, 2nd edn (Harmondsworth, Middlesex, 1986), pp. 213–16.

1885, was a celebrated case of Evangelical zeal.[85] But activism often spilled over beyond simple gospel work. 'Toil, toil, toil', wrote Lord Shaftesbury in his diary for April 1850, 'nor should I lament, could I say fruit, fruit, fruit.'[86] Shaftesbury's efforts in such causes as public health provided a further outlet for Evangelical energy. Wilberforce's campaign against the slave trade and Nonconformist political crusades around 1900 are but the most famous instances of attempts to enforce the ethics of the gospel. A host of voluntary societies embodied the philanthropic urge. Hannah More, the Evangelical authoress of the turn of the nineteenth century, summed up succinctly the prevailing Evangelical attitude. 'Action is the life of virtue', she wrote, 'and the world is the theatre of action.'[87]

Biblicism

The third main feature of the Evangelicals, their devotion to the Bible, has been the result of their belief that all spiritual truth is to be found in its pages. The Bible alone, John Wesley contended, was the source of his doctrine of salvation. 'Let me be *homo unius libri* [a man of one book]', he declared in the preface to his collected sermons of 1746.[88] His brother Charles was so immersed in scripture that in one of his hymns, 'Lord, and is Thine anger gone', twenty-six biblical allusions are crowded into sixty-four lines.[89] Opponents of an early Methodist preacher, he reported, 'said I made my Bible my god!'[90] Another declared that after his conversion the Bible 'seemed an entirely new book'.[91] This frequent experience among Evangelicals led to charges by eighteenth-century opponents that they were subjecting the Bible to arbitrary interpretation under the alleged illumination of the Holy Spirit. The opponents, often maintaining a doughty tradition of Anglican apologetic, claimed to be the more scriptural party in appealing to the bare text.[92] Yet Evangelicals were certain they un-

85. J. C. Pollock, *The Cambridge Seven* (London, 1955).

86. G. B. A. M. Finlayson, *The Seventh Earl of Shaftesbury, 1801–1885* (London, 1981), p. 322.

87. More, *An Estimate of the Religion of the Fashionable World* (London, 1808 edn), p. 146.

88. Heitzenrater, *Wesley*, Vol. 1, p. 149.

89. J. Dale, 'The theological and literary qualities of the poetry of Charles Wesley in relation to the standards of his age', PhD thesis, University of Cambridge, 1961, p. 145.

90. *WV*, Vol. 3, p. 57 (John Nelson).

91. ibid., Vol. 2, pp. 183 f. (George Shadford).

92. W. and T. Ludlam, *Essays Scriptural, Moral and Logical*, Vol.2 (London, 1817),

derstood the Bible clearly. Hence the nineteenth-century Scottish revivalist Brownlow North 'spent hours every day in hard and prayerful study of its pages.'[93] A contemporary evangelist, Henry Moorhouse, was similarly devoted. 'He would not suffer anything, not even a sheet of paper, to be laid upon his Bible. There alone, apart, it must lie, unique, matchless, wonderful, the very mind and presence of the infinite and eternal God.'[94] Evangelicals revered the Bible.

Respect for the Bible did not necessarily lead them into far-fetched views. The passage from the book of Hebrews about a rock following Israel through the wilderness came up for discussion at a conversation party for Cambridge undergraduates led by Charles Simeon. Did the rock really move? 'Oh yes, of course', replied Simeon, 'with a hop, skip and a jump!'[95] Here was no wooden literalness. It is true that doctrinal preoccupations often encouraged an instinct for turning to the New Testament letters in preference to the gospels.[96] Yet Evangelicals did not normally concentrate on obscurities. For the end of the nineteenth century, when the age of the questionnaire was just dawning, we possess a detailed breakdown of texts taken by preachers in a variety of Evangelical pulpits on a Sunday in March 1896. The survey came about because, intriguingly, the journal *Tit-Bits*, on receiving a complaint from a reader about the length of sermons, launched a competition to find the longest—it was, it turned out, a sermon preached at a Primitive Methodist chapel lasting one hour eighteen minutes. *The British Weekly*, an interdenominational paper, repeated the survey and also investigated texts. Three-quarters were drawn from the New Testament. John's gospel was the most popular source, followed closely by the first letter of John and then by the other three gospels. In the Old Testament, most texts came from Psalms, Genesis and Isaiah. None was taken from Philemon, 2 or 3 John, Lamentations, Obadiah, Micah, Nahum, Habakkuk or Zephaniah. The single verse that inspired most sermons was Galatians 2:20 about being crucified with Christ.[97] Certainly there is no evidence here of the deliberate searching out of obscure texts.

------

p. 99, quoted by Walsh, 'Yorkshire Evangelicals', p. 14; cf. G. Reedy, *The Bible and Reason: Anglicans and Scripture in Late Seventeenth-Century England* (Philadelphia, 1985), ch. 5, pt III.

93. K. Moody-Stuart, *Brownlow North: The Story of his Life and Work* (Kilmarnock, [1904]), p. 185.

94. J. Macpherson, *Henry Moorhouse: The English Evangelist* (London, n.d.), p. 94.

95. H. E. Hopkins, *Charles Simeon of Cambridge* (London, 1977), p. 161.

96. For example, N. Anderson, *An Adopted Son* (Leicester, 1985), p. 289.

97. *BW*, 5 March 1896, p. 325; 26 March 1896, p. 379.

There was agreement among Evangelicals of all generations that the Bible is inspired by God. When it came to determining the implications of inspiration, however, there were notable divergences. Henry Venn of Huddersfield referred incidentally in 1763 to 'the infallible word of God' and the Countess of Huntingdon's Connexion confessed its belief in 1783 in 'the infallible truth' of the scriptures.[98] 'The Bible is altogether TRUE', wrote Edward Bickersteth in his extremely popular *A Scripture Help* (1816). 'It is truth without any mixture of error.'[99] Yet in the period up to that date there was no attempt to elaborate any theory of infallibility or inerrancy. On the contrary, there was remarkable fluidity in ideas about the effects of inspiration on the text. The overriding aim of early Evangelicals was to bring home the message of the Bible and to encourage its devotional use rather than to develop a doctrine of scripture. A body of Evangelical opinion, however, began to insist from the 1820s onwards on inerrancy, verbal inspiration and the need for literal interpretation of the Bible.[100] In reaction against the publication of *Essays and Reviews* (1860), a Broad Church manifesto for studying the Bible in the manner of any other book, the newer dogmatic school of thought became more vocal.[101] 'To us', wrote the Baptist C. H. Spurgeon, 'the plenary verbal inspiration of the Holy Scripture is a fact and not a hypothesis.'[102] From the chair of the Congregational Union in 1894, by contrast, G. S. Barrett repudiated the 'crude and mechanical theory of verbal inspiration.'[103] Attitudes to the Bible drew apart until, in the wake of the First World War, the Evangelical world divided into conservatives and liberals primarily on that issue. The importance attributed by Evangelicals to the Bible eventually led to something approaching schism in their ranks.

98. Venn, *Complete Duty*, p. 51. 'The fifteen articles of the Countess of Huntingdon's Connexion', in E. Welch (ed.), *Two Calvinistic Methodist Chapels, 1743–1811* (London, 1975), p. 88.

99. Bickersteth, *A Scripture Help Designed to Assist in Reading the Bible Profitably*, 17th edn (London, 1838), p. 2.

100. W. J. C. Ervine, 'Doctrine and diplomacy; some aspects of the life and thought of the Anglican Evangelical clergy, 1797–1837', PhD thesis, University of Cambridge, 1979, ch. 3; cf. below, pp. 86–91.

101. On Anglicans, cf. J. L. Altholz, 'The mind of Victorian orthodoxy; Anglican responses to "Essays and Reviews", 1860–1864', *Church History*, vol. 51, no. 2 (1982).

102. Spurgeon, *The Greatest Fight in the World* (London, 1896), p. 27, quoted by P. S. Kruppa, *Charles Haddon Spurgeon: A Preacher's Progress* (New York, 1982), p. 374.

103. Barrett, 'The secularisation of the pulpit', in *Congregational Year Book*, 1895, p. 27.

Crucicentrism

The doctrine of the cross, fourthly, has been the focus of the gospel. The Evangelical movement, in the words of Gladstone, 'aimed at bringing back, and by an aggressive movement, the Cross, and all that the Cross essentially implies'.[104] Nothing in the Christian system, according to John Wesley, 'is of greater consequence than the doctrine of Atonement. It is properly the distinguishing point between Deism and Christianity'.[105] The reconciliation of humanity to God, that is to say, achieved by Christ on the cross is why the Christian religion speaks of God as the author of salvation. 'I am saved', wrote an early Methodist preacher, 'through faith in the blood of the Lamb'.[106] There is a cloud of witnesses on the theme. An eighteenth-century Scottish theologian, John Maclaurin, like many subsequent Evangelicals, preached on 'Glorying in the cross of Christ'.[107] 'The death of Christ', according to the clerical manual of 1830, 'in this scriptural and comprehensive view, includes the whole Christian system'.[108] Representative twentieth-century Evangelicals in the Church of England said much the same.[109] Theologians elaborated the point: R. W. Dale, with telling reasonableness in 1875; James Denney, with scrupulous clarity in 1902; John Stott, with contemporary awareness in 1986; and, greatest of all, P. T. Forsyth in a series of vibrant treatises in the early twentieth century.[110] Critics deplored what they saw as an obsession. The Quaker statesman John Bright, having heard G. B. Bubier, a Congregational divine, is said to have murmured to himself, 'The atonement, always the atonement! Have they nothing else to say?'[111] Even those who professed a liberal

---

104. Gladstone, 'The Evangelical movement: its parentage, progress, and issue', *Gleanings from Past Years*, Vol. 7 (London, 1879), p. 207.

105. Wesley to Mary Bishop, 7 February 1778, *The Letters of the Rev. John Wesley, A.M.*, ed. J. Telford, Vol. 6 (London, 1931), pp. 297 f.

106. *WV*, Vol. 1, p. 118 (Christopher Hopper).

107. W. H. Goold (ed.), *The Works of the Rev. John Maclaurin*, Vol. 1 (Edinburgh, 1860), pp. 63–102.

108. Bridges, *Christian Ministry*, p. 320.

109. *R*, 12 January 1934, p. 15 (Stephen Neill). *CEN*, 5 March 1954, p. 8 (Bishop Joost de Blank).

110. Dale, *The Atonement* (London, 1875). Denney, *The Death of Christ* (London, 1902). Stott, *The Cross of Christ* (Leicester, 1986). Forsyth, *The Cruciality of the Cross* (London, 1909); *Positive Preaching and the Modern Mind* (London, 1907); *The Work of Christ* (London, 1910).

111. A. J. Davidson (ed.), *The Autobiography and Diary of Samuel Davidson, D.D., LL.D.* (Edinburgh, 1899), p. 64.

version of Evangelical belief in the twentieth century like the Methodist W. R. Maltby felt compelled to lay great stress on the cross.[112] 'If men are Evangelical Christians at all', declared the Congregationalist Alexander Raleigh in 1879, 'they can say without a shadow of insincerity, "God forbid we should glory, save in the cross of our Lord Jesus Christ . . ."'[113]

Looking back on an interwar childhood in the Brethren, Anne Arnott recalled trying on Christmas Day to escape in imagination to Bethlehem from the ministry which, as always, centred on the crucifixion.[114] The atonement eclipsed even the incarnation among Evangelicals. In 1891 Charles Gore, a rising young Anglo-Catholic, inaugurated a central tradition in Anglican thought by arguing in the Bampton Lectures for the incarnation as the heart of Christian theology.[115] The warning issued to Methodists in the following year is instructive:

> We rejoice in the prominence which is being given to the doctrine of the Incarnation, with all its solemn lessons and inspirations. But we must be careful lest the Cross passes into the background, from which it is the glory of our fathers to have drawn it. Give to the *death* of Christ its true place in your own experience and in your Christian work—as a witness to the real and profound evil of sin, as an overwhelming manifestation of Divine love, as the ground of acceptance with God, as a pattern of sacrifice to disturb us when life is too easy, to inspire and console us when life is hard, and as the only effectual appeal to the general heart of men, and, above all, as the Atonement for our sins.[116]

To make any theme other than the cross the fulcrum of a theological system was to take a step away from Evangelicalism. The Congregationalist James Baldwin Brown, to the dismay of many co-religionists, had already followed

---

112. Maltby, *Christ and his Cross* (London, 1935); cf. W. Strawson, 'Methodist theology, 1850–1950', in R. Davies *et al.* (eds), *A History of the Methodist Church in Great Britain*, Vol. 3 (London, 1983), pp. 217 f.

113. Raleigh (ed.), *Raleigh*, p. 281.

114. Arnott, *The Brethren* (London, 1970 edn), p. 17.

115. Gore, *The Incarnation of the Son of God* (London, 1891); cf. A. M. Ramsey, *From Gore to Temple: The Development of Anglican Theology between 'Lux Mundi' and the Second World War, 1889–1939* (London, 1960).

116. 'Annual address to the Methodist Societies', *Minutes of Several Conversations . . . of the People called Methodists* (London, 1892), pp. 374 f.

the Broad Churchman F. D. Maurice along that path, and by 1897 a Methodist, J. Scott Lidgett, was doing the same.[117] Christopher Chavasse was still urging caution on Anglican Evangelicals about this trend of thought in 1939. 'Let us', he told them, 'keep close to Scripture, and allow the Atonement to explain the Incarnation—Christ was born in order to die . . .'[118] Michael Ramsey, Archbishop of Canterbury, showed he knew his Evangelicals when, in addressing their Keele Congress in 1967, he urged them to recognise that other Anglicans also upheld, in different ways, the 'supreme assertion that in the Cross of Christ alone is our salvation'.[119]

The standard view of Evangelicals was that Christ died as a substitute for sinful mankind. Human beings, they held, were so rebellious against God that a just penalty would have been death. Yet, as Thomas Scott the commentator discovered to his delight, 'Christ indeed bore the sins of all who should ever believe, in all their guilt, condemnation, and deserved punishment, in his own body on the tree'.[120] Belief in a substitutionary atonement originally distinguished Evangelicals from even the strictest divines of other schools. William Law, an outstanding devotional writer drawn on by Scott, among many others, explicitly repudiated the idea that Christ suffered in our stead.[121] Probably the greatest sermon by Robert Hall, Baptist minister in Cambridge at the opening of the nineteenth century and the ablest preacher of his day, was a defence of the doctrine of substitutionary atonement.[122] Its argument was still being repeated, with due acknowledgement of Hall, in a statement of Evangelical principles by the Anglican W. R. Fremantle in 1875.[123] By the 1870s, however, the fear was expressed that substitution was being discarded, and even the leading Wesleyan theologian W. B. Pope was equivocal on the subject.[124] The

---

117. Baldwin Brown, *The Divine Life in Man* (London, [1860]). See also C. Binfield, '"No quest, no conquest." Baldwin Brown and Silvester Home', *So Down to Prayers: Studies in English Nonconformity, 1780–1920* (London, 1977), p. 195. Scott Lidgett, *The Spiritual Principle of the Atonement* (London, 1897); cf. Scott Lidgett, *My Guided Life* (London, 1936), pp. 149–58.

118. *R*, 13 January 1939, p. 26.

119. *CEN*, 7 April 1967, p. 3.

120. Scott, *The Force of Truth* (Edinburgh, 1984 edn), p. 65.

121. Law, *A Serious Call to a Devout and Holy Life*, 20th edn (Romsey, 1816), p. 266.

122. Hall, 'On the substitution of the innocent for the guilty', in O. Gregory (ed.), *The Works of Robert Hall, A.M.*, Vol. 5 (London, 1839), pp. 73–103.

123. Fremantle, 'Atonement', in Garbett (ed.), *Evangelical Principles*, pp. 86–92.

124. E. Steane, *The Doctrine of Christ developed by the Apostles* (Edinburgh, 1872), p. viii. Pope, *The Person of Christ* (London, 1875), p. 51.

humanitarian tone of public opinion was veering against this understanding of the death of Christ. George Bernard Shaw voiced the newer attitude in characteristically searing fashion. 'I detest the doctrine of the Atonement', he once wrote, 'holding that ladies and gentlemen cannot as such possibly allow anyone else to expiate their sins by suffering a cruel death.'[125] In the early years of the twentieth century the teaching was fading from the Methodist pulpit.[126] It survived nevertheless in conservative Evangelical circles, enshrined, for instance, in the statement of faith of the Inter-Varsity Fellowship of Christian Unions. Jesus Christ was there described as dying not only as our representative but also as our substitute.[127] Belief that Christ died in our stead was not uniform in the Evangelical tradition, but it was normal.

The implications of the cross for life were also important for Evangelicals. There was a bond between the atonement and the quest for sanctification. 'All treatises', wrote Henry Venn, '. . . written to promote holiness of life, must be deplorably defective, unless the cross of Christ be laid as the foundation . . .'[128] The motive for spiritual growth was gratitude for Calvary. Preoccupation with the cross led to some exaggerated forms of spirituality. Mrs Penn-Lewis, an early twentieth-century holiness advocate, for example, went about teaching that there must be a decisive experience for the believer of crucifixion of the self.[129] But it was also common for preachers to dwell, as did the Congregationalist David Thomas in the 1840s, on the 'relation of the Atonement to practical righteousness'.[130] By 1908 this line of thought had generated in the mind of the Wesleyan J. E. Rattenbury a sanction for socialism. The gospel declares that human beings are to be considered not for their station, rank or riches but for their potential as sons of God. Consequently, he contended, 'the theology of the cross . . . is well fitted to be the soul of the Collectivist movement'.[131] Richard Heath, an extreme proponent of the social gospel, went further. The vicarious suffering of Christ was for him a symptom of the never-ceasing

---

125. Shaw, 'What is my religious faith?', *Sixteen Self Sketches* (London, 1949), p. 79.

126. I. E. Page (ed.), *John Brash: Memorials and Correspondence* (London, 1912), p. 95. Strawson, 'Methodist theology', pp. 202, 215 ff.

127. D. Johnson, *Contending for the Faith: A History of the Evangelical Movement in the Universities and Colleges* (Leicester, 1979), p. 359.

128. Venn, *Complete Duty*, p. xiii.

129. M. N. Garrard, *Mrs Penn-Lewis: A Memoir* (London, 1930), pp. 26, 168, 197.

130. H. A. Thomas (ed.), *Memorials of the Rev. David Thomas, B.A.* (London, 1876), p. 37.

131. Rattenbury, 'Socialism and the old theology', *Six Sermons on Social Subjects* (London, [1908]), pp. 82 f.

fact of human solidarity in adversity. God was suffering with his creatures.[132] Attention to the cross could lead in diverse directions.

The *theologia crucis* gave rise to debate. For whom did Christ die? For the elect only, as Calvinist believers in particular redemption affirmed? Or for all, as Arminian advocates of general redemption insisted? The Evangelical ranks were riven in the eighteenth century by controversy between Methodists, who were Arminians, and most others, who were Calvinists. By the beginning of the nineteenth century, however, this debate was dying down. Most Evangelicals were content to adopt a 'moderate Calvinism' that in terms of practical pulpit instruction differed only slightly from the Methodist version of Arminianism. Leading Anglican Evangelicals expressed the view in 1800 that redemption is both general and particular. Arminians were right to stress human responsibility to repent and Calvinists right to stress the need for divine grace.[133] 'I frankly confess', wrote William Wilberforce, 'that I myself am no Calvinist, though I am not either an anti-Calvinist.'[134] Discussion of the scope of the atonement became moribund. It was dismissed as mysterious, impractical, a subject ill suited to bringing about conversions. Hence denominations that had maintained a separate existence because of the issue eventually came together. In England the gap between General and Particular Baptists that went back to the early seventeenth century steadily narrowed during the nineteenth, and in 1891 the two bodies formally fused. In Scotland, the Congregational Union, professedly Calvinist, and the Evangelical Union, revivalist and Arminian in style, united in 1897. What Evangelicals agreed on seemed of infinitely greater importance than their disagreements, and their pre-eminent ground of agreement was the cruciality of the cross.

132. M. R. Pease, *Richard Heath, 1831–1912* (n.p., [1922]), pp. 48 ff.

133. J. H. Pratt (ed.), *The Thought of the Evangelical Leaders: Notes of the Discussions of The Eclectic Society, London, during the Years 1798–1814* (Edinburgh, 1978), pp. 165 ff., 505 ff. For the background, see A. P. F. Sell, *The Great Debate: Calvinism, Arminianism and Salvation* (Worthing, 1982).

134. Wilberforce to Robert Southey, 5 December [?], 2519/63, National Library of Scotland, quoted by P. F. Dixon, 'The politics of emancipation; the movement for the abolition of slavery in the British West Indies, 1807–33', DPhil thesis, University of Oxford, 1971, p. 86.

CHAPTER 3

The Essential Evangelicalism Dialectic:
The Historiography of the Early Neo-Evangelical Movement and the Observer-Participant Dilemma

Douglas A. Sweeney

Douglas Sweeney was a precocious graduate student at Vanderbilt University when he published this insightful account of what he called an American evangelical "identity crisis." That crisis, described as "the increasing tension between historic evangelical ecumenism and historic evangelical thought," anticipated later questions about how to integrate Pentecostal, charismatic, and global Protestant-like movements into a general evangelical framework. Sweeney, now Dean of Beeson Divinity School at Samford University in Birmingham, Alabama, is the author and editor of many books, including *Edwards the Exegete: Biblical Interpretation and Anglo-Protestant Culture on the Eve of the Enlightenment* (Oxford University Press, 2015) and, more germane to the subjects here, *The American Evangelical Story: A History of the Movement* (Baker Academic, 2005). The article was published in *Church History* 60 (March 1991): 70–84, and is reprinted here with permission of Cambridge University Press.

*　　　　　*　　　　　*

In the fifty years since the emergence of the neo-evangelical movement, the connotations of the word "evangelical" have changed significantly. Richard Quebedeaux charts an evolution of the movement beginning with the "neo-evangelicalism" of its founders, continuing through the "new evangelicalism" of their children, and on to the more radical evangelicalism typified by contemporary "Young Evangelicals."[1] Although these transitions cannot always be delineated as clearly as Quebedeaux implies, the evangelicalism of the past fifty years has certainly proved more dynamic than static and has managed to wiggle its way out of the grasp of its neo-evangelical founders.

In recent years, evangelicals themselves have risen to a position of prominence in the historiography of their own movement. Leonard Sweet calls this "the most arresting phenomenon in American religious scholarship today." Evangelical scholars "are engaging with and criticizing their own tradition—and thereby setting the scholarly agenda for years to come—by writing the history of evangelicalism."[2] Clearly this is quite a responsibility. Evangelical historians can provide an enormous service to their movement, to the academic community, and to broader culture if they practice their craft honestly and thoroughly; as Sweet quips, "the best attacks are inside jobs."[3] But when personal or institutional agendas are allowed to color a historian's depictions of the movement, no one is served.

It comes as no surprise that evangelical scholars continue to jockey for historiographical position. They hail from varied backgrounds and hold equally varied hopes for the future of their movement. However, these scholars tend to work out of one of two prevailing models. The first and predominant model will be called Reformed. The second will be called Holiness.[4] The aim of this article is to describe the Reformed and Holiness models for early neo-evangelicalism (that of the 1940s and 1950s) as thesis and antithesis, and to look toward a synthesis for the new evangelical historiography. The essay proceeds on the assumption that what Sweet calls the "observer-participant" state of this historiography is as significant as it is remarkable, and that it has matured to a level worthy of critical assessment.[5]

---

1. Richard Quebedeaux, *The Young Evangelicals: Revolution in Orthodoxy* (New York, 1974), pp. 39–41. Though contrasts of this kind aid in describing the development of the post-war evangelical ethos, the neo-evangelical founders called themselves the "new evangelicals." The term, therefore, should not be confused as representing only second generation neo-evangelicals.

2. Leonard I. Sweet, "Wise as Serpents, Innocent as Doves: The New Evangelical Historiography," *Journal of the American Academy of Religion* 56 (1988): 397, 402.

3. Ibid., p. 413.

4. One should certainly avoid locking people up in historiographical boxes. Admittedly, not everyone discussed here falls into one group or the other. However, enough evidence presents itself to categorize these scholars loosely into one of the groups. The labels, furthermore, were not affixed arbitrarily. They are employed in much of the literature, they represent fairly accurately the theological distinctives of each group, and they point to the historical methods used by each group.

5. Sweet, "Wise as Serpents, Innocent as Doves," p. 413.

1.

Scholars such as George Marsden of Duke University, Joel Carpenter of the Pew Charitable Trusts, Mark Noll of Wheaton College, Donald Bloesch of Dubuque Theological Seminary, and Bernard Ramm, most recently of the American Baptist Seminary of the West, represent the Reformed model for neo-evangelical historiography. They tend to approach the history of neo-evangelicalism by discussing the manner in which its intellectual and institutional leaders reformed fundamentalism. Marsden, for example, describes neo-evangelicals as the rebuilders of the "intellectual traditions" of their heritage.[6] Evangelical Douglas Jacobsen has supported this approach in the *Reformed Journal*, writing that evangelicalism's status as an "intellectual religious movement" has always been one of its special concerns. "The core issue" in the emergence of twentieth-century evangelicalism (both in the 1920s to 1930s and in the 1940s to 1950s) "was ideas."[7] Marsden argues, moreover, that although the early neo-evangelical leadership mirrored the "mainstream heritage of fundamentalism" it hoped to infuse mainstream American evangelicalism with an altered form of this heritage. The cultic aspects of fundamentalist militancy were to be abandoned and the fundamentalist attack on modernity was to become sophisticated.[8] Evangelicals, in other words, tried to reform American culture with an intellectually appealing fundamentalism. As Joel Carpenter demonstrates, fundamentalist institutions did indeed provide the incubator from which this new evangelical movement would be hatched.[9] The children of the fundamentalists wanted to keep what they perceived as the best of their heritage and leave the worst behind. Fundamentalist ideas and institutions could prove culturally engaging if only the fundamentalists could clean house.

6. George M. Marsden, "Why No Major Evangelical University?" in *Making Higher Education Christian: The History and Mission of Evangelical Colleges in America*, ed. Joel A. Carpenter and Kenneth W. Shipps (Grand Rapids, 1987), p. 298.

7. Douglas Jacobsen, "Re-visioning Evangelical Theology," *Reformed Journal* 35 (1985): 18.

8. George M. Marsden, "Unity and Diversity in the Evangelical Resurgence," in *Altered Landscapes: Christianity in America, 1935–1985*, ed. David Lotz with Donald W. Shriver and John F. Wilson (Grand Rapids, 1989), p. 67, and "Preachers of Paradox: The Religious New Right in Historical Perspective," in *Religion and America: Spiritual Life in a Secular Age*, ed. Mary Douglas and Steven Tipton (Boston, 1982), p. 155.

9. Joel A. Carpenter, "Fundamentalist Institutions and the Rise of Evangelical Protestantism, 1929–1942," *Church History* 49 (1980): 74 and passim.

The Reformed model for neo-evangelical history shows that evangelicals largely succeeded in reforming fundamentalism.[10] They moved away from their more extreme intellectual assumptions and found a compelling middle ground nearer to the heartland of prefundamentalist evangelicalism.[11] The more evangelicals succeeded in parting with fundamentalism, however, the more they also parted with much of the stability that fundamentalism had provided them. Mark Noll has noted that the academic success experienced by evangelicals in the 1940s "has created a fluid situation where boundaries are not as clear as they once had been."[12] Indeed the altered fundamentalism of the neo-evangelicals proved so culturally accessible and open-ended that according to Marsden, "by 1960 one might classify as 'evangelical' anyone who identified with Billy Graham."[13] To be sure, the Reformed camp still maintains an intellectualist approach to the movement. Donald Bloesch, for example, believes that evangelicals maintain "a definite doctrine."[14] Marsden, also, continues to define evangelicals intellectually (though he admits that "evangelicals will differ . . . over [doctrinal] details").[15] Buttressing the Reformed model, Marsden hails "the triumph—or nearly so" of "Kuyperian

10. James Alden Hedstrom, "Evangelical Program in the United States, 1945–1980: The Morphology of Establishment, Progressive, and Radical Platforms" (Ph.D. diss., Vanderbilt University, 1982), p. 156 argues that "fundamentalism was transcended" in neo-evangelicalism and uses the word "progressive" to describe the new movement.

11. George M. Marsden, "From Fundamentalism to Evangelicalism: A Historical Analysis," in *The Evangelicals: What They Believe, Who They Are, Where They Are Changing*, rev. edition, ed. David F. Wells and John D. Woodbridge (Grand Rapids, 1977), pp. 158, 154.

12. Mark A. Noll, *Between Faith and Criticism: Evangelicals, Scholarship, and the Bible in America* (San Francisco, 1986), pp. 162–163.

13. Marsden, "Preachers of Paradox," p. 156. Marsden has coined the term "open evangelicalism" to epitomize the new spirit the movement took on after its fundamentalist stage. See *Reforming Fundamentalism: Fuller Seminary and the New Evangelicalism* (Grand Rapids, 1987), p. 245.

14. Donald G. Bloesch, *Essentials of Evangelical Theology*, Vol. 1, *God, Authority, and Salvation* (San Francisco, 1978), p. ix.

15. Marsden proposes a five-point doctrinal depiction of evangelical belief. An evangelical trusts in the final authority of Scripture, the real, historical character of God's saving work recorded in Scripture, salvation only through personal trust in Christ, the importance of evangelism and missions, and the importance of a spiritually transformed life. See his introduction in *Evangelicalism and Modern America*, ed. George Marsden (Grand Rapids, 1984), pp. ix–x.

presuppositionalism in the evangelical community."[16] But though powerful Reformed currents may dominate the flow of the evangelical stream, an increasing intellectual openness among evangelicals has allowed for a wealth of theological adaptation.[17]

The Holiness approach to neo-evangelicalism, though not nearly as developed as the Reformed, provides a tempering antithesis to much of what goes on in the establishment historiography (the Reformed approach) today. Typified by scholars such as Timothy Smith of Johns Hopkins University, Donald Dayton of Northern Baptist Theological Seminary, and Leonard Sweet of United Theological Seminary, the Holiness approach argues that evangelicalism has always been more of a dynamic kaleidoscope than the Reformed camp is willing to admit.[18] Rather than looking at the upper echelons of evangelicalism, the Holiness camp seeks to understand the evangelical movement from the bottom up or at the grass roots level.

Donald Dayton (the most vocal of the Holiness scholars) decries what he refers to as the "presbyterianization of evangelicalism and evangelical his-

16. George M. Marsden, "The State of Evangelical Christian Scholarship," *Reformed Journal* 37 (1987): 14.

17. Robert Webber and George Marsden identify fourteen different kinds of evangelicals. Robert E. Webber, *Common Roots: A Call to Evangelical Maturity* (Grand Rapids, 1978), p. 32; Marsden, "Preachers of Paradox," p. 159. More recently, Webber, "Who are the Evangelicals?" *USA Today (Periodical)* 115 (1987): 89 has identified sixteen varieties. See also Webber, "Behind the Scenes: A Personal Account," in *The Orthodox Evangelicals: Who They Are and What They Are Saying*, ed. Robert Webber and Donald Bloesch (Nashville, 1978), pp. 19-20, Bloesch, *The Future of Evangelical Christianity: A Call for Unity Amid Diversity* (Garden City, N.Y., 1983), p. 9, and Joel Carpenter, "The Fundamentalist Leaven and the Rise of an Evangelical United Front," in *The Evangelical Tradition in America*, ed. Leonard I. Sweet (Macon, Ga., 1984), p. 288.

18. Timothy Smith has employed the terms 'mosaic' and 'kaleidoscope' as motifs for the evangelical movement. He depicts evangelicalism not as a doctrinally static twentieth-century phenomenon but in all its glory, so to speak, as a historical, dynamic, and ecumenical movement. Smith and his students have been working for several years on an evangelicalism opus (yet uncompleted). Randall Balmer has suggested recently that a patchwork quilt might provide a more satisfying alternative to Smith's metaphors. He notes that a patchwork quilt exemplifies "folk art rather than fine art" and better symbolizes "the absence of an overall pattern" to evangelicalism. Timothy L. Smith, "The Evangelical Kaleidoscope and the Call to Christian Unity [ecumenical and evangelical antipathy]," *Christian Scholars Review* 15 (1986): 125-140, and Randall Balmer, *Mine Eyes Have Seen the Glory: A Journey into the Evangelical Subculture in America* (New York, 1989), pp. 229-230.

toriography." He argues that the fight for orthodoxy at Princeton Seminary has become the lens through which all subsequent evangelical experience is viewed but asserts that this "fascination" is better understood as a cure for the movement's ills than as a legitimate approach to evangelical history.[19] Dayton claims that the Reformed model for neo-evangelical historiography simply does not work. It projects only the "top half" of the story, the cultural cream. The Reformed camp uses some of the right data (that is, Holiness, Pentecostal, and revivalist sources) but does not allow them to gain interpretive power. Dayton's solution is a new interpretive grid. He and the Holiness camp propose a "people's history" to replace the prevailing elitist history approach.[20] This people's history of evangelicalism has the potential to bear out Timothy Smith's discussion of the "kaleidoscopic diversity of our [evangelical] histories, our organizational structures, and our doctrinal emphases."[21] The social diversification of evangelicalism would prove much more intelligible from the bottom of an evangelical pyramid than from the top. For Dayton, however,

19. Donald W. Dayton, "An Analysis of the Self-Understanding of American Evangelicalism With a Critique of its Correlated Historiography" (Paper delivered at the Wesleyan/Holiness Study Project First Fellows Seminar, Asbury Theological Seminary, 28–30 January 1988), pp. 18–19 and passim (used with permission), and Dayton, "Yet Another Layer of the Onion, Or Opening the Ecumenical Door to Let the Riffraff In," *The Ecumenical Review* 40 (1988): 97 and passim. Dayton uses Bernard Ramm's *The Evangelical Heritage* (Waco, Tex., 1973) as a foil in a number of places. Ramm traces the evangelical heritage from the Reformers through the Scholastics to the Puritans and eventually on through Princeton and into the twentieth century. This epitomizes, according to Dayton, the Reformed bias prevalent among evangelical historians and shows that the Princeton experience has become historiographically determinative. See not only "An Analysis" and "Yet Another Layer," but also Dayton, "The Four-Fold Gospel: Meeting Ground for Holiness, Keswick and Pentecostal Theologies" (Paper delivered at the Wesleyan/Holiness Study Project First Study Conference, Asbury Theological Seminary, 10–11 June 1988) (used with permission).

20. Dayton, "An Analysis," pp. 12–13, 19, and "Yet Another Layer," p. 94. They generally side with Robert Anderson who sees an evangelical social class ladder on which Pentecostals are at the bottom, Holiness groups one rung up, and "evangelicals" on top "as the elite who offer the interpretations and history by which the whole is understood." The people's history would look at evangelicalism "from the bottom up rather than through the projections of the elite" who have taken their interpretive models "from a foreign cultural experience." Dayton, "The Four-Fold Gospel," p. 4, and Robert Mapes Anderson, *Vision of the Disinherited: The Making of American Pentecostalism* (New York, 1979).

21. Smith, "The Evangelical Kaleidoscope," p. 125.

even Smith's kaleidoscope is too rigid a model. Dayton does not find anything like a single, unified movement and announces that "there is no such thing" as "the evangelical movement." While Gordon Harland shouts a hearty "Amen!" Dayton calls for a "moratorium" on the use of the "evangelical" label "because as a label the term is theologically incoherent, sociologically confusing, and ecumenically harmful."[22] Amidst this confusion concerning evangelical identity, even Smith has difficulty coloring in his evangelical kaleidoscope without falling prey to Dayton's charges of incoherence. Smith does indeed draw a historical and theological perimeter around the movement but his descriptions of contemporary evangelicalism do not always fit neatly within even his own boundaries.[23] There is little wonder, then, why the Holiness camp prefers an approach to "evangelicalism" that is essentially antithetical to the Reformed model.

Dayton offers the Holiness/Pentecostal heritage as an alternative to the regnant "Presbyterian" model for evangelical history.[24] Ironically, he argues, "modern evangelicalism" has been a movement "rooted largely in the lower classes" that is only now seeking to "[assert] itself culturally." Charles Finney serves Dayton as a prime example here. When he was converted and expressed a desire for ordination (as a Presbyterian) Finney was pressured to attend Princeton Seminary. He resisted, however, and eventually became a

22. Donald W. Dayton, "The Holy Spirit and Christian Expansion in the Twentieth Century," *Missiology: An International Review* 16 (1988): 403; Dayton, "'Evangelical': More Puzzling Than You Think," *Ecumenical People Programs Papers*, Occasional Paper No. 29 (May 1988), pp. 5-6, and Gordon Harland, "Evangelicalism and Fundamentalism," *Touchstone: Heritage and Theology in a New Age* 5 (1987): 29.

23. Smith, "The Evangelical Kaleidoscope," pp. 125-128, traces the emergence of modern evangelicalism from its origins in the revivals of the eighteenth century and takes a much more inclusive approach to the ensuing history (exemplified in a roster of some contemporary educational institutions he deems "evangelical"). He proposes three characteristics that "have defined evangelicalism in the English-speaking world: the Bible is its authority, the new birth its hallmark, and evangelism its mission." One wonders, however, whether these characteristics find common enough expression in Smith's institutions to justify labelling all the schools "evangelical." Pacific Lutheran University or Calvin College, for example, surely view the new birth in a very different light than, say, the Bible Institute of Los Angeles or even Houghton College. How, then, can one use the new birth to define evangelicalism? (One could ask similar questions of the other two characteristics.)

24. See especially his *Theological Roots of Pentecostalism* (Metuchen, N.J., 1987), in which he expounds on this evangelical legacy.

great New School revivalist. The story of modern evangelicalism, says Dayton, "is in many ways the story of the sons of Finney deciding to go to Princeton after all."[25] Even so, argues Dayton, the bottom-up approach to evangelicalism "works better to describe" even "the real dynamics of Fuller [Seminary] than Fuller's own self-understanding derived from the neo-evangelical vision." Though Fuller's early faculty was largely Reformed and sought to move evangelicalism back into the mainstream, Fuller's student body was recruited primarily through Charles Fuller's "Old Fashioned Revival Hour" radio program. Moreover, argues Dayton, "the repudiation of dispensationalism" proved the "*central*" and driving theological issue at the early Fuller. Stemming from nineteenth-century concerns far removed from Princeton, millennialism was so important to Fuller's early faculty that Carl Henry devoted his most significant early scholarship to the critique of dispensationalism's cultural pessimism. George Ladd spent a career developing a conservative premillennial eschatology that steered clear of dispensationalist accretions. Dayton asserts that while Marsden believes Ernest Sandeen has overstated the case for millennialism as stimulus within fundamentalism and evangelicalism, Dayton believes that Sandeen "understated his case" and that "his thesis is full of even more explanatory power than he understood."[26]

The Holiness camp's most notable complaint is that the Reformed model does not take the nineteenth-century roots of neo-evangelicalism seriously enough. As Sweet notes, "many of evangelicalism's nineteenth century roots were perfectionist and holiness" and few Reformed scholars are very "sure-footed" in this arena.[27] Dayton argues further that the radical vision for social justice promoted by nineteenth-century evangelicals has been blurred by the recent cultural empowerment or "embourgeoisement" of evangelicalism. Though evangelicals historically have been the truly radical Protestants (as against the established liberals "too often willing to be assimilated into the reigning values of the culture"), they have become bourgeois as the neo-

25. Donald W. Dayton, "Response to Marsden, *Reforming Fundamentalism*" (Paper delivered at the Evangelical Theology section of the American Academy of Religion annual conference, Chicago, Illinois, 21 November 1988), pp. 21–22 (used with permission).

26. Dayton, "An Analysis," p. 13; and "Response to Marsden," pp. 14, 16–18. Sandeen, *The Roots of Fundamentalism: British and American Millenarianism 1800–1930* (Chicago, 1979), has postulated that American fundamentalism was produced primarily by a combination of dispensational premillennialism and Old Princeton orthodoxy.

27. Sweet, "Wise as Serpents, Innocent as Doves," p. 400.

evangelical vision has succeeded.[28] Dayton wails with the voice of one crying in the wilderness, "What happened . . . to the [truly] reforming spirit of Evangelicalism?"[29]

2.

It would seem that both the Reformed and Holiness approaches to neo-evangelical historiography are helpful and appropriate as far as they go. The Reformed camp depicts the establishment neo-evangelical founders accurately as predominantly Reformed in outlook. Nevertheless, the neo-evangelical masses have proven to be quite varied and kaleidoscopic in nature. Thus the Holiness camp is correct to point out the vast and less culturally appealing "underbelly" of evangelicalism. However, neither approach by itself has yet provided a complete portrayal of the movement. Furthermore, the contemporary evangelical agenda seems to have distorted both groups' perception of neo-evangelical history in the 1940s and the 1950s.

One problem resulting from this agenda is that scholars from both groups evince a tendency to equate evangelicalism with pristine Christianity. Most of the key players in this historiography have evangelical sympathies. It seems as though these "observer-participants" are trying too hard to make their story attractive. Donald Bloesch, for example, allows that evangelicalism "is not the only form of Christianity" but maintains that "it is the truest and purest form." His definition of an evangelical as one who attests to the centrality of Christ's work as recorded in the Bible, who appropriates the fruit of Christ's labor in his or her own life and who shares a burden to take the gospel to the world applies to Christians of all stripes.[30] Though Bloesch's ecumenical spirit is admirable, his definition proves too loose to be meaningful. As Robert Wuthnow aptly reminds us, fundamentalist beliefs were "shared widely in the population at large" during the early years of the neo-evangelical movement and a relative harmony existed between liberals and conservatives.[31] Though some of the neo-evangelical historiography tends

---

28. Donald W. Dayton, "The Embourgeoisement of a Vision: Lament of a Radical Evangelical," *The Other Side* 23 (1987): 19.

29. Donald Dayton, *Discovering an Evangelical Heritage* (New York, 1976), p. 121.

30. Bloesch, *The Future of Evangelical Christianity*, pp. 5, 17.

31. Robert Wuthnow, *The Restructuring of American Religion: Society and Faith Since World War II* (Princeton, 1988), p. 143.

to speak of evangelicalism and traditional "orthodox" Protestantism synon-ymously, evangelical historians would better serve students of the movement by avoiding this partisanship.[32]

A more serious flaw in both approaches is a tendency to apply contem-porary attitudes and terms to the period of the 1940s and 1950s. Inclusivity, ecumenicity, and pluralism have today become bandwagon concepts among evangelicals. In his discussion of the "New Evangelicalism," Bloesch can now call for a "catholic evangelicalism" that will not only inherit the legacy of the Reformation but "the whole catholic heritage" as well. Bloesch says that evan-gelicalism today "has various meanings, and some of these are ambiguous." He argues that some definitions of evangelicalism prove "too narrow" and finds support in the more historical works of George Marsden who notes that even if one's definition of evangelical "is cleverly formulated and qualified, it will inevitably be inflexible, excluding some who would be 'evangelicals' by more intuitive standards."[33] Joel Carpenter notes Dayton's "scarcely muted glee" concerning the absence of any definable center to evangelicalism.[34] Many scholars are tempted to carry these attitudes into their evaluation of the early days of the evangelical movement, yet this tendency makes for inaccurate history. Marsden defines the movement's "perennial problem" as the fact that "it is not one entity but a coalition of fragmented subgroups, each with its own standards and agenda."[35] Mark Ellingsen argues that one implication of the neo-evangelical program was that "it guaranteed that the Evangelical move-ment would never become a well-defined movement whose outer boundaries could easily be delineated."[36] Carpenter confirms that the early movement "was not a monolithic fundamentalism but rather a broad mosaic . . . with different ethnic and doctrinal heritages."[37]

32. See for example Smith, "The Evangelical Kaleidoscope," p. 125.

33. Bloesch, *Essentials of Evangelical Theology, Volume One*, pp. 8–9, 21; idem, *The Evangelical Renaissance* (Grand Rapids, 1973), pp. 30, 48; and idem, *The Future of Evan-gelical Christianity*, p. 11. Marsden is careful to point out, however, that definitions of evangelicalism also have potential to include "some whose evangelicalism is marginal." Marsden, *Evangelicalism and Modern America*, p. x.

34. Joel A. Carpenter, "Evangelicals: Why Should We Put Up with This Label?" (Paper presented to the presidents of the Christian College Corsortium in Chicago, Illinois, 26 October 1987), p. 2 (used with permission).

35. Marsden, "Why No Major Evangelical University?" p. 299.

36. Mark Ellingsen, *The Evangelical Movement: Growth, Impact, Controversy, Di-alog* (Minneapolis, 1988), p. 100.

37. Carpenter, "Fundamentalist Institutions," p. 63.

Carpenter argues the strongest case for pluralism within earliest neo-evangelicalism. He maintains that both fundamentalist and non-fundamentalist evangelicals shared positions of prominence in the founding of the National Association of Evangelicals (NAE), for example. Though the fundamentalists proved the "most visible and vocal" (and hence have "led interpreters to label the varied traditions involved as 'fundamentalist'"), they ought only to be seen as the "leaven" of the movement and not as constitutive of the entire establishment. It was easy for them to "presume" that their theology would dominate the movement but other evangelicals "then and since, have interpreted their faith differently." These other non-fundamentalist evangelicals did not leave their traditions behind when they joined the NAE. For Carpenter, then, the neo-evangelical movement never lost its doctrinal distinctiveness, "for you can't lose what you never had." Evangelicals have not witnessed the disintegration of their identity since World War II, but have witnessed "the unveiling of [their] true diversity."[38] Carpenter's appropriation of the term "fundamentalist," however, proves too narrow. Although he demonstrates the leavening influence of fundamentalism on all kinds of groups (including Holiness groups) prior to the emergence of neo-evangelicalism, he assumes a rather limited definition of fundamentalism (one that did not include Holiness groups in the first place, for example).[39] Though each tradition did indeed possess reasons of its own for joining or not joining the NAE (or even affiliating with the neo-evangelical movement more generally), each group that did join assented heartily to its rather exclusive and ideologically fundamentalist agenda whether or not it shared the entire fundamentalist heritage.[40]

Marsden writes as though the neo-evangelical leaders themselves promoted a doctrinally ecumenical spirit. In his discussion of the reverberations of the "Black Saturday" event at Fuller Seminary he asserts that "these questions [about inerrancy and self-definition] were especially important since the neo-evangelicals were" trying "to take the lead in building a wider evangelical coalition."[41] Elsewhere Marsden says that the neo-evangelicals, while

38. Carpenter, "The Fundamentalist Leaven," pp. 266–267, 261, 283, and "Evangelicals: Why Should We Put Up With This Label?" pp. 2–3.

39. Carpenter, "The Renewal of American Fundamentalism," pp. 194–205.

40. *Evangelical Action!: A Report of the Organization of the National Association of Evangelicals for United Action* (Boston, 1942), provides a representative account of the neo-evangelical agenda.

41. Marsden, *Reforming Fundamentalism*, pp. 229–230. "The most dramatic moment" in Fuller's history, according to Marsden, Black Saturday (1 December 1962) saw

continuing "to oppose liberalism in theology," were, nevertheless, "willing to reevaluate some of their own theological heritage."[42] According to this construction, outspoken doctrinalists appear atypical or get labeled fundamentalist or neo-fundamentalist in a way that separates them from the heart of the neo-evangelical movement. Carpenter describes a "vast and varied" evangelical "mosaic" of which these fundamentalists comprised "but one segment."[43] Smith also describes "fundamentalists" such as those at the Moody Bible Institute as more distant from the center of evangelicalism than is commonly perceived.[44]

Surely evangelicalism's ideological posture has opened up in recent years. But evangelicals in the 1940s and 1950s, while almost as diverse as the figures in Smith's kaleidoscope, coalesced at the top levels around largely fundamentalist concerns—at least in their official pronouncements. Though the new evangelicals sought with all their might to separate themselves from the fundamentalist "mood," they worked equally hard to carry on the fundamentalist cause.[45] Though Smith's mosaic model has been catching on, it does not fit securely enough over the evangelicalism of the 1940s and 1950s.[46] Webber's

---

the controversy over the seminary's identity (especially as it related to inerrancy) reach its boiling point at a faculty/trustee planning conference in the Huntington Sheraton Hotel. See *Reforming Fundamentalism*, pp. 208–215.

42. Marsden, "From Fundamentalism to Evangelicalism," p. 148.

43. Carpenter, "The Fundamentalist Leaven," pp. 258–259.

44. Smith, "The Evangelical Kaleidoscope," pp. 130–131. Moody Bible Institute, however, was at the organizational center of the neo-evangelical movement from its inception. Indeed, it served as the location where the neo-evangelical founders first strategized.

45. Neo-evangelical intellectual E. J. Carnell is representative here. One of Fuller Seminary's early faculty members, Carnell described his work in 1948 as a "defense of Fundamentalism." Though Carnell, like Carl Henry, Harold John Ockenga and others, sought to avoid the contentious ethos of fundamentalism, he did so from within a fundamentalist frame of reference. Not until the late 1950s did Carnell's view of fundamentalism sour to the point that he could refer to it as "orthodoxy gone cultic." Even then, however, he identified with fundamentalist "orthodoxy." See Carnell, *An Introduction to Christian Apologetics* (Grand Rapids, 1948), p. 8, and *The Case for Orthodox Theology* (Philadelphia, 1959), p. 113.

46. A growing number of analysts, including Billy Graham himself, have used Smith's model in recent years. See, for example, Marsden, *Evangelicalism and Modern America*, pp. viii, x (interestingly, the *Evangelicalism in Modern America* volume was dedicated to Smith); Carpenter, "The Fundamentalist Leaven," p. 258; Cullen Murphy, "Protestantism and the Evangelicals," *The Wilson Quarterly* 5 (1981): 114 (Murphy wrote

sixteen evangelical subcultures certainly thrived but the neo-evangelical sub-culture (a direct descendant of fundamentalism) provided the leadership that would hold the movement together for at least its first two decades.[47] With Jacobsen, evangelical historians can look to "some form of pluralism" as "a more appropriate" strategy for contemporary evangelicalism while admitting that, "until recently, evangelicalism has envisioned itself along strictly monistic lines."[48]

3.

When used in tandem, the Reformed and Holiness approaches to neo-evangelical historiography can complement one another's research and shed light on what Dayton calls "the strange schizophrenia" of contemporary evangelicalism.[49] The neo-evangelical movement seems to have had two divergent but reconcilable personalities. While each historiographical approach has done good work in its own sphere, neither has effectively illuminated the relationship between the different aspects of the evangelical psyche. A thorough interpretation of essential evangelicalism must come to terms with both personalities.

From the beginning pragmatic, evangelistic, and even pietistic impulses propelled a broadly based neo-evangelical movement. A perusal of the "Roster of Delegates" at the first NAE convention makes clear that neo-evangelicals did indeed represent a socially disparate mosaic of Christians.[50] Reformed scholars have had to agree that the neo-evangelical leaders held up a large umbrella.[51] However, in the period at issue the neo-evangelical movement was characterized by a fundamentalist mentality and was intellectually and institutionally exclusive. The founding neo-evangelicals, like all intellectuals who shared the legacy of the fundamentalist-modernist controversies, felt a

---

this article in consultation with Smith); and Kenneth L. Woodward, "The Split-Up Evangelicals," *Newsweek* 99 (26 April 1982): 89.

47. See note 17 above.

48. Douglas Jacobsen, "The Rise of Evangelical Hermeneutical Pluralism," *Christian Scholar's Review* 16 (1987): 325.

49. Dayton, "Yet Another Layer," p. 100.

50. "Roster of Delegates," in *Evangelical Action!* pp. 92–100.

51. Marsden, *Evangelicalism and Modern America*, p. xiv; and Ronald H. Nash, *Evangelicals in America: Who They Are, What They Believe* (Nashville, 1987), p. 24.

need to place themselves on the ideological spectrum. Therefore, their culturally engaging social outlook and their fundamentalist intellectual position stood in constant tension.

As in many religious movements a considerable disparity existed between the rhetorical unity of the neo-evangelical establishment and the reality of its diverse constituency. It is at this point that comments like those of Joel Carpenter on the presumption of the neo-evangelical leaders prove significant. Yes, they did foist a fundamentalist unity on the varied components of the evangelical movement, but at the rhetorical, leadership level this unity stuck.[52] Even though Pentecostals and Holiness groups comprise two thirds of the NAE's constituency, its Reformed intellectual contingency ran the show in the early years and the entire body got along fairly peacefully.[53] Though for such a large and diverse body there were surprisingly few intellectuals, their univocal and largely fundamentalist rhetoric proved a strong enough bond for the entire early movement. Though the movement may never have been as halcyon as Harold Lindsell's "golden age," he does not miss the mark by much in his treatment of the doctrinal unity of early neo-evangelicalism.[54] As Quebedeaux has pointed out, "Evangelicals—as represented by the evangelical establishment, that is—used to be easy to identify" because the neo-evangelical establishment used to be recognized as *"the evangelicals."*[55] Once the rhetorical bond of the establishment was broken in the late 1950s and early 1960s, however, neo-evangelical identity began to unravel.

The question remains as to why this unraveling ever began. Leonard Sweet argues convincingly that "the first generation of new evangelicals, who were themselves second generation fundamentalists, reared children to be their own predicament."[56] Marsden refers to both social and doctrinal problems that led to the breakup of neo-evangelical hegemony.[57] It is the doctrinal factor, however, that usually gets underplayed in explanations of this transition. During the late 1950s and early 1960s the univocal rhetoric of the evangelical intelligentsia turned equivocal. Neo-evangelical attitudes

---

52. Carpenter, "From Fundamentalism to the New Evangelical Coalition," in *Evangelicalism and Modern America*, pp. 12–14.

53. Dayton, "An Analysis," p. 7, and "Yet Another Layer," p. 99.

54. Harold Lindsell, "Evangelicalism's Golden Age," *Moody Monthly* 86 (1985): 113–114.

55. Quebedeaux, *The Worldly Evangelicals*, p. 22.

56. Sweet, "Wise as Serpents, Innocent as Doves," p. 401.

57. Marsden, "Unity and Diversity," pp. 70–71.

concerning modern thought were changing even amidst the new evangelical establishment. As early as 1957 John Walvoord of Dallas Seminary could notice that while many evangelicals held onto the beliefs of the old-time fundamentalists, "many others claiming the same [did] not."[58] Even though the conservatives alarmed at Billy Graham's cooperative evangelism (during and after the 1957 New York crusade) had never wholeheartedly supported the new evangelicalism in the first place, signals of the coming discord may be heard in that controversy nonetheless.[59] In the inerrancy debates at Fuller Seminary in the early 1960s we also see the impossibility of maintaining even the perception of unity among a growing body of evangelical leaders. By 1958 even outsider Sherman Roddy could tell that within the new evangelicalism there was "a vast conspiracy of silence covering an equally vast reorientation of sentiments."[60]

When viewing both sides of this neo-evangelical story at once one can see by what delicate means its identity was held together in the early years. Since the days of the fundamentalist-modernist controversies, the doctrinal statement had taken on primary significance in ecumenical efforts among evangelicals. In contrast to Carl McIntire's American Council of Christian Churches, for example, the NAE accepted members from the Federal Council of Churches provided they affirmed the NAE's doctrinal statement. Randall Balmer notes that "one of the reasons . . . belief is so important to evangelicals

58. John F. Walvoord, "What's Right About Fundamentalism?" *Eternity* 8 (June 1957): 35.

59. Farley Porter Butler, "Billy Graham and the End of Evangelical Unity," (Ph.D. diss., The University of Florida, 1976), claims that Graham's cooperative evangelism marked the end of evangelical unity. Mark Silk ironically shows in "The Rise of the 'New Evangelicalism': Shock and Adjustment," in *Between the Times: The Travail of the Protestant Establishment in America, 1900–1960*, ed. William R. Hutchison (New York, 1989), pp. 278–299, and *Spiritual Politics: Religion and America Since World War II* (New York, 1988), pp. 54–69, 101–107, that Graham's New York crusade symbolized the cessation of mainline insecurity regarding the neo-evangelical resurgence. While by the mid 1950s the new evangelicalism's evangelistic fervor had begun to spread even into the upper echelons of the mainline Protestant establishment, by the early 1960s the new movement's leadership had sanded its edges so smooth that it lost the ability to cut through the liberal establishment. Neo-evangelicalism had become too conventional. It was even beginning to fall out of touch with the popular religious needs of an increasingly unconventional American people.

60. Sherman Roddy, "Fundamentalists and Ecumenicity," *The Christian Century* 75 (1 October 1958): 1110.

may be that they cannot claim any . . . other 'adhesives' as the basis for whatever cohesion exists among them."[61] Because, as Marsden writes, "evangelicals have a very low view of the institutional church" and "ecclesiastical authority," the varied social concerns of the early neo-evangelical movement could find no long-term nexus; though the NAE tried to provide one, its bond proved too weak.[62]

With the rhetorical equivocation of the neo-evangelical establishment, then, the evangelical resurgence lost its direction. It would seem that the new movement's weight had been supported tenuously from the very beginning.[63] The term "neo-evangelical" was replaced gradually by the more generic term "evangelical" and nearly all the characteristics of neo-evangelicalism became less distinctive.[64] As Marsden points out, even a Fuller Seminary graduate returning in the 1960s would have discovered "a general loosening of the evangelical ethos" for "Neo-evangelicalism was no longer a unified movement."[65] Although the neo-evangelical social network held fast in the days of the establishment's ideological unity, its ultimate fragmentation is not surprising in a movement where the pragmatic concerns of a diverse constituency were allowed to tug at delicate cohesives. Whether the vast evangelical constituency "got conned" into the neo-evangelical doctrinal agenda (as Dayton argues) or not, when the fragile unity of the founding neo-evangelicals ended, nothing remained to support the common perception of evangelical unity.[66]

The competing historiographies in our dialectic prove insufficient by themselves to grasp what took place in the new evangelical attempt (and eventual failure) to recast a righteous empire. The Reformed model does not see clearly the definitional trouble latent in the multifarious constituency of the neo-evangelical union from its beginning. The Holiness model does not see clearly the definitive rhetoric of the founding neo-evangelical intelligentsia. Neither model can account adequately for the significance of the "vast reorientation of sentiments" that occurred in the late 1950s and early 1960s. The

---

61. Balmer, *Mine Eyes Have Seen the Glory*, pp. 228–229.

62. Marsden, "Why No Major Evangelical University?" p. 300.

63. Marsden, *Reforming Fundamentalism*, p. 259, writes that "the movement had never sailed far enough from the fundamentalist shores to avoid breaking up on surrounding rocks."

64. Quebedeaux, *The Worldly Evangelicals*, pp. 9, 24.

65. Marsden, *Reforming Fundamentalism*, pp. 245, 260.

66. "An Interview with Donald Dayton," *Faith and Thought* 1 (1983): 31.

jeremiads of first-generation neo-evangelicals such as Harold Lindsell contain some validity: "in many quarters [the new evangelicalism] has ceased to be what its founding fathers intended."[67] Wilbur Smith wrote to Carl Henry in April of 1961, stating, "I greatly regret to have to say that the atmosphere here at [Fuller] is nothing like what you and I knew it to be when the school was started."[68] While this may simply be the complaint of one beginning to find himself on the intellectual outskirts of a progressively more scholarly seminary, it seems more likely a serious reflection of intergenerational vicissitudes within the neo-evangelical movement.

Current neo-evangelical historiography, then, fails to grasp the magnitude of the identity crisis that the sources themselves suggest. Though Carpenter is right to point out that the neo-evangelical intelligentsia's longing for credibility caused it to "distort the meaning of 'evangelical' through the historical mythos [it] created," this distortion and its implications should not simply be run over by the contemporary bandwagon of evangelical pluralism.[69] If the Reformed camp is right about early neo-evangelical intentions then so are the fundamentalists: the new evangelicalism demonstrated little more than an intentional move from toleration to cooperation to accommodation with liberalism (whether one views this positively or negatively).[70] If the Holiness camp is right, then this identity crisis itself simply provides further evidence for the argument that the evangelical establishment has not yet cut its socially harmful ties to Old Princeton.

However, a substantial departure from fundamentalism was not a natural consequence of the neo-evangelical agenda. Rather, much of the fundamentalist heritage remained foundational for the new evangelicalism. As Joel Carpenter sagely suggests, "the fundamentalist leaven helped to make an evangelical united front possible but limited its range."[71] The strange schizophrenia of modern evangelicalism owes to the increasing tension be-

67. Lindsell, "Evangelicalism's Golden Age," p. 113.

68. Smith to Henry, 25 April 1961. Folder 20, Box 16, Collection 8, Records of *Christianity Today*. Billy Graham Center Archives, Wheaton, Illinois.

69. Joel A. Carpenter, "Comments on 'The Four-Fold Gospel'" (Response to a paper by Donald Dayton delivered at the First Study Conference of the Wesleyan/ Holiness Studies Project, Asbury Theological Seminary, 10–11 June 1988), p. 5 (used with permission).

70. For a presentation of the fundamentalist critique of neo-evangelicalism, see Charles Woodbridge, *The New Evangelicalism* (Greenville, S.C., 1969), and idem, *Reaping the Whirlwind* (Collingswood, N.J., 1977).

71. Carpenter, "The Renewal of American Fundamentalism," p. 187.

tween historic evangelical ecumenism and historic evangelical thought. Because theological modernism divided evangelicalism's ecumenical heritage, the neo-evangelicals were forced to decide between an exclusive fellowship within the harbor of historic evangelical doctrine, and historic evangelical piety on the sea of American pluralism. While the founders opted for the former, the story of the unraveling of neo-evangelical identity is the story of their scions setting out to sea.

CHAPTER 4

Evangelical Constituencies
in North America and the World

Mark A. Noll

This chapter reprints almost all of a chapter entitled "Constituencies in North America and the World" that was contained in Mark A. Noll's *American Evangelical Christianity: An Introduction* (Malden, MA: Blackwell, 2001), 29–43. (Reprinted with permission by Wiley.) The indirect stimulus for this effort to discriminate different ways of defining evangelicalism came from introductions to Canadian history, where the history of evangelical movements both closely resemble and significantly diverge from parallel histories in the United States (those differences can be explored more completely in *Aspects of the Canadian Evangelical Experience*, ed. G. A. Rawlyk [Kingston and Montreal: McGill-Queen's University Press, 1997]), to which Noll contributed a chapter entitled "Canadian Evangelicalism: A View from the United States"). The direct stimulus came from the survey described in this chapter, for which George Rawlyk of Queen's University in Kingston, Ontario, provided major guidance, as he had to so many of his fellow Canadians, along with a few Americans, who find Canadian history endlessly fascinating.

*   *   *

Charting the size of the American evangelical constituency at the start of the twenty-first century depends upon which criteria are used for definition. The same dependency of results upon criteria exists for the task of counting evangelicals around the world. Trying out alternative definitions and noting complexities in the defining process itself may look like typical academic obfuscation. It is not. Rather, care over definitions and comparison of results from differing definitions is the only way forward in better understanding who evangelicals are and where they are located. This chapter carries out such an exercise for Canada and the United States; it then goes on to examine a significant survey that makes possible an estimate of the number of evangelicals in over thirty other countries around the world.

There are at least three well-supported strategies for carrying out these tasks. Each method has a persuasive logic of its own, but, not surprisingly, each method yields different results. One is to ascertain how many people tell survey researchers that they adhere to traditional evangelical convictions concerning the Bible, the new birth, and related matters. This method is the technique regularly used by the Gallup Organization in asking people if they have been born again. In somewhat more detail, it has also been used for several recent surveys conducted by the Angus Reid Group of Toronto.[1] A second method is to count the people adhering to the churches and denominations most strongly linked to the historical evangelical and revival movements. This method has been put to especially good use by political scientists, one group of which has published a series of perceptive works on the political behavior of American religious groups.[2] A third method is to figure out how many people

1. For useful discussion of evangelicals, defined as those who say they have been born again, see George Gallup, Jr., and Jim Castelli, *The People's Religion: American Faith in the 90s* (New York: Macmillan, 1989), 92-98; popular reports on religion in Canada using the Angus Reid surveys are found in "God Is Alive—Special Report: The Religion Poll," *Maclean's*, Apr 12, 1993, pp. 32-50; "How Very Different: A poll shows how Canadian and U.S. attitudes vary on family, politics and religion," *Maclean's*, Nov 4, 1996, pp. 36-40; and Mark A. Noll, "Religion in Canada and the United States," *Crux* [Regent College], Dec 1998, pp. 13-25, with commentary by John G. Stackhouse on "Who are the evangelicals?" pp. 26-28. For a sophisticated essay using Angus Reid data, see Andrew S. Grenville, "The Awakened and the Spirit-Moved: The Religious Experiences of Canadian Evangelicals in the 1990s," in *Aspects of the Canadian Evangelical Experience*, ed. G. A. Rawlyk (Montreal and Kingston: McGill-Queen's University Press, 1997), 417-31.

2. For a wide-ranging survey of their results and conclusions, see John Green, James Guth, Lyman Kellstedt, and Corwin Smidt, *Religion and the Culture Wars: Dispatches from the Front* (Lanham, MD: Rowman & Littlefield, 1996). Further examples include Kellstedt and Green, "The Mismeasure of Evangelicals," *Books & Culture*, Jan/Feb 1996, pp. 12-13; Kellstedt and Smidt, "How to Count the Spirit-filled," *Books & Culture*, July/Aug 1996, pp. 24-25; Green, Guth, Kellstedt, and Smidt, "Who Elected Clinton: A Collision of Values," *First Things*, Aug/Sept 1997, pp. 35-40; Green, Guth, Kellstedt, Smidt, and Margaret Poloma, *The Bully Pulpit: The Politics of Protestant Ministers* (Lawrence: University Press of Kansas, 1997); Green, Guth, Kellstedt, and Smidt, "Bringing in the Sheaves: The Christian Right and White Protestants, 1976-1996," in *Sojourners in the Wilderness: The Christian Right in Comparative Perspective*, ed. James Penning and Corwin Smidt (Lanham, MD: Rowman & Littlefield, 1997), 75-91; Green, Guth, Kellstedt, and Smidt, "Evangelicalism," in *The Encyclopedia of Religion and So-*

use the term "evangelical" to describe their own religious beliefs and practices. A research team headed by the sociologist Christian Smith of the University of North Carolina has recently brought out important books and articles on those who use the term "evangelical" for themselves, their churches, and their wider connections.[3]

To indicate how and why these various ways of locating evangelicals overlap, but also contrast, it would be ideal to possess a single research project that uses all three. Fortunately, one recent survey included enough questions to test out all these definitions. An added benefit of the same survey was that it asked virtually the same questions of a large sample of Canadians as well as Americans. For the sake of clarity in defining just who evangelicals are and how many exist in North America, that survey deserves careful attention.

Evangelical Constituencies in the United States and Canada

In October 1996, the Angus Reid Group of Toronto conducted an unusually extensive cross-border poll in which nearly identical questions were asked to 3,000 Americans and 3,000 Canadians.[4] One-fifth of the Canadian interviews were conducted in French, while interviewers used Spanish for 7% of the calls in the United States. The survey included a number of questions about religion, which were originally drafted by the late Canadian historian, George Rawlyk, in an effort to frame questions that came as close to David Bebbington's fourfold definition of "evangelical" as such survey research allows. Yet the poll also gathered information that allowed for counting evangelicals by the other two

---

ciety, ed. William H. Swatos, Jr. (Walnut Creek, CA: AltaMira Press, 1998), 175-78; Green and Guth, "United Methodism and American Political Culture: A Statistical Portrait," in *The People Called Methodists*, ed. William Lawrence, Dennis Campbell, and Russell E. Richey (Nashville: Abingdon, 1998), 27-52; and Green, Guth, Kellstedt, and Smidt, "The 'Spirit Filled' Movements in Contemporary America: A Survey Perspective," in *Pentecostal Currents in American Protestantism*, ed. Edith L. Blumhofer, Russell P. Spittler, and Grant Wacker (Champaign: University of Illinois Press, 1999), 111-30.

3. Christian Smith, *American Evangelicalism: Embattled and Thriving* (Chicago: University of Chicago Press, 1998); Michael Emerson and Christian Smith, *Divided by Faith: Evangelical Religion and the Problem of Race in America* (New York: Oxford University Press, 2000); and Christian Smith, *Christian America? What Evangelicals Really Want* (Berkeley: University of California Press, 2000).

4. I am grateful to Angus Reid and Andrew Grenville for the use of this data and to Lyman Kellstedt for assistance with interpretation.

methods as well. The following paragraphs describe how the three methods were put to work.

(1) **Self-definition.** One question asked directly about self-identity ("Do you consider yourself to be any of the following?" [the answers provided were, "A Charismatic Christian," "A Pentecostal Christian," "An Evangelical Christian," "A Fundamentalist Christian," and "A Liberal or Progressive Christian"]). The following results tabulate as self-defined evangelicals those who responded with any combination of "evangelical," "fundamentalist," "charismatic," or "pentecostal."

(2) **Beliefs.** Several questions inquired about beliefs or practices that have been associated in theological and historical writing with evangelical identity. These were the questions that Rawlyk hoped would come close to operationalizing the Bebbington definition. Four of these questions were tabulated for the following tables. It was, thus, considered a sign of "evangelical" conviction, if

(i) a respondent strongly agreed that "through the life, death and resurrection of Jesus, God provided a way for the forgiveness of my sins" (crucicentrism);

(ii) a respondent strongly agreed that "the Bible is the inspired word of God"; or agreed to whatever degree that "the Bible is God's word, and is to be taken literally, word for word" (biblicism);

(iii) a respondent strongly agreed that "I have committed my life to Christ and consider myself to be a converted Christian" (conversionism); and

(iv) a respondent agreed or agreed strongly that "it is important to encourage non-Christians to become Christians" (activism).

By tallying the number of those who responded positively too all four measures (sometimes three or four), it is possible to obtain a rough picture of the prevalence of traditional evangelical convictions.

(3) **Denominations.** The survey also made it possible to group respondents by ecclesiastical traditions. The categories below follow the important work that Green, Guth, Kellstedt, and Smidt have done on religion and politics in the United States, although the categories are also similar to ones developed by Reginald Bibby and Donald Posterski for Canada.[5]

---

5. See Reginald W. Bibby, *Fragmented Gods: The Poverty and Potential of Religion in Canada* (Toronto: Irwin, 1987); *Mosaic Madness: The Poverty and Potential of Life in Canada* (Toronto: Stoddart, 1990); and *Unknown Gods: The Ongoing Story of Religion in Canada* (Toronto: Stoddart, 1993). Donald Posterski has put Angus Reid survey data to good use in regular columns for the Winnipeg-based periodical, *Christian Week*.

Evangelical Protestants: people who are affiliated with the following churches: Adventist, Alliance, Baptist, Brethren, Church of Christ, Church of God, Mennonite; who identified their denomination or church as charismatic, evangelical, fundamentalist, holiness, pentecostal; or who offered an indeterminate answer to the question of religious affiliation but who could be placed with these churches through other means.

Mainline Protestants: people who responded Anglican, Episcopal, Congregational, Methodist, United Church (Canada); United Church of Christ (U.S.); most Lutherans, most Presbyterians, most Reformed; or who likewise gave an indeterminate answer but who could be placed with these churches through other means.

Black Protestants (U.S. only): As we discuss in greater detail in Chapter Five below, African-American Protestants share many doctrinal and behavioral characteristics with those in evangelical Protestant denominations, but they are treated as a separate category because their responses to almost all social, political, or cultural questions set them apart dramatically from the white evangelicals.

Roman Catholics

Secular/Nominal: These people responded that they were agnostic, atheist, or nothing in particular; also added to this category were those who, though they responded with a religious affiliation, showed no or virtually no religious commitment—for example, people who said they were Baptist, Catholic, or the like, but who rarely prayed, almost never went to church, did not consider religion important, and thought that the idea of God is a superstition.

Other: This is a grab bag category that includes Mormons, Jehovah's Witnesses, Eastern Orthodox, Unitarian-Universalists, Jews, and others not readily classifiable with the other larger groups. (The numbers for all such groups, as well as for members of other religions, even in a survey of 6,000 respondents, is quite low.)

With these general categories we are able to make important comparisons between denominational traditions that are usually considered evangelical and those that are not.

Testing the Definitions

When constituencies defined by these three methods are compared, it is not surprising that a high correlation exists between those who call themselves "evangelical," those who affirm the beliefs historically associated with evangelical movements, and those who are members or adherents of traditionally evangelical denominations. Yet it is also important to stress that this correlation is not absolute. Quite a few people who call themselves evangelical or who belong to traditionally evangelical denominations do not affirm all of the traditionally evangelical beliefs and practices. And many mainline Protestants and Roman Catholics, especially in Canada, affirm all or most of the evangelical beliefs. Brief discussion of the tables that appear below will show how important care in definition actually is.

The first three tables present overall totals for the numbers of evangelicals in the United States and Canada as defined by the three different methods. Table 1 shows that about 19% of Americans use some combination of the labels "evangelical," "pentecostal," "charismatic," or "fundamentalist" for themselves. In Canada the comparable number is 12%.

Table 2 reveals that many more in both countries affirm at least three or four of the traditional beliefs than call themselves "evangelical." Thus, over half of the Americans queried affirmed three or four of these convictions, and slightly over one-fourth of the Canadians.

When comparing the two tables for the two countries, about 60% more Americans than Canadians call themselves "evangelicals," nearly three times as many Americans as Canadians affirm all four traditional evangelical convictions, and about twice as many Americans as Canadians affirm at least three of those convictions.

Table 3 shows that, as with evangelical self-identification and profession of evangelical convictions, there are more Americans than Canadians in the historic evangelical denominations, by a ratio of 2.6 to 1.

TABLE 1: Percentage of population calling themselves "evangelical"

U.S.	CANADA
19	12

TABLE 2: Percentage of population affirming the evangelical beliefs

	U.S.	CANADA
no beliefs	13	33
one belief	14	22
two beliefs	17	17
three beliefs	20	14
four beliefs	36	13

TABLE 3: Percentage of population in various denominational traditions

	U.S.	CANADA
Evang. Prot.	26	10
Mainline Prot.	15	17
Black Prot.	9	—
RC	20	26
Other	10	7
Secular	20	40

The more interesting results surface when the definitions are crossed. Tables 4 and 5 examine those who call themselves evangelicals (or a similar term). In Table 4 it is seen that, not surprisingly, most of the self-identified evangelicals affirm most of the traditional evangelical beliefs. But not all. More than 10% of American self-defined evangelicals and more than 20% of Canadian self-defined evangelicals do not affirm even three of the traditional evangelical convictions. The numbers in Table 5 are even more revealing. While half (Canadian) or more than half (U.S.) of self-defined evangelicals are found in the evangelical denominations, solid minorities are also present among mainline Protestants and Roman Catholics. In Canada a full one-fourth of those calling themselves evangelical are Roman Catholic.

TABLE 4: Percentage of **self-defined evangelicals** who affirm various numbers of evangelical beliefs

	U.S.	CANADA
no beliefs	1	3
one belief	3	6
two beliefs	8	13
three beliefs	15	27
four beliefs	74	51

TABLE 5: Percentage of **self-defined evangelicals** who are found in the various denominational traditions

	U.S.	CANADA
Evang. Prot.	61	50
Mainline Prot.	16	17
Black Prot.	8	—
RC	13	25
Other	1	1

	U.S.	CANADA
Secular	1	7

An even greater blurring of labels occurs when looking at those who affirm three or four of the traditional evangelical convictions, as indicated by Tables 6, 7, and 8. Table 6 reveals that about one-third of Canadians and Americans who affirm three or four of the traditional evangelical beliefs also use the label evangelical for themselves. Tables 7 and 8 show that those who hold to the traditional evangelical beliefs of course show up substantially in the evangelical denominations. But these denominations by no means monopolize the ones who affirm the evangelical convictions. Table 8 is especially striking since it specifies where those who hold the evangelicals beliefs are found ecclesiastically. In the United States 13% of those who affirm all of the survey's four evangelical convictions are African-American Protestants (who only sometimes call themselves "evangelicals"), 14% are found in mainline Protestant churches, and another 13% are Roman Catholics. The distribution is even more counter-intuitive in Canada, where less than half of those who affirm all four evangelical beliefs are found in evangelical denominations, while one-fourth are Roman Catholics and nearly one-fifth are mainline Protestants.

TABLE 6: Percentage of **those affirming 3 or 4 evangelical beliefs** who call themselves evangelicals

U.S.	CANADA
31	33

TABLE 7: Percentage of **those affirming 3 or 4 evangelical beliefs** as found in the various denominational traditions

	U.S.	CANADA
Evang. Prot.	41	30
Mainline Prot.	15	22
Black Prot.	13	—
RC	18	32
Other	6	5
Secular	7	10

TABLE 8: Percentage of **those affirming all 4 evangelical beliefs** as found in the various denominational traditions

	U.S.	CANADA
Evang. Prot.	51	45
Mainline Prot.	14	19
Black Prot.	13	—
RC	13	25
Other	5	7
Secular	4	4

Tables 9 and 10 put the denominational traditions in the spotlight. As Table 9 indicates a slight majority of Canadians in the evangelical denominations call themselves evangelical, but less than half in the American evangelical denominations do so. Significant minorities among mainline Protestants, Roman Catholics, and African-American Protestants also used that self-designation. Table 10 shows the most correspondence between evangelical beliefs and evangelical denominations, but even here the fit is not tight. On the one hand, small minorities in the evangelical denominations do not affirm even three of the evangelical beliefs. On the other hand, large numbers of black Protestants, mainline Protestants, Roman Catholics, and even the miscellaneous category affirm the beliefs.

TABLE 9: Percentage of **those in the various denominational traditions** who called themselves evangelicals

	U.S.	CANADA
Evang. Prot.	44	57
Mainline Prot.	21	12
Black Prot.	17	—
RC	12	11
Other	1	2
Secular	1	2

TABLE 10: Percentage of **those in the various denominational traditions** who affirmed 3 or 4 of the evangelical beliefs

	U.S.	CANADA
Evang. Prot.	88	80
Mainline Prot.	57	37
Black Prot.	79	—
RC	50	34
Other	37	21
Secular	20	7

Implications of the Angus Reid Survey

(1) Precision in terminology is important. It is natural to use the term "evangelical" to mean those who hold certain Christian beliefs and exercise certain Christian practices. It is also legitimate to use the term historically for designating certain churches and religious traditions deriving ultimately from the Reformation and also identifying strongly with more recent revival traditions. But it is also precarious when those two usages are merged without discrimination. As the survey shows, considerable differences result from defining "evangelicals" as those who hold evangelical convictions when compared to defining as "evangelicals" those who identify with the historic Protestant denominations where those beliefs have been most prominent.

(2) The distribution of beliefs and practices traditionally known as "evangelical" is surprisingly wide. As we would expect, a high proportion of those affiliated with explicitly evangelical denominations hold evangelical convictions and a high proportion of all who hold such beliefs are affiliated with evangelical denominations. Yet it is also striking how much mainline and black Protestants contribute to the total of those who hold evangelical beliefs. African-American Protestants, in fact, contribute a higher proportion, relative to their overall population, of those who affirm the evangelical beliefs than do adherents of the mostly white evangelical denominations. It is even more striking how much Roman Catholics contribute to the total of evangelical believers, especially in Canada.

(3) On all issues of belief and practice Canada is now more secular than the U.S. Even with regional variations taken into account, by measures used in the Angus Reid survey, Canada is less religiously active than the United States, and evangelical believers (however measured) are proportionally a much larger part of the population in the United States.

(4) Historical explanations remain important. The considerable differences between Canada and the United States in levels of religious belief and practice pose a major interpretive problem. Although sophisticated surveys like the 1996 Angus Reid poll did not exist a generation ago, earlier, less sophisticated measures nonetheless suggested that until the 1970s Canada actually enjoyed higher rates of religious practice than the U.S.[6] Historical accounts suggest that as far back as the early nineteenth-century, Christian belief and practice were considerably more widespread (and more deeply rooted) in Can-

---

6. As late as the early 1970s, church attendance in Canada, as reported in Gallup polls, was higher than in the United States; in the 1950s and early 1960s it was much higher.

ada than in the United States.[7] If those impressions about earlier situations are valid, it means that Canada has undergone a massive decline in religious practice over just the last thirty years. Some study has gone into that situation for Quebec, almost none for the rest of Canada. For both Christian and academic reasons, study of that secularization is an absolute imperative.

(5) For the United States, the search for evangelical Protestants must proceed cautiously. Each of the methods outlined above provides a valid way for talking about evangelicals, but each must be used carefully to avoid category mistakes and simple uninformed ignorance.

Contemporary Evangelical Constituencies in the World

Over the last several years, the Angus Reid Group of Toronto has included numerous questions bearing on religion in its world-wide comparative surveys as well as in its work in North America. Those surveys make it possible to approach an even more difficult question than the number of evangelicals in North America.[8] That question concerns the number of evangelicals in various individual countries around the world.

Modern survey research yields inexact results. People lie. People say what they think their neighbors would want them to tell the pollsters. Surveys about the Clinton sex scandal illustrate the problem—only a small percentage of Americans said they were interested, but a very large number thought other people were fascinated by l'affaire Lewinsky.

The best survey research firms, like the Angus Reid Group, are aware of these problems. When the good ones present their data, they are at pains to specify degrees of reliability and to highlight doubts about the representativeness of sample populations. The "World Poll" that Angus Reid conducted in 1997 is no exception. In its own publications reporting on results from 33 different nations, it took pains to spell out limitations. For example, in a few of the countries, surveys were restricted to residents in urban areas or to the part of the population that possessed telephones. In addition, the sample size of 500 per country, while entirely adequate for large-scale generalizations, does

7. See, for example, John Webster Grant, *A Profusion of Spires: Religion in Nineteenth-Century Ontario* (Toronto: University of Toronto Press, 1988), 224-25.

8. For exploring Angus Reid's own concerns about morality, modern economic life, and social capital, especially in Canada, see Angus Reid, *Shakedown: How the New Economy Is Changing Our Lives* (Toronto: Doubleday Canada, 1996).

not allow for results to be fine-tuned. Such limitations obviously skew results and qualify the impact of nation-to-nation comparisons.[9]

Yet once necessary precautions have been taken, the Angus Reid World Survey still produced very interesting findings, especially from its queries about religion. The Angus Reid Group's concern for connections between faith and public life, along with strategic exploitation of questions related to political and economic matters, meant that a solid group of religious questions were included in the World Survey. Thus, along with queries about attitudes toward the United States, on politics in the respondents' countries, and on a range of economic and consumer matters, the World Survey included the following questions on religion:

- To what extent is your religious faith important to you in your day-to-day life?
- Are you a Roman Catholic Christian, Christian but not a Roman Catholic, Jewish, or Muslim/Islam?
- Please tell me whether you agree or disagree, moderately or strongly, with the following statement: "I have committed my life to Christ and consider myself to be a converted Christian."
- How often do you pray outside of formal religious services?
- Other than on special occasions such as weddings, funerals, or baptisms, how often did you attend religious services or meetings in the last 12 months?

Of most obvious interest for a book on evangelicals is the question on conversion. A legitimate doubt remains whether the translation of this question into the various languages of the survey measured exactly the same thing that the original might measure in North America. Choice of wording is critical. The translation of the key assertion, for example, used more wooden words for "committed" and "converted" in German-speaking Switzerland ("Ich habe mein Leben Christus gegenüber *verpflichtet* und fühle mich als '*konvertierten* Christen'") than in Germany itself, where a better idiomatic translation was made ("Ich habe mein Leben Jesus Christus *gewidmet* und betrachte mich als *überzeugten* Christen").

Again to set aside details, however, the general results of the poll were significant. The Angus Reid Group tabulated in all 33 countries those respondents

9. General discussion of this world poll is found in *Angus Reid World Monitor*, Issue One, January 1998.

who scored "high" on the religious questions—that is, people who affirmed that religion was very important *and* who prayed at least once a day *and* who attended church at least weekly *and* who have committed their lives to Christ and consider themselves converted Christians. This total, in turn, was divided between non–Roman Catholics and Catholics (in Greece, Ukraine, and Russia, Orthodoxy was substituted for Catholicism). In light of the importance within evangelical traditions of personal commitment to Christ and of the conversion experience, it is tempting to call those who scored "high" on these questions "evangelicals." Yet because that term can be used in so many different ways, it is probably more accurate to call those falling into this Angus Reid category something like Protestant "True Believers" Who Come Close to Traditional Evangelical Definitions.

TABLE 11: Percentage of "True Believers" in 1997 Angus Reid World Survey (ranked by Protestant totals)

	PROTESTANT	ROMAN CATHOLIC	ORTHODOX	TOTAL
United States	28	7		35
South Africa	28	5		33
Brazil	10	15		25
Philippines	10	28		38
South Korea	10	16		26
Canada	8	7		15
Australia	7	5		12
Norway	6	—		6
United Kingdom	5	2		7
Netherlands	5	2		7
Switzerland	4	5		9
Finland	3	—		3
Mexico	3	14		17
Germany	3	4		7
Hong Kong	3	1		4
Taiwan	3	—		3
Indonesia	2	1		3

	PROTESTANT	ROMAN CATHOLIC	ORTHODOX	TOTAL
Sweden	2	1		3
Argentina	2	10		12
Ukraine	1	—	7	8
Czech Republic	1	3		4
China	1	—		1
Malaysia	1	2		3
Greece	1	—	19	20
Italy	1	26		27
Poland	—	22		22
Spain	—	17		17
Belgium	—	4		4
India	—	2		2
Russia	—	—	1	1
France	—	1		1

As indicated in Table 11, the highest proportion of such Protestant "True Believers" is found in the United States and urban South Africa, with substantial segments as well in Brazil, the Philippines, and South Korea. Several other European and North American countries, as well as Australia, have somewhat fewer. On the Catholic side, the highest proportion of "True Believers" is found in the Philippines, Italy, Poland, Spain, South Korea, Brazil, Mexico, and Argentina. Orthodox "True Believers" total 19% in Greece, 7% in Ukraine, and 1% in Russia. When Catholics and non-Catholics are combined, the highest proportion of "True Believers" among the surveyed countries is found in the Philippines. Other countries with more than one-fourth of the population in that same category include the United States (35%), South Africa (33%), Italy (27%), South Korea (26%), and Brazil (25%).

The Angus Reid survey researchers admitted that their work touched only parts of the world, but even with its limitations the poll contains much useful information. Among other conclusions, it indicates that the high proportion of evangelical Christians (however defined) in the United States makes that country very unusual in the world. The Canadian situation, with a proportion of "True Believers" at around 10% of the population, is more typical. The survey also suggests that one of the major opportunities, as well as major challenges, in years to come will be whether Protestant "True Believers" are able to negotiate successfully with Catholic "True Believers," since when considering the world as a whole, there seem to be quite a few more of them than of the Protestant variety.

CHAPTER 5

The Evangelical Discovery of History

David W. Bebbington

The Ecclesiastical History Society, an international but British-based organization for the study of church history in all its aspects, held its fiftieth summer conference at Christ Church, Oxford, in August 2011. To mark the half century of the Society, the president, Professor Sarah Foot, commissioned a number of papers on the historiography of various aspects of the Christian past over the previous half century. This paper on the evangelical dimension was one of them. It takes into account history written about evangelicals by those outside the movement but concentrates on the emergence of new approaches to evangelical history by evangelicals, encompassing the United States and other lands as well as Britain. The word "discovery" in the title is deliberately tendentious: as the paper suggests, the evangelical past had been considered in earlier years, but the most important feature of the story was the emergence of scholarly history writing by evangelicals.

This article originally appeared in Peter D. Clarke and Charlotte Methuen, eds., *The Church on Its Past*, Studies in Church History, no. 49 (Woodbridge, UK: Boydell, 2013), 330–64, and is reproduced by permission of the Ecclesiastical History Society, which holds the copyright to the content.

*   *   *

'From some modern perspectives', wrote James Belich, a leading historian of New Zealand, in 1996, 'the evangelicals are hard to like. They dressed like crows; seemed joyless, humourless and sometimes hypocritical; [and] they

---

I am very grateful to Mark Noll for his comments on this essay and to other friends for discussion of topics in this field.

embalmed the evidence poor historians need to read in tedious preaching'.[1] Similar views have often been expressed in the historiography of Evangelical Protestantism, the subject of this essay. It will cover such disapproving appraisals of the Evangelical past, but because a high proportion of the writing about the movement was by insiders it will have more to say about studies by Evangelicals of their own history. Evangelicals are taken to be those who have placed particular stress on the value of the Bible, the doctrine of the cross, an experience of conversion and a responsibility for activism. They were to be found in the Church of England and its sister provinces of the Anglican communion, forming an Evangelical party that rivalled the high church and broad church tendencies, and also in the denominations that stemmed from Nonconformity in England and Wales, as well as in the Protestant churches of Scotland. Evangelicals were strong, often overwhelmingly so, within Methodism and Congregationalism and among the Baptists and the Presbyterians. Some bodies that arose later on, including the (so-called Plymouth) Brethren, the Churches of Christ and the Pentecostals (the last two primarily American in origin), joined the Evangelical coalition. These dynamic groupings spread over the parts of the globe inhabited by people of British stock. From the outbreak of the Evangelical Revival in the eighteenth century onwards, they obeyed their own imperative of preaching the gospel. By the second half of the nineteenth century they were culturally dominant in Britain, the United States and other lands of British settlement. Although their ascendancy subsequently decayed in most areas of the British Isles, there was ample compensation in the extension of their influence into many other regions of the world through the missionary movement.[2] Evangelicals also penetrated the European continent, affecting the religious life of most of its countries. Excellent work has been done on some branches of the Evangelical movement on the Continent,[3] but

1. James Belich, *Making Peoples: A History of the New Zealanders; From Polynesian Settlement to the End of the Nineteenth Century* (Auckland, 1996), 135.

2. The series 'A History of Evangelicalism' is the most convenient source for an overview. So far it contains three volumes: Mark A. Noll, *The Rise of Evangelicalism: The Age of Edwards, Whitefield and the Wesleys* (Leicester, 2004); John Wolffe, *The Expansion of Evangelicalism: The Age of Wilberforce, More, Chalmers and Finney* (Nottingham, 2006); and David W. Bebbington, *The Dominance of Evangelicalism: The Age of Spurgeon and Moody* (Leicester, 2005). Two further volumes on the twentieth century are in preparation.

3. E.g. Sébastien Fath, *Une autre manière d'être chrétien en France: Socio-histoire de l'implantation baptiste (1810–1950)* (Geneva, 2001); W. Reg Ward, *The Protestant Evangelical Awakening* (Cambridge, 1992); Gregory L. Nichols, *The Development of Russian Evangelical Spirituality: A Study of Ivan V. Kargel* (Eugene, OR, 2011).

this essay concentrates on history written about its adherents in the English-speaking world and the missions it generated. It offers an evaluation of the work written about Evangelicals of all types during the period since the foundation of the Ecclesiastical History Society in 1961.

Before the 1960s Evangelicals were generally averse to history. Many of them suffered from a disinclination to explore the life of the mind, preferring to concentrate on the more pressing task of evangelism.[4] The present, not the past, was the time in which people were converted. The eschatology most favoured amongst conservative Evangelicals, a form of premillennialism, encouraged belief in the imminent return of Christ to earth. If the second advent was likely at any time, scholarly enterprise appeared a waste of energy.[5] Furthermore there was an aspect of the Evangelical worldview that inhibited specifically historical work. The time that mattered was that of the earliest church. The first century provided, through the New Testament, authoritative teachings to obey and noble examples to follow. Subsequent Christian generations were notoriously inclined to degeneration and so, for many, were barely worth attention. Consequently when in the 1940s a group of British Evangelicals did create a centre for scholarly research, Tyndale House, Cambridge, it concentrated on biblical studies and effectively excluded church history from its purview.[6] One of its moving spirits, F. F. Bruce, who was to go on to occupy the Rylands Chair in Biblical Criticism and Exegesis at Manchester from 1959, was exceptional in writing three historical volumes on early Christianity, but even he had declared ten years before that 'if Church History teaches one thing more than another, it is that there is a constant tendency to deterioration'.[7] History was, if anything, at even more of a discount in the United States, where a strident Fundamentalism displaying overt hostility towards the academy had made a far greater impact on the Evangelical world. Although by the 1940s a number of 'neo-Evangelicals' were inching their way back towards greater engagement with scholarship, progress was especially slow in the discipline of

4. Mark A. Noll, *The Scandal of the Evangelical Mind* (Grand Rapids, MI, 1994).

5. Timothy Weber, *Living in the Shadow of the Second Coming: American Premillennialism, 1875–1925* (New York, 1979). The same premillennial school of thought predominated long after 1925.

6. Thomas A. Noble, *Research for the Academy and Church: Tyndale House and Fellowship; The First Sixty Years* (Leicester, 2006).

7. Frederick F. Bruce, 'Church History and Its Lessons', in *The Church: A Symposium*, ed. J. B. Watson (London, 1949), 178, quoted by Tim Grass, *F. F. Bruce: A Life* (Milton Keynes, 2011), 73.

history. As late as 1982 Mark Noll, a leading American Evangelical historian, was deploring 'the generally weak sense of history among most evangelical groups'.[8] Even the past of the Evangelical movement itself was alien territory.

Yet over the years beginning in 1961 the situation was transformed. Evangelicals—or at least a growing number of scholars in their ranks—became interested in their own past. Books were published, organizations formed and conferences held. By 1994 Harry S. Stout, Professor of History at Yale, could claim that, whereas in the 1970s 'evangelicalism was not a field of scholarly inquiry', by 1994, when he was writing, 'it certainly has become one'.[9] Stout was considering the United States alone, but his comment applied also to Britain, Australia and elsewhere. Although there were important contributions from outside the Evangelical movement, the achievement was largely the fruit of exploration by Evangelicals of their past. They had made a discovery of their own history. This essay examines the process. It considers first the state of the historiography of the Evangelical movement in the years preceding the upsurge of interest. Earlier historical work on aspects of the Evangelical world did exist, but much of what was produced was popular and unscholarly. The second topic is the ways in which existing patterns of writing were changed from the 1960s onwards; the general trend was towards markedly higher standards of scholarship. Then there will be a discussion of the major innovations in writing about the Evangelical movement over the period. So, thirdly, there will be assessment of the impact of religious developments on Evangelical historiography. The fourth section will analyse changes in historical fashion that affected writing about Evangelicals. The overall aim will be to explain the reasons for the growth and character of Evangelical historical studies over the last half-century.

In the first place, the prevailing model in the study of the Evangelical past before 1961 was denominational history. In Britain history societies had existed within the various Nonconformist bodies since around the opening of the twentieth century. The Baptist Historical Society, for example, had been founded in 1908 for the purpose, among others, of 'holding Meetings to Discuss Obscure Points'.[10] There was a similar pattern in America, where

---

8. Wheaton, IL, Wheaton College, Billy Graham Center, Archives of the Institute for the Study of American Evangelicals [hereafter: ISAE], 'Proposal for a Planning Grant: An Institute for the Study of American Evangelicalism' (typescript, Wheaton, IL, 1982), 1. I am grateful to Eric Brandt for his assistance with research in these archives.

9. ISAE, Harry S. ['Skip'] Stout to ISAE Advisors, 29 May 1994.

10. Circular announcing a meeting to establish the Baptist Historical Society, April

the equivalent Baptist organization had been formed as long before as 1853. Methodists, Congregationalists, Presbyterians and even Huguenots possessed their counterparts. Quakers, on the fringe of the Evangelical movement, and Unitarians, definitely beyond the fringe, had their own organizations too. The aim of these historical agencies was to defend the principles of their parent bodies. Evangelical Anglicans, though possessing no historical society, fitted the mould by reissuing in 1951 G. R. Balleine's history of the Evangelical party, first published in 1908, with a preface expressing the hope that the book would remain 'a vindication of the historic Evangelical tradition in the Church of England'.[11] There was therefore a longstanding custom of, as it were, slicing the history of Protestantism longitudinally, by denomination. The rarity of horizontal slicing into different periods meant that the common ground occupied by Evangelicals in the relatively recent past was obscured. Methodists, who owed their existence to the Evangelical Revival, focused their historical interest almost exclusively on John Wesley, with perhaps a side-glance for his brother Charles. Thus the Methodist denominational association was (and is) called the Wesley Historical Society. Consequently, at least down to the 1950s, there was little attention to the decades after Wesley's death in 1791. The chief exceptions were the four ground-breaking but rather uncritical studies of the relationship of Methodism to labour history by the minister Robert Wearmouth, published between 1937 and 1957.[12] In America William Warren Sweet, though himself a Methodist minister, deliberately tried to counteract the same dominance of confessional history by refusing to allow his graduate students at the University of Chicago to write dissertations about their own denominations, thereby producing a generation of scholars with a broader vision who flourished in the third quarter of the twentieth century—Robert Handy, Winthrop Hudson, Sidney Mead.[13] Among them there were signs, as

---

1908, quoted by Faith Bowers, 'Centenary History of the Baptist Historical Society: Part 1: 1908–2008', *Baptist Quarterly* 42 (2008), 325–39, at 325.

11. G[eorge]. R. Balleine, *A History of the Evangelical Party in the Church of England* (London, 1951), v.

12. Robert F. Wearmouth, *Methodism and the Working-Class Movements of England, 1800–1850* (London, 1937); idem, *Methodism and the Common People of the Eighteenth Century* (London, 1945); idem, *Methodism and the Struggle of the Working Classes, 1850–1900* (Leicester, 1954); idem, *The Social and Political Influence of Methodism in the Twentieth Century* (London, 1957).

13. Sidney E. Mead, 'Professor Sweet's Religion and Culture in America: A Review Article', *Church History* 32 (1953), 33–49, at 41–2; James L. Ash Jr, *Protestantism and the American University: An Intellectual Biography of William Warren Sweet* (Dallas, TX, 1982), 103.

in Handy's volume about the United States and Canada in the Oxford History of the Christian Church series, that religious history could be illuminated by treating Evangelicals as a distinct sector.[14] Yet the institutional pattern of higher education in America, whereby most church history was taught and written in seminaries and departments affiliated to specific religious bodies, meant that the subject retained its overwhelmingly confessional stance. History was treated as a branch of denominational apologetics.

Biography was another common feature of Evangelical historical work in the middle years of the twentieth century. The practice of commemorating the recently dead persisted, often generating anecdotal volumes with such titles as *Passion for Souls*.[15] Figures from the remoter past attracted some attention, with Wesley predictably looming large. Wesley was manipulated to fit the preconceptions of his Methodist biographers so that their twentieth-century priorities could bask in the glow of his authority. Thus the most popular American biography of Wesley in the 1950s was written by Francis J. McConnell, a bishop in the Methodist Episcopal Church whose mind had been moulded by the school of philosophy sometimes labelled 'personalism', according to which personality is the ultimate metaphysical principle. In his book Wesley is described as having been 'profoundly interested in human values' and eager for the 'release of higher human possibilities'.[16] Even when historical work aspired to higher scholarly standards, it was often cast in biographical form. The most telling study of Evangelical Anglicanism published around mid-century, though not presented as a biography, illustrates the point. G. C. B. Davies's book *The Early Cornish Evangelicals* (1951), despite its title, was almost exclusively concerned with Samuel Walker of Truro.[17] There were symptoms of change, for there was already the start of a tendency to examine the theology of Wesley in its intellectual context. Harald Lindström's *Wesley and Sanctification* (1946), though concentrating again on the single individual, is an early instance of a series of fruitful studies of the thought of the founder of Methodism.[18] When L. E. Elliott-Binns, a broad-

---

14. Robert T. Handy, *A History of the Churches in the United States and Canada*, Oxford History of the Christian Church (Oxford, 1976).

15. Kenneth Hulbert, *Passion for Souls: The Story of Charles H. Hulbert, Methodist Missioner* (London, 1959).

16. Francis J. McConnell, *John Wesley* (New York, 1939), 310, quoted by Richard Heitzenrater, *The Elusive Mr. Wesley*, 2 vols (Nashville, TN, 1984), 2:203.

17. G[eorge]. C. B. Davies, *The Early Cornish Evangelicals, 1735–60* (London, 1951).

18. Harald Lindström, *Wesley and Sanctification* (London, 1946).

minded Evangelical clergyman who had also written on Erasmus and Pope Innocent III, published in 1953 an account of the eighteenth-century revival, he expressed dismay that his source biographies were often 'the works of pious admirers, lacking in critical ability and with no apparent desire to verify their statements'.[19] He was not going to add to their number, but his scrupulosity was unusual. Biography, often tending to hagiography, remained a living genre among Evangelicals.

That was true of a specific department of Evangelical historical writing, missionary studies. Biographies depicting the heroic deeds of their pioneering subjects were almost as much the norm in the middle of the twentieth century as they had been in the middle of the nineteenth. In 1947 A. G. Pouncy published an account of the career of Henry Martyn, the scholar who left Cambridge at the opening of the nineteenth century in order to blaze a gospel trail into Iran. An Evangelical publisher issued it with the subtitle 'The First Modern Apostle to the Mohammedan'.[20] Complementing the biographies were institutional histories published by the various agencies, denominational and undenominational. The Bible Churchmen's Missionary Society, for example, published a record, again in 1947, of its first quarter-century. The tone of the book can be gauged from the foreword's explanation that the society's missionaries were eager to 'get to grips with the devil in the strongholds of paganism by unsheathing therein the sword of the Spirit'.[21] Although the book did include descriptions of setbacks, it was primarily a story of successive triumphs designed to foster further support for the society. The one major work that broke out of the constrictions of missionary advocacy was Kenneth Scott Latourette's magisterial *History of the Expansion of Christianity* (1937–47). Latourette, a Baptist minister on the faculty of Yale Divinity School, discussed the advance of the faith over its two thousand years in seven volumes, allocating the sixth to the nineteenth century and the seventh to the twentieth.[22] His expertise in Chinese history ensured that he treated missions in the context

19. L[eonard]. E. Elliott-Binns, *The Early Evangelicals: A Religious and Social Study* (London, 1953), 5.

20. A[nthony]. G. Pouncy, *Henry Martyn, 1781–1812: The First Modern Apostle to the Mohammedan* (London, 1947).

21. Daniel H. C. Bartlett, Foreword to W[alter]. S. Hooton and J. Stafford Wright, *The First Twenty-Five Years of the Bible Churchmen's Missionary Society (1922–47)* (London, 1947), ix.

22. Kenneth S. Latourette, *A History of the Expansion of Christianity*, 7 vols (New York, 1937–47).

of their host cultures far more than his contemporaries. In general, however, the history of the worldwide spread of Evangelical religion remained an intellectual backwater.

The place of Evangelicalism in mainstream historiography was marginal, particularly in Britain. It is true that the eighteenth-century Evangelical Revival claimed a place in British textbooks just as the contemporary Great Awakening was discussed in their American equivalents. G. M. Young, a fellow of All Souls College, Oxford, also gave weight to the formative influence of Evangelical religion over Victorian England in his luminous study, *Portrait of an Age* (1936). A boy born in 1810, he pointed out on his opening page, 'found himself at every turn controlled, and animated, by the imponderable pressure of the Evangelical discipline'.[23] It became conventional to acknowledge the role of Evangelical faith in the temper of the era. A post-war collection of BBC talks on the Victorian age included two, by Charles Smyth of Cambridge and Gordon Rupp, later of the same university, on the Anglican and Nonconformist varieties of Evangelicalism.[24] Acknowledgement, however, did not lead on to analysis. In the 1950s the Victorian era, still languishing under a shadow of sneering disapproval, was accorded only limited academic scrutiny. The place of Evangelicals in nineteenth-century Britain remained shrouded in obscurity, with few apart from Lord Shaftesbury receiving attention.[25] The twentieth century, according to leaders of historical opinion, was a period for recollection rather than record. Since the United States possessed so much shorter a past, the centuries when Evangelicals were active were more carefully researched. Eminent historians such as Richard Hofstadter of Columbia University could not fail to take account of the movement, so that, for example, his study of *Anti-intellectualism in American Life* (1963) treats the Evangelical spirit as 'the most powerful carrier' of the phenomenon he examines.[26] More sympathetic accounts could also be found in mainstream history. In 1959 William G. McLoughlin Jr of Brown University successfully argued in his *Modern Revivalism* that the religious revivals beloved by Evangelicals had been 'more

23. G[eorge]. M. Young, *Victorian England: Portrait of an Age*, 2nd edn (London, 1957), 1.

24. Charles Smyth, 'The Evangelical Discipline', and Gordon Rupp, 'Evangelicalism of the Nonconformists', in *Ideas and Beliefs of the Victorians: An Historic Revaluation of the Victorian Age* (London, 1949), 97–104, 105–12.

25. The frequently reprinted J[ohn]. L. and Barbara Hammond, *Lord Shaftesbury* (London, 1923), had put Shaftesbury on the intellectual map.

26. Richard Hofstadter, *Anti-intellectualism in American Life* (London, 1964), 47.

significant than social historians have yet acknowledged'.[27] The most thorough coverage of Evangelicalism in a national history, however, was to be found in the first volume of Manning Clark's massive *History of Australia*, appearing in 1962.[28] Clark, as the unbelieving son of an angular Evangelical Anglican clergyman,[29] saw Evangelicalism as one of the three great contending forces in the Australian past alongside the Enlightenment and Roman Catholicism. Yet the internal history of the movement was little illuminated either in Clark's volumes or elsewhere. Although in lands outside Britain there was rather more recognition of the role of the Evangelical movement in the national past, the detail of its life usually seemed beneath serious academic notice.

The second section of this essay can usefully address the ways in which the mid-twentieth-century legacy of historiography relating to Evangelicalism was adapted in later years. The existing pattern—high on denominational history, life stories and missionary successes but low in mainstream history—certainly persisted in the decades from the 1960s onwards, but with striking modifications. Denominational studies became notably more scholarly. The transformation was most obvious in Methodist history, where a new edition of Wesley's works achieved much higher standards of precision from the appearance of the first volume in 1975.[30] Reg Ward, the editor of the journals in Wesley's works, John Wigger, David Hempton and others wrote works that put Methodism—British, American and global—squarely within the parameters of conventional history.[31] *A History of the Methodist Church in Great Britain*, published in four volumes between 1965 and 1988, included chapters of great quality, perhaps the most valuable being a study in volume 1 by John Walsh, fellow of Jesus College, Oxford, who also wrote illuminatingly on the broader Evangelical movement.[32] Congregationalism was similarly served in England

27. William G. McLoughlin Jr, *Modern Revivalism: Charles Grandison Finney to Billy Graham* (New York, 1959), vi.

28. Manning Clark, *The History of Australia*, 6 vols (Parkville, Vic., 1962–87).

29. Manning Clark, *A Historian's Apprenticeship* (Parkville, Vic., 1992), ch. 1.

30. John Wesley, *The Appeals to Men of Reason and Religion and Certain Related Open Letters*, ed. Gerald R. Cragg, *The Works of John Wesley*, Vol. 11 (Oxford, 1975). The series continues.

31. W[illiam]. R. Ward, *Religion and Society in England, 1790–1850* (London, 1972); John H. Wigger, *Taking Heaven by Storm: Methodism and the Rise of Popular Christianity in America* (New York, 1998); David Hempton, *Methodism: Empire of the Spirit* (New Haven, CT, 2005).

32. John Walsh, 'Methodism at the End of the Eighteenth Century', in Rupert Davies, A. Raymond George and Gordon Rupp, eds, *A History of the Methodist Church*

by Clyde Binfield, whose long editorship of the *Journal of the United Reformed Church Historical Society* ensured a succession of perceptive articles. There were authoritative monographs on the Presbyterians of North America by, for example, Mark Noll on the leaders of Princeton Seminary and Richard Vaudry on the Free Church in Canada.[33] Baptists were particularly well served by a series of nearly twenty publications on the Baptist Heritage in Atlantic Canada issued from 1979 under the inspiration of Jarold K. Zeman, who had received an academic formation at Charles University in Prague before the Communist takeover of Czechoslovakia forced him to emigrate.[34] Newer religious bodies also began to attract their historians: Harold Rowdon on the Brethren in England, Edwin Harrell on the Disciples of Christ in America and Walter Hollenweger on the Pentecostals worldwide opened fresh paths where others have followed.[35] At the same time denominational loyalties were fading,[36] so that Evangelical history relating to more than one denomination seemed a more natural unit of historical study. Yet writing about specific denominations did survive, and, while much of it continued to be designed for internal consumption and some of it tolerated low standards of research, several historians were engaging powerfully with the issues raised by a wider historiography.

Biography has also been affected by an improvement in scholarly standards. It must be admitted once more that a great deal of more popular writing has remained immune to the trend. A biography of Charles Haddon Spurgeon, the greatest of Victorian preachers, appeared in 1992. The author, Lewis Drummond, formerly president of Southeastern Baptist Theological Seminary in North Carolina, provided a full scholarly apparatus and conceded that his subject had weaknesses, but he was eager to draw lessons, turned aside to vindicate the mir-

---

in Great Britain, 4 vols (London, 1965–88), 1:275–315; J[ohn]. D. Walsh, 'Origins of the Evangelical Revival', in *Essays in Modern English Church History in Memory of Norman Sykes*, ed. G[areth]. V. Bennett and J[ohn]. D. Walsh (London, 1966), 132–62.

33. Mark A. Noll, *Princeton and the Republic, 1768–1822: The Search for a Christian Enlightenment in the Era of Samuel Stanhope* (Princeton, NJ, 1989); Richard W. Vaudry, *The Free Church in Victorian Canada, 1844–1861* (Waterloo, ON, 1989).

34. Jarold K. Zeman, *Open Doors: Canadian Baptists, 1950–1990* (Hantsport, NS, 1992).

35. Harold H. Rowdon, *The Origins of the Brethren, 1825–1850* (London, 1967); David Edwin Harrell Jr, *A Social History of the Disciples of Christ*, 1: *Quest for a Christian America: The Disciples of Christ and American Society to 1966* (Nashville, TN, 1966); Walter J. Hollenweger, *The Pentecostals* (London, 1972).

36. Robert Wuthnow, *The Restructuring of American Religion: Society and Faith Since World War II* (Princeton, NJ, 1988).

acle of the feeding of the five thousand and even gave an account, without any sense of anomaly, of the entry of Spurgeon into heaven.[37] Yet a growing number of biographers have illuminated whole areas by writing about individuals. One of them, John Pollock, an Evangelical Anglican clergyman, managed to bridge the gulf between the popular and the academic in his well-rounded study of William Wilberforce.[38] Henry Rack of the University of Manchester performed the same feat to produce the standard life of John Wesley in 1989.[39] Eighteenth-century Methodists have fared better than most other categories of Evangelical: Charles Wesley, John Fletcher and Francis Asbury have all received penetrating biographical treatment in the recent past.[40] The high proportion of attention to the eighteenth century, in some measure reflecting a general preoccupation of historians in the early twenty-first century, is nowhere better illustrated than by the scholarship lavished on Jonathan Edwards, the New England Puritan divine who is often hailed as 'America's theologian'. The Yale edition of the works of Edwards, begun in 1959, spawned a cottage industry of conferences, collo-quia and collections on Edwards, culminating in the masterly biography by George Marsden.[41] There are also excellent biographies of later figures such as the leader of the Free Church of Scotland, Thomas Chalmers, the nineteenth-century American evangelist D. L. Moody, his twentieth-century successor Oral Roberts and the British social gospeller Hugh Price Hughes, but they are less thick on the ground than for the earlier period.[42] Biographical work, especially on the eighteenth century, has greatly improved over the last fifty years.

The academic revolution in the historiography of Evangelicals is nowhere more evident than in missionary studies. The prime agent of change was An-

37. Lewis Drummond, *Spurgeon: Prince of Preachers* (Grand Rapids, MI, 1992), 715, 44, 771 respectively.

38. John Pollock, *Wilberforce* (London, 1977).

39. Henry D. Rack, *Reasonable Enthusiast: John Wesley and the Rise of Methodism* (London, 1989).

40. Gareth Lloyd, *Charles Wesley and the Struggle for Methodist Identity* (Oxford, 2007); Patrick Streiff, *Reluctant Saint? A Theological Biography of Fletcher of Madeley* (Peterborough, 2001); John H. Wigger, *American Saint: Francis Asbury and the Methodists* (Oxford, 2009).

41. George M. Marsden, *Jonathan Edwards: A Life* (New Haven, CT, 2003).

42. Stewart J. Brown, *Thomas Chalmers and the Godly Commonwealth in Scotland* (Oxford, 1982); James F. Findlay Jr, *Dwight L. Moody: American Evangelist* (Chicago, 1969); David Edwin Harrell, *Oral Roberts: An American Life* (Bloomington, IN, 1985); Christopher Oldstone-Moore, *Hugh Price Hughes: Founder of a New Methodism, Conscience of a New Nonconformity* (Cardiff, 1999).

the Evangelical share of churchgoers increased from 30 to 37 per cent.[50] Although there was a decline in absolute numbers of Evangelical worshippers, they had become a larger proportion of the Christian community at prayer. Likewise in the United States the mainline churches lost ground to those identifying themselves as Evangelical. Awareness of Evangelicals as a sector of the American population made rapid strides after Jimmy Carter, elected president in 1976, was identified as coming from their ranks. Evangelicals began to enjoy salience as a political constituency to be courted or reviled.[51] There was also a growing consciousness that the burgeoning Protestants of the Third World, the long-term fruit of the missionary movement, were overwhelmingly Evangelical by conviction. Hence Evangelicals as a grouping enjoyed much more prominence than in the past. The public, especially in America, wanted to read about them and mainstream publishers became keen to issue books on Evangelical themes. A milestone was the publication in 1980 by Oxford University Press in New York of George Marsden's *Fundamentalism and American Culture*, a study of the warping of popular Evangelicalism into hardline Fundamentalism in the United States.[52] The huge success of Marsden's path-breaking book helped ensure that Oxford in New York welcomed titles on Evangelical subjects for the rest of the period. Other academic presses followed suit, with McGill-Queen's University Press in Canada, for instance, generating a long sequence of 'Studies in the History of Religion', many with Evangelical subject-matter. The expansion of Evangelicalism in the later twentieth century undergirded the growth of historical work on the movement.

At the same time Evangelicals discovered history as a career option. The movement had long fostered entry to the ministry and the other professions, but, with the expansion of higher education after the Second World War, rapid in North America but also happening elsewhere after some delay, academia offered fresh opportunities. A generation of American graduate students with backgrounds in conservative denominations pursued history as a vocation. Timothy L. Smith, who composed the first major work in the efflorescence of Evangelical historiography, *Revivalism and Social Reform* (1957), was a minister

50. Peter Brierley, *The Tide Is Running Out: What the English Church Attendance Survey Reveals* (London, 2000), 27; idem, ed., *UK Christian Handbook, Religious Trends No. 2* (London, 1999), 12.3.

51. Wuthnow, *Restructuring of American Religion*, ch. 8.

52. George M. Marsden, *Fundamentalism and American Culture: The Shaping of Twentieth-Century Evangelicalism, 1870–1925* (New York, 1980).

of the Church of the Nazarene, a Holiness denomination.[53] George Marsden was the son of a minister of the Orthodox Presbyterians who had split from mainline Presbyterianism in the wake of the Fundamentalist disputes the historian chronicled. Mark Noll came from a Conservative Baptist home.[54] Martin Marty at Chicago, William Hutchinson at Harvard and Sydney Ahlstrom at Yale all provided supervision on Evangelical topics for doctoral candidates, who in due course went on to mentor a further generation of aspirants in the field. In Britain a key agency was the Inter-Varsity Fellowship (IVF) that bound together Christian Unions, groups of Evangelical students, in the universities. It launched professional groups for graduates, the Christian Medical Fellowship being the largest, and added one in the early 1960s for historians. Although for many years the Historians' Study Group did little more than hold a couple of small gatherings a year, it fostered the idea that historical research and teaching could be a sphere for Christian enterprise. One of the earliest pieces of writing to explore Evangelical history as a distinct genre was an unpublished Cambridge prize essay of 1962 by Haddon Willmer, later Professor of Theology at Leeds, on the Evangelical movement in England between 1785 and 1835.[55] Willmer, the son of a conservative Baptist minister, was active at university in the Cambridge Inter-Collegiate Christian Union. The IVF, which established equivalents in most other countries in the Commonwealth and some beyond, also nurtured scholars in other parts of the world. At an international conference on Evangelical history in Sydney in 1997, nearly all the dozen people round the table found that they had IVF backgrounds.[56] The rise of Evangelical historical scholarship, which was parallel to the advance of conservative Protestants in several other academic disciplines,[57] was a global phenomenon.

Their enterprise established a number of institutional bases. The Historians' Study Group in Britain evolved into the autonomous Christianity and History Forum with its own bulletin, its sixth issue publishing in 2010 articles

53. Timothy L. Smith, *Revivalism and Social Reform: American Protestantism on the Eve of the Civil War* (Nashville, TN, 1957).

54. Maxie B. Burch, *The Evangelical Historians: The Historiography of George Marsden, Nathan Hatch and Mark Noll* (Lanham, MD, 1996), 5, 3.

55. Haddon Willmer, 'Evangelicalism, 1785 to 1835', Hulsean Prize essay, University of Cambridge (1962).

56. Personal experience.

57. D. Michael Lindsay, *Faith in the Halls of Power: How Evangelicals joined the American Elite* (New York, 2007), chs 3–4.

on Evangelical interactions with the Huguenots, the novel and the empire.[58] The Forum paled in significance, however, by comparison with its sister organization in North America, the Conference on Faith and History, founded in 1968 by Richard V. Pierard and Robert D. Linder, graduate students at the University of Iowa. The Conference could draw on the network of Christian colleges in North America as well as the smaller number of Evangelicals holding posts in secular institutions and so grew to number over six hundred members.[59] Its periodical, *Fides et Historia*, existed primarily to 'stimulate or provoke dialogue among evangelical Christian historians' rather than to encourage research on any sector of religious history,[60] but from its earliest years it generated papers on the history of the Evangelical movement and their proportion grew over time. In Australia an Evangelical History Association, sharing the American organization's concern with fellowship but more centrally focused on the history of the movement, was launched in 1987 under Stuart Piggin, soon to become master of Robert Menzies College at Macquarie University in Sydney.[61] It issued the periodical *Lucas*, produced an *Australian Dictionary of Evangelical Biography* and published collected volumes of papers. Most important of all was the Institute for the Study of American Evangelicals at Wheaton College, Illinois. Originating as no more than informal meetings between young friends in academia such as Mark Noll and Nathan Hatch, in 1979 the group held a successful conference at Wheaton on the Bible in America, afterwards publishing the papers, and three years later set up the Institute to organize more gatherings.[62] The momentum of the series of conferences, which regularly led to volumes published with academic imprints, was sustained by annual consultations that doubled as holidays *en famille* on the coast of New England complete with games of softball. The result, as George Marsden put it, was the creation of 'an informal network of colleagues who have become the closest of friends and hence have accomplished by con-

58. *Christianity and History Bulletin*, no. 6 (Summer 2010), 7–43.

59. 'The Conference on Christianity and History', http://www.huntington.edu /cfh/fides.htm, accessed 1 August 2011.

60. Robert D. Linder, 'Editorial', *Fides et Historia* [hereafter *FH*] 2 (1969), 2.

61. Geoffrey R. Treloar, 'History as Vocation: Stuart Piggin as Evangelical Historian and Historian of Evangelicalism', in *Making History for God: Essays on Evangelicalism, Revival and Mission in Honour of Stuart Piggin, Master of Robert Menzies College, 1990–2004*, ed. Geoffrey R. Treloar and Robert D. Linder (Sydney, 2004), 3–34, at 14.

62. Nathan O. Hatch and Mark A. Noll, eds, *The Bible in America: Essays in Cultural History* (New York, 1982).

certed effort what none of them could have done alone'.[63] The emergence of Evangelical history probably owes as much to family games as to high-level intellectual developments.

Nevertheless, innovations in the sphere of theology did have an impact on historical studies. Evangelicals had been accustomed to repudiate tradition, seeing it as a sinister force undermining a pure biblicism. Gradually during the period some of their leaders became more friendly towards the concept. F. F. Bruce realized 'the prevalence of tradition' among Brethren assemblies which believed themselves to be free from its influence and so expounded the value of early Christian traditions in a lecture series of 1968.[64] The Baptist Barrie White, principal of Regent's Park College, Oxford, was willing, in a booklet of 1976, to treat tradition as a condensing of the work of the Holy Spirit in the past and thus as carrying a measure of authority for subsequent practice.[65] In the United States, where the Evangelical school in the Episcopal Church had long been in eclipse, there was from the 1970s a novel upsurge of enthusiasm for liturgy that drew many towards the traditional. Robert E. Webber of Wheaton College was the central figure, joining an Episcopal congregation and urging a rediscovery of the common roots that bound Evangelicals to the church's past.[66] Although he was the son-in-law of Harold Lindsell, the author of *The Battle for the Bible* (1976) and champion of a stern inerrancy designed to buttress the sole authority of the Bible, Webber published an influential series of books commending high church worship as the correct complement to Evangelical belief. Addressing the common fear of Evangelicals that the venture might elevate tradition over Scripture, he pointed out that tradition meant no more than 'passing on', whether a truth or a practice. The proper perspective on Christ, the church, worship and spirituality was within what Webber called 'the paradigms of history', how each of them had been viewed in the past.[67] A fascination with the links between the New Testament and the present, a form of history-mindedness, was springing up. In such a context the Evangelical past itself could not fail to exert a stronger appeal over minds associated with the movement.

63. ISAE, George Marsden, 'ISAE: Retrospect and Prospect—June 1994'.

64. F[rederick]. F. Bruce, *Tradition Old and New* (Grand Rapids, MI, 1970), 9.

65. B[arrington]. R. White, *Authority: A Baptist View* (London, 1976), 23–6.

66. Robert E. Webber, *Common Roots: A Call to Evangelical Maturity* (Grand Rapids, MI, 1978).

67. Robert Webber, *Ancient-Future Faith: Rethinking Evangelicalism for a Postmodern World* (Grand Rapids, MI, 1999), 180–1, chs 4, 8, 11, 14.

A more specific set of intellectual influences played over the growth of Evangelical historiography. The Conference on Faith and History, together with its organizational equivalents in other lands, was centrally preoccupied in its early years with the relationship of theology to the discipline of history. 'Is there a Christian approach to history?' asked an article in the second volume of *Fides et Historia* in 1969.[68] The aim was to bridge the gulf between an Evangelical allegiance and the academic enterprise. At one level the object was the typical Evangelical desire to witness to the faith; at another it was to develop what came to be called a 'Christian mind'. The most significant theological stimulus in this direction came, perhaps remarkably, from the Netherlands. A number of Dutch neo-Calvinist theologians developed a school of thought that called for the subjection of all areas of human activity to the lordship of Christ. Its leading exponent, Abraham Kuyper, founder of a separatist Dutch Reformed movement in 1892 and Prime Minister of the Netherlands from 1901 to 1905, set out his vision in the Stone Lectures of 1898 at Princeton Seminary, published as *Lectures on Calvinism*.[69] The impact of this point of view on English speakers was hugely reinforced by American exponents, especially the theologian Cornelius Van Til, a son of Dutch immigrants to the United States who contended for the importance of presuppositions in intellectual exploration. It followed that believers must adopt distinctively Christian premises when undertaking any discipline such as history.[70] The school of Kuyper shaped the thought of C. T. McIntire of the Institute for Christian Studies at Toronto, at one time a leading theorist of history in Evangelical circles.[71] Van Til deeply swayed George Marsden, who believed that 'the very facts of history differ for the Christian and the non-Christian historian'.[72] Calvin College, where Marsden taught, was a bastion of this point of view. During the 1970s a small Christian Studies Unit propagated the same standpoint in Britain, but its deepest influence was always felt in the Netherlands itself, helping in 1989 to inspire the creation there of an Association of Christian Historians.[73] Although this ideological position

---

68. Charles J. Miller, 'Is There a Christian Approach to History?', *FH* 2 (1969), 3–15.

69. Abraham Kuyper, *Lectures on Calvinism* (Grand Rapids, MI, 1931).

70. John Frame, *Cornelius Van Til: An Analysis of His Thought* (Phillipsburg, NJ, 1995).

71. C. T. McIntire, 'The Focus of Historical Study: A Christian View', *FH* 14 (1981), 6–17, esp. 10, 11.

72. George M. Marsden, 'The Spiritual Vision of History', *FH* 14 (1981), 55–66, at 56.

73. *Christianity and History: An International Newsletter*, no. 2 (1991), 1–3.

was applicable to all genres of history, political and economic as much as religious, and although several advocates, including Marsden, modified their loyalties over time, it fostered self-confidence among Evangelical historians. They came to believe that they could study their own past with an emphasis on what they themselves considered important, the theological and the spiritual. Neo-Calvinism was a potent reinforcer of Evangelical history.

Yet Calvinism also generated opposition to the rise of academic historiography among Evangelicals. During the second half of the twentieth century there was a striking resurgence of specifically Reformed theology in the English-speaking world. Under the leadership of Martyn Lloyd-Jones and J. I. Packer, confessional Calvinism gathered force, first in Britain, and then, partly through the *Banner of Truth* magazine and publishing house, across the globe. The editor of the magazine, Iain Murray, once Lloyd-Jones's assistant minister, believed that history books ought to subserve the twin causes of advancing spiritual religion and promoting Reformed orthodoxy. He preferred history with heroes, as a book of his with that title published in 2009 confirmed.[74] Murray was championing a more traditional style of Evangelical historiography. In 1994–5 there was an instructive controversy about how history should be written. In a review in the *Banner of Truth*, Murray censured Harry S. Stout of Yale, a regular participant in the programmes of the Institute for the Study of American Evangelicals, for having embraced the norms of social and cultural history and so having surrendered to the 'unregenerate mind'.[75] Another reviewer in the magazine criticized Stout's biography of the evangelist George Whitefield for 'being obsessed with finding the slightest flaw in the character of a spiritual giant'.[76] Stout, himelf a firm Calvinist, replied vigorously that he and professionals like him followed the evidence, not dwelling on 'devotional or hagiographic themes'. The Bible itself did not hide the faults of its characters. If social and cultural history was illegitimate, 'there is no room for Christians in the secular academy'.[77] Murray responded that 'to write the lives of eminent Christians with minimum notice of the things which meant *most* to them, and without which their lives cannot be understood, is to mislead'.[78] It was an issue of priorities. For Murray, selecting the achievements of Evangelicals was designed to edify and evangelize; for Stout, portraying Evangelicals in their

---

74. Iain H. Murray, *Heroes* (Edinburgh, 2009).
75. Iain H. Murray, in *Banner of Truth*, July 1994, 8.
76. David White, in *Banner of Truth*, March 1994, 29.
77. Harry S. Stout, in *Banner of Truth*, March 1995, 7–10, at 7, 8.
78. Iain H. Murray, in *Banner of Truth*, March 1995, 10–11, at 11.

the genesis of the Evangelical movement must be situated.[88] Reg Ward demonstrated that Evangelical history has to be international in scope.

A further tendency in the churches of the period, especially strong among Evangelicals, was a rising eagerness to relate the Christian gospel to its cultural setting. Missiologists, among whom Andrew Walls was the most historically informed, took the initiative in relating the spread of the faith to the attitudes of its recipients, hoping to reveal the best ways of maximizing converts.[89] It was the genius of Lesslie Newbigin, a United Reformed Church minister who had served as a bishop in the Church of South India, to relate this body of thinking to the circumstances of the West. In his brief but powerful book, *The Other Side of 1984*, published by the British and World Councils of Churches in 1983, Newbigin argued that the Western churches must penetrate behind the debilitating effects of the Enlightenment if they were to recover their missionary vigour in articulating public truth.[90] His summons led to the Gospel and Our Culture movement which held a conference at Swanwick in 1992, published the conference papers and maintained an ongoing network.[91] The interaction of gospel and culture was becoming a central topic for reflection among Evangelicals and a wider Christian constituency. Historiography displayed similar symptoms. George Marsden's *Fundamentalism and American Culture* had already, in 1980, shown by its very title an appreciation of the need to locate Evangelical developments in their broad setting.[92] Hymns attracted attention, notably in Sandra Sizer's *Gospel Hymns and Social Religion* (1978), as a key way in which Evangelicals expressed themselves in an art form.[93] On the other side of the Atlantic, my *Evangelicalism in Modern Britain* (1989), though perhaps best known for its effort to define the word 'Evangelical', attempted to show how the movement had been shaped by the changing cultural ambience.[94] Regent's Park College, Oxford, set up a Centre for the Study of

88. See John Walsh, 'Profile: W. R. Ward; Methodist Historian and Historian of Methodism', *Epworth Review* 22 (1995), 41–6.

89. See n. 43 above.

90. Lesslie Newbigin, *The Other Side of 1984: Questions for the Churches* (London, 1983).

91. Hugh Montefiore, ed., *The Gospel and Contemporary Culture* (London, 1992); 'The Gospel and Our Culture', http://gospel-culture.org.uk/intro.htm, accessed 3 August 2011.

92. See n. 52 above.

93. Sandra S. Sizer, *Gospel Hymns and Social Religion: The Rhetoric of Nineteenth-Century Revivalism* (Philadelphia, PA, 1978).

94. D[avid]. W. Bebbington, *Evangelicalism in Modern Britain: A History from the 1730s to the 1980s* (London, 1989). On the thesis of ch. 1 of this book, see Michael G.

Christianity and Culture, its first conference in 1996 taking 'Culture and the Nonconformist Tradition' as its theme. The resulting book, according to one of the editors, reported on the experience of Nonconformists in 'balancing their absorption of the culture of their time, with the creation of their own distinctive subcultures'.[95] Popular culture was not neglected in subsequent writing, with such studies as an account of the enormously popular Cornish Methodist fiction by the three Hocking siblings, Silas, Joseph and Salome.[96] The two-way process of culture influencing religion and religion influencing culture became a common historical theme.

A final trend in the churches took place in the area of spirituality. Its normative form among many Evangelicals had long been that propagated by the Keswick movement, according to which holiness was to be discovered through the exercise of faith. The hold of Keswick teaching, however, slackened during the 1960s, when there arose an entirely different model of piety associated with charismatic renewal, encouraging free expression in worship, a search for bodily wholeness, close personal relationships and a willingness to embrace authentic living in the secular world.[97] The topic of spiritual practice became a major preoccupation. A whole series of pamphlets, the Grove Spirituality booklets, explored the subject from an Anglican Evangelical standpoint from 1982 onwards.[98] Historians affected by renewal naturally paid attention to religious experience in the past. Ian Randall, tutor at the Baptist Spurgeon's College in London and the author of *Evangelical Experiences* (1999), an account of inter-war English Evangelical spirituality, had himself been touched by the charismatic movement.[99] Likewise in America a new and thorough

---

Haykin and Kenneth J. Stewart, eds, *The Emergence of Evangelicalism: Exploring Historical Continuities* (Nottingham, 2008), published in the United States as *The Advent of Evangelicalism: Exploring Historical Continuities* (Nashville, TN, 2008).

95. Jane Shaw, 'Introduction: Why "Culture and the Nonconformist Tradition"?', in eadem and Alan Kreider, eds, *Culture and the Nonconformist Tradition* (Cardiff, 1999), 6.

96. Alan M. Kent, *Pulp Methodism: The Lives & Literature of Silas, Joseph & Salome Hocking, Three Cornish Novelists* (St Austell, 2002); Martin Wellings, '"Pulp Methodism" Revisited: The Literature and Significance of Silas and Joseph Hocking', in Peter Clarke and Charlotte Methuen, eds, *The Church and Literature*, Studies in Church History 48 (Woodbridge, 2012), 362–73.

97. D[avid]. W. Bebbington, 'Holiness in the Evangelical Tradition', in Stephen C. Barton, ed., *Holiness Past and Present* (London, 2003), 298–315, at 308–14.

98. The first was Peter Adam, *Living the Trinity* (Bramcote, 1982).

99. Ian Randall, *Evangelical Experiences: A Study in the Spirituality of English Evangelicalism, 1918–1939* (Carlisle, 1999).

account of the Great Awakening was written by Thomas S. Kidd, a member of a Baptist church with a distinctly charismatic ethos. Unlike many previous commentators, Kidd laid particular stress on the radical Evangelicals who went in for dreams and portents.[100] Revivalism was increasingly studied for its own sake rather than for the light it cast on such themes as social control. A leading historian of eighteenth-century Canada, George Rawlyk, drew attention to the formative role of the revivalist Henry Alline in the country's Maritime provinces.[101] Rawlyk, who was a core member of the circle around the Institute for the Study of American Evangelicals, became fascinated by religious experience in the past and wrote *Canada Fire* (1994) to show the radical credentials of revivalists from his home country.[102] Janice Holmes demonstrated the importance of revivals in late nineteenth-century Britain and Ireland and a range of scholars of Evangelicalism swamped the 2008 volume of Studies in Church History with accounts of revivalism in the modern period.[103] Spirituality and revival were in the air; they also appeared increasingly in the historiography. It was another way in which religious developments affected the writing of Evangelical history in the period.

The historiography of the movement, however, was also shaped by broader trends in the world of scholarship. To this, the fourth aspect of the subject, we now turn. The long-term twentieth-century shift of history towards techniques and concepts drawn from the social sciences necessarily had a major impact. Some of the best work on religion in the modern world was achieved by applying sociological methods. In England the *oeuvre* of Hugh McLeod, beginning with *Class and Religion in the Late Victorian City* (1974), showed how much could be revealed about religion when the central category of analysis

---

100. Thomas S. Kidd, *The Great Awakening: The Roots of Evangelical Christianity in Colonial America* (New Haven, CT, 2007).

101. George A. Rawlyk, *Ravished by the Spirit: Religious Revivals, Baptists and Henry Alline* (Montreal, 1984); idem, *Henry Alline: Selected Writings*, Sources of American Spirituality (New York, 1987).

102. George A. Rawlyk, *The Canada Fire: Radical Evangelicalism in British North America* (Montreal, 1984). On Rawlyk, see Mark A. Noll, 'George Rawlyk's Contribution to Canadian History as a Contribution to United States History: A Preliminary Probe', *FH* 32 (2000), 1–17, also in Daniel C. Goodwin, ed., *Revivals, Baptists, and George Rawlyk*, Baptist Heritage in Atlantic Canada 17 (Wolfville, NS, 2000), 29–51.

103. Janice Holmes, *Religious Revivals in Britain and Ireland, 1859–1905* (Dublin, 2000); Kate Cooper and Jeremy Gregory, eds, *Revival and Resurgence in Christian History*, Studies in Church History 44 (Woodbridge, 2008).

was class and there was copious use of statistics.[104] Few Evangelical historians practised this type of history, although one, Nigel Scotland, contributed to the adjacent subdiscipline of labour history by writing a study of agricultural labourers' trade unionism in East Anglia in the later nineteenth century. It was notable for giving ample space, as labour historians rarely did, to the ideas of the Primitive Methodists who formed the trade union vanguard.[105] A social scientific theory much in vogue during the 1960s and 1970s, the notion of manipulation of the lower classes by the upper classes, was applied to Evangelical religion. 'Revivals', wrote Paul E. Johnson in an influential study of early nineteenth-century Rochester, New York, that appeared in 1978, 'provided entrepreneurs with a means of imposing new standards of work discipline and personal comportment upon themselves and the men who worked for them, and thus they functioned as powerful social controls.'[106] Likewise an account of the Clapham Sect around William Wilberforce by Ford K. Brown, published in 1961, dwelt on its efforts to discipline the lower orders and, most famously, E. P. Thompson in his *Making of the English Working Class* two years later depicted Methodist preachers as using 'emotional violence' to turn converts into docile workers and loyal subjects.[107] Those with Evangelical sympathies found this picture far from compelling. Two of them were responsible for powerful ripostes. Reg Ward showed in *Religion and Society in England, 1790–1850* (1972) the extent to which Methodism in early industrial England was a radical force, sapping the foundations of church and state, and Nathan O. Hatch, in his book *The Democratization of American Christianity* (1989), laid bare the populism of Evangelical and related movements in the early national period of the United States that caused alarm to the new country's elites.[108] Although the first of these works was less effective than the second in redirecting the flow of historical writing, both struck powerful blows at the model of social manipulation by religion.

104. Hugh McLeod, *Class and Religion in the Late Victorian City* (London, 1974).

105. Nigel Scotland, *Methodism and the Revolt of the Field: A Study of the Methodist Contribution to Agricultural Trade Unionism in East Anglia, 1872–1896* (Gloucester, 1981).

106. Paul E. Johnson, *A Shopkeeper's Millennium: Society and Revivals in Rochester, New York, 1815–1837* (New York, 1978), 138.

107. Ford K. Brown, *Fathers of the Victorians: The Age of Wilberforce* (Cambridge, 1961); E[dward]. P. Thompson, *The Making of the English Working Class* (Harmondsworth, 1968; first publ. 1963), 418.

108. Ward, *Religion and Society*; Nathan O. Hatch, *The Democratization of American Christianity* (New Haven, CT, 1989).

The theory of social control was a symptom of the permeation of Marxist ideas into academia. Thompson, though coming from a Methodist background, had embraced a sophisticated form of Marxism with a strong cultural component.[109] A few other British historians with Marxist convictions wrote about aspects of the Evangelical movement. A. Allan Maclaren, for example, published in 1974 a study of religion in Aberdeen at the time of the Disruption of the Scottish church from that standpoint.[110] Its claims about the dearth of working-class involvement in Presbyterianism were later to be undermined by Peter Hillis.[111] Although research findings moulded by Marxist premises rarely endured, the legacy of Karl Marx played a significant role in the emergence of Evangelical historiography. Perhaps surprisingly, Marxism acted as a beacon for Evangelical historians. Those Evangelicals who gave any thought to historical theory in the 1960s and even in the 1970s normally accepted uncritically the prevailing objectivist model of history being the patient collection of brute facts from relevant sources.[112] According to John Warwick Montgomery of Trinity Evangelical Divinity School, Deerfield, Illinois, probably the best known exponent of an Evangelical philosophy of history at the time, Marxist rewritings of history were 'gross examples' of the solipsistic fallacy that 'there is no objective reality outside myself'.[113] For the younger generation who were discovering history as a vocation, however, Marxist successes in the academy showed that committed history was acceptable. 'If neo-Marxists can write neo-Marxist history', asked George Rawlyk in 1993, 'why should not evangelical Christian historians . . . write from an evangelical Christian perspective?'[114] The ideas of Marx began to be treated temperately in Evangelical writing about history. C. T. McIntire, for instance, wrote appreciatively of Marx's insight into human culture-making capacity and in my *Patterns in History* (1979) there is

109. On Thompson, see David Hempton and John Walsh, 'E. P. Thompson and Methodism', in Mark A. Noll, ed., *God and Mammon: Protestants, Money and the Market, 1790–1860* (New York, 2002), 99–120.

110. A. Allan Maclaren, *Religion and Class: The Disruption Years in Aberdeen* (London, 1974).

111. Peter Hillis, 'Presbyterianism and Social Class in Mid-Nineteenth-Century Glasgow: A Study of Nine Churches', *Journal of Ecclesiastical History* 32 (1981), 47–64.

112. Peter Novick, *That Noble Dream: The 'Objectivity Question' and the American Historical Profession* (Cambridge, 1988).

113. John Warwick Montgomery, *The Shape of the Past: A Christian Response to Secular Philosophies of History* (Minneapolis, MN, 1975), 8.

114. George A. Rawlyk, 'Writing about Canadian Revivals', in Edith L. Blumhofer and Randall Balmer, eds, *Modern Christian Revivals* (Urbana, IL, 1993), 208–26, at 219.

a sympathetic appraisal of the Marxist view of history.[115] Marxist historical scholarship blazed a trail which Evangelicals were eager to follow.

The rise of women's history, followed by gender history, was one of the most striking phenomena of historiography during the late twentieth century. Accounts of women's part in religious history began to flow from the press, though sometimes it was accused of being, especially in America, more committed to feminism than to scholarship. In Britain, however, the earliest significant study of an Evangelical topic was written by Olive Anderson of Westfield College, London, precisely to show that female preaching in the 1860s owed more to pre-millennialism than to feminism.[116] The best monograph in the field was actually by a man, Frank Prochaska, whose *Women and Philanthropy in Nineteenth-Century England* (1980) documented the work of Evangelical societies.[117] The publication of Leonore Davidoff and Catherine Hall's *Family Fortunes* (1987), examining religious as well as other roles of men and women in nineteenth-century house-holds, already marked a shift towards a more sophisticated gender history.[118] Evangelicals themselves lagged behind in Britain, not publishing illuminating critical history about women until the eve of the twenty-first century.[119] Part of the explanation lay in the division of opinion among Evangelicals about the role of women, crystallized over the issue of female ordination. My commissioned article on nineteenth-century Evangelical women appearing in 1984 in the journal circulating among graduates from Christian Unions carefully avoided taking sides in the debate.[120] The theme first occurred on the conference schedule of the Institute for the Study of American Evangelicals in 1993.[121] In the following year there appeared Susan Juster's *Disorderly Women*, an account of the prominence of women among

115. McIntire, 'Focus of Historical Study', 12–13; David Bebbington, *Patterns in History* (Leicester, 1979), ch. 6.

116. Olive Anderson, 'Women Preachers in Mid-Victorian Britain: Some Reflexions on Feminism, Popular Religion and Social Change', *Historical Journal* 12 (1969), 467–84.

117. F[rank]. K. Prochaska, *Women and Philanthropy in Nineteenth-Century England* (Oxford, 1980).

118. Leonore Davidoff and Catherine Hall, *Family Fortunes: Men and Women of the English Middle Class, 1780–1850* (London, 1987).

119. Linda Wilson, *Constrained by Zeal: Female Spirituality among Nonconformists, 1825–1875* (Carlisle, 2000).

120. D[avid]. W. Bebbington, 'Evangelicals and the Role of Women, 1800–1930', *Christian Arena* 37 (1984), 19–23.

121. ISAE, 'ISAE History Research: Consultations', 14–15.

New England Free Baptists in the Revolutionary era, and three years later Catherine Brekus's *Strangers and Pilgrims*, exploring female preaching in America down to 1845.[122] Women became and remained central to historiography about Evangelicals. Men considered as male fared less well, in that the rising theme of masculinity was rarely examined on either side of the Atlantic. Two studies of the representation of men in the writings of the Victorian preacher Charles Haddon Spurgeon and William Booth, the founder of the Salvation Army, are exceptions.[123] Despite the small inroads into masculinity, the content of writing about Evangelicalism was transformed in the area of gender during the period.

So too was discussion of Evangelicals and race. In the United States the civil rights movement prompted a sustained reassessment of the place of racial divisions in the national past. The scrutiny of slave religion led to novel findings such as the extent of black preaching to whites and the prevalence of mixed black and white worship before the Civil War.[124] The intertwining of the subsequent racial discrimination in the South with the Evangelical religion of the oppressors and of the oppressed was freshly explored.[125] Perhaps the most striking development in the historiography was a turn from treating the civil rights movement as a largely secular phenomenon to emphasizing, as Mark Noll put it in 2008, 'the strength of the African-American religion that drove the movement'.[126] More generally, black studies became more widespread, producing such classics as Evelyn Brooks Higginbotham's *Righteous Discontent: The Women's Movement in the Black Baptist Church, 1880–1920* (1993).[127]

122. Susan Juster, *Disorderly Women: Sexual Politics and Evangelicalism in Revolutionary New England* (Ithaca, NY, 1994).

123. Laura Lauer, 'William Booth: Saint or Charlatan?', and Andrew Bradstock, '"A Man of God Is a Manly Man": Spurgeon, Luther and "Holy Boldness"', in Andrew Bradstock et al., eds, *Masculinity and Spirituality in Victorian Culture* (Basingstoke, 2000), 194–208, 209–25.

124. Mechal Sobel, *Trabelin' On: The Slave Journey to an Afro-Baptist Faith* (Princeton, NJ, 1979), 190–9; John B. Boles, ed., *Masters & Slaves in the House of the Lord: Race and Religion in the American South, 1740–1870* (Lexington, KY, 1988).

125. Paul Harvey, *Redeeming the South: Religious Cultures and Racial Identities among Southern Baptists, 1865–1925* (Chapel Hill, NC, 1997); idem, *Freedom's Coming: Religious Culture and the Shaping of the American South from the Civil War through the Civil Rights Era* (Chapel Hill, NC, 2005).

126. Mark A. Noll, *God and Race in American Politics: A Short History* (Princeton, NJ, 2008), 135.

127. Evelyn Brooks Higginbotham, *Righteous Discontent: The Women's Movement in the Black Baptist Church, 1880–1920* (Cambridge, MA, 1993).

Works on indigenous peoples, including Native Americans and Australian Aborigines, increasingly engaged with the role of Evangelical missionaries among them.[128] In British historiography the issue of race focused mainly on the subject of the abolition of the slave trade. Traditionally this was a topic where the Evangelicals came to the fore as the leaders, under Wilberforce, of the campaign against the trade. They still appeared in that role in the probing analysis by Roger Anstey, professor at the University of Kent at Canterbury and a Methodist, in 1975.[129] The subsequent growth in coverage of the topic, however, had the effect of stressing the agency of other groups and circumstances, even in a collection of essays in memory of Anstey.[130] It was only with the appearance of Christopher Leslie Brown's *Moral Capital* (2006) in time for the bicentenary of abolition that the Evangelicals were reinstated to prominence, though it was now an earlier group and with more carefully delineated motives.[131] At a more popular level William Hague's biography of Wilberforce (2007), with the sub-title 'the life of the great anti-slave trade campaigner', and even more the film *Amazing Grace* (2006) helped consolidate the place of Evangelical religion in the process of abolition.[132] The Evangelical record on issues surrounding race relations was increasingly valued in America and intermittently stressed in Britain.

There was again a transatlantic difference over the theme of nationhood. For Americans, the question of how the diverse elements in a new land were forged into a nation was a matter of perennial importance; British historians of the recent past, by contrast, long left the equivalent issue to the medievalists and early modernists. A longstanding American tradition saw Evangelical religion as an agent of social integration in the early republic. Its hold on the historiography was, if anything, strengthened during the period. Mark Noll's *America's God* (2002) recounted how the Second Great Awakening exercised a pervasive influence on society, so that, for example, in 1840 there were more

128. E.g. William G. McLoughlin Jr, *Cherokees and Missionaries, 1789–1839* (New Haven, CT, 1984); John W. Harris, *One Blood: 200 Years of Aboriginal Encounter with Christianity; A Story of Hope*, 2nd edn (Sutherland, NSW, 1994).

129. Roger Anstey, *The Atlantic Slave Trade and British Abolition, 1760–1810* (London, 1975).

130. *Anti-Slavery, Religion and Reform: Essays in Memory of Roger Anstey*, ed. Christine Bolt and Seymour Drescher (Folkestone, 1980).

131. Christopher Leslie Brown, *Moral Capital: Foundations of British Abolitionism* (Chapel Hill, NC, 2006).

132. William Hague, *William Wilberforce: The Life of the Great Anti-Slave Trade Campaigner* (London, 2007).

than twice as many Methodist sermons heard per capita as letters delivered.[133]
Daniel Walker Howe's volume on the years 1815–1848 in the Oxford History of
the United States confirmed the general verdict that the Evangelical movement
brought 'civilization and order' to America.[134] In Britain the subject of national
identity became a popular theme only as the devolution debate gathered momentum and particularly after the publication of Linda Colley's *Britons* (1992),
a book which attributed a primary role to Protestantism in integrating the
diverse parts of the United Kingdom during the eighteenth century. Already,
however, the question had been broached in volume 18 of Studies in Church
History, which was devoted to the theme of *Religion and National Identity*
(1982).[135] The president of the Ecclesiastical History Society who chose that
theme, Keith Robbins, subsequently delivered a series of Ford Lectures touch-
ing on the topic, issued a collection of essays about it and wrote the volume
of the Oxford History of the Christian Church on twentieth-century Britain
with the title *England, Ireland, Scotland, Wales* (2008).[136] Evangelicalism had
its place in Robbins's analyses, but it was far more prominent in R. Tudur
Jones's study of Wales between 1890 and 1914, *Faith and the Crisis of a Nation*
(1981–2; ET 2004).[137] A collection of essays on religion and national identity
in Wales and Scotland confirmed that Evangelicalism was closely bound up
with the sense of nationhood in each.[138] The amplest treatment of the Evangelical factor in nationhood, however, was in Callum Brown's book *The Death
of Christian Britain* (2001). In a work of marked originality, Brown contended
that Evangelicalism shaped the discourse, and therefore the identity, of the
British people between 1800 and the sudden onset of secularization in the

133. Mark A. Noll, *America's God: From Jonathan Edwards to Abraham Lincoln*
(New York, 2002), 201.

134. Daniel Walker Howe, *What God Hath Wrought: The Transformation of America, 1815–1848*, Oxford History of the United States (New York, 2007), 188.

135. Stuart Mews, ed., *Religion and National Identity*, Studies in Church History
18 (Oxford, 1982).

136. Keith Robbins, *Nineteenth-Century Britain: Integration and Diversity* (Oxford,
1988); idem, *History, Religion and Identity in Modern Britain* (London, 1993); idem,
England, Ireland, Scotland, Wales: The Christian Church, 1900–2000, Oxford History
of the Christian Church (Oxford, 2008).

137. R. Tudur Jones, *Faith and the Crisis of a Nation: Wales, 1890–1914* (Cardiff,
2004; first publ. in Welsh 1981–2).

138. Robert Pope, ed., *Religion and National Identity: Wales and Scotland, c. 1700–
2000* (Cardiff, 2001).

1960s.[139] At a single bound, British historiography caught up with its American counterpart in relating Evangelical religion to national identity.

Advances in the history of ideas also impinged on Evangelical historiography. The discussion of Evangelical theology was in a backward state for much of the period. Bernard Reardon of the University of Newcastle, the author of the most frequently used text on nineteenth-century religious thought in Britain, confined Evangelicalism to an introductory section, pointing out its 'weaknesses'. 'Intellectually it was narrow', he wrote, 'and naïvely reactionary.'[140] That judgement reflected the paucity of research that had hitherto been undertaken in the field. America had been better served in the past with a series of monographs on the decline of Calvinism,[141] but even in the United States there was a dearth of up-to-date studies until Bruce Kuklick's *Philosophers and Churchmen* (1985).[142] Stimulus to further work came chiefly from three directions. In the first place, the historians of science found it essential to engage with theology. Thus in 1991 John Hedley Brooke, in pushing forward the study of religion and science in the eighteenth and nineteenth centuries, explored Evangelical themes in some detail.[143] Four years later a conference under the auspices of the Institute for the Study of American Evangelicals brought together historians of science, including Brooke, and historians of theology to produce a collection of essays on *Evangelicals and Science in Historical Perspective* (1999).[144] Secondly, the history of political thought, the main genre in the study of ideas normally encountered by historians, prompted some of them to take a parallel interest in the history of religious thought. In particular, the novel methods in the history of political thought entailing placing authors in their intellectual milieu championed by Quentin Skinner at Cambridge inspired a few to apply similar techniques to Evangelical theologians. A collec-

139. Callum Brown, *The Death of Christian Britain: Understanding Secularisation 1800–2000* (London, 2001).

140. Bernard M. G. Reardon, *Religious Thought in the Victorian Age: A Survey from Coleridge to Gore* (London, 1980; first publ. 1971), 29.

141. Frank H. Foster, *A Genetic History of the New England Theology* (Chicago, IL, 1907), and Joseph Haroutunian, *Piety versus Moralism: The Passing of the New England Theology* (New York, 1932), are the classic studies.

142. Bruce Kuklick, *Philosophers and Churchmen: From Jonathan Edwards to John Dewey* (New Haven, CT, 1985).

143. John Hedley Brooke, *Science and Religion: Some Historical Perspectives* (Cambridge, 1991).

144. David N. Livingstone, D. G. Hart and Mark A. Noll, eds, *Evangelicals and Science in Historical Perspective* (New York, 1999).

tion of papers on the subject, showing an awareness of the limitations as well as the potential of Skinnerian methods in the intellectual history of religion, appeared in 2009.[145] And thirdly some historical theologians, with Alan Sell prominent among them in Britain and E. Brooks Holifield in America, laid bare hitherto unexplored dimensions of Evangelical thought.[146] One of the most illuminating, because it opened up non-Anglican Evangelical theology with unprecedented clarity, was Mark Hopkins's *Nonconformity's Romantic Generation* (2004).[147] Sell, Hopkins and others began to fill up the gaps left by Reardon. Earlier Evangelical ideas were at last coming into their own.

It has to be admitted that the most radical historical approaches of the age did not take root in Evangelical studies. Apart from Callum Brown, few students of Evangelical history drew on post-modernist practice. That is primarily because so many of the specialists in the field were themselves Evangelicals. In general the Evangelical world reacted with horror at the challenge of postmodernism to cherished assumptions. In particular its characteristic denial of any single intended meaning in texts alarmed those who saw the Almighty as the primary author of Scripture. Evangelicals published such works as *Truth Decay: Defending Christianity against the Challenges of Postmodernism.*[148] Only a handful of bolder souls in the Evangelical movement, such as Robert Webber, were willing to endorse a postmodern understanding of the world, and virtually none of them was a historian.[149] Nevertheless the post-modern questioning of received practice constituted a stirring of the historiographical waters. In 2010 there appeared a collection of essays, *Confessing History*, which asked whether faith needed to be applied more drastically to the study of the past. Perhaps, the authors suggested, history had been unduly limited by its

145. Alister Chapman, John Coffey and Brad S. Gregory, eds, *Seeing Things Their Way: Intellectual History and the Return of Religion* (Notre Dame, IN, 2009).

146. Alan F. Sell, *Defending and Declaring the Faith: Some Scottish Examples, 1860–1920* (Exeter, 1987), and many subsequent titles; E. Brooks Holifield, *Theology in America: Christian Thought from the Age of the Puritans to the Civil War* (New Haven, CT, 2003).

147. Mark Hopkins, *Nonconformity's Romantic Generation: Evangelical and Liberal Theologies in Victorian England*, Studies in Evangelical History and Thought (Carlisle, 2004).

148. Douglas Groothuis, *Truth Decay: Defending Christianity against the Challenges of Postmodernism* (Downers Grove, IL, 2000).

149. Webber, *Ancient-Future Faith*, esp. 29–34. An exception was Stanley Grenz, an Evangelical who was sympathetic to postmodernism and, although primarily a theologian, also wrote history.

confinement to a professional straitjacket.[150] In due course that point of view was likely to produce more drastic reassessments of the Evangelical past. The period under review, however, had already, as we have seen, witnessed at least two significant advances in method associated with the Evangelical discovery of history. One was a recognition that history is a matter of perspectives on the past; the other was fresh attention to culture as a subject for historical investigation. Both innovations, though showing little or no postmodern inspiration, were parallel to the postmodernist enthusiasms for perspectives and culture, and sometimes they were put into practice even in advance of contemporary fashion. So the practitioners in the Evangelical school of history were by no means retrogressive in their methodological assumptions.

There was, therefore, a transformation of Evangelical history over the half-century between 1961 and 2011. At the opening of the period Evangelicals themselves neglected their history, producing chiefly denominational apologias, edifying biographies and missionary hagiographies. Evangelicals in Britain, and in some measure those elsewhere, did not figure prominently in mainstream historical literature. These patterns altered over the fifty years, with denominational, biographical and missionary studies all becoming much more scholarly and Evangelicalism sometimes (though by no means consistently) occupying an enhanced position in general histories. Religious changes affected the volume of Evangelical history, with Evangelicals increasing as a proportion of the churchgoing population, adherents of the movement pursuing careers in history and some of them creating effective institutional bases. The acceptance of tradition and the influence of neo-Calvinism helped promote their study of the past, though not without criticism from the Calvinist camp. Broader religious developments impinged on the type of history they wrote: the ecumenical imperative led to more cooperative studies and less anti-Catholic content; global links fostered international coverage; the theme of gospel and culture rose to prominence and equally spirituality came to the fore. At the same time scholarly trends shaped the way the history of Evangelical movements was written. Methods and models from the social sciences were applied to the Evangelical past while Marxism both impinged on written history and showed committed scholarship was possible. The rise of women's and gender history, race issues and national identity changed the content of

150. Eric Miller, 'Introduction: A Tradition Renewed? The Challenge of a Generation', in John Fea, Jay Green and Eric Miller, eds, *Confessing History: Explorations in the Christian Faith and the Historian's Vocation* (Notre Dame, IN, 2010), 9. I am grateful to Andy Tooley for this reference.

Evangelical studies, each of these themes attracting historians from outside the movement to explore aspects of its record. The history of Evangelical ideas began to be nourished by advances in the history of science, the history of political thought and historical theology. And if postmodernism exerted little effect, Evangelical historians could claim to have anticipated its twin concerns for perspectives and culture. By the end of the period, historians in general were paying growing attention to the history of the Evangelical movement, though there was much scope for further growth. Among Evangelical scholars themselves, the previous neglect of their past was over: they had made a discovery of history.

CHAPTER 6

Re-examining David Bebbington's Quadrilateral

ROUNDTABLE

Objections have been made to the characterization of evangelicalism in terms of emphasis on the four attributes of conversion, activism, Bible, and cross—"a quadrilateral of priorities." It could seem too precise, unduly limiting the movement, or too open-ended, allowing those without its typical convictions to come under its umbrella. At the twenty-fifth anniversary of the publication of David Bebbington's book *Evangelicalism in Modern Britain*, in 2014, during two academic conferences, six scholars offered assessments of the quadrilateral from different points of view. Afterward the author was permitted to respond to each of them. The debate allowed considered evaluation of how evangelicalism can best be understood.

The participants expressed their concerns, as well as their appreciation, from many points on the interpretive compass.

Charlie Phillips, the convener, is a senior analyst and national program officer at the Maclellan Foundation, Memphis, Tennessee. His PhD dissertation under David Bebbington examined the theological achievements of Edwards Amasa Park, a leading nineteenth-century Congregationalist. His introduction provides details on the academic meetings that generated this roundtable.

Kelly Cross Elliott is an associate professor of history at Abilene Christian University and a scholar of the British Empire, especially as it took shape in India. Her response explores the outworking of evangelicalism among missionaries and native Indians in the nineteenth century.

Thomas S. Kidd, Vardaman Distinguished Professor of History at Baylor University and prolific author of books and articles on many phases of American history, especially the colonial era, draws on the history of the eighteenth-century Great Awakening to ask if reliance on the Holy Spirit should not transform the Bebbington quadrilateral into a pentagon.

otherwise be obscured by its apparently intellectualist properties. Timothy Larsen (Wheaton College) gracefully chaired the first panel. At balmy Pepperdine, Darren Dochuk (Washington University in St. Louis) looked at recent evangelical experience to ask whether any other elements ought to be added to the admittedly sturdy four-part construct. Molly Worthen (University of North Carolina at Chapel Hill) challenged the helpfulness of the generally "static" usage of the quadrilateral since 1989, while acknowledging that its application in *EMB* was far more nuanced. And Bebbington's great friend, Mark Noll (Notre Dame)[1] wondered if his own nominalist affliction disqualified him from the very "task of assessing . . . the four-fold definition." I think not. Jonathan Yeager chaired the panel. David Bebbington's gracious but still pointed response to each of the papers closes this special section of the journal.

Jonathan and I were confident that having first-rate minds test Bebbington's quadrilateral in a manner that might advance the very scholarship he so well embodies would be a better way to honor our friend and mentor than mere hagiography. We are deeply grateful to each of the panelists for their well-considered papers collected here, for the assistance of the professional societies sponsoring the panels, for the generous help of Donald Yerxa in collecting the panel papers, and for the financial support of the Maclellan Foundation, Inc., in making the panels themselves possible. It is our hope that we have successfully extended our personal gratitude to David Bebbington through this excellent work by his professional colleagues because their academic scholarship honors him in a manner he will value profoundly.

The Bebbington Quadrilateral Travels into the Empire

Kelly Cross Elliott

Over the twenty-five years since its publication in 1989, David Bebbington's *Evangelicalism in Modern Britain* has achieved an enviable status. It is simultaneously a venerable standard in scholarly conversations about British religious history, yet also fresh and provocative enough to incite the kind of lively debate evidenced in this roundtable. In *Evangelicalism in Modern Britain* Bebbington examines the contours of British evangelical religion over more than two centuries, finding that the character of the movement developed and changed

---

1. Bebbington joked at Pepperdine that in answering challenging questions from inquisitors he often looks first to his WWMS bracelet: "What Would Mark Say?"

over time in response to shifts in British high culture. He further outlines a quadrilateral of traits common to evangelical religion through these centuries, making it possible to identify connections and make comparisons between evangelicals across time. Conversionism, crucicentrism, activism, and biblicism might look quite different in Jonathan Edwards's eighteenth-century guise than in John Stott's twentieth; nevertheless, these four characteristics stand out as markers that identify a core faith.[2]

This essay follows the Bebbington quadrilateral out of Britain and into the Empire as evangelical missionaries carried it abroad, beginning in the late eighteenth century. In the imperial mission field, evangelicalism encountered new influences and took on a variety of forms. Yet the four most central characteristics of the faith remained, and culture continued to influence the shape of evangelical religion. If one reframes Bebbington's original argument within the context of recent scholarship of British imperialism, which has focused particularly on the interactive and mutually constitutive nature of metropolitan center and imperial periphery, the question that naturally arises is: How did British evangelical religion change over time in response to the changing assumptions, not only of Western and British civilization, but also to the cultures and complex interactions of the foreign mission field?

The Baptist Missionary Society's work, begun famously at Serampore in Bengal by William Carey in 1795, unfolded in a new cultural context, very different from the British environment in which evangelical religion had grown. Over the course of the nineteenth century, the particular problems and complexities of the Indian mission field deeply shaped the character of missionary evangelicalism. The Baptist mission in Bengal and the Indian Christian churches that formed there tested the cohesiveness of evangelical religion as it jostled against many of the central assumptions of British imperialism. In particular, the activism of colonial Christians starkly illuminated the contradictory attitudes of British Christians who saw evangelistic efforts as a natural outgrowth of conversion, yet doubted the ability of those outside of European civilization to spread the gospel or build their own religious institutions.

It is not difficult to find all four characteristics of "Bebbingtonian evangelicalism" among Bengali Baptist converts in early nineteenth-century India. The classic evangelical conversion narrative, originally associated with writers like John Wesley and David Brainerd, finds echo in the testimony of Gokul, one of the first converts at Serampore. A Bengali sudra, Gokul encountered

2. D. W . Bebbington, *Evangelicalism in Modern Britain: A History from the 1730s to the 1980s* (London: Routledge, 1989), 1–17.

the gospel in 1800 when British missionary John Thomas, a medical doctor, set a dislocated shoulder for Gokul's friend Krishnu, preaching all the while. Yet Gokul did not care for Christianity at first. "Displeased that the bible did not agree with some of his notions," Gokul "discontinued his visits" to the missionaries after initial interest. Yet, as Gokul later told William Carey, "his mind was so uneasy that he could scarcely get sleep for two months . . . his heart was all sinful." Once he accepted Christ, Gokul had "no other hope" and declared himself "willing to leave all God forbids, when he knows it, and to do all that is commanded, when he knows it. All this he said with many tears," as Carey recorded. This account of Gokul's transformation aligns with the normative evangelical conversion story—initial resistance to the gospel followed by consciousness of sin, fear of damnation, and finally, confident joy and relief in salvation.[3] Like Sampson Staniforth, whose conversion narrative Bebbington cites, Gokul experienced spiritual "agony, guilt" and then "immense relief" once he came to believe in the missionary message.[4]

Gokul's conversion story is provided through the voice of William Carey, but similar accounts also appear in Bengali Christians' own words. A new convert wrote to the Baptist Missionary Society (BMS) leadership in 1802: "I Petumber Singh (60 years of age) write to thank friends for writing and to send our Christian greetings . . . I was born a Hindu, early left home, and became a sinner. I found no salvation in Hindu ceremonial, but by God's grace his true Gospel has brought me cleansing and peace."[5] Though less emotive than many accounts, Petumber's explanation of how he became a Christian is typical of evangelical emphasis on conversion. The testimony of Bengali Baptist convert Sebuk-ram provides another striking example of evangelicalism in the Indian context. In a letter to a Scottish Baptist preacher written c. 1800, the newly-baptized Sebuk-ram demonstrates his adoption of at least three of the four qualities Bebbington identifies as central to evangelical religion. Describing his conversion after reading the New Testament, Sebuk-ram emphasizes Christ's substitutionary sacrifice on the cross and his own feeling of compulsion to share the gospel message once he embraced it:

3. William Carey's diary, December 22, 1800, quoted in Eustace Carey, *Memoir of William Carey, D.D.* (London: Jackson and Walford, 1836), 437–38; and E. Daniel Potts, *British Baptist Missionaries in India, 1793–1837: The History of Serampore and Its Missions* (Cambridge: Cambridge University Press, 1967), 35.

4. Bebbington, *Evangelicalism*, 5.

5. Southern Baptist Historical Library and Archive (Nashville), Baptist Missionary Society Manuscripts, Missionary Correspondence, Petumber Singh, Box IN/10.

I . . . examined the book [a New Testament left by British missionary William Ward and Indian convert Krishnu]. I saw it contained the only way of holiness, and that God for sinful men in his own body, bearing sufferings, had completed the sacrifice . . . The same night two or three friends getting together, and throwing open the door of our hearts, we confessed that we had committed the blackest crimes, and wept much. We confessed to each other, that our Lord Jesus Christ was truly the Son of God, the Saviour of sinners: we really believed this, and making it certain in our minds, with a loud voice we called out in faith, "Oh! Lord! Where art thou! Oh! Saviour, save us." Then closing our eyes, we saw through our tears, the light which the Holy Spirit had shed in our hearts. Thus possessing a mind fixed in faith, we were brought to hate all transgressing and sin, all evil connexions and works, the gods and goddesses; all the evil customs of this wicked world; so that hearing of them our ear tingled, and seeing them we turned another way. This we considered as the pouring out of the Holy Spirit, and through the mercy of the Lord Jesus Christ our mind became prepared . . . This is now my desire, and day and night, full of fear, this is my prayer to God, that I may be constantly ready to proclaim this gospel.[6]

Here we see conversionism—Sebuk-ram's description of his consciousness of sin, his tears, and the coming of salvation as the illumination of the Holy Spirit—crucicentrism—his realization of Christ's bodily suffering for sinful human beings—and activism—his strong desire to share the gospel with others. And while he does not reference biblicism directly, it is significant that Sebuk-ram's change of heart came after reading the New Testament.[7] Sebuk-ram's contemporary, an itinerant preacher named Vrinda-vuna, foregrounds the role of the biblical text more clearly in his description of his own conversion and continuing struggle against sin. Writing to the missionaries and the church at Serampore in 1814, he confesses, "My body, through my sinfulness, is fast moldering to the dust, but

6. Letter from Sebuk-ram to Rev. George Barclay, Kilwinning, Scotland, quoted in *The Periodical Accounts of the Baptist Missionary Society*, Vol. VI: 30 (London: Button, 1801), 11–12.

7. Bebbington, *Evangelicalism*, 5. See also Bruce Hindmarsh's discussion of similar narratives, including Native American conversions under David Brainerd's ministry, as well as conversions in Sierra Leone in "Patterns of Conversion in Early Evangelical History and Overseas Mission Experience," in Brian Stanley, ed., *Christian Missions and the Enlightenment* (Grand Rapids, Mich.: Eerdmans, 2001), 71–98.

though so sinful, having received God's holy word, my mind thirsting, I go as to a sea and drink; but drinking a little, I thirst and go again . . . My worshipping of idols in this way was a very great sin; but when I received the bible from [British missionary] Mr. Chamberlain, my second birth was accomplished."[8] Such testimony nicely reflects Bebbington's markers of the evangelical faith and certainly would have resonated with any contemporary Western evangelical.

Similar examples of Indian converts adopting British evangelicalism's central characteristics abound in the sources of the BMS, often appearing in what are apparently the converts' own words. Of course, it is important to ask questions about the mediated nature of these accounts.[9] Mission texts were crafted to reflect a specific worldview and to persuade readers to support a particular religious purpose. It is hardly surprising that Indian Christian testimony within these publications should employ literary forms and terminology common to British evangelicalism. Missionary sources, however, also suggest that the transmission of the evangelical quadrilateral into the imperial mission field was a deeply complex process. Evangelicalism was no whole-cloth Western import accepted without question by colonized subjects. Rather, just as the British cultural environment molded evangelical religion in Britain, the interaction of Indian, missionary, and metropolitan concerns deeply influenced the shape of Christianity in India. Conversionism, biblicism, and crucicentrism all appear in Indian Christianity. But it is the activism of colonial Christians that reveals most about the complicated and ambivalent nature of the relationship between British evangelicalism and mission churches in the Empire.

Indian Activism at Serampore, 1800–1820s

Activism, "the expression of the gospel in effort," was a typical response when a newly saved sinner accepted Christ.[10] New Christians felt compelled to work for the conversion of others and spent their energies daily in this task. The Brit-

---

8. *Periodical Accounts* Vol. V: 28, 445–46.

9. Gareth Griffiths notes that "the voice of the native subject to the pen of the mission recorder was only the first step in a long process of control exercised over the record of the lives of . . . converts." Griffiths, "Trained to Tell the Truth: Missionaries, Converts, and Narration," in Norman Etherington, ed., *Missions and Empire*, The Oxford History of the British Empire Companion Series (Oxford: Oxford University Press, 2005), 153. See also Peggy Brock, "New Christians as Evangelists," in *Missions and Empire*, 132–52.

10. Bebbington, *Evangelicalism*, 3.

ish evangelical preachers who, after the example of John Wesley, rode hundreds of miles while studying and preaching sermons every day of the week had their counterparts in India. In 1814 British missionary J. Leonard described the work of Indian preachers in and around Calcutta as "indefatigable," declaring that "it would take a whole day to do justice to a week's work of these men":

> Sebuk-ram preaches in twenty different places during the week, some of which are seven miles distant. He crosses and recrosses the river every day. Bhagvut preaches at eleven, in and about the town; Neeloo at about ten; and Manik at six . . . [These] Brethren preach regularly during the week in forty-seven different houses; and are invited to many more, but their time does not admit of their accepting these invitations.[11]

Like their fellow evangelicals in Britain, many Indian converts dedicated their new lives to God, and their activism was vital to the spread of Christianity in India. Such "indigenous preachers," as Peggy Brock has argued, acted as "the footsoldiers of the advance" of the gospel in the Empire.[12] Where European agency failed due to ill health, cultural barriers, language difficulties, and expense, native agency thrived. The activism of Indian Christians, Baptist missionary William Ward declared in 1803, was "the grand desideratum that [was] to move the Hindoo nation."[13] The trio of early missionaries at Serampore stressed the efficacy and abilities of Indian Christians almost from the beginning of their work. William Carey wrote in 1806: "When we consider their superior acquaintance with the language, the circumstances, the ideas and reasonings of their fellow-countrymen, & with the snares which surround them, everything else being equal, how much more effectually must they speak to the heart, than a European can possibly do!"[14] The missionaries' confidence in Indian activism led them to emphasize the need to build indig-

---

11. Leonard to William Ward, Calcutta, April 13, 1814, quoted in *Periodical Accounts* Vol. V: 28, 431–32. This laundry list of evangelistic efforts makes close comparison to British accounts of the same period. See Bebbington, *Evangelicalism*, 10–11.

12. Brock, "New Christians as Evangelists," 132.

13. William Ward's journal, March 6, 1803, quoted in *Periodical Accounts* Vol. II: 12, 370. Ward's reflections here follow his hearing the first sermon preached by an Indian convert, Petumber Singh.

14. Carey et al., to BMS, Serampore, August 31, 1806, quoted in E. Daniel Potts, *British Baptist Missionaries in India*, 33. The Serampore Trio were William Carey, Joshua Marshman, and William Ward.

also between one generation and the next. As the British cultural context of evangelicalism changed from Enlightenment to Romantic, the pragmatic, self-reliant missionaries who had begun their work in the 1790s, now deeply affected by their relationships with colonial Christians and their experience of the Indian context, found their commitment to indigenous agency challenged by a generation more inclined to publicity, fund-raising, and the dominance of European leadership and cultural forms in mission churches.[19]

The consequence of this divergence of views within the Baptist Missionary Society was, ultimately, a significant change in the Society's policy toward indigenous agency and leadership. Where the Serampore missionaries had encouraged the activism of colonial converts, the next generation of leaders in London, and the new generation of missionaries they sent to India, openly questioned the fitness of Indian Christians for preaching, teaching, and pastoring churches. The BMS leadership wrote plaintively in 1822 of the convert Krishnu Pall's lack of success as an independent evangelist in Malda, where he had been working for twenty years. "Perhaps, if it were possible for the Society to associate some brother from this country with this faithful and interesting Hindoo [sic] teacher, we might, under the divine blessing, witness pleasing results," ran the *Annual Report*, penned by the BMS secretary. "Experience has fully proved that native talent is employed to most advantage, when aided and directed by the judgment of a European Missionary."[20] This statement marks a clear digression from the policy Serampore had adopted less than twenty years before. Eustace Carey, one of the second generation of Baptist

19. This pattern is in keeping with Bebbington's contention that "cultural diffusion within Evangelicalism was normally a matter of percolation down the social scale" and that "spatial variation" resulted from "differing degrees of proximity to the sources of fresh waves of opinion, and especially to London." The BMS of the 1790s was dominated by Northamptonshire mechanics, while the next generation was more urbane, educated, and middle class. Thus the younger generation adopted humanitarian attitudes and approaches while the older generation remained fixed on a more traditionally nonconformist approach to church autonomy and mission work. Bebbington, *Evangelicalism*, 274.

20. *Annual Report* 1822, 2. It is significant that the writers of the Report did not base this conclusion on any information they had received from Serampore, whose missionaries remained confident in Krishnu and native agency generally. Rather, this statement follows a complaint that "no intelligence has reached us, for some time past, from Malda. It appears still to be occupied by Krishnu." Hearing nothing, the BMS committee assumed the worst. Further, it seems not to have occurred to them that European missionaries in India were faring no better at the time.

missionaries in India and William Carey's nephew, likewise doubted the ability of Indians, who were "only newly awakened from heathen superstition," having had "little previous mental culture," to preach effectively. At best, he thought, native ministers would "be but partially competent to make known, defend, and exemplify the gospel."[21] Similarly, General Baptist Amos Sutton argued that Indians' conscience and habits—which, he posited, were not so well developed as the Europeans'—would make them "idle and unfaithful" ministers. He further declared that he had never met an Indian preacher who could "be depended upon when alone," without the watchful accompaniment of a European missionary.[22] The shape that the Bebbington quadrilateral was allowed to take in the Empire was thus deeply marked by the contemporary currents of British imperial culture—a culture whose assumptions about the superiority of British civilization and agency jangled uncomfortably against evangelical rhetoric of Christian brotherhood and unity.

Yet this is not the end of the story. For in the mid-nineteenth century, faced with falling conversion numbers and ebbing funds, the Baptist Missionary Society changed direction again, returning to its original confidence in the activism of colonial Christians. "It becomes our duty once more to revise the principles on which we are conducting our enterprise," declared the 1855 *Annual Report*. "Its founders, from the hour that they fairly embarked in it, boldly avowed their conviction that the evangelization of the heathen was to be carried on by native converts. They relied on European agency only to do the preparatory work, and to assist and direct the movements of those who were raised up, by their instrumentality, to preach the gospel. It can scarcely be questioned that in later days we have considerably departed from this practice."

Furthermore, the Society's emphasis on European evangelists and the importation of British cultural forms had created stilted, dependent churches. Now the Baptist Missionary Society advocated a return to Serampore's convert-centered model, not only because of financial exigencies, but also because of practical results, citing "the fact, which almost every missionary confirms, that the larger proportion of converts is the fruit of native agency."[23]

---

21. Eustace Carey quoted in Potts, *British Baptist Missionaries*, 34.

22. Amos Sutton quoted in Potts, *British Baptist Missionaries*, 34.

23. *Annual Report 1857*, 14. The repentant and self-deprecating tone of this report is quite striking; the leadership later expressed their gratitude that "amidst all our mistakes, deficiencies, and shortcomings, thanks be to God, His kingdom is rapidly spreading throughout the world," 14–5. The same reference to deviation from original policy appears in the 1860 report: "The system adopted by the Serampore brethren

Evidence from the imperial mission field countered the racial assumptions of British culture: Indian preachers were, in fact, capable and effective mission-aries, and the gospel flourished when presented in its own cultural context.[24] Thus it appears that, at least in some instances, the imperial context shaped missionary evangelicalism even more than British culture at home did, for the BMS continued to pursue indigenous leadership and independence, and most crucially, persisted in this course even as contemporary British culture grew more racist in the later part of the nineteenth century.[25] The shape evangelicals took in the Empire was thus conditioned by both colonial and metropolitan cultures.

The Bebbington Quadrilateral and the Work of the Holy Spirit

Thomas S. Kidd

The work of the Holy Spirit has been one of the most controversial issues in evangelical Christianity since evangelicalism's advent in the 1730s and 1740s. The issue remains controversial today, illustrated by periodic disputes between "cessationists" and "continuationists." The most fascinating recent such con-flict occurred in October 2013, when anti-charismatic pastor John MacArthur hosted his "Strange Fire" conference to coincide with the release of his book of

---

undoubtedly was to constitute the missionary an overseer, who was to superintend a band of native agents, itinerating through a given district, and to instruct the churches to choose their pastor from among themselves. And if that system has subsequently been somewhat departed from, the directors of all missionary societies are now fast returning [to] it." *Annual Report* 1860, 6–7. On the problem of dependency, see Ed-ward Bean Underhill's letter to the Baptist Missionaries of Bengal in *The Minutes and Reports of a Conference of the Baptist Missionaries of Bengal* (Calcutta, Baptist Mission Press, 1855), 99–100.

24. Missionary C. B. Lewis wrote in 1871 that the "trim model of an English church" many in the British public hoped to see in India was "an artificial thing. It owes its existence to foreign benevolence, and its shape to foreign civilization, and, with the failure of foreign resources, it must necessarily fall to pieces." *Annual Report* 1872, 9–10.

25. Andrew C. Ross, "Christian Missions and Mid-Nineteenth Century Change in Attitudes to Race: The African Experience," in Andrew Porter, ed., *The Imperial Horizons of British Protestant Missions, 1880–1914* (Grand Rapids, Mich.: Eerdmans, 2003), 85–105; Douglas Lorimer, *Colour, Class and the Victorians: English Attitudes to the Negro in the Mid-Nineteenth Century* (New York: Holmes & Meier, 1978).

the same name. MacArthur deplored the influence of charismatics who ostensibly believe in the leading of the Holy Spirit outside of the authority of scripture. "If Scripture alone were truly their final authority," MacArthur writes, "charismatic Christians would never tolerate patently unbiblical practices—like mumbling in nonsensical prayer languages, uttering fallible prophecies, worshipping in disorderly ways, or being knocked senseless by the supposed power of the Holy Spirit."[26]

Setting aside the issue of glossolalia, which appeared only occasionally in the era of the First Great Awakening, MacArthur's remaining concerns sound strikingly similar to points of contention raised against the Methodists, led by the Wesley brothers and George Whitefield, and other evangelicals at the beginning of the evangelical movement. In honoring the twenty-fifth anniversary of David Bebbington's monumental *Evangelicalism in Modern Britain*, and its celebrated "quadrilateral," I am a bit embarrassed to critique or qualify anything about it—it might be better simply to say I am thankful for the book, and for David, and then let David talk about whatever he wants. But I think he would rather engage in a discussion about how to define evangelicalism, so let me get to my point: from the outset of the movement, belief in the active, immediate ministry of the Holy Spirit was precisely what made evangelical Christianity as novel and controversial as it was. It was not just that the new evangelicals tested the limits of what one might expect from the Spirit on a daily basis, in terms of assurance, comfort, understanding, and guidance. The new evangelicals also had fundamental points of disagreement with their adversaries—especially Anglican opponents—about the doctrine of the Holy Spirit.

This is also not only a matter of emphasizing the work of the Holy Spirit as the illuminator of scripture, or as the agent behind conversion (biblicism and conversionism being two elements of the quadrilateral). The ministry of the Spirit was arguably the most distinctive, controversial, and energizing principle behind the piety of the new evangelicals. The Spirit led them into a previously unknown world of wonders that prompted talk of the eschaton. That emphasis on the Spirit was also at the heart of critics' attacks on evangelicals, who admittedly downplayed and moderated their concepts of the Spirit's work by the mid-1740s. Nevertheless, as I researched my biography *George Whitefield: America's Spiritual Founding Father*, I became even more convinced that an emphasis on the Spirit was a "Distinguishing Mark" of

---

26. http://www.charismanews.com/opinion/watchman-on-the-wall/42368-pastor -macarthur-what-are-you-afraid-of (accessed 12/9/2014).

evangelicalism, to borrow Jonathan Edwards's phrase. An accent on the Spirit certainly deserves to be included in any four-point definition of evangelicalism—at least evangelicalism of its eighteenth-century variety. As Whitefield wrote four years before his death: "To be filled with the Holy Ghost. That is the grand point."[27]

In their focus on the Holy Spirit, evangelicals were hardly promoting a new doctrine. They believed they were recovering biblical doctrine and practice, and one could certainly see versions of their pneumatology among earlier Catholic and Protestant groups. But placing the work of the Spirit at the center of their ministry and piety was a greater departure from their immediate Protestant forbears than biblicism, activism, or crucicentrism, and along with their belief in rapid, discernible conversion, was the tenet of the evangelicals that set them apart from many of their predecessors and other Protestant communities at the time.

I can only briefly suggest the ways that the ministry of the Spirit helped to define evangelical spirituality; indeed, I will only focus on some aspects of the issue in George Whitefield's career itself. Whitefield discovered the ministry of the Spirit during his conversion travail, and he relished the presence of the Spirit as a newly-converted student at Oxford. This emphasis emerges in the original editions of his published journals, but more intriguingly, in his brief unpublished 1736 diary that now resides at the British Library. In jottings running from March to June, most entries spoke of the Holy Spirit's presence—over and over, he wrote that he was "full of the Holy Ghost," or felt "joy in the Holy Ghost," sometimes for hours on end. On May 6 he exulted that he experienced "joy in the Holy Ghost Grace Grace Free Grace." The Holy Spirit was an emotionally and mentally tangible presence to him. Whitefield often spoke to private meetings of friends, noting that the Holy Spirit assisted him in knowing what to say. On one occasion, the Spirit enabled him "to apply all the promises made to the Apostles to us." The Spirit once "suggested" to him "things just applicable to what we were discoursing," and the Spirit even "put words into my mouth," he noted. He concluded that one of the Spirit's ministries to believers was "to point out appropriate particular texts to our particular circumstances."[28]

27. Whitefield to W. P., Dec. 30, 1766, in John Gillies, ed., *The Works of the Reverend George Whitefield* (6 vols., London: Dilly, 1771), III, 343.

28. Whitefield, Diary, Mar. 3, 6; Apr. 6; May 6, 30, 31; June 23, 1736, British Library. On Whitefield and the Holy Spirit, see also David Jull, "George Whitefield and the Great Awakening: A Pentecostal Perspective," *Asian Journal of Pentecostal Studies* 14:2

As Whitefield's ministry in England and Wales exploded in 1739, he learned of rumors circulating that he had gone entirely mad, that he claimed to be the Holy Ghost himself, and that he had "walked bareheaded through Bristol streets singing psalms." Whitefield certainly did not claim to be the Holy Spirit, but he did emphasize the distinction between those who had received the Spirit and those who had not. At one meeting, he observed: "some were so filled with the Holy Ghost, that they were almost unable to support themselves under it. This, I know, is foolishness to the natural and letter-learned men." William Seward told a Methodist friend that "Brother Whitefield has had joy in the Holy Ghost without intermission for three years."[29]

Whitefield's stress on the indwelling Holy Spirit alienated some potential allies. For example, Bishop Joseph Butler became increasingly uncomfortable with what he heard about the Methodists' ministry, and in August 1739 he met with John Wesley and upbraided him for enthusiastic excesses. He singled out Whitefield in particular: "Mr. Whitefield says in his *Journal* [for February 11, 1739], 'There are promises still to be fulfilled in me.' Sir, the pretending to extraordinary revelations and gifts of the Holy Ghost is a horrid thing, a very horrid thing."[30]

At the same time, dissenting pastor and celebrated hymn-writer Isaac Watts wrote to the Bishop of London, Edmund Gibson, expressing similar concerns about Whitefield's claims of special revelations from the Holy Spirit. In personal conversation, Whitefield had confirmed to Watts that he occasionally received impressions in his mind—thoughts or messages, often in response to prayer—which, he knew with certainty, came from God. Watts warned him against the "danger of delusion."[31]

(July 2011): 256–71. On the primacy of the Holy Spirit among evangelicals, see Timothy Larsen, "Defining and Locating Evangelicalism," in Timothy Larsen and Daniel J. Treier, eds., *The Cambridge Companion to Evangelical Theology* (Cambridge: Cambridge University Press, 2007), 10–12.

29. Whitefield, *A Continuation of the Reverend Mr. Whitefield's Journal: From his Arrival at London, to his Departure from Thence on his way to Georgia* (London, J. Hutton, 1739), 79–80; William Seward to Joseph Stennett, Apr. 17, 1739, in Graham C. G. Thomas, ed., "George Whitefield and Friends: The Correspondence of Some Early Methodists," *National Library of Wales Journal* 27:1 (1991): 293.

30. "Wesley's Interview with Bishop Butler, August 16 and 18, 1739," in W. Reginald Ward and Richard P. Heitzenrater, eds., *The Works of John Wesley*, Bicentennial ed., vol 19, *Journals and Diaries* II (Nashville, Tenn.: Abingdon, 1990), 471; Arnold A. Dallimore, *George Whitefield: The Life and Times of the Great Evangelist of the Eighteenth-Century Revival* (2 vols., London: Banner of Truth, 1970), I, 342–44.

31. Isaac Watts to the Bishop of London, Aug. 15, 1739, Thomas Milner, ed., *The*

of application, its influence parallels that of Clifford Geertz's 1966 definition of religion as "a system of symbols which acts to establish powerful, pervasive, and long-lasting moods and motivations."[35]

Bebbington's definition supported the larger argument of his book that the moods of British evangelicalism changed over time, and that these moods succeeded one another through Enlightenment, Romantic, and Modernist patterns. After 1989 the quadrilateral definition acquired a life of its own, extracted from the larger argument of Professor Bebbington's book. While initially presented as a point of departure for that larger argument, Bebbington's definition became associated with scholarship that approached religion as an intellectual system rather than an affective enterprise. As a result, an impression remains that exponents of "lived religion" who follow Geertz in their interest in the emotional components of religion are deeply at odds with Bebbington's interest in belief. This is ironic. In fact, Bebbington's larger argument about Enlightenment, Romantic, and Modernist moods in evangelicalism complements the Geertzian approach to religion in important respects and might even be described as an application of Geertz's argument about "powerful, pervasive, and long-lasting moods" to the history of British evangelicalism. Seen in this light, Bebbington's thumbnail characterization of the four parts of evangelical doctrine is less an argument about the primacy of belief over affect than it is a succinct description of the symbolic system embodied through evangelical moods. Something other than belief lies at the crux of the difference between Bebbington's approach and that of "lived" religionists. But first, a few comments are in order about why belief may have emerged as a contentious issue for lived religionists.

I take the liberty of focusing on American religious history to explain why I think that, with respect to the role of belief in religion, Bebbington's work is closer to that of lived religionists than might first appear to be the case. While important overlap exists in religious histories and historiographies of Britain and the U.S., the sheer abundance of religion in the U.S. and the pursuit of "lived religion" in American religious historiography have led to sharp questions about the importance of belief, and to sharp questions about the relevance of intellectual history. On the surface of some of these discussions, it might appear that belief really *is* the issue. For example, in his 1996 book on devotion to St. Jude in the early and mid-twentieth century, Robert Orsi, the most celebrated proponent of lived religion, recounts his own experience, while circling over La Guardia, of surprising himself with a desperate prayer

---

35. Clifford Geertz, "Religion as a Cultural System," in Michael Banton, ed., *Anthropological Approaches to the Study of Religion* (London: Routledge, 1966), 4.

to the saint. "I am not a devout, but I promised to tell this story at the time, and here it is," Orsi writes in the preface to his book. "I would still say to the women who asked me that I do not believe in St. Jude. But what's belief got to do with it?"[36]

It might seem off-topic to begin discussion of Bebbington's definition of evangelical belief with this challenge to belief from a book on American Catholicism. But I would suggest that some of the heat around the issue of belief comes from impatience, if not resentment, at the long history of American protestant disdain for Catholicism. In asserting the superiority of their own beliefs over the course of the last four centuries, more than a few American evangelicals set out to make Catholics feel ashamed of what they believed. I venture to say that this history of abuse stands behind some of the questions about belief as a category in religion. While these questions about belief as a category may be important, they may have arisen as a means of elevating discourse, and as a better alternative than saying, "Protestant beliefs are superstitions, too."

In fact, Orsi is *very* interested in religious belief. In the book on St. Jude, he spends several chapters discussing the role that belief plays in the lives of Jude's devout, explaining how ideas about Jude changed with the circumstances of people's lives. Orsi also delves into the psychology of religious belief in his concluding chapters and applies it to the history of devotion to Jude. He treats belief in Jude with no less empathy—or sympathy—than Bebbington treats the beliefs of evangelicals. Despite what Orsi wrote in his preface, belief has much to do with Orsi's presentation of devotion to Jude.

Turning to the place of belief in the lived religion approach to evangelicalism, here again there are more similarities to Bebbington's work than one might expect. To be sure, many of these works are informed by ethnographic theory and by methods of participant-observation that set them apart from Bebbington's project—a point to which I will return in a moment. But in treating belief as an essential ingredient of religion that brings people together and defines them as a group, there is significant agreement, though lived religionists may downplay it.

Marie Griffith's *Born Again Bodies* (2004) is a good example. Though primarily concerned with evangelical bodies and the display of affect through bodily activity, Griffith cannot help but acknowledge the unifying power of belief among the evangelicals she studies. Simply put, they express adherence

36. Robert A. Orsi, *Thank You, St. Jude: Women's Devotion to the Patron Saint of Hopeless Causes* (New Haven, Conn.: Yale University Press, 1996), xxi.

to biblicism and crucicentrism through diet and exercise. Indicative of that adherence, Griffith identifies an array of "Christian exercise programs" popular in the U.S. at the end of the last century: "Believercise, Word-a-Cise, Cross Training, Jehobics, Praise Aerobics, and more." Regarding what participants wear and how their muscles develop, Griffith asserts that, "it would be difficult to say how Christian aerobics is different from other programs at any local gymnasium."[37] Yet commitment to evangelical belief is explicit in the names of these programs, and must be obvious to everyone involved. It is hard to imagine that instructors affiliated with Word-a-Cise would miss the opportunity to begin or end each class with a passage from scripture, or that Christian Cross Trainers do not link gain through pain to Jesus's suffering on the cross.

Griffith's discussion of Christian dieting makes it clear that belief factors into this ascetic practice. For example, Christian diet maven Mab Graff Hoover meditates on Paul's letter to the Colossians. And her application of scripture leads her to the rhetorical question: "Can I imagine myself picking up a grease-filled, chocolate covered donut, and saying, 'I eat this in the name of the Lord Jesus?'" Doctrine is important, and not always freely interpreted. We learn that controversy regarding how to correctly express the doctrine of the Trinity led to "furor" over Weigh Down, "the largest Christian diet plan on the market" at the turn of this century. Insistence on a precisely accurate statement of trinitarian doctrine inspired the creation of the spinoff organization, Thin Within.[38]

In *When God Talks Back* Tanya Luhrmann addressed the role of belief in American evangelicalism very directly. Belief is essential for the evangelicals in the Vineyard churches Luhrmann studied, but as she explained, belief is a practice as well as an object of faith. Belief develops through time and effort for these evangelicals, and virtually everyone who commits to the practice of believing becomes more skillful at it. Beginners are encouraged to pray to God for what they want, as specifically as possible. Not just a new car, but a red convertible. If the red convertible does not materialize, Luhrmann explains how practitioners are schooled to ask what God is trying to communicate. Luhrmann is far more interested in the *practice* of belief, and in the latitude believers have in expressing themselves, than in the doctrines of evangelical orthodoxy that Vineyard members uphold. Nevertheless, ministers *do* explain theology, members *do* participate in Bible study, and the peril of unbelief is ab-

37. R. Marie Griffith, *Born Again Bodies: Flesh and Spirit in American Christianity* (Berkeley: University of California Press, 2004), 178–79.

38. Ibid., 208–9, 182.

solutely fundamental. "After all," Luhrmann writes, "theologically conservative Christians are supposed to believe that the Bible is literally true, and they do."[39]

Such recent work on the affective aspect of American evangelicalism is not at odds with Bebbington's quadrilateral thesis. Perhaps because every scholar working in the field knows the four essential elements of evangelical orthodoxy, they take adherence to these elements for granted! I would submit that the real differences between Bebbington's approach and that of the lived religionists lie in the areas of method and theories of culture formation. Most obviously, Orsi, Griffith, Luhrmann, and other lived religionists incorporate ethnographic methods involving participant-observation. Bebbington's book, on the other hand, focuses on analysis of texts. While lived religionists seek engagement with live informants, Bebbington's concentration on texts invites analysis of evangelical writings over a long period of historical time. But overemphasizing these differences would do disservice all around. Luhrmann, Griffith, and Orsi all incorporate texts and cultural history into their ethnographic studies. Conversely, Bebbington's insight and sensitivity to evangelical cultures are directly related to his own experience as a participant-observer of evangelical life.

The crucial difference lies in assumptions about how culture is formed. Bebbington argues for a top-down "pattern of diffusion." As he wrote in his concluding chapter, "Ideas originating in high culture have spread to leaders of Evangelical opinion and through them to the Evangelical constituency." Ordinary people shaped these ideas to their own circumstances and tastes, but the impetus in the formation of evangelical cultures comes from highly educated professional thinkers. To quote Professor Bebbington, "Popular Protestantism has been remoulded in turn by the Enlightenment of Locke, the Romanticism of Coleridge and the Modernism associated with, among other, the Bloomsbury Group."[40]

Lived religionists, by contrast, are interested in how religious cultures are formed from below. Daughters of immigrants struggling with the conflict between traditional Catholic mores and assimilation to American culture constructed the cult of St. Jude. White middle-class evangelicals bind their anxiety about race, consumption, and material abundance through fitness and diet directed toward Jesus. Members of Vineyard churches in Palo Alto and Chicago, moved by loneliness and feelings of incompleteness, invest time and energy

---

39. T. M. Luhrmann, *When God Talks Back: Understanding the American Evangelical Relationship with God* (New York: Alfred A. Knopf, 2012), 84–85; quotation from 89.

40. Bebbington, *Evangelicalism in Modern Britain*, 273.

in practicing communication with God. There are no Lockes, Coleridges, or Virginia Woolfs here—no great minds whose ideas filter down to shape the tenor of popular culture. The philosophers of culture in lived religion books are the postmodern theorists upon whom the authors of these books rely to interpret evangelicals.

Beyond these differences, I think it important to consider how the two sides might be combined to advance scholarly understanding of evangelicalism. Bebbington's attention to Locke, Coleridge, and Virginia Woolf enables him to clarify what the terms Enlightenment, Romanticism, and Modernism mean, thereby setting up his insightful application of these terms to show how British evangelicalism changed over time. But these intellectual elites may have crystalized what people around them were already thinking and feeling. The importance of these great thinkers for understanding popular religious history can be appreciated by emphasizing their indebtedness to surrounding society. Great thinkers advance ideas that influence others, but they also refine ideas people are already thinking, and conceptualize inchoate feelings prevalent around them. In other words, Bebbington's emphasis on the importance of philosophers who conceptualize the forces of cultural formation can aid the lived religionists' attention to how those forces emerge in society. And *vice versa*.

The last point I would make is that beliefs do practical work. Practicing adherence to belief maintains a person's framework of perception and judgment. Given strong adherence to conversionism, biblicism, activism, and crucicentrism among evangelicals, we should press the question of exactly what work this adherence does. I would suggest that, not least among other things, the work of belief keeps skepticism and relativism at bay, and that this purpose helps explain why the honed-down belief system of evangelicalism emerged when it did from the practical piety of Puritanism. The commonsense realism of Scottish thinkers played a major role in this emergence, as Bebbington explains. But the skepticism advanced most articulately by David Hume, and abroad in a variety of popular movements, loomed as large to these evangelical founders as the rationalism of John Locke. Commonsense rationalism did the work of defending against Humean skepticism, and demand for this work never disappeared. Coleridge called in Reason (with a capital R) when Lockean reason (with a small r) became insufficient. Subsequently, fundamentalists insisted on the propositional expression of doctrine to block the exit to relativism through Romanticism. Whatever else they do, the four tenets of evangelical orthodoxy operate together as a defense against skeptical inquiry.

This excessively brief comment departs from the direction of Bebbington's work. But it does so as my effort to honor his emphasis on the intellectual history of evangelicalism and its importance for understanding evangelicalism as a lived religion.

Revisiting Bebbington's Classic Rendering of Modern Evangelicalism at Points of New Departure

DARREN DOCHUK

I am sure there are more up-to-date ways of measuring a scholar's impact, methods beyond my stuck-in-the-2000s mindset: perhaps the volume of re-tweets they generate, or the speed with which they can light up the blogo-sphere. But for me, Google and Wikipedia suffice. Punch in "David Bebbington" and you get a good read on things: he is everywhere—on page after page of Google's reserve. Type the same name into Wikipedia and you are enticed to visit not one but two pages devoted almost exclusively to the man: his own biography, and the databank's entry on "evangelicalism." In the latter case, Wikipedia's treatment of the term begins with extensive rehashing of Bebbington's four-fold classification: conversionism, biblicism, crucicentrism, and activism. "This definition has been influential," Wikipedia's anonymous scribe concludes somewhat hastily, as if to suggest that the reader need not read on; Bebbington explains it all.[41] By these sure-fire means we can see that David Bebbington has indeed generated wide influence. I might have prepped for this piece by thumbing through the footnotes of recent histories of evan-gelicalism to tally the number of times I came across this simple concession: "See Bebbington, pp. 2–3." But such unscientific research would merely have confirmed what we already know: that this shorthand is ubiquitous, and that two generations of religious historians have authored texts with Bebbington by their side. He has allowed us to avoid the knotty details while he did the heavy lifting. I confess *Evangelicalism in Modern Britain* was a later discovery for me—a long overdue follow-up to frequent borrowing of one paragraph. Having digested the book now on a few different occasions, I have come to appreciate the richer portrait of evangelicalism that this exemplary text offers beyond the specifics of the quadrilateral. I would like to encourage us not to forget this big-picture offering.

41. See http://en.wikipedia.org/wiki/Evangelicalism (accessed 8/1/2014).

Still, what about the specifics? Twenty-five years later, do they necessitate serious questioning? My gut-level response to this query is the same today as it was when I first signed on to this panel: NO, absolutely NOT! Bebbington got it right, so why tamper with a good thing? In four beautifully concise points, he managed to boil evangelicalism down to its theological essence, an essence that has remained remarkably intact for three hundred years. It is also worth noting that as much as he used pages 2–3 of his book to isolate evangelicalism's four cores, he used pages 3–19 to unpack them in very nuanced terms. And from pages 20 to 276 he tracked these essentials across three centuries and through a dizzying array of doctrinal, cultural, and political switchbacks and debates. The point being: Bebbington's brilliant four-fold definition was and remains serviceable because of its concreteness *and* its pliability—because of its identification of four timeless principles, still the backbone of this movement, and its cautious handling of the manner in which these principles have functioned differently across generations.[42]

It is in the spirit of pliability that I would like to move past the gut level to something substantive. I will do so by raising a few curiosities about the theological characteristics that Bebbington stresses (or downplays) in his quadrilateral, then by raising other possible common denominators that might help scholars glue evangelicalism together as a cultural force. I hope these prompts will allow Bebbington to comment on his analysis of evangelicalism in light of recent historical and historiographical trends, and (speaking selfishly here) help historians of post-1930s evangelicalism and society find focus and definition in a movement and an era that defy both.

The first cluster concerns the theological emphases that Bebbington did and did not accept into his definition of evangelicalism. As already mentioned, *Evangelicalism in Modern Britain* deftly balances concreteness and elasticity; its quadrilateral is determinative but also broad enough to allow for subtle distinctions and shifting priorities. Bebbington notes, for example, that while Methodists, Presbyterians, and Baptists have always seen "conversionism" and "activism" as essential calls, they have long debated how best to achieve the former and perform the latter. And while in the nineteenth century "biblicism" trumped the other three emphases, in the twentieth "activism" rose to the top. This give-and-take is effective—but provocative as well: might Bebbington have placed more emphasis on other traits, traits that have risen to prominence

42. D. W. Bebbington, *Evangelicalism in Modern Britain: A History from the 1730s to the 1980s* (London: Routledge [reprint], 2002), 3.

in evangelicalism during the twentieth century? Do some of the features of evangelicalism submerged in Bebbington's model deserve foregrounding and first-tier status?[43]

For instance, what about evangelicals' steady emphasis on the work of the Holy Spirit, evidenced most clearly in the holiness-Pentecostal tradition? In this roundtable discussion Thomas Kidd issues a challenge to take seriously eighteenth-century evangelicals' emphasis on the ministry of the Holy Spirit as a defining mark. Kidd cites George Whitefield's career as evidence of the way this theological accent set him and his followers apart. We can identify plenty of other preachers and laypeople to illustrate the same point for the twentieth century, suggesting a continuous strand in the history of evangelicalism that deserves definitional emphasis.

Indeed, especially for the twentieth century—an epoch in American religion that began with the outpouring of Spirit-filled worship among black and white seekers in Los Angeles and ended with proliferating displays of Spirit-filled, multicultural piety in booming communities far beyond Southern California—it seems limiting to marginalize pneumatology. Bebbington's own coverage of twentieth-century British religion reveals a similar rising trajectory of restorationist yearning, among Welsh working folk at the dawn of the era and among urbane Londoners toward its end. As he observes, by the 1970s these yearnings "after the dynamic of the first-century church" had become "a powerful force in British Christianity." We can ask, then: powerful enough to warrant inclusion as a fifth definitional pillar?[44]

To be sure, evangelicals have never agreed on the specifics of the Holy Spirit's indwelling. Quite the contrary, the particulars have often stirred up controversy, during the twentieth century especially (consider the National Association of Evangelicals' debate over the Assemblies of God's appeal for membership, and continued fundamentalist backlash against charismatic influences). But that is the point. The heat proves the stakes are high, and that right understanding of the Spirit is considered absolute for right Christian living. In this sense I see value in J. I. Packer's six-fold definition of evangelicalism, which includes "the lordship of the Holy Spirit" as essential for the brethren.[45]

Packer's definition (the value of which Bebbington acknowledges) contains yet a sixth essential: fellowship. Bebbington notes the central importance of

43. Ibid., 4.

44. Ibid., 197, 229.

45. Ibid., 4; Packer, *The Evangelical Anglican Identity Problem* (Oxford: Latimer House Studies, 1978), 20.

fellowship, but he folds it into his category of activism, a logical yet in light of twentieth-century developments partially satisfactory choice. Lord Shaftesbury's nineteenth-century call for "toil, toil, toil" on behalf of the gospel was also a command for his Christian contemporaries to bear witness to the core of their faith—a personal relationship with Jesus—through the nurturing of strong relationships with each other . . . voluntarily, across boundaries of church distinction and beyond the pale of powerful states. Functional in one respect— collective action being more efficient than independent initiative—the fellowship imperative was also ideational, a Tocquevillian truth about free individuals flourishing in community that cut to the heart of what evangelicals stood for.

The Lausanne Covenant, a useful summation of late-twentieth-century evangelical thought, reminds us of this. Framing its introduction, animating each of its fifteen suppositions, are declarations for one creed of a subjectively intense communalism and corporate Christianity:

- *We, members of the Church of Jesus Christ . . . praise God for his great salvation and rejoice in the fellowship he has given us with himself and with each other.*
- *The church is the community of God's people rather than an institution. . . .*
- *We affirm that the Church's visible unity in truth is God's purpose.*
- *Evangelism summons us to unity, because our oneness strengthens our witness. . . .*
- *We who share the same biblical faith should be closely united in fellowship, work and witness.*
- *We pledge ourselves to seek a deeper unity in truth, worship, holiness and mission.*
- *Thus a growing partnership of churches will develop and the universal character of Christ's Church will be more clearly exhibited.*[46]

Another reminder comes via emerging scholarship on twentieth-century evangelicalism, which drives home the argument that fellowship, the quest for self-meaning and authenticity through complete commitment to the whole, is a distinguishing mark of evangelicalism, not merely an add-on. As historians have demonstrated, for some (Mennonite Brethren, for instance) entry into the evangelical fold comes through affinity and association, not just shared theological truths. Their truths are indeed widely shared, leaving any Mennonite

46. http://www.lausanne.org/content/covenant/lausanne-covenant (accessed 12/15 /2014).

Though he takes a slightly different tack, stressing consumer goods and celebrity pastors over church songsters, Todd Brenneman's *Homespun Gospel* effectively presses for this same kind of recalibration. Especially by the late twentieth century (but is this any different than the eighteenth or nineteenth?), he asserts, evangelicalism's defining appeal was to a "culture of emotionality" and "religiosity as a practice of sentimentality instead of . . . intellectual discovery." Where words could no longer do enough to unify evangelicalism's sprawling constituency, feelings did plenty. Further illustration of this comes by way (once again) of the Lausanne Movement and its most recent treatise for global evangelicalism, delivered at Cape Town in 2010. Although it would be wrong to overstate the difference, one cannot help but be struck by how this document—more so than the original of 1974—seeks to confess faith and action through a tug at the heart. "Love" is its axiom, "Discerning" and "Living" the buzzwords of a document that commands evangelicals to "bear witness" in a "pluralistic, globalized world" crying out for Christ. No scandal of the evangelical mind, this is, rather, symptomatic of a renewed "new evangelicalism" that recognizes where its greatest strength always lies: in its ability to stir souls into communion with the Spirit and one another.[55]

Speaking of "bearing witness" in a "globalized world" and market-sensitive preachers delivering homespun gospels, can we call evangelicalism a *method*? After all, the term's origin is in this very thing: a specific mode of interpreting, interacting with, and engaging the world. Bebbington's text is, understandably, saturated with explication of the evangelical ways of doing the Lord's work. "The Evangelical movement," Bebbington carefully elucidates, "was permeated by Enlightenment influences." It fully embraced "the empiricist method" and made it "habitual"; it fostered certainty that knowing came through exploration and "experience," tried and true; it tired quickly of abstracts, and had little time for those (in "the scholastic camp") who "spent their time spinning cobwebs of discourse that obscured reality"; it reasoned and sought to engineer a Christian world out of first principles, and an on-the-ground business know-how for philanthropy, education, and industry, "regular methods of mission" ("house-to-house visitation" at the grassroots, through

---

55. Todd M. Brenneman, *Homespun Gospel: The Triumph of Sentimentality in Contemporary American Evangelicalism* (New York: Oxford University Press, 2013). See also Jay Green's incisive review of *Homespun Gospel* in *Christianity Today*, http://www .christianitytoday.com/ct/2014/april/trouble-with-touchy-feely-faith.html?paging=off (accessed 8/1/2014). See, for instance, Cape Town Commitment, http://www.lausanne. org/en/documents/ctcommitment.html#p2-1 (accessed 8/1/2014).

"a large and heterogeneous machinery of organizations" at the macro-level), and immediate and broad impact. At its roots and in its mature form, British evangelicalism was sentimental, sure, and as struggles over science played out, and it self-corrected, it also reoriented toward a heavier supernaturalism. But steeped as it was in "Newtonian cosmology," it remained tuned to the schematic and pragmatic, and the bottom-line result. It remains so tuned today.[56]

Again, this portrait of evangelicalism as quintessentially modern in method is not novel. Yet in light of Bebbington's incredibly colorful rendering of the movement and the ongoing labor of scholars like Kathryn Lofton, Timothy Gloege, R. G. Robins, and Brendan Pietsch, it deserves repeating. Thanks to Lofton's prodding, we've been forced to think anew about Protestant thinkers and activists at the turn of the twentieth century, less in liberal-conservative binaries of belief than in terms of method. Lofton's subjects, predominantly "theological modernists," were defined by their "overt allegiance to the inherent virtues of method" and "preoccupation with intellectual procedures over consequences." Evangelicals of the kind that Gloege and Pietsch examine—capitalist innovators and dispensational premillennialists, all members of Moody's camp—deserve their own distinctive label as "modernists" for their embrace of an epistemology that rejected the consequences of theological modernism but nevertheless practiced—indeed, championed, more so than their liberal cousins—"multiple strategies" for engaging the modern world (see Robins) that included pioneering and brokering power on the "modern commercial landscape" (see Gloege), advancing an "epistemic method" of "parsing texts and dissecting time" (see Pietsch), managing knowledge production through highly technical, even technocratic, strategies, and maximizing the analytics and disciplines of applied science in the pursuit and defense of knowable truth. More than ever, the apologetics and general certainty this system creates in (and demands of) its practitioners today seems to place evangelicals at odds with their more hesitant non-evangelical counterparts.[57]

56. Bebbington, *Evangelicalism in Modern Britain*, 57–59, 70–71, 91, 117–19.

57. Kathryn Lofton, "The Methodology of the Modernists: Process in American Protestantism," *Church History* 75:2 (June 2006): 379–80; R. G. Robins, *A. J. Tomlinson: Plainfolk Modernism* (New York: Oxford University Press, 2004), 19. Here I am borrowing (with their permission) from drafts of Brendan Pietsch's introduction to his forthcoming book on dispensational modernism and Timothy Gloege's introduction to his forthcoming book on late-nineteenth-century evangelicalism and corporate capitalism, both in the author's possession.

It also maps them onto a particular geography. Might we, thirdly, do more to think about and define in first-tier terms evangelicalism as a *place*, or an *ethos*? In his outstanding ethnography of 2008, James Wellman uses the metaphor of an onion to describe the layers of evangelical character and commitment (in comparison to liberal ones), and emphasize the totalizing nature of this worldview. His subjects' doctrine captivates him, but no more so than the broader moral terrain that dictates their logics and demographics and rituals and aesthetics, and claims to power. Representative of different layers of the onion, all of these elements nevertheless work together to create one entity—evangelicalism—as something definable by its look, scent, and feel as much as by its suppositions.[58]

Bebbington may be less willing than Wellman to deprioritize theology, but he too, it is worth pointing out, paints modern British evangelicalism in the same beautifully textured ways, always with an eye for thick description. His attention to cultural contexts—economic and moral geographies in which evangelicalism flourished—is especially noteworthy. Take, for instance, a few lines spliced from one section in Chapter 2, a chapter titled "Knowledge of the Lord":

- *In the proliferating cottage meetings of early Evangelicalism it was often women who took the lead in prayer and praise, counsel and exhortation.*
- *The places where Evangelicalism struck deepest root were usually of certain particular kinds. Where artisans were most numerous, vital religion was most likely to do well. Therefore, areas springing into life with proto-industrial employment for the skilled worker, townships like Paddiford Common in 'Janet's Repentance' with weaving and mining as the chief occupation were ideal territory.*
- *In particular, artisans who prided themselves on avoiding dependence on the landed order for their daily bread would assert their self-reliance by giving the new message a hearing—and perhaps more. Evangelism was most effective where deference was weakest, whether in town or countryside.*[59]

In these evocative passages we are exposed to a historian who thinks theologically (hence the chapter title) yet writes like an anthropologist. Not unlike Wellman, his prose seeks to unpack ideas (not to reduce them to something

---

58. James K. Wellman, Jr., *Evangelical vs. Liberal: The Clash of Christian Cultures in the Pacific Northwest* (New York: Oxford University Press, 2008).

59. Bebbington, *Evangelicalism in Modern Britain*, 26–27.

merely functional) and make them essences of a place. Bebbington can be further inspiration, then, for a wave of scholarship on evangelicalism, that has stressed its potency as a system of being tied to particular sectors and spaces, not just sets of belief. Other emerging scholars are offering us similarly rich "definitions" of evangelicalism that make it increasingly impossible to differentiate between doctrines and the circumstances that give them meaning. A movement of born-again people, evangelicalism (as we see in Bebbington's passages) has always been a product of born-again landscapes (1880s steel towns, 1920s advertising hubs, 1950s suburbs, current global, urban, and rustbelt frontiers), and all of the peculiar anxieties and disruptions and opportunities—and notions of time now and beyond—that these emerging sites have created. I am, no doubt, preaching to the choir. But I think we should continue to strive for a reading of evangelicalism that opens up its definition to a full range of mitigating factors, right down to the soil that has cultivated its adherents' labor and daily bread, and that pays attention to all of its "things in their entanglements."[60]

There is much to add here, but the modest takeaway is that as belief and behavior, aesthetic and method, identity, sense of soil, and cosmic ambition, evangelicalism is something that expects of and defines for its members *everything*. Our attempt to study and even categorize it thus demands a multilevel approach that takes this fullness into account. Much more than a conduit for the quadrilateral, and something meant for our convenience, David Bebbington's illustrious book about British evangelicals can and should be considered one of our "how-to" guides in the pursuit of this type of layered historical scholarship.[61]

60. I am borrowing from Courtney Bender's charge for scholars of religion to pay more attention to "things in their entanglements." See Courtney Bender, *The New Metaphysicals: Spirituality and the American Religious Imagination* (Chicago: University of Chicago Press, 2010), 44.

61. For two recent examples of this type of multilevel approach to evangelicalism, see Robert Wuthnow, *Rough Country: How Texas Became America's Most Powerful Bible-Belt State* (Princeton, N.J.: Princeton University Press, 2014), 457; Lydia Bean, *The Politics of Evangelical Identity: Local Churches and Partisan Divides in the United States and Canada* (Princeton, N.J.: Princeton University Press, 2014), 19.

Noun or Adjective?
The Ravings of a Fanatical Nominalist

MARK A. NOLL

For some time I resisted invitations to take part in the worthwhile task of assessing David Bebbington's four-fold definition of evangelicalism. That definition, along with the book where it first appeared and whose twenty-fifth anniversary we celebrated in 2014, *Evangelicalism in Modern Britain: A History from the 1730s to the 1980s,* have more than merited all the attention they have both received.[62] My reason for hesitating lies elsewhere. As Bebbington has known since he graciously asked me for comment on a pre-publication draft of parts of that book, my strongly nominalist predispositions have never taken kindly to realist notions like "evangelicalism," "fundamentalism," "the Enlightenment," "Romanticism," "modernism," or "post-modernism." Where others have written as if these collective nouns describe truly existing entities about which histories can be written, I have regarded them much more as convenient mental shorthand referring to bundles of specific traits characterizing specific people, communities, or traditions that offer a sharper focus for researching and narrating their historical development. To take part in any assessment of the four-fold definition would, therefore, require me to explain to others, Bebbington, and indeed myself why someone with my strongly nominalist prejudices finds some aspects of his essentialist definition of evangelicalism a problem.

But spelling out such complaints could leave the impression that I thought debilitating flaws crippled either the definition or the book in which it appeared. That impression would be false since I yield to no one in general admiration for what Bebbington has written. The research for everything he attempts is so extensive, the documentation so precise, the architectonics so clear, and the overall effect so exceedingly useful that no difference in background presuppositions should qualify heart-felt appreciation. In my view, *Evangelicalism in Modern Britain* deserves a place alongside Timothy L. Smith's *Revivalism and Social Reform: American Protestantism on the Eve of the Civil War* (1957) and George Marsden's *Fundamentalism and American Culture* (1980) as the three books most responsible for fueling the general renewal of historical scholarship on evangelical Christian expressions in the modern English-speaking world. Besides, the four-fold definition has

---

62. D. W. Bebbington, *Evangelicalism in Modern Britain: A History from the 1730s to the 1980s* (London: Unwin Hyman, 1989).

self-described historical "splitter," so brutally attacked the distinguished English historian, Christopher Hill, whom Hexter derided as a "compulsive lumper."[67] Although I am myself certainly a splitter and although I do intend to rave against what strike me as difficulties posed to historical writing by essentialist realism, I am also exceedingly grateful for what I have learned from *Evangelicalism in Modern Britain* and also for how its four-fold definition has caught on.

As a thesis, I call on pithy statements from quite different publications. The first appears in a recent exchange between two of the very best historians of African Christianity, J. D. Y. Peel and Derek Peterson, which arose in a discussion of Peterson's fine recent book, *Ethnic Patriotism and the East African Revival*.[68] Although Peel obviously admired the book, that admiration was tempered by a feeling that Peterson had allowed his very extensive research in local sources to obscure the fact that "the Revival *did* have an overall, unifying trajectory." Despite Peterson's praiseworthy focus on particular local situations, Peel concluded that "the general or overall questions posed by the Revival's remarkable translocal appeal go largely unanswered."[69]

Peterson replied that what has routinely been described as "the East African Revival" should better be understood as an outgrowth of the "organizational energy" of Joe Church, William Nagenda, and their colleagues. That energy, in Peterson's view, "constructed the Revival . . . Without Joe Church at one's elbow, it is difficult to draw the line between the Revival and other [East African] innovations in Christianity." After comparing what his diligent research discovered in several different locations with what he termed the construction project of Joe Church et al., Peterson concluded: "I am not convinced that the Revival ever was a movement."[70] Based on the evidence presented in his book, I think Peterson is right.

The second source for my thesis comes from the riveting opening sentence with which Steven Shapin introduced a 1998 book that itself inaugurated a new series on the history of science from the University of Chicago

---

67. Hexter's review of Hill appeared first in the *Times Literary Supplement*, October 24, 1975, and was reprinted in his *On Historians: Reappraisals of Some of the Masters of Modern History* (Cambridge, Mass.: Harvard University Press, 1979), 227–51 (242 for "compulsive lumper").

68. Derek R. Peterson, *Ethnic Patriotism and the East African Revival: A History of Dissent, c. 1935–1972* (New York: Cambridge University Press, 2012).

69. J. Y. D. Peel, "Book Debate," *Social Sciences and Missions* 27 (2014): 274.

70. Peterson, "Book Debate," *Social Sciences and Missions* 27 (2014): 275.

Press: "There was no such thing as the *Scientific Revolution* and this is a book about it."[71] Based on the careful presentation of evidence in that book, Shapin's apparently outlandish statement also proved persuasive. So, indebted to both Peterson and Shapin, here is my thesis: "There is no such thing as evangelicalism and David Bebbington has provided the best possible definition for it."

My specific complaint about "evangelicalism" as a noun does not primarily concern any of the four characteristics of the Bebbington definition. To be sure, "conversion" does raise a delicate question about at least a few of the Reformed, Lutheran, and Anglican/Episcopal Christians who obviously belong in any history of British, American, or Canadian evangelicalism, but who never experienced a classic evangelical conversion. The reverse problem confronts historical writing about the recent past because of the substantial numbers of Roman Catholics who have experienced conversions of the evangelical type but who, as John Stackhouse pointed out in Kingston, fit awkwardly into connected histories of evangelicalism.

Admittedly, the difficulty involved in using general characteristics to define the subject for a historical study is not a trivial side issue. As some readers will remember, the Angus Reid Group in 1996 conducted an extensive survey of 3,000 Americans and 3,000 Canadians where the questions about evangelical definition that had been debated at Kingston the previous year came more sharply into focus. Through the influence of George Rawlyk, the Angus Reid surveyors had included four questions that were keyed to the Bebbington definition. The results were just disconcerting enough to give pause. For the United States, 51 percent of those who answered the four questions positively (in other words, who defined themselves as evangelicals according to the Bebbington criteria) belonged to denominations historically viewed as evangelicals, 14 percent belonged to mainline Protestant churches, and 13 percent were African-American Protestants. But 13 percent of those who affirmed all four were Catholics, and 4 percent claimed no religious affiliation. For Canada, there was less alignment with the traditional organizational categories that historians of Christianity usually put to use. Thus, 45 percent of Canadians who affirmed all four of the Bebbington characteristics adhered to evangelical denominations, and 19 percent belonged to mainline Protestant churches, but a full 25 percent were Catholics.[72] If results from such a survey were the only

71. Steven Shapin, *The Scientific Revolution* (Chicago: University of Chicago Press, 1998).

72. For fuller discussion of these and related results, see Mark A. Noll, "Constit-

consideration that historians used to select topics to research and narrate, it would indicate a real problem, since there are no existing histories of either Canadian evangelicalism or American evangelicalism that include a prominent, if minority, place for Roman Catholics.

Yet for most purposes, the four-fold characterization works very well to designate traits that have been correctly regarded as characterizing individuals, groups, traditions, organizations, denominations, and actions as evangelical. About such individuals, groups, traditions, organizations, denominations, and actions, it is certain that histories can be written. *Evangelicalism in Modern Britain* is, in fact, full of such narratives.

By contrast, an entity designated as "evangelicalism" does not work well for historical research or historical narratives. The issue, I believe, can be reduced to a consideration of traits as opposed to a consideration of essences. In a realist view, there exists such a thing as evangelicalism. By contrast, in a nominalist view, there exist only traits that can legitimately be named as evangelical.

The nominalist-realist difference does not make much of a difference for titles. Few were bothered when Timothy Smith's book on American Protestantism said very little about southern Presbyterians, hard-shell anti-mission Baptists, or immigrant Mennonites, though these groups were certainly Protestant. Similarly, Donald Dayton was one of the few critics seriously to object to the fact that George Marsden's fundamentalism relegated holiness Protestants to the background and said very little about Pentecostals, even though holiness and Pentecostal movements shared kin networks with the Protestants upon whom Marsden did concentrate.[73] Likewise, the great success of *Evangelicalism in Modern Britain* arises from the fact that its narratives illuminate the development of individuals, groups, movements, and social actions that clearly shared evangelical traits and whose histories could be traced by noting connections among these individuals, groups, and movements.

When, however, that book referred to evangelicalism as an entity with agency, there were difficulties, which can be specified through three illustrations. First, John Coffey's contribution to the Haykin and Stewart volume, *The Advent of Evangelicalism*, took exception to the sharp divide that Bebbing-

---

uencies in North America and the World," in *American Evangelical Christianity: An Introduction* (Malden, Mass.: Blackwell, 2001), 29–43.

73. For example, Donald Dayton, "The Search for the Historical Evangelicalism: George Marsden's History of Fuller Seminary as a Case Study," *Christian Scholar's Review* 23 (1993): 12–33.

ton drew between seventeenth-century Puritanism and eighteenth-century evangelicalism. Coffey quoted what he regarded as the offending phrases in *Evangelicalism in Modern Britain* when he defined the problem: Bebbington's "language is unusually emphatic. Evangelicalism was the product of 'a revolution in taste' and was 'created' by the Enlightenment. It was 'a new movement,' a 'metamorphosis.' The implication is that even if evangelicalism evolved from Puritanism, the two are nevertheless different species."[74]

As an equal-opportunity critic Coffey also objected to an effort I had earlier made to distinguish seventeenth-century Puritans from eighteenth-century evangelicals: thus, Noll describes "Puritanism as 'a traditional religion of traditional European Christendom.' Each of [the] three features of this 'traditional religion' that Noll mentions were certainly present in mainstream Puritanism . . . But there were [also] powerful counter-currents within Puritanism."[75] Against such statements depicting discontinuity between the seventeenth and eighteenth centuries, Coffey offered a good deal of counter evidence. For example, some Puritans proclaimed a strong doctrine of assurance of the sort that Bebbington described as appearing freshly on the scene with evangelicalism. And quite a few Puritans were fissile, populist networkers of the sort that I said came into existence only when evangelicals appeared on the scene.

Coffey's insistence on the diversity of both Puritans in the seventeenth century and evangelicals in the eighteenth drove his critique. Yes, of course, discontinuous elements also existed, but without specifying what traits were under consideration or what broad or narrow currency such traits enjoyed, it made little sense to speak flatly of either discontinuity or continuity between Puritans and evangelicals. In my view, Coffey was correct.

But so, in my view, was Bebbington correct when at the end of the Haykin-Stewart volume he responded to Coffey. In that response, he conceded that Coffey saw correctly that revivalism as such did not begin in the eighteenth century but could be traced to Scottish communion seasons of the early seventeenth century. Yet Bebbington went on to note that Coffey himself had conceded that a widespread sentiment anticipating revival did constitute something new in the eighteenth century: "So the expectation of regular revival that has been so prominent a mark of modern evangelicalism was born . . . Although revivals of the type experienced from the 1730s onwards were known in previous years, showing a tangible continuity, the Evangelical

74. John Coffey, "Puritanism, Evangelicalism, and the Evangelical Protestant Tradition," in *Advent of Evangelicalism*, 254.

75. Ibid., 263.

Revival was novel both because of its scale, and because it created an eager anticipation of more awakenings."[76]

The Coffey-Bebbington exchange was productive in the very best way. But it was productive because of how it descended into particulars. If evangelicalism is defined as a form of Protestant Christianity for which revivals are important, it was not new. But if evangelicalism is defined as a form of Protestant Christianity where the expectation of revival dominated, then it was new. In other words, historical knowledge advances—as it definitely did in this exchange—by giving up a realistic picture of evangelicalism (as a thing outside of time and space) in favor of a nominalist picture (as an agreed-upon designation for a certain collection of traits that can be researched and narrated in their times and places).

My second example highlights an instance where Bebbington himself offered a splitter's refinement to improve upon a lumping assertion made in *Evangelicalism in Modern Britain*. One of the most helpful contributions of that book was the way it specified several traits usually associated with the Enlightenment as also characterizing evangelicalism. With particularly effective examples, he spelled out the strong emphasis on experience—on practical experimentation—that characterized evangelicals in an age where much of the intellectual tone had been set by Sir Isaac Newton's experimental methods. A sub-section of my book, *The Rise of Evangelicalism: The Age of Edwards, Whitefield and the Wesleys*, pays tribute to Bebbington's account by trying to summarize in brief compass his persuasive account of those Enlightenment-evangelical connections.[77]

The example concerns the dislike that most evangelicals in the eighteenth and early nineteenth centuries expressed for the proposals of John Hutchinson, a Yorkshire Anglican who thought that the science of Sir Isaac Newton led inevitably to materialism. In reaction, Hutchinson developed a view of the physical universe strictly from the Hebrew scriptures. Using the double meaning in Old Testament Hebrew for expressing the terms "weight" and "glory," Hutchinson offered a thoroughly biblical alternative to Newtonian science. Yet despite its intensely biblical character, which might seem to align with one of Bebbington's four evangelical characteristics—and, one might add, despite the predilection of later evangelicals to favor something like the biblical literalism that Hutchinson exemplified—evangelicals of Hutchinson's era (and later) rejected his proposal.

76. Bebbington, "Response," in *Advent of Evangelicalism*, 423.
77. Noll, *Rise of Evangelicalism*, 140–41.

In *Evangelicalism and Modern Britain* things become cloudy when Bebbington refers to the particular stress on experience as simply "Enlightenment influences" and to the corresponding trait as simply "Evangelical convictions." Thus, because "the Evangelical movement . . . was permeated by Enlightenment influences," there was "in the eighteenth century and long into the nineteenth no hint of a clash between Evangelical religion and science . . . Admittedly a few Evangelicals in the Church of England were attracted by Hutchinsonianism, a system of belief rejecting Newton's views on the ground that the Bible contains a complete system of natural philosophy . . . [William] Romaine was weaned from Hutchinsonianism as his Evangelical convictions deepened. . . ."[78]

My objection to this narrative depends upon accepting Bebbington's persuasive account that traced specific traits of the Enlightenment to traits among evangelicals that certainly had been shaped by the era's rage for experiment. Thus, in this case and following Bebbington's lead, my splitter's rendition would have concluded that "Romaine was weaned from Hutchinsonianism *as his evangelical predilection for empirical experience* deepened."

But, thankfully, in a paper published in 1999 on British evangelicals and science Bebbington did a much better job of correcting than I have just done in making what he wrote earlier more specific. Here is his second account in a passage that meets high nominalist standards:

> It might be supposed that the rival Hutchinsonian scheme of natural philosophy drawn from the Hebrew text of the Bible would appeal to evangelicals. Certainly William Romaine, the earliest evangelical Anglican to occupy a London pulpit, used his single series of lectures as Gresham Professor of Astronomy to assail Newtonian philosophy on Hutchinsonian lines. . . . But Thomas Haweis was more representative in being initially attracted by the devotional spirit of the Hutchinsonians but then alienated by their High Church sacramentalism. [John] Wesley was fascinated by their strangely cabalistic scheme but found it untenable. So it was Newtonianism that claimed the allegiance of nearly all the branches of the evangelical community.[79]

78. Bebbington, *Evangelicalism in Modern Britain*, 57.

79. David W. Bebbington, "Science and Evangelical Theology in Britain from Wesley to Orr," in David N. Livingstone, D. G. Hart, and Mark A. Noll, eds., *Evangelicals and Science in Historical Perspective* (Oxford: Oxford University Press, 1999), 125–26.

An evangelical is:

1. an orthodox Protestant
2. who stands in the tradition of global Christian networks arising from the eighteenth-century revival movements associated with John Wesley and George Whitefield;
3. who has a preeminent place for the Bible in her or his Christian life as the divinely inspired, final authority in matters of faith and practice;
4. who stresses reconciliation with God through the atoning work of Christ on the cross,
5. and who stresses the work of the Holy Spirit in the life of an individual to bring about conversion and an ongoing life of fellowship with God and service to God and others, including the duty of all believers to participate in the task of proclaiming the gospel to all people.[84]

As a definition provided for a book of theology, it was perhaps appropriate for Larsen to list five factors for designating an undifferentiated evangelical. But his ideal type was, in my view, sharpened when he added the recognition of a specific historical network to his designation of abstractly presented traits.

As another example, Alister Chapman's contribution to the Bebbington–Ceri Jones collection on recent British history offered a sophisticated answer to the question posed by his title: "Evangelical or Fundamentalist? The Case of John Stott."[85] Beginning with the definitions that Bebbington set out for "evangelicalism" and "fundamentalism" in that book's introduction, Chapman went on to sharpen his question through astute distinctions. Concerning the public dispute over fundamentalism that attended Billy Graham's much-publicized visit to England in 1955, Chapman writes: "The controversy shows the importance of understanding fundamentalism and evangelicalism in their particular historical contexts." Then in describing various Britons who at different times and for different reasons stuck the label of "fundamentalism" on Stott, he writes that "the term was . . . slippery. . . . With no agreed referent, fundamentalism was a word that could easily be applied to

---

84. Timothy Larsen, "Defining and Locating Evangelicalism," in Timothy Larsen and Daniel J. Treier, eds., *The Cambridge Companion to Evangelical Theology* (New York: Cambridge University Press, 2007), 1–14 (quotation, 1).

85. Alister Chapman, "Evangelical or Fundamentalist? The Case of John Stott," in *Evangelicalism and Fundamentalism in the United Kingdom*, 192–208.

any theologically conservative Protestant."[86] As he made these observations about the plasticity of abstract nouns, Chapman drafted the best kind of history. Instead of a quick and snarky "it all depends" of the sort I might have offered, Chapman patiently, and with full attention to a complex biography, spelled out the specific reasons why John Stott recognized himself as an evangelical and why some of his critics could call him a fundamentalist. The result was a masterful account that, with careful attention to specific traits, fleshed out the skeleton that Bebbington's definition of evangelicalism had earlier provided.

David Bebbington's achievement with *Evangelicalism in Modern Britain* as well as his four-fold definition of evangelicalism will easily survive any criticism that I might make. My sole aim has been to point out how a brilliant definition of enduring usefulness could be made a little bit more specific and a little bit more useful if a little bit more consideration were shown to those of us afflicted with the nominalist gene.

"Defining Evangelicalism: Questions That Complement the Quadrilateral"

Molly Worthen

Anyone who writes or teaches about evangelicals has to take up the task of deciding who counts as one. As with any complex and controversial term, the definition we choose depends on our audience. The great virtue of David Bebbington's "quadrilateral" is that it works well with so many different audiences, from academic conferences to cocktail parties. What's more, Bebbington's four bullet points—the Bible, the born-again experience, evangelism, and the cross—generally play well with believers themselves. In this definition, there is no hint of the political connotations or the anti-intellectualism that has sent so many Christians running from the evangelical label. And we are left with a set of qualities that we can find in Jim Wallis or Jerry Falwell, in the eighteenth century or the twenty-first.

Yet this definition has come to have a simple and static character—one that is at odds with the nuanced role it originally played in *Evangelicalism and Modern Britain.* But then, over-simplification is often the cost of popularization. And it can sometimes be a problem. Lately my research has concerned

86. Ibid., 195, 198.

conservative Protestants in twentieth-century America. As I got into my archival work and interviewed a wide variety of evangelicals, I found that Bebbington's bullet points did not always give me the tools that I needed. Even the "born-again experience"—supposedly the essence of evangelicalism—turned out to be less than an ironclad indicator. Some evangelicals have always viewed conversion as an incremental process rather than an instantaneous rebirth. And don't get me started on what different conservative Protestants say they mean by "biblicism." Yet I wanted to corral Christian communities that seemed to be moving through history in related ways, struggling with the same problems, even if they found different solutions. I needed a dynamic framework, a definition that identified agents of change—because as we know, in some ways the corners of Bebbington's quadrilateral have held fairly constant over the centuries, but in other ways they are constantly in motion. I found myself wanting to label as "evangelical" traditions that share common roots in the Pietist aftermath of the Reformation, or the eighteenth- and nineteenth-century Anglosphere revivals, alongside self-described evangelicals. I'm talking about groups that often strenuously object if you call them an evangelical to their face: Mennonites, Churches of Christ, and other groups that may reject so-called evangelical bona fides and proudly claim an independent history and identity.

What I found is that there is a constellation of Protestant traditions that often disagree about matters of dogma, about frankly almost everything except the divinity of Christ, but who seem to have been part of the same conversation over the centuries. They seem to have a stake in what one another gets up to—because they orbit around the same questions. If they don't share a single statement of faith, they do share a set of worries and concerns. And they are alike in that they have to sort out these worries in the absence of a single central authority to guide them. *Sola scriptura* sounds simple enough, but it's not a very clear source of authority in practice.

Three elemental concerns unite the Protestants that I am labeling evangelical: how to repair the fracture between spiritual and rational knowledge; how to assure salvation and a true relationship with God, or "meet and know Jesus," as some evangelicals say; and how to resolve the tension between the demands of personal belief and the constraints of a secularized public square. These are all problems of intellectual and spiritual authority, and they took on a new edge in the modern era, which I'm dating from the mid-seventeenth century, the time of the rebirth of reason and the first hints of our present-day notions of "religious" and "secular." Like Bebbington, I see evangelicalism as a thoroughly modern movement.

I want to acknowledge that none of these worries, on their own, is unique to evangelicals. But in combination, and in the absence of a magisterial arbiter capable of guiding believers through uncertainties and disagreements, I think these concerns have shaped a distinctive spiritual community. Sure, Catholics and liberal Protestants sometimes stay up at night pondering these things too, but they have a commanding intellectual authority. Roman Catholics dispute the Vatican, but the "Roman" part of their name still means something. Liberal Protestants tend to allow the goddess of reason to rule over the Bible (or to rule, relatively untroubled, in her separate sphere). I am grossly oversimplifying and generalizing here, but simplifications and generalizations often serve a purpose. And I'm convinced that no matter how many nuances and caveats you care to add, the evangelical anxiety about personal salvation and communion with the divine, faith and reason, and the secular public square is different from anxieties that other Christians have—because of their confused and contradictory relationship to intellectual authority.

This is a historian's definition, meant to account for the patterns of history, rather than a believer's self-description that tries to relay evangelicals' internal perspective in language that they might use themselves. And it's a little too unwieldy to win many converts: I'm suggesting only that it came in handy for me, as I explored my own research questions. But I have been encouraged by evangelical readers' reactions to *Apostles of Reason*, in which I lay all this out. Most of the feedback that I've received—from evangelicals ranging from conservative Southern Baptists to liberal Nazarenes—has been positive. What they seem to appreciate is the way in which this framework allowed me to tease out the relationships between different evangelical communities and explain how some have come to wield disproportionate influence over others. I argued that some evangelicals, particularly those in the Reformed inerrantist tradition, gained cultural and political power by coming up with seductive answers to those three questions that I mentioned—questions that jibed with contemporary movements in modern Western culture.

This definition helped me try to do in the American context what Bebbington did so persuasively in *Evangelicalism in Modern Britain*: to argue that evangelicals have never stood apart from mainstream culture, but have always been caught up in it and responded to the intellectual and cultural trends of their time. I found that it became easier to trace their relationship to the wider world if I defined them in terms of a universal human problem—anxiety about authority—rather than Christian doctrine.

I used the word "Western," and that word is a crucial qualifier. In writing this book I spent some time describing American evangelicals' engagement with non-Western Protestants through missions, the Lausanne movement, charismatic renewal, and other modes of outreach. I became increasingly aware that my definition broke down upon leaving the northern half of the Western Hemisphere.

I don't mean to suggest that there is a firm divide between the Western world and everywhere else. Centuries of trade, travel, and imperialism have forced non-Western cultures to grapple with Western ideas and assumptions (and vice versa). But, as my American subjects learned when they got out into the world and talked to non-Western Christians about their concerns and visions for the global church, often they do not share the same anxieties that Western evangelicals do.

As American evangelicals began to work more closely with Christians in newly independent societies, as they witnessed the fires of revival and non-Western Christians' intimate struggles with the supernatural, many realized that their own assumptions about social change and religious experience fell apart outside the dominion of Enlightenment reason and the legacy of the fundamentalist-modernist battles. Today, the globalization of Protestantism has made it harder than ever to define the term "evangelical."

Many Christians in the Global South care more about warding off witches or insuring the fate of unbaptized ancestors than combating the fiends of secularism. While they affirm the authority of the Bible, Christians outside the developed West do not agonize so much over the nature of that authority or its clash with the claims of the Enlightenment. They do not equate "the social gospel" with godless socialism. They read scripture through the lens of their own cultural contexts. According to Orlando Costas, an evangelical theologian born in Puerto Rico, the "reality of poverty, powerlessness, and oppression . . . [provides the context where t]he emphasis on the content of the gospel and the teaching of the biblical text rather than on formal questions of authority and the philosophical presuppositions behind a particular doctrine of inspiration is freeing evangelical theology in the Two-Thirds World."[87]

Growing numbers of conservative Protestants from abroad and from immigrant churches at home are joining Christian student groups on secular campuses in the United States and attending American evangelical colleges and seminaries. On some campuses, Asian-American members—particularly those of Korean descent—dominate the membership of evangelical student

87. Orlando E. Costas, "Evangelical Theology in the Two-Thirds World," in Joel A. Carpenter and Wilbert R. Shenk, eds., *Earthen Vessels: American Evangelicals and Foreign Missions, 1880–1980* (Grand Rapids, Mich.: Eerdmans, 1990), 241, 247.

associations and represent the largest nonwhite population in American evangelical seminaries.[88] Sometimes these students identify with the traditional concerns of American evangelicals. But often they bring their own interpretations of Christian heritage and the implications of the gospel for public life. Self-segregation along ethnic lines remains a powerful force, but I do think they are changing the conversation. I've spoken with faculty and administrators who tell me this is happening. Particularly in Pentecostal circles—where the global scope of the movement demands a cross-cultural, multiracial perspective—nonwhite and non-American theologians are publishing some of the most adventurous and sophisticated cultural theology in evangelicalism today.

Is it possible to come up with a definition for "evangelical" that works today, in the twenty-first century, across all times and places? I would love to have one. No matter how many of us nit-picking scholars complain about the trouble with defining the term "evangelical" and say we should chuck it altogether, lots of people, outsiders and believers alike, are going to keep using the word. I'm afraid we're stuck with it.

The Evangelical Quadrilateral: A Response

DAVID W. BEBBINGTON

It is a pleasant task to respond to the six panelists who considered the evangelical quadrilateral at the conferences in Washington and at Pepperdine in 2014. In some ways it is surprising, and certainly a cause for gratitude, that the subject is still considered worth discussing twenty-five years after the publication of *Evangelicalism in Modern Britain*. But perhaps in another way it is not surprising, because the introductory chapter of the book was designed merely to summarize what everybody knew. The idea that the quadrilateral was breaking fresh ground did not occur to the author, who was trying to capture the consensus of opinion among existing writers on the subject. In some measure that goal seems to have been achieved, for even the contributors to a volume assessing the case outlined in Chapter 2 of the book, several of them critically,

---

88. Rebecca Y. Kim, *God's New Whiz Kids? Korean American Evangelicals on Campus* (New York: New York University Press, 2006); Elaine Howard Ecklund, *Korean American Evangelicals: New Models for Civic Life* (New York: Oxford University Press, 2006), 6.

Thomas Kidd, the Quadrilateral at Origin

Thomas Kidd, the historian of the Great Awakening and the biographer of George Whitefield, raises an issue derived from his detailed work on the origins of the movement. He is happy that early evangelicals were concerned with Bible, cross, conversion, and activism, but sees another attribute as equally important among them. In the 1730s and 1740s, he points out, they regularly insisted on the role of the Holy Spirit in bringing about the quickening of new birth. The evidence he adduces in his two books can leave no doubt about that.[94] At the start of the evangelical movement, he therefore suggests, it displayed a fifth salient characteristic. To strengthen his case, it can be said that the movement showed the same additional feature at other times and places. Thus in Elliott's paper Sebuk-Ram is noted as having stressed the Holy Spirit in India around 1800, mentioning the work of the Spirit twice within a short passage. So it is clear that an emphasis on the third person of the Trinity can often be discerned within the evangelical movement.

Yet it cannot be conceded that the ministry of the Spirit was consistently on a par with the other prominent features of evangelicalism. Characteristics need to have existed over time if they are to be treated as valid marks of the whole movement. There may be variation in the degree of stress, but some emphasis is called for. The Holy Spirit, however, was not always given prominence. Thus in the 1920s, when the Pentecostals, a growing sector of the evangelical movement, did give a large place in thought and experience to the Spirit—and largely *because* Pentecostals accorded the Spirit this honor—the fundamentalists did not. They went further. They denounced the Pentecostals for misleading their hearers by unduly magnifying the role of the Spirit in the Christian's life. The Pentecostals, claimed the fundamentalists, were distracting people from Christ by constantly pointing to the Spirit.[95] The fundamentalists were a species of evangelicals, but they opposed any special place for the Holy Spirit. Consequently, it would be a mistake to claim that the ministry of the Spirit has always been a leading feature of evangelicalism.

Even at the start of the evangelical movement there are indications that some were wary of according what they considered undue importance to

---

94. Thomas S. Kidd, *The Great Awakening: The Roots of Evangelical Christianity in Colonial America* (New Haven, Conn.: Yale University Press, 2009); *George Whitefield: America's Spiritual Founding Father* (New Haven, Conn.: Yale University Press, 2014).

95. Gerald W. King, *Disfellowshiped: Pentecostal Responses to Fundamentalism in the United States, 1906–1943* (Eugene, Ore.: Pickwick, 2011)

the signs of the Spirit's presence. Isaac Watts, the Congregational divine and hymn-writer, Kidd notes, criticized Whitefield for claiming special revelations of the Spirit. While at the height of the early Great Awakening some radicals showed a liking for signs and wonders induced by the Spirit, more moderate evangelicals looked askance on exaggerated spiritual claims. Thus teaching about the Holy Spirit actually divided the early evangelicals. That doctrine did not serve as a uniting factor, an essential of any feature that could be considered a hallmark of the entire movement. Even at its origin, evangelicalism evinced four salient characteristics rather than five.

Amanda Porterfield, the Quadrilateral in Theory

More theoretical questions surrounding *Evangelicalism in Modern Britain* form the subject of Amanda Porterfield's contribution. She enquires how the method establishing the quadrilateral relates to other approaches to the study of religion. Porterfield contends that it is a mistake to neglect the ideas of evangelicalism, and that is shared ground. The intellectual history of the movement is essential to grasping its place in the past. Its ideas formed much of its identity. On the other hand, however, ideas are not separate from society. As Porterfield points out, society shapes thinkers. Thus the leading English evangelical of the later twentieth century, John Stott, was molded by his experience of Rugby School.[96] Society also creates a willingness to welcome new thought. Holiness teaching took hold in England from the 1870s, for example, in part because of dissatisfaction with the slow rate of evangelical growth.[97] So ideas and society should be seen as parts of a whole.

The quadrilateral is not just about beliefs. It is true that the convictions that Christ saves through the atonement, that the Bible contains all that is necessary for salvation, and that a person must be born from above are irreducibly theological assertions. Yet activism is primarily about deeds, conversion is an event in life, and the Bible has to be read. All of these evangelical priorities concern behavior. Even the doctrine of the cross entails motivation for a Christian lifestyle founded on gratitude for redemption. Although, then, the

96. Alister Chapman, *Godly Ambition: John Stott and the Evangelical Movement* (Oxford: Oxford University Press, 2012).

97. D. W. Bebbington, *Evangelicalism in Modern Britain: A History from the 1730s to the 1980s* (London: Unwin Hyman, 1989), 152.

quadrilateral draws attention to ideas, it is not meant to exclude conduct.[98] The approach adopted in *Evangelicalism in Modern Britain* is therefore, as Porterfield observes, much closer to the school of thought identified with "lived religion" than might be supposed.

The method undergirding the book does not rely on texts alone. The primary sources are often printed publications, but Porterfield is right that the author was self-consciously a participant-observer. I have undertaken fieldwork on evangelical (and other) congregations since 1965 by recording the content of services. The notes describe not just what is said in the sermon, but also features of congregations like the proportion of ladies wearing hats and the number of arms raised in worship. The set of notebooks forms a continuous run covering nearly half a century.[99] They often cast light on the long-term characteristics of evangelicalism. Thus at the Baptist church in which I was brought up, a solitary text was displayed at the front: "We preach Christ crucified." Asking myself why that alone was selected helped identify the salience of crucicentrism in the evangelical movement. So contemporary observation contributed to the genesis of the quadrilateral.

Porterfield notes that *Evangelicalism in Modern Britain* tries to bring out cultural processes that are top-down. The diffusion of the values of the Enlightenment, Romanticism, and what the book calls "Modernism" in and around the movement gives the book its structure. They are envisaged as gradually spreading downward and outward from cultural innovators to wider numbers. The lived religion school insists, by contrast, that religion is formed from below, by ordinary people in the course of their everyday existence. Yet, as Porterfield also proposes, the two approaches can be integrated. It is definitely the case that evangelicalism embraced groups on the lower rungs of the social ladder who were immensely creative. Thus the Cokelers, a sect living in north Sussex from the later nineteenth into the following century, added some unusual articles to their impeccably evangelical creed. Believing in the supreme value of "oneness," they discouraged marriage as a symptom of "twoness"—and so tended to die out. But they also believed in wearing Sussex "smocks," the white working clothes of agricultural laborers, long after others discarded such apparel, for the costume became a symbol of

---

98. *Contra* Todd M. Brenneman, *Homespun Gospel: The Triumph of Sentimentality in Contemporary American Evangelicalism* (New York: Oxford University Press, 2013), 156–57.

99. They are used in D. W. Bebbington, "Evangelicals and Public Worship, 1965–2005," *Evangelical Quarterly* 79 (2007): 3–22.

purity.[100] The local way of life formed religious practice. Yet acknowledging such developments does not entail abandoning the top-down element in cultural processes affecting evangelicalism. There has been a trickle-down process, as *Evangelicalism in Modern Britain* tries to show, from a cultural elite to a mass public.[101] That was crucially formative within the movement. High culture created the "spectacles behind the eyes" through which the world was viewed. Hence the optimism of the Enlightenment generated postmillennialism and the pessimism of the Romantic spirit fostered premillennialism, so establishing alternative eschatologies. Because ordinary folk create their own religious practice does not mean that they are immune to a pervasive cultural mood.

Certainly there is no intention in *Evangelicalism in Modern Britain* to do battle with Clifford Geertz, the prevailing influence on the lived religion school, or any of its other exponents. It is crucial, as Geertz would recommend, to examine local evangelical creativity in detail and depth. That is what is attempted in my *Victorian Religious Revivals*, an account of awakenings in local communities throughout the English-speaking world.[102] Nevertheless, as is argued in the historiographical chapter of that book, there are many twentieth-century models for the study of religion that ought to be discarded. In particular the "religion and society" school, seeing religion as an epiphenomenon of a class society, should be superseded. That is to reject a point of view espoused equally by Marxists and by right-wingers upholding a determinism of money and power. Their perspective is mistaken precisely because it leaves out of account the religious experience of ordinary people. In that book I recommend an alternative model, one called "culture and piety." Culture encompasses the whole of everyday life; piety highlights the Christian spirituality lived out in that context. Hence I agree with Porterfield that there is much more theoretical common ground between my methods and that of Geertz than might be imagined from *Evangelicalism in Modern Britain* alone.

---

100. Peter Jerrome, *John Sirgood's Way: The Story of the Loxwood Dependants* (Petworth, U.K.: Window Press, 1998).

101. It is analyzed in D. W. Bebbington, "Evangelicalism and Cultural Diffusion," in Mark Smith, ed., *British Evangelical Identities Past and Present*: Volume 1: *Aspects of the History and Sociology of Evangelicalism in Britain and Ireland* (Milton Keynes, Pentworth, U.K.: Paternoster, 2008), 18–34.

102. D. W. Bebbington, *Victorian Religious Revivals: Culture and Piety in Local and Global Contexts* (Oxford: Oxford University Press, 2012).

Darren Dochuk, the Quadrilateral in Time

Darren Dochuk concentrates on a particular period of time, the twentieth century, for his evaluation of the quadrilateral. There are several topics covered in the second half of his paper on which, as he says, we entirely concur. Evangelicalism was indeed marked by sentiment, flexibility of method, and an ethos varying according to place. Sentiment was commonly as much a part of evangelical life as intellect, a case now made out more fully by Todd Brenneman.[103] Experience, felt emotion, was not, however, independent of conversion but its fruit. Sentiment was a consequence of hearts strangely warmed. Nor was it constant: a few evangelical groups made a virtue of an absence of feeling. So it does not qualify as a factor in the delineation of the evangelical movement. Again, evangelicals were often strikingly willing to adopt novel methods. Their zeal to transmit the gospel meant that they were unusually eager to take up fresh techniques such as radio and film so that by all means they might save some. But this innovative capacity was no more an independent attribute than sentiment, for it was a corollary of activism. Evangelicals sought the best means of passing on their message in successive generations. And evangelical religion has regularly reflected its specific place, something that *Victorian Religious Revivals* tries to illustrate. The seven awakenings discussed in the book were all profoundly shaped by their settings. So there is much agreement with Dochuk on specific points.

There is more divergence when Dochuk proposes that certain features common in twentieth-century evangelicalism should be seen as defining qualities of the movement as a whole. Like Thomas Kidd on the origins of the movement, Dochuk discerns an emphasis on the ministry of the Holy Spirit as an evangelical distinctive. Certainly it was common among twentieth-century evangelicals, especially those swayed by Pentecostalism or charismatic renewal. Yet, as was commented previously, the Holy Spirit was not always prominent among evangelicals. We can go further. Sometimes there were deliberate efforts to downplay the work of the Spirit. Thus in the course of my fieldwork in the 1970s, I visited a strong and highly evangelical Baptist church in Bournemouth, England, which was trying to hold back the tide of the charismatic movement. The members of the congregation were instructed not to sing a verse in a Trinitarian chorus expressing adoration of the Holy Spirit for fear of diverting our gaze away from Jesus Christ. An emphasis on the Spirit was by no means a universal attribute of evangelicals. It cannot be treated as a characteristic on the same level as the points of the quadrilateral.

103. Brenneman, *Homespun Gospel.*

Nor can fellowship. Dochuk contends that the spirit of togetherness was as much a mark of the movement as anything else. It is true that fellowship was frequently an evangelical trait. Early Methodists, for example, were defined by their meeting weekly in classes. Yet a communal emphasis was by no means a consistent attribute of evangelicalism. Many have claimed, on the contrary, that isolation of particular people, each alone before the Almighty, is more typical of evangelical ways. Mark Hutchinson and John Wolffe, for instance, have written about individualism as a fifth note of evangelicalism.[104] That estimate of the importance of prioritizing single persons reflects the standard criticism of the evangelical party in the Church of England: it lacked a sense of churchmanship. If that view is valid, it follows that evangelicals, as individualists, are at the opposite pole from emphasizing fellowship. Although there is no good reason to add individualism to the list of evangelical characteristics, a truth lurks here: because of the high rank attributed to conversion, evangelicals did normally stress particular persons at least as much as any corporate expression of the Christian life. Consequently fellowship cannot be seen as another hallmark of all evangelicals. Rather, sometimes the individual and sometimes togetherness received greater weight among them.

Dochuk draws attention to the strength of premillennial eschatology in twentieth-century American evangelicalism. The dispensational version of premillennialism looms especially large. Yet that has not always been the case. In the eighteenth century postmillennial teaching was common and its premillennial equivalent was rare. So premillennialism itself cannot justifiably be treated as a persistent element in evangelicalism. Dochuk, however, provides a modification of his case. Evangelicals, he avers, were "an intensely expectant lot," upholding *some* form of eschatology. But even that formula does not carry conviction. During the nineteenth century the postmillennial hope elided with the secular idea of progress, eventually ceasing altogether to be other-worldly. Advance, according to such broad-minded evangelicals as Hugh Price Hughes, would take place within this world and the Christian hope would merge into social reconstruction. An assertive eschatology was not always firmly grasped by evangelicals. It joins Dochuk's other candidates for addition to the way of characterizing evangelicals as a feature prominent in the twentieth century but not consistently so before. All of them prevailed at a particular time, but not throughout the course of evangelical history. The quadrilateral remains a four-sided device.

104. Mark Hutchinson and John Wolffe, *A Short History of Global Evangelicalism* (Cambridge: Cambridge University Press, 2012), 19.

Apostles of Reason, is not dwelt on in *Evangelicalism in Modern Britain*.[107] Yet authority was often at issue among British evangelicals, too. Over 150 years Anglican evangelicals held an annual Islington Clerical Meeting precisely to set out an official line on ecclesiastical issues. Eminent speakers delivered pronouncements that functioned rather like the deliverances of a magisterium.[108] And Worthen makes an important point that we share over the composition of the evangelical movement. In late twentieth-century America, she shows, it encompassed not just those of Reformed and Methodist pedigree but also groups such as sections of Mennonites and Churches of Christ. Neither originated as evangelical bodies, but they became so over time. So there is much common ground in our analyses.

Yet we do disagree. Worthen explains that the quadrilateral proved inadequate in her exploration of the debates taking place in the late twentieth-century evangelical world. The quadrilateral, she submits, provides a characterization that is "static." The category of "born again" does not fit all evangelicals because some saw conversion as incremental. And biblicism is too imprecise to be illuminating. On each of these questions I should not wish to concede. The quadrilateral is intended to be dynamic, not static, altering with the times. As Dochuk remarks, it has "functioned differently across generations." Conversion among evangelicals can indeed be gradual, but that is fully acknowledged in *Evangelicalism in Modern Britain*. The process varied enormously between denominations and at different points in time, often encompassing slow and unconscious varieties. As for biblicism, the pages of Worthen's book give eloquent testimony to its centrality in the evangelical movement. The debates over inerrancy were symptoms of the unfading priority of scripture. I should wish to stand by the value of the quadrilateral.

Perhaps a suggestion may be allowed. Worthen concentrates on the anxieties of what in *Apostles of Reason* she calls "the evangelical imagination."[109] Its preoccupations were the relation of faith and reason, the question of personal salvation and the tension between personal belief and the public square. She concedes that the content of these debates was not unique to evangelicals, for similar issues rocked the Roman Catholic Church during the same period.

---

107. Molly Worthen, *Apostles of Reason: The Crisis of Authority in American Evangelicalism* (New York: Oxford University Press, 2014).

108. D. W. Bebbington, "The Islington Conference," in Andrew Atherstone and John Maiden, eds., *Evangelicalism and the Church of England in the Twentieth Century: Reform, Resistance and Renewal* (Woodbridge, Suffolk: Boydell Press, 2014), 48–67.

109. Worthen, *Apostles of Reason*, chap. 11, especially page 264.

My suggestion is that the *way* in which these issues were addressed more than their content reflects a distinctive evangelical ethos. That is because the theme of faith and reason reflects an emphasis on the Bible, the subject of personal salvation arises from concern with the cross and conversion, and the personal belief/public square antithesis emerges from strains over contrasting modes of activism. Consequently, these anxieties derive from biblicism, crucicentrism, conversionism, and activism. The debates discussed in *Apostles of Reason* illustrate the prominence of the aspects of the quadrilateral.

Conclusion

The commentators on the quadrilateral have raised a series of questions that stimulate much further thought but not a significant change of mind. Its four elements do seem to reflect the nature of evangelicalism. There is no persuasive call to add to their number and certainly no reason to drop any of them. Perhaps to my surprise, I find I want to uphold a modern equivalent of the Vincentian canon. In the fifth century Vincent of Lérins taught that Christian truth was what was believed *ubique, semper et ab omnibus*: everywhere, always, and by all. I still believe that emphases on cross, Bible, conversion, and activism reflect the reality of the evangelical movement *ubique, semper et ab omnibus*.

CHAPTER 7

Evangelicals and Unevangelicals: The Contested History of a Word

Linford D. Fisher

In this article Linford Fisher, associate professor of history at Brown University, subjects conventions about writing "evangelical history" to sharp chronological and conceptual scrutiny. In his view, static, "essentialist," or "transhistorical" definitions miss the fluidity, dynamism, and flexibility of a concept that has passed through three general stages (meaning basically anti-Catholic, expressing "true" or active Protestant faith, and in the twentieth century used to denote a univocal concept). This article, which is abridged here, can be read in its entirety in *Religion and American Culture* 26, no. 2 (Summer 2016): 184–226. It is used here by permission of the editors of *Religion and American Culture*.

Besides over a dozen articles and book chapters, Professor Fisher is the author of *The Indian Great Awakening: Religion and the Shaping of Native Cultures in Early America* (Oxford University Press, 2012) and coauthor of *Decoding Roger Williams: The Lost Essay of Rhode Island's Founding Father* (Baylor University Press, 2014).

*　　　*　　　*

> *"Not Evangelical"! and who is this,*
> *With serpent's tongue, that dares the sentence hiss?"[1]*
> —Day K. Lee, Universalist minister, 1841

1. Day K. Lee, "Universalists Are Not Evangelical Christians," *Evangelical Magazine and Gospel Advocate* 12, no. 7 (February 12, 1841): 56. The *Evangelical Magazine and Gospel Advocate* was a Universalist periodical. The quotation given here is the opening two lines of a longer satirical critique of conservative Protestants for excluding Universalists from the "evangelical" fold in the antebellum era. Lee served as a minister in

Francis Peabody was offended. Representatives from a wide variety of Protestant denominations in Boston had come together in January 1912 to organize and attend one of the popular "Men and Religion Forward" crusades that were taking the country by storm. With a motto of "More Men for Religion; More Religion for Men," the movement intended to rescue Protestant churches from feminization by getting males of all ages back into the pews. The Boston program was sponsored by a broad assortment of Protestant men's organizations (including the Young Men's Christian Association) and invited the participation of virtually every Protestant denomination, with at least one notable exception: the Unitarians. The rationale for excluding Unitarians, as Peabody, a Harvard professor and practicing Unitarian, protested in *The Christian Register* was that its planners felt that "the movement would therefore be more effective if it were definitely 'evangelical.'"[2] Pittsburgh Unitarian minister L. Walter Mason was equally irate, so he immediately fired off a twelve-page pamphlet addressing the issue head-on, as the title suggested: *Are Unitarians Evangelical?*

Mason's answer to his own question, perhaps surprisingly to modern readers, was an unambiguous "yes." And this was not the first time Unitarians had been denied the title of "evangelical." When the Inter-Church Conference on Federation was held in New York City in 1905, Unitarian delegates were excluded because, as the officers of the conference explained, although Unitarians were "regarded as Christians," they "are not 'evangelical.'"[3] Mason had protested in 1905, and he did the same in 1912. For Mason, to be "evangelical" was to devote oneself primarily to the teachings of Jesus as found in the first four books of the New Testament, or the Gospels. Unitarians were therefore even more evangelical than their supposedly evangelical detractors, since conservative Protestants (in his view) fixated on the Pauline epistles and historic creeds drawn from them. "Unitarians," he reasoned, "because they draw their chief inspiration from Jesus as expressed in the Gospels, are pre-eminently the evangelical people."[4] In this way, Mason performed a brilliant reversal, essen-

---

Universalist churches in Salem, Massachusetts, and Brooklyn, New York. Abel Thomas, *A Century of Universalism in Philadelphia and New York* (Philadelphia, 1872), 332.

2. Francis Peabody, Letter to the Editor, *Christian Register*, January 18, 1912, as quoted in L. Walter Mason, *Are Unitarians Evangelical?: Or Orthodoxy Based Upon the Teaching of Paul, Unitarianism Based Upon the Teaching of Jesus* ([Pittsburgh], 1912), 2. I am grateful to Tim Grundmeier for securing a copy of Mason's booklet from the Moody Memorial Library at Baylor University.

3. Ibid., 3.

4. Ibid.

tially inverting who was in and who was out by juxtaposing the "Orthodox" (his Protestant critics) with "the evangelicals" (Unitarians).

Mason's surprising protest draws back the curtain on the often overlooked, contested, and varied history of the use of the word "evangelical." Historians and political pundits alike seem perfectly comfortable using the term with reference to theologically conservative Protestants between the eighteenth century and the present, often in ways that assume an identifiable core or center that was unchanged across centuries. Far from ever having a stable, fixed meaning, however, "evangelical" has always been a contested and elastic term in western Christian history, as Mason's analysis suggests.

In part, this identification of a stable "evangelicalism" throughout American history is a result of a particular set of developments, both historically and historiographically, which historians themselves helped to shape. Although scholars used the word "evangelical" in academic articles dating from the mid-to-late nineteenth century, starting in the late 1960s and 1970s—during the height of self-conscious conservative Protestant political, cultural, and social mobilization—historians took an increasingly active interest in thinking about the possible historical roots of such a movement.[5] Such interest in the academy was also the result of the recovery of American religious history in the 1960s and 1970s, all of which led to an outpouring of articles and books on the topic of identifying and understanding "evangelicals" in American history.[6]

5. "Evangelical" insiders, too, sought to construct historical continuities between the 1970s and prior epochs in American religious history. See, for example, Donald W. Dayton, *Discovering an Evangelical Heritage* (New York: Harper & Row, 1976).

6. For the renewed interest in American religious history, see Henry F. May, "The Recovery of American Religious History," *The American Historical Review* 70, no. 1 (October 1964): 79–92. Notably, however, in 1964, "evangelicals" barely registered in May's recovery project regarding America's religious past (he only uses the term once, in a footnote). A decade later, that had changed drastically. For scholarship on historical "evangelicals" in the 1970s, see as a representative sample: Rhys Isaac, "Evangelical Revolt: The Nature of the Baptists' Challenge to the Traditional Order in Virginia, 1765 to 1775," *The William and Mary Quarterly* 31, no. 3 (July 1974): 345; John B. Boles, *The Great Revival, 1787–1805: The Origins of the Southern Evangelical Mind* (Lexington: University Press of Kentucky, 1972); James Brewer Stewart, "Evangelicalism and the Radical Strain in Southern Antislavery Thought During the 1820s," *The Journal of Southern History* 39, no. 3 (August 1, 1973): 379–96; Stephen E. Berk, *Calvinism versus Democracy; Timothy Dwight and the Origins of American Evangelical Orthodoxy* (Hamden, Conn.: Archon Books, 1974); Drew Gilpin Faust, "Evangelicalism and the Meaning of the Proslavery Argument: The Reverend Thornton Stringfellow of Virginia,"

In short, the discovery by historians of "evangelicals" in American history corresponded to the rise of a particular kind of American evangelicalism in the 1970s that needed a historical explanation.[7]

Since the 1970s, a *doctrinal*, or "essentialist," understanding of what "evangelical" has signified has largely been the default definition for historians and contemporary political commentators, which often involves an attempt to create uninterrupted continuity with the past in service of the present.[8] The prime example of this is David Bebbington's now classic 1989 study, *Evangelicalism in Modern Britain: A History from the 1730s to the 1980s*, from which comes the most often-cited definition of evangelicalism. Bebbington identifies four defining traits of evangelicals: conversionism: "the belief that lives need to be changed";

The Virginia Magazine of History and Biography 85, no. 1 (January 1, 1977): 3–17; David F. Wells and John D. Woodbridge, eds., *The Evangelicals: What They Believe, Who They Are, Where They Are Changing* (Nashville: Abingdon Press, 1975).

7. Although it is outside the parameters of this essay, it is important to note that, since the 1970s, historians have applied the label "evangelical" to groups that rarely claimed it, like the large majority of African Protestants, slave and free, in American history; the large number of women who were involved in conservative American Protestant social reform but who seem to have been less concerned with the specific label and identity of "evangelical"; and even Christianized American Indians in the colonial period. See, for example, Catherine A. Brekus, *Sarah Osborn's World: The Rise of Evangelical Christianity in Early America* (New Haven: Yale University Press, 2013); Paul Harvey, *Freedom's Coming: Religious Culture and the Shaping of the South from the Civil War through the Civil Rights Era* (Chapel Hill: University of North Carolina Press, 2005); Julius H. Rubin, *Tears of Repentance: Christian Indian Identity and Community in Colonial Southern New England* (Lincoln: University of Nebraska Press, 2013), 117.

8. D. Bruce Hindmarsh, *John Newton and the English Evangelical Tradition: Between the Conversions of Wesley and Wilberforce* (New York: Oxford University Press, 1996), 8–9. This vein of scholarship has been occasionally challenged, even from within the subfield of evangelical scholarship. See, for example, D. G. Hart, *Deconstructing Evangelicalism: Conservative Protestantism in the Age of Billy Graham* (Grand Rapids, MI: Baker Academic, 2005); Donald W. Dayton and Robert K. Johnston, *The Variety of American Evangelicalism*, 1st edition (Knoxville: University of Tennessee Press, 1991); Robert Krapohl and Charles H. Lippy, *The Evangelicals: A Historical, Thematic, and Biographical Guide* (Westport, Conn: Greenwood, 1999). For important but dated discussions of the historiography of evangelicalism, see Leonard I. Sweet, "The Evangelical Tradition in America," in *The Evangelical Tradition in America* (Mercer University Press, 1984); Leonard I. Sweet, "Wise as Serpents, Innocent as Doves: The New Evangelical Historiography," *Journal of the American Academy of Religion* 56, no. 3 (October 1, 1988): 397–416.

activism: "the expression of the gospel in effort"; biblicism: "a particular regard for the Bible"; and crucicentrism: "a stress on the sacrifice of Christ on the cross."[9] Although Bebbington's "evangelical quadrilateral" continues to be widely cited— indeed, the National Association of Evangelicals (founded in the U.S. in 1942) also uses it in its official self-definition—scholars have gone to great lengths to further clarify what they see as a continuous movement over time.[10] This is partly because Bebbington's four features are often insufficient to adequately separate "evangelicals" from Protestants more generally in many eras of American history. Some historians have added additional traits to what it means (or meant) to be "evangelical," such as an emphasis on the Holy Spirit in revival, belief in original sin, justification by faith, substitutionary atonement, and sanctification through the power of the Holy Spirit (for a total of nine important elements).[11] Others offer roughly analogous "theological emphases" as "preconditions" for evangelical belief and identity that are shared by insiders across time and space.[12]

History is rarely so tidy, however; movements even less so. The limitations in transhistorical, doctrinal-based definitions of what it meant to be "evangelical" become especially evident when one considers the long and surprising history of this word from the early modern period through the mid-twentieth century, or roughly 1500 through 1950. From the Protestant Reformation through the early twentieth century, to be "evangelical" was most often a Protestant-inflected way of being in the world, not necessarily a fixed doctrinal position to which to assent (even though particular theological positions and practices were often important to those who employed the term). It was a flexible and dynamic idiom, intended to communicate a relative biblical authenticity by those who wielded it. As Chicago Divinity School professor Gerald B. Smith noted in 1922, to be "evangelical" was not simply to be Prot-

9. David W. Bebbington, *Evangelicalism in Modern Britain: A History from the 1730s to the 1980s*, new edition (Routledge, 1989), 3.

10. "What Is an Evangelical?" http://www.nae.net/church-and-faith-partners /what-is-an-evangelical, accessed 9/20/13.

11. Thomas S. Kidd, *The Great Awakening: The Roots of Evangelical Christianity in Colonial America* (New Haven: Yale University Press, 2007), xiv; Mark A. Noll, *The Rise of Evangelicalism: The Age of Edwards, Whitefield and the Wesleys* (IVP Academic, 2004).

12. Mark Hutchinson and John Wolffe, *A Short History of Global Evangelicalism*, 1st ed. (Cambridge University Press, 2012), 10–11. W. R. Ward has suggested that a cluster of shared ideas existed across confessions and geographies by the early eighteenth century, which formed an "evangelical hexagon." See W. R. Ward, *Early Evangelicalism: A Global Intellectual History, 1670–1789* (Cambridge University Press, 2006), 4.

estant, but to be seriously Protestant, that is, to give "evidence of a profounder religious life."[13] Therefore, to be "evangelical" was at once a critique and a practice; it was a pursuit of experiential purity, but that purity was incessantly relative to the other modes of Christianity that were out there. Additionally, the word often represented an eminently flexible category of relative comparison capable of being wielded by a surprisingly wide array of individuals. It was used by faithful insiders, brandished polemically by outsiders, imposed on groups who would never have claimed it themselves, appropriated by groups and individuals considered by insiders to be "unevangelical," and used in descriptive ways by historians, scholars of religion, and, later, political pundits. It is a term that has been associated over time (either through appropriation or imposition) with a wide swath of conservative Protestant groups, of course, but also Catholics, Christian Scientists, Unitarians, Universalists, and even Buddhists and Hindus.

In particular, this essay seeks to recover three overlooked dimensions of the use of the word "evangelical": first, the firmly Protestant and even anti-Catholic implication of the term that spanned the history of Protestantism from the 1520s to the twentieth century; second, the relative authenticity, "true-Christian" usage, which contained within it a strong "primitivist" impulse with reference to New Testament Christianity; and third, the contested nature of the word, particularly in the nineteenth and early twentieth centuries, when "evangelical" identity supposedly started to become more recognizable. This is not to deny the possibility of like-minded connection-making in particular eras, or that many "evangelical" leaders and laypersons believed that doctrine was essential to their identity and movement. To highlight these three historical aspects of the use of the word "evangelical" is simply to restore the dynamism, multiplicity, and contestation over time to this history that transhistorical doctrinal definitions largely fail to sufficiently recognize. To be "evangelical" meant different things to different people across time and space, and its meanings and usages changed over time. Nineteenth-century "evangelical" concerns were different from twentieth-century concerns, which were both different from the eighteenth century. Our understanding of the use of the word "evangelical" must, at minimum, accurately reflect these changes over time and varying contexts. We need to recognize that "evangelical" was almost always a polemical, contested, and constructed term and idea rather than something objectively existing in a timeless past.

13. Gerald Birney Smith, "The Spirit of Evangelical Christianity," *The Journal of Religion* 2, no. 6 (November 1, 1922): 627.

Although the history of the use of the word "evangelical" is less an or-derly progression from one meaning to the next and more of layers of accre-tions over time, there are several key turning points that can be identified. Sustained use of the word "evangelical" started with the sixteenth-century Protestant reformers as a way to designate themselves as the true Christians. By the late seventeenth century, usage of the word was highly variable, of-ten with reference to Protestantism, the New Testament era, or notions of relative true-Christianity; such references were almost always adjectival or adverbial ("evangelical prayers"). It was not until the late eighteenth and early nineteenth centuries that a distinct, self-conscious, nominal usage ("evan-gelical" as a noun) came into circulation, but again, largely retaining older meanings of Protestant and "true-Christian." In the early nineteenth century, the word also began to have a more direct association with evangelization and missionary activity, particularly in a global context. But the nineteenth century usages of the word were highly contested, with various movements and groups—like Universalists, Unitarians, and Christian Scientists—making claim to the word, which largely had a positive, true-Christian connotation. By the 1890s, the word "evangelical" came to encompass almost every single Protestant group, by some estimates. This widespread appropriation and ap-plication disintegrated during the opening decades of the twentieth century. By the 1940s, a new iteration of "evangelicalism" laid exclusive claim to the word, and others who had previously appropriated the term as a positive way to mark true Christianity largely conceded the word to this particular vein of theologically and politically conservative Protestantism. But throughout the preceding centuries, the word had been widely contested, had multiple and overlapping meanings, and served as a convenient shorthand for true-gospel Christianity.

"Evangelical" as Protestant and Anti-Catholic

Looking at the use of the word "evangelical" in its various historical contexts suggests it has often referenced a specifically Protestant identity vis-à-vis Ca-tholicism. This is partly because the first widespread early modern use of the word was by the first "Protestant" reformers in the 1520s. As historians and theologians have often pointed out, the origins of the word "evangelical" are rooted in the New Testament. The Greek word *euangelion* means simply "gos-pel," or "good news." The word itself was most associated with the Christian gospel—the idea of God incarnate for the salvation of humanity—in most of

Christian history. Medieval and early modern usage, however, likely emerged more directly from the Latin variants of the word, including *evangelica*. . . .

Although such Latin uses of "evangelical" were widespread throughout ancient Christianity and medieval Catholicism (simply with reference to "gospel"), in the early modern period the term quickly took on a new inflection in the 1520s. Early leaders of what became the Protestant movement identified a distinctive approach to Christian practice and theology that they often believed was more gospel-centered, Bible-based, and authentic than Catholicism, for which they often used the descriptor "evangelical." Protestant reformers such as Martin Luther, William Tyndale, and Menno Simons all repeatedly used the word within a decade of each other in the 1530s, indicating how rapidly the word came into usage in a wide variety of contexts (Germany, England, and the Netherlands). Protestant creeds such as the Second Helvetic Confession (1566) repeatedly invoke "evangelical" to describe the project of recovering what they saw as authentic Christian belief and practice. Scholars of the early modern period have long recognized and repeated this designation of early Protestants as "evangelicals" in part because this was, from very early on, a term associated with the Reformation.

Nonetheless, an older understanding of the meaning of "evangelical" persisted among Catholics, who refused to simply surrender the term to Protestants—which is not entirely surprising given its ancient usage. As just one example, the Jesuit priest Alonso de Sandoval, serving in Cartagena (Colombia) in the early seventeenth century, published a catechism for enslaved Africans who arrived in his city that purported to be a *catechismo evangelico* ("evangelical catechism") for the "Ethiopians."[14] . . . But the vast majority of post-1520s early modern usage was with reference to an emerging Protestantism.

This "Reformational" use of "evangelical" had several meanings and defining characteristics. First, at the broadest possible level, these Protestant reformers believed they were living in an "evangelical dispensation" that was inaugurated with the coming of Jesus and the new covenant between God and his people as described in the New Testament. The gospel dispensation was one of grace that contrasted starkly with the Old Testament and the old covenant of works. Second, many Protestants viewed the core message of this evangelical/gospel-centered dispensation as having been obscured or cor-

---

14. Alonso de Sandoval, Francisco de Lyra, and Bartolomé Arteaga, *Naturaleza, policia sagrada i profana, costumbres i ritos, disciplina i catechismo evangelico de todos los etiopes* (En Sevilla, por Francisco de Lira impresor, 1627). See also José de Acosta, *Historia natural y moral de las Indias* (Madrid: R. Anglés, 1894), 348.

rupted in the medieval period, and they were now part of a new movement to return to a New Testament–based, gospel-centered Christianity. So while the "evangelical dispensation" might reach back to the New Testament, it was being recovered anew in the early modern period with the rise of Protestantism. The contrast between "legal" and "evangelical" was repeated dozens of times in early modern English texts and sermons that had these dual contrasts between the Old Testament and New Testament, between Catholicism and gospel Christianity. Even John Locke contrasted the "Mosaical" law and the "Evangelical Law of God" in his writings.[15] This Reformational usage of the word set the tone for the following three hundred years within Protestantism: that of using "evangelical" as a tag of gospel- and New Testament–centered Christianity.[16] . . .

This basic presumption of "evangelical" as "Protestant" even in non-German-speaking contexts continued far longer than previously recognized.[17] This association was stated clearly when the New Hampshire Assembly passed its full state constitution in 1784. Article Six of Part One of the Constitution (the Bill of Rights) explicitly connected "evangelical" with "Protestant": "As morality and piety, rightly grounded on **evangelical** principles, will give the best and greatest security to the government . . . the people of this state have the right to impower . . . the support and maintenance of public **protestant** teachers of piety, religion, and morality."[18] . . .

Some of the institutional apparatus that conservative Protestant "evangelicals" began to build in the mid-nineteenth century included within its framing a clear sense of being Protestant, in a strongly comparative, anti-Catholic way. In 1838, Samuel S. Schmucker, a professor at Gettysburg Theological Seminary, published a pamphlet titled *Plan for Protestant Union*, which proposed

15. See, for example, John Locke and Robert McNamee, "John Locke to James Tyrrell, 14 August 1690," July 1, 2013, http://www.e-enlightenment.com/item/lockjoO Uo040110_1key001cor.

16. The various definitions in the *Oxford English Dictionary* reflect these various uses as well. See entry for "evangelical," *OED Online*, accessed September 27, 2012.

17. See, for example, Andrew Croswell, *What Is Christ to Me, If He Is Not Mine? Or, A Seasonable Defence of the Old Protestant Doctrine of Justifying Faith* (Boston, 1745), 34.

18. New Hampshire State Constitution, Part 1, Article 6, http://www.lonang.com /exlibris/organic/1784-nhr.htm, accessed March 18, 2013. Emphasis added. Notably, the phrase "evangelical principles" was replaced with "high principles" at some point in the nineteenth century, although the official online copy of the Constitution does not note when this substitution was made. http://www.nh.gov/constitution/billofrights .html, accessed March 18, 2013.

a collection of interdenominational Protestant churches who would agree to a central, conservative, Protestant creed, while still remaining within their respective denominations. Although Schmucker's ideas found little traction in the U.S., he was one of the seventy-five American clergymen who traveled to London to help form the Evangelical Alliance, founded in 1846 as a means of bringing about international Protestant cooperation. The aims of the Evangelical Alliance were broad, but central to its foundation and early activity was a strong and public repudiation of "Popery," perhaps spurred on by the passage of the Catholic Emancipation Act in Great Britain in 1829. In 1851, the Glasgow Committee of the Evangelical Alliance held an essay competition for the best paper "against Romanism," for which the Rev. J. A. Wylie of Edinburgh won the prize for an essay titled "The Papacy."[19] . . .

"Evangelical" as True-Christianity and Primitivist

Another common (and related) usage of "evangelical" over the past five hundred years has been to simply denote practices, feelings, and beliefs as more authentic, biblical, and true-Christian than other possible ways of enacting Christianity. For most of the early modern period (and, indeed, even up through the early nineteenth century), "evangelical" was not something one *was* as much as it was a way to describe a supposedly correct orientation to Christian practices and beliefs. Consequently, the word was invoked in a way that, while it included doctrinal content, was a way to signify to the reader the nature of authentic Christianity (from the perspective of the writer). What is surprising is the longevity of such usages through the nineteenth century and even beyond and the fact that it was used in this way by a wide variety of individuals who would in no other way be considered to be "evangelical" by current scholars.

Because "evangelical" was commonly used as a way of describing the authenticity of what one did, from the early sixteenth through the late eighteenth centuries, "evangelical" was almost always used adjectivally, as a descriptor of something else. Rarely did it stand on its own as a noun.[20] In many ways,

---

19. John W. Ewing, *Goodly Fellowship: A Centenary Tribute to the Life and Work of the World's Evangelical Alliance, 1846–1946* (Marshall, Morgan & Scott, 1946), 26, 49. . . .

20. Some historians have recognized this usage. Hutchinson and Wolffe, for example, parenthetically recognize that the actual word "evangelical" "has a much longer history, as both a noun and an adjective." This important insight goes relatively unex-

"evangelical" also had a deeply primitivist strain to it, with the New Testament (and especially the Gospels) as its foremost referent. To be "evangelical" was to lay claim to the closest possible approximation of New Testament Christianity—a religious orientation that by default delegitimized Catholicism in the process but also could serve polemical purposes in intra-Protestant debates. . . .

Looking at the usage of the word in this context helps us to reassess the supposed origins of "evangelicalism." Scholars point to the First Great Awakening (1730s–1740s; often termed the "Evangelical Awakening" by British scholars) as the beginnings of a discernible movement called "evangelicalism."[21] But a few historians have increasingly pushed back in time the search for origins to include the mid-seventeenth-century religious revitalization movements within Lutheranism, often referred to as "Pietism," or even earlier, with the published works of Johann Arndt, starting with *True Christianity* (1605).[22] Between 1680 and 1740, according to some historians, a major transition was taking place across Continental Europe, the British Isles, and British North America. Noting the various strands of Continental Pietism and the ways it paralleled developments in the British Isles and even North America, historian W. R. Ward asserted that "by the early eighteenth century a recognisable evangelicalism had emerged from different confessional starting points."[23]

The main emphases of these vastly disparate and geographically disconnected groups of people seem to have been an interest in revivalism, a more emotive, dramatic experience of conversion, and a desire to connect with other

plored and essentially has no bearing on how the authors understand the eighteenth century as the supposed origins of the movement. Hutchinson and Wolffe, *A Short History of Global Evangelicalism*, 6.

21. This is so widespread in the literature that only a representative sample can be given here. The most recent definitive work on global evangelicalism makes Jonathan Edwards and the 1730s the official start of "evangelicalism," with the Continental pietistic reforms of the late seventeenth century as "the prehistory of the evangelical movement." Hutchinson and Wolffe, *A Short History of Global Evangelicalism*, 25. See also Kidd, *The Great Awakening: The Roots of Evangelical Christianity in Colonial America*; Douglas A. Sweeney, *The American Evangelical Story: A History of the Movement* (Baker Academic, 2005); Ward, *Early Evangelicalism*; Jonathan M. Yeager, ed., *Early Evangelicalism: A Reader* (Oxford University Press, USA, 2013).

22. W. R. Ward is perhaps the strongest advocate for locating the origins of "evangelicalism" prior to the Evangelical Revival / First Great Awakening. See, for example, Ward, *Early Evangelicalism*, 6–7.

23. Ibid., 3.

like-minded people. But aside from these foci, there is little to distinguish these early eighteenth-century "evangelicals" from other Protestants in this time period except that they were at times the "hotter sort of Protestants," as Patrick Collinson so aptly called the puritan radicals of Elizabethan England a century and a half prior.[24]

Perhaps historians have been misled by the use of the word "evangelical" in this time period, but a close examination reveals a fundamental continuity between the sixteenth, seventeenth, and eighteenth centuries in terms of a primarily Reformational, true-Christian usage of "evangelical." Cotton Mather (whom historians have sometimes identified as the first "American evangelical"), in his two-volume history of New England church history, *Magnalia Christi Americana* (1702), uses "evangelical" thirty-nine times in a wide variety of ways.[25] Mostly the term is used with reference to "true-gospel-order," or being gospel-centered, which resonates with a Reformational usage; that is to say, for Mather "evangelical" is a descriptor to indicate authentic Christianity, in his view. . . .

Similarly, the revivalism surrounding the Great Awakening also spurred a minor flurry of periodicals devoted to documenting the spread of the revivals and to the cultivation of the inner spiritual life, most notably the *Christian History* and the *Christian Monthly History*. Historians have called these publications—in particular Thomas Prince's *Christian History*—the "first evangelical magazines," and Mark Noll has suggested that "Evangelical self-consciousness increased measurably as articles from the magazines were circulated, read publicly and reprinted in other papers."[26] Although there seemingly was an increased transatlantic awareness of like-minded believers in this time period, particularly regarding revivalism, it is not self-evident why this should be labeled "evangelical" or tied to late-twentieth-century conservative Protestants in terms of doctrinal continuity. Given the relatively short duration of these revivalist periodicals, and without the benefit of knowing what comes later in the nineteenth and twentieth centuries, it makes more sense to take them at

24. Patrick Collinson, *The Elizabethan Puritan Movement* (Jonathan Cape, 1967), 27.

25. On Cotton Mather as an early "evangelical," see Richard F. Lovelace, *The American Pietism of Cotton Mather: Origins of American Evangelicalism* (Wipf & Stock Publishers, 2007); Rick Kennedy, *The First American Evangelical: A Short Life of Cotton Mather* (Grand Rapids, Michigan: Wm. B. Eerdmans Publishing Co., 2015).

26. Noll, *The Rise of Evangelicalism*, 118. See also Susan Durden O'Brien, "A Study of the First Evangelical Magazines, 1740–1748," *The Journal of Ecclesiastical History* 27, no. 3 (1976): 255–75.

face value and in their contexts as what they present themselves to be, namely, publications that document the spread of revivalistic Protestantism for the encouragement of Christians on both sides of the Atlantic.[27] . . .

As gauged from the use of the word "evangelical," a transition to something more fully self-conscious and intentional did not take place until the late eighteenth century or early nineteenth century. One gauge of this is that, by the early nineteenth century, for the first time there was a proliferation of periodicals and associations and institutions with the word "evangelical" in their names, a usage that referenced an organizational self-consciousness in addition to being Protestant, Lutheran, or true-gospel. Although perhaps inflected with pro-Protestant, true-Christian assumptions, organizations and publications like the Evangelical Alliance, the Massachusetts Evangelical Missionary Society, the *Evangelical Magazine*, the *Vermont Evangelical Magazine*, and the *Evangelical Magazine and Missionary Chronicle* represented self-conscious attempts to associate under the umbrella of particular orientations to the life of faith and to the world, often in ways that transcended denominational boundaries. Additionally, nominative usages now coexisted alongside of ongoing adjectival and adverbial usages; writers refer to "evangelical Christianity" and "evangelical believers" in a way that seems to be a somewhat distinct mode of identification from prior centuries.[28]

27. As Hindmarsh notes, "none of the revival magazines lasted beyond 1748." D. Bruce Hindmarsh, *The Evangelical Conversion Narrative: Spiritual Autobiography in Early Modern England* (New York: Oxford University Press, 2005), 72. This is not to say that the Great Awakening should not be understood as a time of change. I am merely suggesting that with regard to parsing the origins and history of a distinct, self-conscious evangelicalism that feels "modern" and contemporary, neither the usage nor the self-conscious organization yet existed in the 1740s or even 1750s other than around ideas related to revivalism.

28. In England, organization under the umbrella of "evangelical" slowly reached a level that was not possible in the United States, simply because of the lack of an established church. Between roughly 1789 and 1850, there was an identifiable "Evangelical Party" within the Church of England that contrasted to the "High Party" and attracted a growing number of parishioners and ministers who wished to renew the church from within, not simply to leave it for a splinter movement, like Methodism. Members of the "Clapham Sect"—which worked to bring about the end of the slave trade in the British Empire—were associated with this "evangelical" movement within Anglicanism. Evangelical parties also existed within the Church of Ireland and the Episcopal Church of Scotland. George Reginald Balleine, *A History of the Evangelical Party in the Church of England* (Longmans, Green, and Co., 1908), vii. See also Bebbington, *Evangelicalism in Modern Britain*, 75–150.

By the early nineteenth century, the word "evangelical" took on yet another strong layer of meaning as it became increasingly associated with evangelization and missionary activity—particularly in a global context—than had previously been the case. The spread of Protestant Christianity at home and afar gained some urgency starting in the late sixteenth and early seventeenth centuries and reached a noticeable peak in the early nineteenth century. This often—although not always—occurred in tandem with those who increasingly self-identified with movements that were labeled "evangelical."[29] Dozens of missionary societies sprang into being in the opening decades of the nineteenth century, the most prominent of which in the U.S. was the American Board of Commissioners for Foreign Missions in 1810. Protestants took these developments as nothing less than the divine hand of God at work. . . . In this way, "evangelical" was frequently used to refer to persons or activities related to spreading Christianity (where later Christians might have used "evangelistic").

Importantly, however, evangelistic activity was hardly the exclusive domain of more activistic, revivalist, theologically conservative Protestants. Catholic missionaries still operated globally, and, indeed, even some of the Protestant missionary agencies and their missionaries were less revivalistic and more rationalistic. This included the Society for Propagating the Gospel among Indians and Others in North America, founded in Boston in 1787. Additionally, when Joseph Smith was building the Church of Jesus Christ of Latter-day Saints in the 1830s, he authorized the Twelve Apostles to appoint "'evangelical ministers' in large branches of the Church" to aid in the spread of Mormon restorationist principles and the supernatural giving of the Book of Mormon, even though Mormons otherwise never claimed to be (nor were perceived as) "evangelical" in the conservative Protestant sense.[30] Similarly, Catholic publications affirmed the "good morals and evangelical life" of Jesuit

---

29. Often overlooked in the discussions of Protestant missionary efforts are the various seventeenth- and eighteenth-century missionary societies, such as the New England Company (1649), the Society for the Propagation of the Gospel in Foreign Parts (1701), and the Scottish Society for the Propagation of Christian Knowledge (1709), and the Society for Propagating the Gospel among Indians and Others in North America (1787). See Linford D. Fisher, "'Not in Our Neighborhood': American Indians, the Founding of the SPGNA, and the Turn to International Missions in the Early Republic," *Common-Place* 15, no. 3 (2015). And for missionary attempts to the American Indians, see Linford D. Fisher, *The Indian Great Awakening: Religion and the Shaping of Indian Cultures in Early America* (New York: Oxford University Press, 2012).

30. Richard Lyman Bushman, *Joseph Smith: Rough Stone Rolling* (Random House LLC, 2007), 261.

priests, namely, "the zeal with which they labour for the salvation of souls."[31] And in 1908, Isidor Jacobs wrote a short essay in which he noted that some Christian ministers opposed Christian Science because "it is not an evangelical Christian sect," primarily because its practitioners "deny the divinity of Christ." However, he argued, since "evangelical churches" were those that "proclaim the glad tidings," Christian Science fit the definition perfectly, since Christian Scientists were spreading their teachings to those who had not heard them before, including Jews.[32]

Therefore, the meanings associated with the use of the word "evangelical" had grown by accretion over time, although in ways that were not universally agreed upon. It was a way for Protestants to distinguish themselves from Catholics; to denote particular true-Christian, primitivist practices; to signify a particular approach to reformed revivalism; to identify a particular branch in the Church of England; and a way of identifying Protestants who took seriously their Bibles, faith, piety, their own conversions, and the conversions of others. This took place in a new nineteenth-century oppositional context of liberal Protestantism and, as always, vis-à-vis Catholicism. Throughout, an older early modern adjectival and adverbial usage persisted. . . . Older meanings and usages of the word coexisted with newer ones intending to communicate an authentic, stand-above-the-crowd Christianity.

"Evangelical" as a Contested Category

Perhaps the most interesting component of the word "evangelical" is simply its highly contested history. Using the relatively fixed notion of a post-1970s "evangelicalism," historians have seemingly forgotten that, even in the nineteenth and early twentieth centuries, the appropriation and application of "evangelical" was surprisingly contentious, as a mostly desirable point of identification by groups and individuals who would not at all fit contemporary definitions of "evangelical." There simply was no one agreed-upon definition of what "evangelical" was, and a close reading of the sources reveals a robust conversation and contestation regarding the term.[33] Humorously, one critical

31. "Title 'Jesuit,'" *The Jesuit; Or, Catholic Sentinel* 1, no. 1 (September 5, 1829): 2.
32. Isidor Jacobs, "Christian Science from the Jewish View-Point," in *The Christian Science Journal*, vol. 26 (Christian Science Publishing Society, 1908), 215.
33. For a representative sample, see "Evangelical Preaching," *Christian Disciple* 4, no. 11 (November 4, 1816); "Evangelical Christians," *Universalist Watchman, Repository*

writer in 1867 who signed his/her name simply as "Unevangelical" defined "evangelical" as "the unrestrained liberty of private judgment."[34]

If one feature of the nineteenth century religious landscape was that "evangelical" became a way to draw particular lines demarcating more authentically serious and biblical Christians from the others (who, by implication, were less serious and less biblical), such line drawing was always subjective and contested. This can be seen most plainly in the various denominational listings and compendia that began appearing in the late eighteenth century. Some authors enumerated the various denominations in the United States without distinguishing categorically between the various groups. Such was the case when a "General Summary of the Principal Religious Denominations in the United States" was published in *The American Almanac and Repository of Useful Knowledge* in 1836.[35]

Some self-styled Protestant "evangelicals," however, wanted to be more nuanced, and often wrote as if such distinctions were easily made. In 1844, the American Presbyterian Robert Baird (himself invested in the American Bible Society and the American Sunday School Union) published a series of essays he had first written serially for a specifically European audience that was a bit flummoxed at the religious landscape in America.[36] In organizing and categorizing the denominations, Baird laid all of his partisan cards on the table. His first five books of *Religion in America* take the reader through the progression of church development in America from the opening years of colonization through the early national period. Baird then gives his particular

and *Chronicle* 16, no. 26 (January 11, 1845): 206; "On the Term Evangelical," *Christian Reformer; or Evangelical Miscellany* 1, no. 1 (July 1, 1828); "Evangelical Preaching," *Christian Advocate* 64, no. 1 (January 3, 1889): 1; "Evangelical; What Is It?," *New York Evangelist* 71, no. 36 (September 6, 1900): 6; "Evangelical Religion," *The Independent . . . Devoted to the Consideration of Politics, Social and Economic Tendencies, History, Literature, and the Arts* 9, no. 427 (February 5, 1857): 4; "Evangelical Christianity Contrasted with Rational Christianity," *The Utica Christian Repository* 2, no. 9 (September 1823); "Term 'Evangelical,'" *Washington Theological Repertory* 8, no. 15 (October 1, 1827): 681.

34. Unevangelical, "Evangelical," *German Reformed Messenger* 32, no. 32 (April 10, 1867): 2.

35. "General Summary of the Principal Religious Denominations in the United States," *The American Almanac and Repository of Useful Knowledge* (1836), 138ff.

36. Robert Baird, *Religion in America: Or an Account of the Origin, Relation to the State, and Present Condition of the Evangelical Churches in the United States: With Notices of the Unevangelical Denominations* (Harper & Brothers, 1844).

interpretation of the denominational landscape in the 1840s by devoting an entire book to "The Evangelical Churches in America" (Book VI) before turning to the "Unevangelical Denominations in America" (Book VII).

Baird's listing of "Evangelical Denominations" included most of the usual suspects later historians have tended to lump together, such as Baptists, Presbyterians, Methodists, and others; somewhat more surprisingly, Baird also included Quakers. [37] His list of "Unevangelical Denominations" included the Roman Catholic Church, Unitarians, Universalists, Swedenborgians and Tunkers, Jews, Rappists, Shakers, Mormons, Atheists, Deists, Socialists, and a few other groups like the Christian Connexion (who were Unitarian Baptists and the largest of these unevangelical groups after Catholics) and the Fourrierists.[38] Where *The American Almanac* saw an undifferentiated spectrum of American religious affiliation, Baird perceived a religious world sharply divided between "evangelicals" and "unevangelicals."

With regard to the "Evangelical Denominations," Baird struggled to articulate precisely what made them unique. Lacking any distinctive doctrinal core to highlight, Baird at times resorted to bland truisms, stating that "evangelical Protestant Churches" are churches "whose religion is the Bible, the whole Bible, and nothing but the Bible," a judgment most of the "Unevangelical Denominations" would have contested.[39] Likely realizing the inadequacy of such a definition, a few pages later Baird suddenly lists in exquisite detail the specific theological tenets of evangelical denominations that essentially lay out a Calvinistic, theologically conservative Protestant Christianity—entirely resonant with his own Presbyterian tradition.[40] But once again, Baird has to include several caveats, in this case noting that the Methodists and "some smaller bodies" reject predestination as well as the effectual keeping by God of the individual "through faith unto salvation."[41] Twelve years later, Baird's definition was once again far more simplistic: "When we speak of the great bulk of the Churches in American being Evangelical, we simply mean that they teach the doctrines of the Reformers of the sixteenth century, of the Apostles, and of the Saviour himself; the sum of which is, that there is salvation only through faith in Jesus Christ, as the 'Lamb of God which taketh away the sin

---

37. For a full listing of Baird's "Evangelical" churches, see Baird, *Religion in America*, xii.

38. Baird, *Religion in America*, xii.

39. Ibid., 270.

40. For a full listing, see ibid., 289–90.

41. Ibid.

of the world.'"[42] In this one definition, Baird boiled down "evangelical" identity to a firmly Protestant, primitivist vision of simple Jesus-centered focus on individual salvation, even as he admitted that some American "evangelicals" would balk at such a reduction of their religion.

The most important evidence of the elasticity of the term "evangelical," in fact, is the way in which it was appropriated by groups that were not usually considered so by other conservative Protestant denominations (nor by later scholars). Historian Nathan Hatch has suggested that in the late eighteenth and early nineteenth centuries, "rationalistic Christians—many of them Unitarians and Universalists—argued against evangelical orthodoxy by appealing to the Bible."[43] While this is certainly true in some cases, Unitarians and Universalists also used another overlooked strategy: inserting themselves *within* the "evangelical" orthodoxy by showing themselves to be more authentically faithful to the Bible than other conservative Protestants. . . .

In the nineteenth century, Unitarians and Universalists published magazines that contained "evangelical" in their titles. This led to the confusing situation in which Methodists, Presbyterians, Unitarians, and Universalists all published periodicals called the *Evangelical Repository* in the antebellum period. One had to be a close reader to recognize the slight doctrinal differences. The Unitarians published *The Evangelical Repertory* (1823–1824), *The Evangelical Repository* (1827–1828), and the *Utica Evangelical Magazine* (1828–1848), among others, while the Universalists published the *Evangelical Luminary* and the *Evangelical Universalist*. If theologically conservative, missionary-minded Protestants had their *Evangelical Magazine* (with two different versions being published in London and the United States in the late eighteenth and early nineteenth centuries), the Unitarians had their own, but with a titular addition that made them even more true-gospel-centered: *Evangelical Magazine and Gospel Advocate*. Even the *Universalist Watchman, Repository and Chronicle* ran essays encouraging emphases that other conservative Protestants might have imagined to be their own exclusive terrain, such as "evangelical conversion."[44]

---

42. Robert Baird, *State and Prospects of Religion in America: Being a Report Made at the Conference of the Evangelical Alliance, in Paris, August 25th, 1855* (London: Edward Suter, 1855), 58.

43. Nathan O. Hatch, *The Democratization of American Christianity* (New Haven: Yale University Press, 1989), 181–82.

44. "Evangelical Conversion," *Universalist Watchman, Repository and Chronicle* 3, no. 16 (August 13, 1831): 121.

The contestation over who could legitimately claim title to the word "evangelical" sometimes included newer movements on the American religious landscape, including Christian Science. Founded and cultivated in the late nineteenth century by Mary Baker Eddy on the principles of "the Mind is All-in-All" and "Mind Cure"—and the corollary that sin and sickness were illusions—Christian Science quickly gained adherents through Eddy's *Science and Health* (1875) and the founding of the First Church of Christ, Scientist, in Boston in 1879.[45] Although many more conservative Christians dismissed it as a dangerous and misleading form of Christian expression (the 1890 Religious Census listed them as "Non-Orthodox"), Christian Science leaders and other observers occasionally maintained that they were within the "evangelical" umbrella. . . .

But the most surprising use of the word "evangelical" in the nineteenth century was actually with reference to non-Christians. In the mid-1890s, the liberal Catholic theologian Merwin-Marie Snell published two essays in *The Biblical World* titled "Evangelical Hinduism" (1895) and "Evangelical Buddhism" (1896).[46] Tapping into the late-nineteenth-century collective American fascination with Asian religions symbolized in the World's Parliament of Religions as part of the World's Fair in Chicago in 1893, Snell's personal study of world religions led him to apply the term "evangelical" to certain Hindu and Buddhist traditions.[47] For Snell, these particular strands of Hinduism and Buddhism were evangelical because they taught the "*way of faith*," the subtext of which is clearly a reference to the ways in which they were more primitivist and authentic relative to the other Buddhist and Hindu sects around them (at least as defined through the lens of Snell's Christianity). But Snell also identified these particular Hindu and Buddhist sects as "evangelical" because of their particular emphasis on "salvation." With regard to Hinduism, he contended that "its plan of salvation is so thoroughly evangelical" that you only need to

45. Mary Baker Eddy, *Science and Health* (Boston: Christian Science Pub. Co., 1875), chap. 6.

46. Merwin-Marie Snell, "Evangelical Hinduism," *The Biblical World* 6, no. 4 (October 1, 1895): 270–77; Merwin-Marie Snell, "Evangelical Buddhism," *The Biblical World* 7, no. 3 (March 1, 1896): 182–88.

47. Snell's definition of evangelical was broad and encompassing, even within the Christian tradition: it is the impulse within Christianity in which "tired alike of the theological disputations, ceremonial complexities, casuistic moral laws, painful self-disciplines, and politico-ecclesiastic intrigues, men sought to throw aside all these things and to take refuge in a simple religion of loving trust in an all-sufficient personal human Saviour." Snell, "Evangelical Hinduism," 270–71.

replace the Vedic literature with the Bible, and the names of Rama and Krishna with Jesus, and the notion of a "triune cosmic operation in the Deity" with the Trinity, and one would be able to include it "as an irreproachable member of the evangelical family of churches."[48]

When Unitarians, Universalists, Christian Scientists, and even Catholics on behalf of Hindus and Buddhists used the term "evangelical," they were making a claim to a pure and authentic practice of religion, one that was in most cases Christianity-properly-understood-from-the-Gospels. Not all Unitarians, Universalists, and Christian Scientists laid claim to the word "evangelical," of course, but the claim is consistent enough and spans enough time (more than a century, in the case of Unitarians and Universalists) to illustrate that—no matter what historians have recently imposed in terms of doctrinal uniformity across time and space—in the nineteenth century the word had a sufficiently positive and elastic association that a surprisingly wide array of denominations and individuals fought over the right to use it legitimately.

Between the mid-nineteenth century and the early twentieth century, then, the trend regarding the use of "evangelical" by more broad-minded Christians tended toward *inclusivity*, not exclusivity. This was true even of some conservative Protestants, who occasionally included Unitarians and Universalists within the evangelical fold. When Philip Schaff, the Swiss-born Protestant church historian, compiled his masterful three-volume *Creeds of Christendom* in 1877, the eighth chapter of Volume One listed out the "Creeds of Modern Evangelical Denominations." Included in that list were the expected groups like the Congregationalists, Baptists, and Methodists; also included as "evangelical," however, were Quakers, Unitarians, Universalists, and the Catholic Apostolic Church (Irvingites)—all of which, notably, were part of the "Unevangelical" denominations according to Baird thirty years prior.[49] . . .

So ubiquitous was the use and application of the word "evangelical" for Protestants by the late nineteenth century, the term itself almost lost any sense of distinctive meaning. In 1890, the U.S. Federal Government began including a more detailed denominational classification in its decennial census. This census report, much like Baird's survey fifty years prior, divided American Prot-

48. Snell, "Evangelical Hinduism," 277.

49. Philip Schaff, *The Creeds of Christendom: The History of Creeds* (Harper, 1877), xv. Although, given Schaff's Germanic background, he may well have been using "evangelical" in a more classically Protestant vein (which, if so, merely highlights the continued vagueness of the term).

estants into "Evangelical" and "Non-Evangelical" categories. Of the 14,002,475 Protestants identified, a full 13,869,483 were listed as "Evangelical"; only 132,992 American Protestants were counted as "Non-Evangelical"—less than one percent of the total U.S. Protestant population.[50] This meant that in 1890, slightly more than 99 percent of American Protestants were labeled as "evangelical," which reveals the flexible, constructed nature of the term and the category, as well as the way in which the word had essentially lost its meaning apart from broader Protestant identity.

H. K. Carroll, who was in charge of the religious data collection and analysis for the 1890 census, explained some of the difficulties in denominational classification. Despite clearly listing who was in and who was out, Carroll admitted that "it is not easy to define clearly and to apply discriminatingly the term 'Evangelical.'"[51] Universalists were "evangelical" in his assessment, while Unitarians were not, primarily based on how rationalistic he perceived them to be. His classifications—like Baird's before him—were "more or less arbitrary," Carroll admitted, "and due allowance should be made for this fact."[52]

This purported pan-evangelical heyday did not last long, however. The 1906 federal report of "Religious Bodies" in the U.S. entirely dropped "evangelical" as an overarching category.[53] Other changes were afoot, too. One way of gauging when "evangelical" shifted from a widely-Protestant true-gospel-notion to one that more resembles contemporary understanding is when these other "unevangelical" groups gave up the title for themselves.[54] Unitarians and Universalists had been claiming the word "evangelical" from their very inception as distinct religious organizations in the early nineteenth century, something that continued into the early twentieth century, despite their repeated

50. H. K. Carroll, *The Religious Forces of the United States, Enumerated, Classified, and Described on the Basis of the Government Census of 1890* (New York: The Christian Literature Co., 1893), xlvi–xlvii; "Religious Aspect of the Last United States Census," in *The Christian Yearbook* (Dayton, OH: Christian Publishing Associates, 1894), 20–21. The "Non-Evangelical" denominations included Church of the New Jerusalem, Friends (Hicksite), German Evangelical Protestant, and Unitarians.

51. Carroll, *The Religious Forces of the United States, Enumerated, Classified, and Described on the Basis of the Government Census of 1890*, xviii.

52. Ibid., xlvi.

53. United States Bureau of the Census and William Chamberlin Hunt, *Religious Bodies: 1906* (U.S. Government Printing Office, 1910), 30–31. There is a category for "Evangelical Bodies" within the listing of Protestant groups, but it only contains two denominations: the Evangelical Association and the United Evangelical Church.

54. My thanks to Jeff Wilson for pushing me to think in this direction.

and insulting exclusion from the "evangelical" fold.[55] However, the in-print protests by Francis Peabody and L. Walter Mason in 1912 (mentioned in the introduction), amidst the growth of evangelicalism and its more culturally conservative counterpart, fundamentalism, seem to have been the beginning of the end in many ways.[56] In 1918, Francis Peabody wrote a letter to the *New York Times* complaining that the Young Women's Christian Association (YWCA) was using an "Evangelical test" to weed out non-evangelicals—particularly Unitarians—for leadership positions. Despite persistent rejection from the YWCA and its counterpart, the Young Men's Christian Association (YMCA), Unitarian churches for several decades had "unstintingly supported both organizations."[57] Peabody took the YWCA and YMCA to task for insisting on hair-splitting doctrinal distinction during real war-time need (that a "cup of cocoa shall be poured by none but evangelical hands"). He suggested instead that both organizations live up to their professed Christianity, thereby saving themselves from "disingenuous orthodoxy."[58] But not once did Peabody insist that Unitarians were "evangelicals," too, as he had in 1912.

Within half a century after Mason's short printed protest in 1912, the Unitarians and Universalists had given up the fight entirely. . . .

*　　　　　*　　　　　*

Although it is difficult to pin down a precise turning point, by the 1940s a particular era of contestation over the meaning of the term "evangelical" largely came to a close. Although the sources and roots of this slow shift were multiple, the rise of Protestant fundamentalism as a more culturally militant form of "evangelicalism" seems to have shaped public discourse surrounding what it meant to be "evangelical" and cast "evangelicalism" in a more narrow, tightly defined, negatively tinged way. The simultaneous rise of the Social Gospel in the late nineteenth and early twentieth centuries alongside of Holiness and

---

55. The U.S. Federal Census of 1890, for example, listed only four "Non-Evangelical" denominations; with 67,749 members, Unitarians were the most numerous of the four. Carroll, *The Religious Forces of the United States, Enumerated, Classified, and Described on the Basis of the Government Census of 1890*, xlvii; "Religious Aspect of the Last United States Census," 21.

56. Mason, *Are Unitarians Evangelical?*

57. Francis G. Peabody, "War No Time for Sectarianism," *New York Times*, March 31, 1918, 62.

58. Ibid.

Pentecostal movements only accentuated the multiplicity of new Protestant pathways. The perceived public humiliation of "fundamentalism" as enshrined in the Scopes (Monkey) Trial held in Dayton, Tennessee, in 1925, while perhaps not *the* turning point, surely hints at a slow but sure slide in the popularity of "fundamentalist" and "evangelical" as a positive point of identification and organization for a growing number of Protestant Christians. This shift in sentiment is captured in part by the noted writer and satirist H. L. Mencken, who in his 1925 obituary of William Jennings Bryan (a professed fundamentalist and three-time presidential candidate who served as the public prosecutor in the Scopes Trial) in *The Baltimore Evening Sun*, smirked that "evangelical Christianity, as everyone knows, is founded upon hate, as the Christianity of Christ was founded upon love."[59]

In the United States, the 1930s brought a growing chorus of more culturally engaged but theologically conservative Protestants who forcefully defended a particular set of ideas regarding the actual label of "evangelical," all of which culminated in the founding of the National Association of Evangelicals in 1942 by self-stylized "Neo-Evangelicals" along with formation of the Evangelical Theological Society in 1949.[60] Similarly, in the United Kingdom, the *Evangelical Quarterly* from 1929 published essays that attempted to establish a particular perspective on issues that was identifiably "evangelical," as one essay by A. MacDonald proclaimed in 1932: "Modern Thought and the Evangelical Standpoint."[61] These efforts, along with the meteoric rise of Billy Graham and his nationally prominent evangelistic campaigns, seemed to make a convincing claim to this particular word and association that more theologically liberal Protestants and other Christian "outsiders" were willing to give up.

Nonetheless, that did not stop the greatest Protestant theologian of the twentieth century, Karl Barth—who was surely not very sympathetic with the

59. H. L. Mencken, "Obituary of William Jennings Bryan," *The Baltimore Evening Sun*, July 27, 1925.

60. One example of the defense of one version of an "evangelical" worldview in the 1930s is Frank E. Gaebelein, "An Evangelical's Defense," *The North American Review* 232, no. 1 (July 1, 1931): 26–32. "Neo-Evangelical" was actually a term that had already been used in England in the 1860s in an attempt to revive a flagging Evangelical Party faction within the Church of England. In a sense, this only further illustrates the point that the goal is always yet an even more authentic true expression of Christianity. Mark Smith and Stephen Taylor, *Evangelicalism in the Church of England c. 1790–c. 1890: A Miscellany* (Boydell Press, 2004), 302.

61. A. MacDonald, "Modern Thought and the Evangelical Standpoint," *The Evangelical Quarterly* 4.4 (Oct. 1932): 349–58.

theological outlook of American or British "evangelicals"—from publishing his lectures at Princeton University and the University of Chicago in 1962 under the title *Evangelical Theology*. His use of "evangelical" was simultaneously consistent with a historical German usage of the term and a mocking reference to American conservative Protestants who claimed the term as their own.[62] Even if the 1940s marked the mostly successful appropriation by one strain of conservative Protestants of the term "evangelical," those who claimed the label were surprisingly diverse in their politics and social stances, as recent scholarship has demonstrated.[63] It was not until the culture wars of the 1970s and the rise of the Moral Majority in the late 1970s that evangelicalism took on a more familiar shape, both in terms of cultural stances (anti-abortion) and political mobilization. But even in the post-1970s era, denominations and movements that either self-identified as or were labeled "evangelical" proliferated along a diverse spectrum of practices, social activism, theological nuances, cultural stances, and, more recently, political allegiances.[64] Therefore, it is important that historians and political commentators not simply read backward into the eighteenth and nineteenth centuries the supposed doctrinal (and political) consensus of post-1970s evangelicalism. The history and usage of the term over time itself reminds us that the word has always been in flux, applied in relative ways and for polemical purposes, and was always elastic enough that people and movements could slip in and out of association with the term.[65]

62. Karl Barth, *Evangelical Theology: An Introduction* (New York: Holt, Rinehart and Winston, 1963).

63. As just a representative sample, see: D. K. Williams, *God's Own Party: The Making of the Christian Right* (New York: Oxford University Press, 2010); Darren Dochuk, *From Bible Belt to Sunbelt: Plain-Folk Religion, Grassroots Politics, and the Rise of Evangelical Conservatism* (New York: W. W. Norton, 2011); Molly Worthen, *Apostles of Reason: The Crisis of Authority in American Evangelicalism* (New York: Oxford, 2013); Steven P. Miller, *The Age of Evangelicalism: America's Born-Again Years* (New York: Oxford University Press, 2014); Matthew Avery Sutton, *American Apocalypse: A History of Modern Evangelicalism* (Belknap Press, 2014).

64. On the varieties of evangelicalism, see Randall Balmer, *Mine Eyes Have Seen the Glory: A Journey into the Evangelical Subculture in America* (New York: Oxford University Press, 1989); Dayton and Johnston, *The Variety of American Evangelicalism*; Christian Smith, *Christian America? What Evangelicals Really Want*, 1st edition (Berkeley: University of California Press, 2000); Christian Smith, *American Evangelicalism: Embattled and Thriving*, 1st ed. (University of Chicago Press, 1998).

65. See, for example, David Hempton, *Evangelical Disenchantment: Nine Portraits of Faith and Doubt* (Yale University Press, 2008). . . .

And such elasticity is still ongoing. The rise of Pentecostalism in the open-ing decade of the twentieth century, the charismatic movement of the 1960s, and the spread of various forms of locally-inflected Protestantism globally all continue to raise questions about to whom the label "evangelical" should be applied.[66] And, notably, when Jorge Mario Bergoglio was proclaimed Pope Francis on March 13, 2013, some religious commentators soon dubbed him the "evangelical pope," by which they referred, in part, to his "Christ-centeredness," implicitly contrasting "Christ-centeredness" to something less Christ-centered and, therefore, more Catholic and less truly Christian.[67]

Indeed, to equate what it has meant to be "evangelical" across time and space with four or five or nine or even twenty beliefs misses the rich and diverse ways the word has been used between the sixteenth century and the present. If there is any continuity in the use of the word "evangelical" through-out history, it is this relative, primitivist, comparative, and contestable sense of being more true to the gospel than others, at least as defined within that particular cultural moment. Although this usage might often elude historians today, those who wielded the term and those who were excluded by it in past times saw it perfectly clearly. In 1848 George Washington Burnap, pastor of the First Independent Church of Baltimore, gave a series of lectures on the topic of "Popular Objections to Unitarian Christianity." Burnap opened the fifth lecture, titled "Unitarianism Evangelical Christianity" this way: "I am this evening to speak to you of the epithet *Evangelical*, as arrogated by certain

---

66. For a strong argument regarding the internationally-coherent nature of "global evangelicalism"—despite the lack of evangelical self-definition by some of these global Protestants—see Hutchinson and Wolffe, *A Short History of Global Evangelicalism*.

67. George Weigel, "The Christ-Centered Pope: The Catholic Church and the World Wrestle with an Evangelical Papacy," *National Review Online*, accessed Oc-tober 3, 2013, http://www.nationalreview.com/article/359042/christ-centered-pope -george-weigel. The ongoing online debates and hand-wringing over the definition and history of what it means to be "evangelical" also illustrate the nebulous and ephemeral quality of the term, even in the present. See, for example, Bradley Wright, "What, Exactly, Is Evangelical Christianity?" *Black, White and Gray*, accessed Novem-ber 17, 2013, http://www.patheos.com/blogs/blackwhiteandgray/2013/03/what-exactly -is-evangelical-christianity/; Fred Clark, "'What Is an Evangelical?' Part 3,947 . . . ," *Slacktivist*, accessed November 18, 2013, http://www.patheos.com/blogs/slacktivist /2012/10/03/what-is-an-evangelical-part-3947/; "An Evangelical Manifesto: The Washington Declaration of Evangelical Identity and Public Commitment," May 7, 2008, http://www.anevangelicalmanifesto.com/docs/Evangelical_Manifesto_Sum mary.pdf.

classes of Christians, and denied to others." The use of the word "evangelical," Burnap noted, "is intended to intimate the idea of a special purity of doctrine and sanctity of life as belonging to those who claim it. Its denial is intended to cast a reproach on those from whom it is withheld, of laxity of doctrine, and a life less scrupulously exact."[68]

Voices like Burnap's warn us that the term and category "evangelical" have been highly constructed and contested over time, and we have largely used them as if they are not. The backwards reading of the term (starting in the 1970s) has a particular genealogy and—if we are honest—serves purposes that are both historical (providing an easy, although imprecise, shorthand) and confessional (giving legitimacy to "evangelicalism" in the present). At minimum, we should stop pretending that four core beliefs can adequately apply to an incredible diversity of individuals, denominations, and movements between 1680 and the present who may or may not have laid claim to such a term (especially as we understand it today). In our current paradigm, there is no room for Unitarians, Universalists, or Christian Scientists as "evangelical." That alone should tell us we have missed something.

Even in 1900, after more than a century of struggle over the meaning of the word, one astute American observer noted that "to be evangelical means one thing in England, and quite another thing in this land; it means one thing to a conservative Calvinist and quite another to a liberal; one thing at Princeton, another at Andover or Yale."[69] If people in the past were often talking past each other with regard to the contested meaning of "evangelical," the problem with our current static, homogenizing use of the term is that it creates a historical fiction in which people in the past are speaking in unison, when they were not.

68. George Washington Burnap, *Popular Objections to Unitarian Christianity: Considered and Answered in Seven Discourses* (Boston, 1848), 93.
69. "Evangelical; What Is It?," 6.

PART II

The Current Crisis: Looking Back

The four essays that follow do not attempt a complete or definitive assessment of the now famous 81 percent of American "evangelicals" that many media identified as voting for Donald Trump in November 2016. Among such efforts, which continue to proliferate, one of the fullest and most discerning has been provided by John Fea, *Believe Me: The Evangelical Road to Donald Trump* (Eerdmans, 2018). But even the best cannot explain everything that was pertinent—for example, how much of the 81 percent represented votes *against* Hillary Clinton more than *for* Donald Trump. The essays that follow by Michael Hamilton, D. G. Hart, Kristin Kobes Du Mez, and Fred Clark have a more specific purpose tailored to the structure of this book. They do seek to explain the evangelical-Trump phenomenon, but, at the same time, they also attend to the knotty questions of definition explored in the book's first part.

CHAPTER 8

A Strange Love?
Or: How White Evangelicals Learned
to Stop Worrying and Love the Donald

MICHAEL S. HAMILTON

After two decades on the faculty of Seattle Pacific University, Michael Hamilton is now Vice President for Programming and Special Initiatives at the Issachar Fund. He has written many illuminating articles on the history of American evangelicalism, including "How a Humble Evangelist [Billy Graham] Changed Christianity as We Know It" (*Christianity Today*, April 2018), and on histories of evangelicalism, including "Whoring after the Gods of Babylon? Or Pining for the Fleshpots of Egypt" (*Fides et Historia* 48, no. 1 [Winter/Spring 2016]). His essay here was written expressly for this book.

*   *   *

Eighty-one percent. Every person who studies, writes about, or thinks about white evangelicals knows immediately what this number refers to—the unexpected finding of a Pew survey that 81 percent of white evangelicals voted for Donald Trump in the 2016 US presidential election.[1] Fourteen months into his presidency, white evangelical support for him remained strong. Seventy-eight percent told Pew pollsters that they approved of Trump's job performance—double the approval rate of the public in general.[2]

1. Gregory A. Smith and Jessica Martínez, "How the Faithful Voted: A Preliminary 2016 Analysis," Pew Research Center, November 9, 2016, http://www.pewresearch.org /fact-tank/2016/11/09/how-the-faithful-voted-a-preliminary-2016-analysis/.
2. Alec Tyson, "Disagreements about Trump Widely Seen as Reflecting Divides over 'Other Values and Goals,'" Pew Research Center, March 15, 2018, http://www.pew

Outsiders were surprised that people known for public piety and a strict personal moral code had such enthusiasm for a philandering, church-avoiding businessman. Many insiders were shocked to learn that the vast majority of people who attended their churches and supported their organizations were undisturbed not only by Trump's irreligion and sexual immorality but also by his blatant racism, unapologetic misogyny, dishonest business practices, disregard for truth, undisguised narcissism, violent language, and bullying behavior.

A common reaction among these insiders has been disbelief. Dan Reid, longtime editorial director at InterVarsity Press, said to me, in a tone of exasperation, "How can Trump have gotten eighty-one percent? I don't know a single person at IVP who voted for Trump!" Thomas Kidd, a widely read historian of evangelicalism whose opinions are found at two places in this book, believes that the recent dominance in America of the political definition of "evangelical" has resulted in many white Americans being counted as evangelical who are not truly evangelical by religious measures. "I suspect," says Kidd, "that large numbers of these people who identify as 'evangelicals' are really just whites who watch Fox News and who consider themselves religious."[3]

Who Are These Trump-Supporting White Evangelicals?

The Pew election polls do indeed identify evangelicals solely by asking them if they are white and consider themselves "evangelical" or "born-again" Christians. But there is no basis for the supposition that if the term "evangelical" were strictly limited to those who hold a traditional set of theological beliefs about the Bible, Jesus, salvation, conversion, and the importance of the church and its work, the percentage of white evangelicals who have supported Trump would be reduced. Two evangelical polling organizations, Barna and Lifeway, have respectively found that theological evangelicals are more, or at least equally, likely to support Trump as are the "evangelicals" identified by the political pollsters.[4] And Pew polls have found that higher levels of church

research.org/fact-tank/2018/03/15/disagreements-about-trump-widely-seen-as-reflecting-divides-over-other-values-and-goals/.

3. Thomas S. Kidd, "Roy Moore and the Confused Identity of Today's 'Evangelical' Voter," *Vox*, December 13, 2017, https://www.vox.com/first-person/2017/11/22/16686614/roy-moore-evangelical-voter.

4. "Notional Christians: The Big Election Story in 2016," Barna, December 1,

attendance correlate with stronger levels of Trump support.[5] No matter how "evangelical" is defined—theologically, denominationally, or by self-identification—once evangelicals are sorted by race, the non-Hispanic white group overwhelmingly approves of Trump. And they do so in far higher numbers than whites in any other religious group.

The main reason white evangelicals support Trump is because they are so strongly committed to the Republican Party, and they have been for many years now. Both the Pew polls and the Barna polls show no significant difference in evangelical levels of support for the evangelical George W. Bush, the Episcopalian-turned-Baptist John McCain, the Mormon Mitt Romney, and the unchurched nominal Protestant Donald Trump. Trump's extreme style and behavior, which are so far outside evangelical norms, make evangelical approval appear stranger than it really is. Evangelicals favor most Republican Party policies, and if one disregards Trump's style, his policies actually line up quite well with current Republican patterns.

Why Are White Evangelicals Such Ardent Republicans?

White evangelical leaders in the North have leaned Republican for a long time, at least since Dwight L. Moody in the post–Civil War era. But the current era of aggressive white evangelical political mobilization was launched by Republican Party activists in the 1960s. Searching for new groups of potential Republican voters in the wake of the Barry Goldwater debacle, party organizers began courting theologically conservative religious leaders who had grown increasingly uncomfortable with social changes in America. GOP recruiter Morton Blackwell observed that white evangelicals were "the greatest tract of virgin timber on the political landscape." He and his colleagues believed that conservative evangelical social views could be politicized and then harvested for conservative Republican candidates. The outlines of a deal soon emerged.

2016, https://www.barna.com/research/notional-christians-big-election-story-2016/; Bob Smietana, "Many Who Call Themselves Evangelical Don't Actually Hold Evangelical Beliefs," LifeWay, December 6, 2017, https://lifewayresearch.com/2017/12/06/many-evangelicals-dont-hold-evangelical-beliefs/.

5. Gregory A. Smith, "Among White Evangelicals, Regular Churchgoers Are the Most Supportive of Trump," Pew Research Center, April 26, 2017, http://www.pewresearch.org/fact-tank/2017/04/26/among-white-evangelicals-regular-churchgoers-are-the-most-supportive-of-trump/.

If the Republican Party gave religious leaders political access and supported white evangelical causes—conservative morality in public schools, freedom of private schools, outlawing abortion—the white evangelical leaders would politicize their religious movement on behalf of the Republican Party and its entire range of issues.[6]

One can see the Republicans keeping their part of the bargain in Fox News, the independent propaganda arm of the GOP. There is no inherent reason for it to be religious, but the editors are always careful to include Christian concerns. Every December they run stories on the latest outrage in the so-called War on Christmas. Likewise, the massively popular commentator Bill O'Reilly (recently revealed to be a serial sexual predator) freely called himself a Christian. Thomas Kidd's hunch may have been partly right—there likely are political conservatives who have gradually been persuaded by Fox News to think of themselves as Christians.

White evangelical attachment to the Republican Party is not driven by their theology. Most African Americans who hold the same evangelical beliefs vote for Democrats. In the 1930s, most southern white evangelicals were voting for Franklin Roosevelt just because he was a Democrat and *despite* the New Deal. Yet even conservative economic policies were not a necessary implication of evangelical belief. White evangelicals in western Canada in the 1930s organized a successful political party, Social Credit, around redistributionist socialistic economic policies.

Likewise, it is not simply a matter of the rank and file playing follow-the-leader. White evangelical Republican voting is as much a bottom-up phenomenon as a top-down phenomenon. Historian Nathan Hatch conclusively demonstrated that the people in populist American religious movements like evangelicalism choose their leaders by voting with their feet.[7] One can therefore become an evangelical leader only by appealing to values that the evangelical audience already holds. Once attained, leadership is exercised in more dialogical fashion, by give-and-take with the audience.

This process was perfectly demonstrated in the 2016 Republican primaries. Evangelical leaders had a number of candidates to choose from. When large groups of them gathered to seek a consensus, the only clear pattern that emerged was that hardly any of them favored Trump. But to everyone's

---

6. William Martin, *With God on Our Side: The Rise of the Religious Right in America* (New York: Broadway, 1996), quotation on 191.

7. Nathan O. Hatch, *The Democratization of American Christianity* (New Haven: Yale University Press, 1989).

surprise, Trump got more white evangelical votes in several early primaries than the evangelical candidates Ted Cruz, Ben Carson, and Mike Huckabee. It did not take long for evangelical leaders to follow evangelical voters into the Trump camp. James Dobson, the culture-wars-obsessed founder of Focus on the Family, originally endorsed Cruz. Dobson criticized Trump for his willingness to tolerate same-sex marriage, which Dobson declared a "nonnegotiable" issue.[8] But when his audience made their preference clear, Dobson followed his audience and became one of Trump's most outspoken and influential apologists. Undaunted by the obvious fact that Trump was not, by evangelical standards, even remotely a Christian, Dobson helped invent and promote the fiction that Trump had recently and miraculously had a conversion experience. Trump was now—praise the Lord!—"a baby Christian."[9]

What Is the Nature of White Evangelical Politics?

In fact, white evangelical voters are comfortable with Trump precisely because he embodies and articulates their deepest social concerns, which turn out to be disconnected from their theology. Historian David Bebbington's influential four-part description of evangelical essentials (the "Bebbington Quadrilateral") tilts toward the theological—biblicism, crucicentrism, conversionism, and activism in spreading the first three. But separate from its theology, American white evangelical Christianity has a political character that also boils down to four essential elements—Christian nationalism, Christian tribalism, political moralism, and antistatism. Call this the white evangelical political quadrilateral.

Christian nationalism is the engine that drives white American evangelical politics. It is the ideology (ideology being an interconnected system of beliefs, theories, and sociopolitical goals) that the United States is intended by God to be a Christian nation. This ideology posits that America had a uniquely Christian past and has a uniquely Christian future. But in the present, the enemies of God—internal and external—deny America's Christian past and threaten its future. This is why evangelicals believe that politics is fundamen-

8. "Dr. James Dobson Endorses Ted Cruz for President," *YouTube*, February 17, 2016, https://youtu.be/NldPotQNiWQ.

9. "Dr. James Dobson on Donald Trump's Christian Faith," *Dr. James Dobson's Family Talk*, accessed February 13, 2019, http://drjamesdobson.org/news/dr-james -dobson-on-trumps-christian-faith.

tally about using power—political and military—to suppress God's enemies and the threat they pose to God's plan for America.

Christian tribalism is the white evangelical form of identity politics. Feminist literary scholar (and devout Episcopalian) Catharine Stimpson defines identity politics as "a group's assertion that it is a meaningful group; that it differs significantly from other groups; that its members share a history of injustice and grievance; and that its psychological and political mission is to explore, act out, act on and act up its group identity."[10] This fits white evangelical self-understanding in every particular. Its sense of injustice and grievance is located in the belief that powerful elites in America are using their cultural and political power to restrict and weaken the churches and to steer the nation in a secular direction. This sense of injustice and grievance has been rising since 1962 when the US Supreme Court decided that prayer in public schools is unconstitutional. It reached a fever pitch fifty years later with the contraceptive mandate in the Patient Protection and Affordable Care Act of 2010 and the 2015 Supreme Court decision establishing that same-sex couples have a constitutional right to marry. White evangelicals do not imagine that the Christian nation will consist only of white evangelicals, but they do seem to envision that their tribe will be like the Levites in ancient Israel, setting the religious, moral, and therefore political tone for the nation as a whole.

Political moralism is the white evangelical view that political policies ought to uphold Christian moral values. Government should enforce Christian morality by punishing immoral behavior rather than by incentivizing or enabling good behavior. For white evangelicals, sexual morality is at the top of their values pyramid. The bedrock principle is that any kind of sexual activity outside of marriage between one man and one woman is an absolute wrong. This explains why they are beside themselves about same-sex marriage, why they oppose government support for distribution of contraception, why they oppose sex education in public schools except for preaching abstinence, and why the number-one focus of local men's ministry groups is avoiding pornography.[11]

10. "Identity Politics," Merriam-Webster.com, accessed February 13, 2019, https://www.merriam-webster.com/dictionary/identity%20politics.

11. The home page of Every Man Ministries (https://www.everymanministries.com), whose men's ministry resources are used by major white evangelical churches like Saddleback, lists as its top eleven video topics, in this order, "Porn, Lust, Marriage, Leadership, Temptation, Sex, Relationship, Fantasy, Faith, Family, Fatherhood."

Political moralism also helps explain evangelical opposition to abortion. Contrary to their rhetoric, white evangelicals are not generally pro-life. To give just one example, they usually prefer military action over peaceful diplomacy, even knowing that warfare always kills noncombatant men, women, children, and unborn babies. Unqualified opposition to abortion was originally a Catholics-only phenomenon. In the 1960s, white evangelicals actually allowed for abortion *if the woman's doctor recommended it.*[12] But when California adopted this policy in 1967, the number of abortions increased far beyond everyone's expectations. It was obvious that the decision-making had gotten out of the hands of doctors and into the hands of women, who were now using abortion as a method of on-demand birth control. Evangelicals, always uncomfortable with how birth control permitted women to engage in immoral sexual activity without consequences, soon migrated to the Catholic view that abortion is equivalent to murder.[13] This made it easy to think about abortion as a self-evident either/or moral choice. It also made abortion an ideal Republican Party tool for solidifying political loyalty.

Finally, white evangelical political ideology incorporates an antistatist view of the role of government. Sermon after sermon in white evangelicalism insists that the role of government is to defend the nation against external enemies, establish and maintain internal order, and punish evildoers. The obligation of citizens is to obey authority, except when government contravenes God. In the late nineteenth century, more than a few white evangelical leaders aligned themselves with Theodore Roosevelt's view that government was an agent of the people to work for positive social change. But after the First World War, white evangelical leaders in the North almost universally associated government social reform with socialism and communism. They were therefore uncomfortable with Franklin Roosevelt's New Deal, because they thought a larger government threatened the church's freedom and therefore outweighed any good that social programs might do. But white evangelicals are not libertarians. Their political moralism dictates that a larger and more interventionist government is good when used to restrain immorality and punish evildoers. White evangelicals are generally more troubled by expanding government programs that provide free food to mothers and their small children than they

12. Christian Medical Society, "A Protestant Affirmation on the Control of Human Reproduction" (1968), *Journal of the American Scientific Affiliation* 22 (June 1970): 46–47.

13. Kristin Luker, *Abortion and the Politics of Motherhood* (Berkeley: University of California Press, 1984).

are by expanding government prisons or expanding the size and firepower of local police forces.

Why Do White Evangelicals Approve of Trump?

Christian nationalism is the engine that drives the vehicle of white evangelical politics; it is also the power source for the other components of that vehicle—their tribalism, their political moralism, and their antistatism. To use a different metaphor, Christian nationalism is the framework, or worldview, within which their tribalism, political moralism, and antistatism come together, function, and make sense. We have strong empirical evidence for this in a sophisticated postelection study by sociologists Andrew Whitehead, Samuel Perry, and Joseph Baker. They established a measure for adherence to Christian nationalism, through answers to six questions on a national survey, and discovered that Christian nationalism is the single strongest independent predictor of a Trump vote. Regardless of age, sex, income, education, political party, or theology, those who believe in Christian America were far more likely to vote for Trump. The authors found that the "religious vote" for Trump "was primarily the result of Christian nationalism."[14]

For vast numbers of Americans, the story takes an even darker turn. The authors confirmed a large body of earlier work establishing significant positive relationships between Christian nationalism and Islamophobia, nativism, antiblack prejudice, and sexism. And they showed that these forms of prejudice are mediated into politics via the belief that American is, and should be, a Christian nation.[15] So, when white evangelicals envision a Christian America, it is an America controlled and dominated by white male Christians; an America that restricts or excludes non-Christian religions because they are defined as un-American; an America that subordinates women to men because this is mandated by the Bible; and an America that discriminates against sexual minorities because they violate Christian morality and are therefore un-American.

Christian nationalist ideology helps explain several features of contemporary white evangelical politics that both insiders and outsiders find con-

14. Andrew L. Whitehead, Samuel L. Perry, and Joseph O. Baker, "Make America Christian Again: Christian Nationalism and Voting for Donald Trump in the 2016 Presidential Election," *Sociology of Religion: A Quarterly Review*, January 25, 2018, 18, https://doi.org/10.1093/socrel/srx070.

15. Whitehead, Perry, and Baker, "Make America Christian Again," 2, 18–19.

fusing. And in doing so, it helps explain why white evangelicals continue to be among Trump's strongest and most dependable supporters. Consider these curiosities:

- In 2011, only 30 percent of white evangelicals agreed that immorality did not disqualify politicians from public office, and 64 percent agreed that strong religious beliefs are "very important" in a presidential candidate. Three weeks before the 2016 election, these numbers had completely flipped—72 percent said that immorality did not disqualify a politician, and only 49 percent said that a candidate's religious views were important.[16]
- The nation's founders greatly feared lodging too much power in one person's hands, and the nation's two-party political system is based on the premise that both parties are legitimately American. But white evangelicals are not put off by Trump's obvious authoritarian tendencies, including his repeated threats to use governmental power to silence his political opponents.
- White evangelicals' loudest complaint is that their religious freedom is being threatened by the government, but increasingly they want to use the government to deny religious freedom to Americans who are Muslim.[17]
- White evangelicals favor unilateralism in foreign policy and are quick to advocate using military force. They distrust diplomacy, despite its object of settling disputes peacefully. If America is God's uniquely chosen nation, then America's self-interest is God's plan. The goal is not to settle disputes, the goal is to win them.

Whitehead and his colleagues learned that the ideology of Christian nationalism demands preservation of America's Christian identity "*irrespective of the means by which such a project would be achieved.*"[18] Up close, this may look like violation of American constitutional principles or moral hypocrisy, but from a distance it makes perfect sense. If Christian America is God's plan,

16. "Backing Trump, White Evangelicals Flip Flop on Importance of Candidate Character—PRRI/Brookings Survey," PRRI, October 19, 2016, https://www.prri.org/research/prri-brookings-oct-19-poll-politics-election-clinton-double-digit-lead-trump/.

17. Peter Beinart, "When Conservatives Oppose 'Religious Freedom,'" *Atlantic*, April 11, 2017, https://www.theatlantic.com/politics/archive/2017/04/when-conservatives-oppose-religious-freedom/522567/.

18. Whitehead, Perry, and Baker, "Make America Christian Again," 19.

its enemies are God's enemies. The method God uses to thwart his enemies and fulfill his plan is unimportant.

Other parts of the white evangelical political quadrilateral help explain other hard-edged dimensions of white evangelical politics. Tribalism helps explain the persistent white evangelical belief in the importance of white superiority. In the 1960s, *Christianity Today* affected a moderate tone on race relations but was much more critical of the civil rights movement and civil rights legislation than of racial segregation. African American Dolphus Weary recalled white students at Los Angeles Baptist College (now Master's College) laughing and cheering in 1968 when Martin Luther King Jr. was assassinated.[19] White evangelical racism was reinforced when the Southern Baptist Convention (SBC) became part of the white evangelical tribe in the 1980s. This meant that at the same time white southerners were transferring their antiblack attitudes from the Democratic Party to the Republican Party—Richard Nixon's infamous "Southern Strategy"—they were also bringing them into evangelicalism. The SBC has since, on several occasions, apologized for its racist history.[20] But the telling point on this issue is that despite frequent resolutions urging government action on issues like abortion or same-sex marriage, the SBC never advocates for government action to curb racial discrimination.

Political moralism helps explain white evangelicalism's preference for female subordination, euphemized as "complementarianism." In 1984, the SBC officially declared that women could not be pastors because they were the sex that sinned in Eden.[21] More significantly, as historian Kristin Du Mez explains in chapter 10 below, white evangelical angst over the way feminism and its doctrine of gender equality are destroying godly masculinity is long-standing. To combat this, white evangelicals recently developed a doctrine that God intends men to be warriors while women are to play the complementary role of passivity.[22]

19. Curtis J. Evans, "White Evangelical Protestant Responses to the Civil Rights Movement," *Harvard Theological Review* 102, no. 2 (2009): 261–69; Edward Gilbreath, "Catching Up with a Dream: Evangelicals and Race 30 Years after the Death of Martin Luther King, Jr.," *Christianity Today*, March 2, 1998, https://www.christianitytoday.com /ct/1998/march2/8t3020.html.

20. Barry Hankins, *Uneasy in Babylon: Southern Baptist Conservatives and American Culture* (Tuscaloosa: University of Alabama Press, 2002).

21. "Resolution on Ordination and the Role of Women in Ministry," Southern Baptist Convention, 1984, http://www.sbc.net/resolutions/1088.

22. See below, 236–42.

No wonder that before the election James Dobson fretted that the thought of a Hillary Clinton presidency "haunts my days and nights."[23] She symbolized opposition to every tenet of Christian nationalism. But opposition to Clinton was not decisive. Du Mez's startling conclusion about white evangelicals' support for Trump's aggressively sexist masculinity applies equally to white evangelicals' support for Trump's racism, authoritarianism, xenophobia, advocacy of violence, hatred of Muslims, bullying manner, and disregard for American constitutional principles: "In the end, many evangelicals did not vote for Trump despite their beliefs, but because of them." A certain percentage of the 81 percent of white evangelicals who voted for Trump believe that he may be the agent of God's salvation for Christian America. From the Christian nationalist point of view, the fact that more Americans voted for Clinton than for Trump highlights the peril of the situation. The future of Christian America hangs by a thread, and the democratic process poses a grave threat. This is no time for theological or constitutional fastidiousness. It is time for extraordinary leaders to launch extraordinary measures.

23. "Dr. James Dobson on Donald Trump's Christian Faith."

CHAPTER 9

Live by the Polls, Die by the Polls

D. G. HART

D. G. Hart, Distinguished Associate Professor of History at Hillsdale College, has written many books on many topics, including evangelical Christianity, Presbyterianism, Calvinism, J. Gresham Machen, H. L. Mencken, the study of religion in modern American universities, and more. His complex understanding of American evangelicalism is indicated in the titles of some of his books: *From Billy Graham to Sarah Palin: Evangelicals and the Betrayal of American Conservativism* (Eerdmans, 2011); *The Old-Time Religion in Modern America: Evangelical Protestantism in the Twentieth Century* (Ivan Dee, 2003); and *Deconstructing Evangelicalism: Conservative Protestantism in the Age of Billy Graham* (Baker Academic, 2005). The essay that follows was written especially for this book.

*　　　　*　　　　*

However journalists and academics may assess the contemporary fortunes of evangelicalism in the United States, the sector of Protestantism that arose after World War II as an alternative (if not rival) to the Protestant mainline is persisting in remarkable ways. In a recent story for the Pew Research Forum, Gregory A. Smith and David Masci gave reason to believe that no matter how damaged evangelicalism's reputation is after the 2016 presidential election, born-again Protestants continue to be more resilient than mainline Protestants (and Roman Catholics). At 25.4 percent of the population, evangelicalism (as defined by association with evangelical-type churches, born-again status, and race) "is the nation's single largest religious group, exceeding the size of the nation's Catholic (20.8%), mainline Protestant (14.7%) and religiously unaffiliated (22.8%) populations."[1] This does not mean that evangelicalism defined this way has been growing. Since 2007, in fact, when 74 percent of born-again white Protestants were gearing up to cast votes for John McCain (compared to 78 percent for Mitt Romney in 2012, and the dreaded 81 percent who supported Donald Trump),[2] evangelicalism has dropped to 26.3 percent (according to a slightly different way of counting the national population). Yet again, in comparison to other Christians in the United States, evangelicalism defined by church adherence or responses to pollsters is not experiencing as dramatic a decline—the mainline went from 18.1 percent in 2007 to 14.7 percent in 2014, and Roman Catholics, from 23.9 to 20.8 percent during the same years.[3] American white evangelicalism may still decline thanks to unsavory associations with the Trump administration—akin to the fatigue that some born-again Protestants experienced with George W. Bush and the Iraq War. Even so, by the signs that pundits and researchers have used for the better part of four decades, the coalition of conservative Protestants that Harold John Ockenga corralled and that Billy Graham inspired not only defeated the mainline but remains a force to reckon with in publishing, advertising, communications, higher education, social services, and politics.

The dark side of these statistics, to borrow a phrase from James Bratt, however, is a religious identity that is a mile wide and an inch deep. The tests that pollsters use for evangelicalism are similar to those of joining a church. Respondents simply answer a set of questions. But the content of the questions differs considerably. In fact, the tactics used increasingly by researchers to discern religious identity rely on self-evaluation and then questions designed by social scientists about the most important markers of faith. It is a bottom-up method that fits well evangelicalism's populism. According to some measures, the most important evangelical beliefs and practices are affirming the Bible as the word of God (98 percent), following Christ's teaching in personal life (97 percent), holding that Christianity is the only way to eternal life (96 percent), witnessing to others (94 percent), and experiencing new

---

1. Gregory A. Smith and David Masci, "5 Facts about U.S. Evangelical Protestants," Pew Research Center, March 1, 2018, http://www.pewresearch.org/fact-tank/2018/03/01/5-facts-about-u-s-evangelical-protestants/.

2. Gregory A. Smith and Jessica Martínez, "How the Faithful Voted: A Preliminary 2016 Analysis," Pew Research Center, November, 9, 2016, http://www.pewresearch.org/fact-tank/2016/11/09/how-the-faithful-voted-a-preliminary-2016-analysis/.

3. Smith and Masci, "5 Facts about U.S. Evangelical Protestants."

birth (93 percent).[4] This contrasts significantly with church membership vows that require affirmations of the Trinity, Scripture, Christ's work as redeemer, the sacraments, and submission to church government.

The contrast between quantifying poll numbers and counting church members raises a basic question about the efforts of Ockenga and Graham—did the desire to become a large conservative Protestant organization that could rival the mainline churches fundamentally compromise evangelicalism? If so, the answer has implications both for the origins of postwar, largely white evangelicalism in the United States and for its apparent recent hypocrisy in producing voters for Donald Trump. From the very beginning, evangelicalism's leaders did not press (except in the case of biblical inerrancy) doctrines that would narrow the movement. Conservative Protestantism needed a minimal set of doctrinal affirmations. Yet, that basis for conforming to the evangelical profile was not going to blossom into a deep or profound expression of Christianity. Roughly thirty years later, when America's bicentennial coincided with "the year of the evangelical," the creation of a religious identity that could attract a wide swath of American Protestants sent signals to pollsters and political operatives that evangelicalism was an identity that could attract advertisers (on cable television and in publishing) and even determine elections. With those dynamics at work, the support that President Trump received from evangelicals (whether in good standing or not) was an outcome that should not have surprised anyone. From the outset, evangelicalism had the potential to be exploited by democratically elected government officials because its markers were so porous and relatively easy to quantify.

When Number Crunching Became a Blessing

Whether coincidental or providential, measuring the demographic heft of evangelicalism and the formation of the Moral Majority occurred simultaneously. In 1979, the same year that GOP strategists persuaded Jerry Falwell (the elder) to head up the Moral Majority, the editors of *Christianity Today* cooperated with George Gallup Jr. to survey evangelical beliefs in the United States. The results included data that indicated more than a third of Americans had had a "life-changing religious experience" (with 50 million declaring that

---

4. "Global Survey of Evangelical Protestant Leaders," Pew Research Center, June 22, 2011, http://www.pewforum.org/2011/06/22/global-survey-of-evangelical -protestant-leaders/.

Jesus Christ was the reason for change); 80 percent professed that Jesus is divine, and 84 percent held that the Ten Commandments "are valid today."[5] One writer for the magazine concluded cheerfully that with evangelicals composing one-fifth of the population, they were "clearly a powerful religious force in society."[6] Gallup's results also encouraged the magazine's editors and readers with the hopeful projection that the 1980s were shaping up to be "the decade of the evangelicals, because that is where the action is." The editors added that evangelicals "understand their own faith better, are far more ready to speak out to others about their faith, and place high priority on winning others to their evangelical faith."[7] When Gallup repeated his survey of Americans a decade later, he found that the 1980s had indeed lived up to its billing. By 1989 evangelicals (defined by the Gallup questions) accounted for 31 percent of the population.[8]

Soon sociologists and political scientists entered the quantification arena and confirmed the impression that evangelicalism was a significant factor in all aspects of American society. James Davison Hunter was not as optimistic about evangelical fidelity as Gallup. His book *Evangelicalism: The Coming Generation* (1987) presented born-again Protestants as orthodox believers under siege whose faithfulness could well collapse under modernity's weight. Even so, his next book, *Culture Wars: The Struggle to Define America* (1991), put evangelicals squarely in the orthodox party of Americans who (along with conservative Roman Catholics and Jews) were striving to uphold older American ideals on family, education, art, law, and politics. Soon thereafter came the research of John C. Green, James L. Guth, Corwin E. Smidt, and Lyman A. Kellstedt, who crafted surveys to assess evangelicalism's influence on electoral politics. Throughout the late 1980s and into the years of George W. Bush's presidency, these political scientists explained electoral results according to their careful measures of Christian belief added to church belonging and doctrinal emphases (they carved evangelical identity out from the generic Protestant designation that had dominated political science). After the election of George H. W. Bush in 1988, they observed that the "most committed Evangelicals

5. "The *Christianity Today*–Gallup Poll: An Overview," *Christianity Today*, December 21, 1979, 1666.

6. "Who and Where Are the Evangelicals?" *Christianity Today*, December 21, 1979, 1671.

7. "We Poll the Pollster," *Christianity Today*, December 21, 1979, 1664.

8. George Gallup Jr. and Jim Castelli, *The People's Religion: American Faith in the 1990s* (New York: Macmillan, 1990), 92.

oppose gay rights and tend to be conservative Republicans."[9] By 2000, when Bush's son won a highly contested election against Vice President Al Gore, they concluded that the Christian Right was "a significant voting bloc, and is probably as important to the [Republican] party as black Protestants, Jews, and secular voters are to the Democrats."[10]

Whether these findings always encouraged evangelicalism's religious leadership—pastors, theologians, seminary professors, editors—the recognition of born-again Protestantism's stature by pollsters and social scientists fostered a measure of pride in belonging to a movement so large. But by 2016, with indications of supermajority forms of support for Donald Trump, evangelical pundits began to see polling data more as a curse than a blessing. Andy Crouch wrote for *Christianity Today* almost a month before the November election that political strategy had become "its own form of idolatry—an attempt to manipulate the levers of history in favor of the causes we support." To make alliances with those "who seem to offer strength" was to compromise "dependence on God."[11] That was a plausible warning, but one that seemed to be completely absent from evangelicalism (except for those in the Jim Wallis–Tony Campolo wing) for the better part of four decades, a period when born-again Protestants inhabited the largest and most vigorous space in the most powerful nation in the world's religious landscape.

What Could Possibly Have Gone Wrong?

Observers of contemporary religion in the United States have various theories for white evangelical support for Donald Trump—from nationalism, xenophobia, and racism to hypocrisy and sinfulness. One explanation that eludes most assessments is that evangelicalism was so broad and thin that while its numbers impressed, it lacked mechanisms to distinguish legitimate from illegitimate born-again faith.

9. Kellstedt et al., "Grasping the Essentials: The Social Embodiment of Religion and Political Behavior," in *Religion and the Culture Wars: Dispatches from the Front*, ed. John C. Green et al. (Lanham, MD: Rowman & Littlefield, 1996), xv.

10. Guth et al., "God's Own Party: Evangelicals and Republicans in the '92 Election," *Christian Century*, February 17, 1993, 174.

11. Andy Crouch, "Speak Truth to Trump," *Christianity Today*, October 10, 2016, https://www.christianitytoday.com/ct/2016/october-web-only/speak-truth-to-trump.html.

For instance, academics who teach at Fuller Seminary and Wheaton College and editors and writers at *Christianity Today* may be uncomfortable with charismatic television celebrities Jim and Tammy Bakker and Joel Osteen and proponents of the prosperity gospel, but despite the criticisms that some of them made, none had the authority as an official gatekeeper to declare these evangelical outliers to be outside of the movement as instances of what Ross Douthat calls "bad religion," that is, heterodox versions of orthodox Christianity.[12] In fact, the evangelical tent, as measured by the pollsters, is so big that Osteen came in eighth on a top-ten list of figures whom evangelicals trusted for political endorsements (he was the only pastor on the list, two slots above Jerry Falwell Jr.).[13] In addition, Kate Bowler argues that though distinct from evangelicalism, the prosperity gospel often grew out of born-again Christianity.[14] Meanwhile, John Wigger's book on the Bakkers, as the title indicates (*The Rise and Fall of Jim and Tammy Bakker's Evangelical Empire*), places their "ministry" within the orbit of evangelicalism.[15]

In the end, the breadth of evangelical identity is a function of disregard for the institutional church. Despite their own history of error and hypocrisy, Christian communions (at least conservative ones) have mechanisms for controlling the quality of ministers and determining a faith sufficient for belonging. They even have the levers for excluding wayward officers and members. Depending on whom you read, evangelicalism has usually favored the informal over the formal, the parachurch over the ecclesial. It is, as Nathan Hatch argued, an inherently populist faith, which could explain why in evangelical circles numbers matter more than structures.[16] The result is that any American who self-applies the label winds up an evangelical. The paradox for evangelicals is this: more law and order of the kind that institutional churches have traditionally supplied would have prevented them from the embarrassment of Trump. At the same time, without the numbers, no one would have noticed or cared how they voted.

12. Ross Douthat, *Bad Religion: How We Became a Nation of Heretics* (New York: Free Press, 2012); see especially chap. 6.

13. Kate Shellnutt, "The 10 Celebrities Evangelicals Trust Most and Least on Politics," *Christianity Today*, March 19, 2018, https://www.christianitytoday.com /news/2018/march/10-celebrity-political-endorsements-evangelicals-trust-most.html.

14. Kate Bowler, *Blessed: A History of the American Prosperity Gospel* (New York: Oxford University Press, 2013).

15. John Wigger, *The Rise and Fall of Jim and Tammy Bakker's Evangelical Empire* (New York: Oxford University Press, 2017).

16. Nathan O. Hatch, *The Democratization of American Christianity* (New Haven: Yale University Press, 1989).

CHAPTER 10

Donald Trump and Militant Evangelical Masculinity

KRISTIN KOBES DU MEZ

Kristin Kobes Du Mez, a professor of history, gender studies, and urban studies at Calvin College, is the author of *A New Gospel for Women: Katharine Bushnell and the Challenge of Christian Feminism* (Oxford University Press, 2015). In her current research, she has written extensively on questions of feminism, gender identity, progressive Christians in politics, and the 2016 presidential election. The following is a slightly revised version of an essay first published in *Religion and Politics* (January 17, 2017). It is republished with the permission of *Religion and Politics*, an online journal of the John C. Danforth Center on Religion and Politics at Washington University in Saint Louis.

*   *   *

The fact that "family values" conservatives continue to rally around Trump has bewildered many people, including a number of evangelicals themselves.

Trump, after all, is a man who boasted of his "manhood" on national television, who incited violence at his rallies, and bragged of assaulting women. He is a man who spoke in the chapel of a Christian college in Iowa—my alma mater, no less—and claimed that he could "stand in the middle of 5th Avenue and shoot somebody" and not lose voters.[1]

Certainly, his behavior did little to dissuade the 81 percent of white evangelicals who voted for him, a constituency that proved key to his victory.

Yes, there were Supreme Court appointments and fears about religious freedom to consider, and a longstanding alliance with the Republican Party to

---

1. Jeremy Diamond, "Trump: I Could 'Shoot Somebody and I Wouldn't Lose Voters,'" *CNN*, updated January 24, 2016.

contend with. But even so, how could the self-professed "Moral Majority" embrace a candidate who seemed to flaunt his own cruelty?

The truth is, many evangelicals long ago replaced the suffering servant of Christ with an image that more closely resembles Donald Trump than many would care to admit. They've traded a faith that privileges humility and elevates "the least of these" for one that derides gentleness as the province of wusses. Having replaced the Jesus of the gospels with an idol of machismo, it's no wonder many have come to think of Trump himself as the nation's savior.

Indeed, white evangelical support for Trump can be seen as the culmination of a decades-long embrace of militant masculinity, a masculinity that has enshrined patriarchal authority, condoned a callous display of power at home and abroad, and functioned as a linchpin in the political and social worldviews of conservative white evangelicals. In the end, many evangelicals did not vote for Trump despite their beliefs, but because of them.

The roots of this ideology can be traced back to the 1970s, a decade in which evangelicals began to stake a new claim on politics and culture. As they mobilized around "family values" issues, defining masculinity and femininity was central to their task. James Dobson was one of the earliest and most influential proponents of this effort. The psychologist rose to fame with his 1970 book *Dare to Discipline*, but it was five years later, in *What Wives Wish Their Husbands Knew about Women*, that he began to articulate his gender ideology: men and women differed "biochemically, anatomically, and emotionally." To wit, men like to "hunt and fish and hike in the wilderness"; women prefer to "stay at home and wait for them." More significantly, "men derive self-esteem by being *respected*; women feel worthy when they are *loved*."

In 1980, in his *Straight Talk to Men and Their Wives*, Dobson blamed feminists for calling into question "everything traditionally masculine," for tampering with the "time-honored roles of protector and protected," and for denigrating masculine leadership as "macho." He saw this as a crisis of gender, but also as a threat to national security. For the sake of the nation, a "call to arms" was needed, a reassertion of the "Judeo-Christian concept of masculinity" in the face of feminists' "concerted attack on 'maleness.'"

To understand how changing gender roles could imperil the nation, the politicization of evangelical Christianity must be placed in the context of Cold War politics, and against the backdrop of the Vietnam War.

Evangelicals staunchly opposed communism, and their reasons for doing so were many: communists were anti-American, anti-God, and they threatened God-given rights and the integrity of the family. A strong military was necessary to ward off the communist peril, and strong men were essential to a strong military.

But the rising generation caused reason for concern. Young men sporting long hair and flowered shirts dodged the draft, shunned authority, and shirked their duty to protect America from the threat of global communism. The Vietnam era would emerge as a pivotal moment in the relationship between American evangelicals and the U.S. military. In the 1940s and 1950s, evangelicals had often looked askance at the military, which they saw as a source of moral corruption for young men. But as Anne Loveland has argued, evangelicals who supported U.S. military action in Vietnam came to hold the military itself in high (and often uncritical) esteem.[2]

In this climate, gender was never a purely domestic issue. Evangelical opposition to the Equal Rights Amendment (ERA) in the 1970s and early '80s bears this out, according to Donald Mathews and Jane De Hart.[3] To evangelicals, the ERA challenged the very foundation of the conservative Christian worldview: the idea that gender was a sacred, God-given certainty in an uncertain, fluctuating world. Opposition to the ERA quickly emerged as a key plank in their "family values" platform. But the ERA was also an issue of national security. Evangelicals claimed the ERA would destroy women's femininity by forcing them to be "like men"—competitive and career-driven, sexually promiscuous—and, most alarmingly, by forcing them to take up arms in military combat. The ERA, then, would not only "masculinize" women, but would also remove from men their obligations of provision and protection, rendering American defenses vulnerable.

Evangelicals like Dobson responded with a clarion call to turn back the tide of impending chaos by reasserting moral absolutes and reestablishing a "Christian civilization." Defining and defending distinct gender roles was at the heart of this effort, providing conservative evangelicals a clear identity against secularists, feminists, and other liberals.

But by the end of the 1980s their cause seemed to be coming undone. The fall of the Soviet Union and abrupt resolution of the Cold War had upended their presumed place in the world, economic conditions were making it increasingly difficult for men to fulfill their role as providers, and a growing

2. Anne C. Loveland, *American Evangelicals and the U.S. Military, 1942–1993* (Baton Rouge, LA: Louisiana State University Press, 1997).

3. Donald G. Mathews and Jane Sherron De Hart, *Sex, Gender, and the Politics of ERA: A State and the Nation* (New York: Oxford University Press, 1992).

acceptance of feminism in society at large meant that evangelicals experienced the "new world order" as more than a little disorderly.

Identifying a renewed "crisis of masculinity," evangelicals responded by launching the wildly popular Promise Keepers movement in 1990. Promoted by Dobson, the movement quickly took hold; at its height in 1997, Promise Keepers drew more than 800,000 men to Washington, D.C., for its national rally.

Reflecting the unsettled times, Promise Keepers called for a new Christian masculinity, an alternative both to the "softer," modern version they found lacking, and to the "macho" version they feared had become outmoded. Their solution: the archetype of the "Tender Warrior."

Authors like Steve Farrar, Gordon Dalbey, and Stu Weber—all white evangelical men—pioneered this "Tender Warrior" motif. Significantly, all three looked to Vietnam for the source of masculine identity. In *Healing the Masculine Soul* (1988), Dalbey, the son of a naval officer, admitted to having neglected the image of the war hero as his blueprint for manhood by joining the Peace Corps and becoming a supporter of feminism, civil rights, and the antiwar movement. Only later did he conclude that manhood "requires the warrior." In *Point Man: How a Man Can Lead His Family* (1990), Farrar compared a father's task of protecting his sons from feminization to that of a "point man" leading his troops through the dangers of Vietnam. And in 1993's *Tender Warrior: God's Intention for a Man*, Weber—a former Green Beret—opened with a scene depicting the terrors of Vietnam, and explained how God designed men to be providers, protectors, and warriors.

In words that would echo through the movement, Weber insisted that God himself was unmistakably "the Warrior of both testaments." Forget "gentle Jesus, meek and mild"—Jesus was "the ultimate man."

But with Democratic president Bill Clinton sending the military on "emasculating" peacekeeping missions, and with debates raging about women in combat and gays in the military, the crisis only deepened. Before long a new slate of books on evangelical masculinity appeared, offering instructions on how to raise properly masculine sons in a "feminized" culture. Abandoning any lip service to "tenderness," these books championed an unabashedly aggressive, testosterone-driven masculinity.

In *Raising a Modern-Day Knight* (published in 1997 by Dobson's Focus on the Family), Robert Lewis offered a detailed guide to help boys attain a "biblically grounded" manhood in a culture where men were "being stripped of their maleness by a modern, secular, feminist culture." Turning to the "age of knights"—a time rife with powerful symbols of "virile manhood"—Lewis advised staging elaborate manhood ceremonies involving expensive steak dinners and commemorated by symbols of "great value," such as "a Bible, a shotgun or a plaque."

In 2001 Dobson himself joined the growing outcry against a "war against boys" in America. In his *Bringing Up Boys* he again criticized a "small but noisy band of feminists" who attacked "the very essence of masculinity." He derided "feminists and other social liberals" who wanted to make boys more like girls, and men more like women—"feminized, emasculated, and wimpified." *Bringing Up Boys* found a receptive audience, quickly selling more than a million copies.

Also in 2001, Douglas Wilson's *Future Men* insisted that boys must be raised to be warriors. Central to Wilson's "definition of masculinity" was the concept of dominion; like Adam, all men were "created to exercise dominion over the earth." To this end it was "absolutely *essential* for boys to play with wooden swords and plastic guns," and "young boys should obviously be trained in the use of real firearms." Indeed, Wilson called for a "theology of fist fighting."

Perhaps the most influential evangelical book to appear in 2001 was John Eldredge's *Wild at Heart*. Amplifying themes articulated by earlier authors, Eldredge insisted that the difference between men and women resided at the level of the soul. And masculinity, according to Eldredge, was thoroughly militaristic. God created men to long for "a battle to fight, an adventure to live, and a beauty to rescue."

Women's role was a passive one: women yearned to be fought *for*. They possessed something "wild at heart," but it was "feminine to the core, more *seductive* than fierce."

But society offered confusing messages to men, according to Eldredge: "Having spent the last thirty years redefining masculinity into something more sensitive, safe, manageable and, well, feminine, it now berates men for not being men." A "crisis in masculinity" pervaded both church and society because a "warrior culture"—"a place for men to learn to fight like men"—no longer existed.

"If we believe that man is made in the image of God," Eldredge wrote, then we must remember that "the Lord is a warrior." Aggression was "part of the masculine design"; men were "hardwired for it." Attempts to pacify men only emasculated them: "If you want a safer, quieter animal, there's an easy solution: castrate him." Yes, "a man is a dangerous thing," he wrote, but the very strength that made men dangerous also made them heroes.

Only months after *Wild at Heart* debuted, terrorists struck the United States. Almost overnight Eldredge's call for "manly" heroes developed a deep and widespread cultural resonance.

The moral certitudes of the "War on Terror"—framed by evangelical president George W. Bush—abruptly replaced the post–Cold War malaise. Once again America needed strong, heroic men to defend the country, at home and abroad.

Evangelicals, many of whom had never strayed from Cold War gender constructions, stood at the ready to address these new conditions. "When those two planes hit the Twin Towers on September 11, what we suddenly needed were masculine men," Farrar wrote in his 2005 book *King Me*. "Feminized men don't walk into burning buildings. But masculine men do. That's why God created men to be masculine." In no uncertain terms he repudiated the earlier "Tender Warrior" motif: "The trend today is to major on the 'tender' and minor on the 'warrior,'" but "in the trenches you don't want tenderness."

It is not difficult to imagine how evangelicals, steeped in literature claiming that men were created in the image of a warrior God, might be receptive to sentiments like those expressed by the late Jerry Falwell, in his 2004 sermon "God Is Pro-War." In fact, surveys demonstrate that traditionalist evangelicals are more likely than other Americans to approve of U.S. engagement in a preemptive war, support military action against terrorism, and condone the use of torture.[4]

This brand of militant masculinity also helps explain the lack of outrage on the part of many evangelicals when it comes to Trump's character issues. Dobson himself, one of Trump's most influential evangelical supporters, urged fellow Christians "to cut him some slack." More tellingly, the Rev. Robert Jeffress, pastor of First Baptist Church in Dallas and stalwart Trump

---

4. "The Religious Dimensions of the Torture Debate," Pew Research Center, April 29, 2009, updated May 7, 2009, http://www.pewforum.org/2009/04/29/the-religious -dimensions-of-the-torture-debate/; Ronald E. Brown, R. Khari Brown, and Aaron W. Blasé, "Religion and Military Policy Attitudes in America," *Review of Religious Research*, Vol. 55, No. 4 (December 2013): 573–95; Zeynep Taydas, Cigdem Kentmen, and Laura R. Olson, "Faith Matters: Religious Affiliation and Public Opinion about Barack Obama's Foreign Policy in the 'Greater' Middle East," *Social Science Quarterly*, Vol. 93, No. 5, Special Issue: Social, Economic, and Political Transition in America: Retrospective on the "Era of Obama" (December 2012): 1218–42.

supporter, explained his endorsement of the unconventional candidate in this way: "I want the meanest, toughest, son-of-a-you-know-what I can find in that role, and I think that's where many evangelicals are."[5]

Ominously, though, there is a fine line between merely speaking of brute force and enacting violence. Less than a month after the election, a 28-year-old white man shot up a D.C. pizzeria with a military-style assault rifle. He said he was in search of a child sex slave ring linked to Hillary Clinton, which turned out to be a hoax generated by fake news reports. Chillingly, he cited one of his favorite books, *Wild at Heart*, in a post-arrest interview with *The New York Times*.[6]

On the role of gender in the 2016 election, most observers have scrutinized Clinton's appeal—or lack thereof. But more revealing is Trump's testosterone-fueled masculinity, which aligns remarkably well with that long championed by evangelicals. What makes a strong leader? A virile (white) man. And what of his vulgarity? Infidelity? Bombast? Even sexual assault? Well, boys will be boys.

In retrospect, drawing attention to these perceived negatives may have been a fatal error on the part of the Clinton campaign, for among those who embrace this sort of militant masculinity, such character traits paradoxically testify to Trump's fitness for the job.

Trump appeared at a moment when evangelicals feel increasingly beleaguered, even persecuted. Issues related to gender—from the cultural sea change on gay marriage to transgender bathroom laws to attacks on the Hyde Amendment and promotion of the contraceptive mandate—are at the center of their perceived victimization. The threat of terrorism looms large, American power isn't what it used to be, and nearly two-thirds of white evangelicals harbor fears that a once-powerful nation has become "too soft and feminine."[7]

In Donald Trump, they have found the leader they have been looking for.

5. Trip Gabriel and Michael Luo, "A Born-Again Donald Trump? Believe It, Evangelical Leader Says," *New York Times*, June 25, 2016; Robert P. Jones, "The Evangelicals and the Great Trump Hope," *New York Times*, July 11, 2016.

6. Adam Goldman, "The Comet Ping Pong Gunman Answers Our Reporter's Questions," *New York Times*, December 7, 2016.

7. Emma Green, "Why White Evangelicals Are Feeling Hopeful about Trump," *The Atlantic*, December 1, 2016.

CHAPTER 11

The "Weird" Fringe Is the Biggest Part of White Evangelicalism

Fred Clark

Fred Clark, a graduate of Eastern Baptist Seminary, blogs regularly at *Slacktivist*. This essay was posted on *Patheos* on April 23, 2018. It is used by permission of the author.

*   *   *

"Never mind Fox," says the subhead for Ruth Graham's latest, "Trump's most reliable media mouthpiece is now Christian TV."

Graham's "Church of the Donald" is in *Politico*, but she's not a typical cult-of-savvy *Politico* writer.[1] She's a veteran religion reporter, and a good one—someone with a deep, longstanding knowledge of white evangelicalism and the various corners of its subculture. This piece is, on one level, just a work of basic reporting, a kind of guided tour of that world for *Politico* readers who might not be acquainted with it.

But I think this piece might be more eye-opening for white evangelical readers—for people who *are* already familiar with that world—because what Ruth Graham highlights here is the way that a lot of conventional thinking about evangelicalism gets it backwards. That conventional thinking may once have been true, but it no longer is—and hasn't been for some time.

Evangelicalism is, notoriously, a big umbrella, but we've usually thought of the core of it as being, you know, Billy Graham and such. Mainstream white evangelicals have long thought of themselves as exactly that—the main stream

1. Ruth Graham, "Church of the Donald," *Politico*, May/June 2018, https://www
.politico.com/magazine/story/2018/04/22/trump-christian-evangelical-conservatives
-television-tbn-cbn-218008.

and the mainstream of evangelicalism. They were the embodiment of and the arbiters of evangelical normalcy and respectability.

Yes, the subculture also included lots of other, smaller, less important branches—televangelists, prosperity preachers, faith healers, snake-handlers, "Bible-prophecy scholars," Reconstructionist neo-Confederates, spiritual warfare obsessives, Ken Ham, Bob Jones, Pat freaking Robertson, etc. But those smaller fringe aspects of evangelicalism were not *typical* of the movement as a whole. Mainstream evangelicals might begrudgingly acknowledge that they were a part of the extended family, rolling their eyes at news of the latest embarrassment from *The 700 Club*, but they always insisted that those distant relatives were less consequential than the mainstream.

After all, as the great scholar of American evangelicalism George Marsden put it, an evangelical is "someone who likes *Billy Graham*"—not someone who likes Pat Robertson. Robertson may have his little cable TV show, but he rarely makes the pages of *Christianity Today*. His books aren't assigned in classes at Wheaton or Calvin, or at Fuller or TEDS [Trinity Evangelical Divinity School]. He's not regarded as influential or revered by any of the important evangelical institutions like InterVarsity or the National Association of Evangelicals. He's part of the fringe.

But what Graham's "Church of the Donald" illustrates is that this supposed "fringe" is vastly larger and far, far more influential than any of those supposedly mainstream institutions or their leaders. CBN [Christian Broadcasting Network] is bigger, more central, and more typically representative of American white evangelicalism than *Christianity Today* or Wheaton College or the National Association of Evangelicals.

It's really the old-guard "mainstream" that is now the fringe—the marginal, inconsequential, only begrudgingly accepted faction of the larger family whose presence in it is a source of embarrassment for the rest. That mainstream still thinks of itself as the bastion of the most influential and most authoritative evangelical "leadership," but those leaders lack what the leading voices of the weird fringes have: actual followers.

This fact has largely escaped notice by the leaders of "mainstream" evangelicalism—the folks I've sometimes called the "faculty lounge." The shrinking, diminishing role of their leadership might be described as the shift from them representing all Americans who "like Billy Graham" to their representing, primarily, those Americans who like *George Marsden*. (See the Postscript below.)

Robert Jones of the Public Religion Research Institute understands that the center of gravity has shifted away from the old-guard "mainstream" to what was once dismissed as the "fringe," but he hasn't yet lost the habits of the old reality. Listen to how he describes the new evangelical leadership in Graham's piece:

> Trump has actually delivered the goods in Washington, especially for this particular strain of evangelicals. And he has brought more televangelists and Christian broadcasters into his inner circle than any president before him. [Paula] White, arguably his closest spiritual adviser, hosted a show that aired on TBN [Trinity Broadcasting Network] and BET [Black Entertainment Television] for years. His lawyer, Jay Sekulow, has his own daily call-in radio show on a Christian network. Trump's faith advisory board, announced during the campaign, included many members drawn from the world of television ministry, including Ken and Gloria Copeland, who have headed a daily program since 1989; Tony Suarez, who hosts a talk show on TBN's Hispanic-oriented network; Jentezen Franklin and Robert Jeffress, whose sermons air as their own programs on TBN; and Mark Burns, who founded the web-based NOW Network. Johnnie Moore, another advisory board member, is a communications consultant who has worked with clients including CBN. "If you look at his evangelical advisory council, it's people with media connections, more than broad church-based connections," Robert Jones, CEO of the Public Religion Research Institute, says. "That's a weird slice of the evangelical world."

"Weird" is probably an inescapable word when considering people like the Copelands, but if it's meant to describe them as an atypical aberration, then it's also a misleading word here. These "people with media connections" rather than "broad church-based connections" are not merely a "*slice* of the evangelical world." They *are* that world. They are the majority of it.

It's the former "mainstream" that is now weird, that now consists only of a non-representative "slice."

The evaporating tributary of the former mainstream sent representatives of its no-longer representative brand of evangelicalism to a big "consultation" in early April 2018 at—where else?—Wheaton College. It was a gathering of people who like George Marsden. It was a vanguard without an army, a gathering of leaders without followers.

Postscript: For the record: *I* like George Marsden. Quite a bit. He is an irreplaceable, essential interpreter of 20th-century white evangelicalism. I think that admiring George Marsden is admirable. I also recognize that most white evangelicals have never heard of him and that, outside of the walls of the faculty lounge, Pat Robertson matters far, far more than he does. Heck, John Hagee matters far more than he does.

I also like and admire Mark Noll—another terrific scholar of American evangelicalism who inevitably gets mentioned in the next breath after any mention of Marsden. I think Noll's *The Scandal of the Evangelical Mind* is one of the most perceptive descriptions of white evangelicalism ever produced. That was a book that "everybody" in mainstream evangelicalism read when it came out 20+ years ago, becoming a runaway best seller for the respected mainstream evangelical publisher Wm. B. Eerdmans. It sold nearly *35,000* copies.

Contrast that with, for example, the World's Worst Books, which have sold more than 65 million copies so far.[2]

I'm not suggesting that selling only 35,000 copies means it wasn't really read by "everybody" in mainstream evangelicalism. I'm suggesting that means it *was*. That's the problem.

---

2. Fred Clark, "Left Behind Index (The Whole Thing)," *Patheos*, Nov. 5, 2015, http://www.patheos.com/blogs/slacktivist/2015/11/05/left-behind-index-the-whole-thing/.

PART III

The Current Crisis: Assessment

The five essays in part 3 maintain the dual focus on questions about defining evangelicalism and questions arising from contemporary American politics. They do so, however, from different perspectives. Thomas Kidd is a widely published historian with major books on George Whitefield and the colonial Great Awakening; Timothy Keller is pastor emeritus of Redeemer Presbyterian Church in New York City, a congregation with a widely diverse membership; Molly Worthen is a historian and commentator on recent American history, especially involving evangelicals; Jemar Tisby is a graduate student who has already made strong contributions in explaining the place of African Americans in evangelical history; and Brian Stiller, a Canadian, is Global Ambassador of the World Evangelical Alliance. Together their contributions do not "resolve" historical or contemporary difficulties, but they do flesh out the possibilities—as well as the challenges and conundrums—of evangelical history, now and in the past.

CHAPTER 12

Is the Term "Evangelical" Redeemable?

Thomas S. Kidd

Thomas Kidd, Vardaman Distinguished Professor of History at Baylor University, is a prolific historian, with well-received books on many eighteenth-century American subjects, including George Whitefield, the Great Awakening, religion and the American Revolution, Benjamin Franklin, and Patrick Henry; but also Muslims in America; Baptists in America; and more. He has also been one of the most reliable authors of op-ed columns and other commentary on evangelicals and contemporary American politics. Portions of the following essay, which gets at the heart of a question many people have been asking, appeared originally at the *Evangelical History* blog of the Gospel Coalition.

*   *   *

News stories about white evangelical support for Donald Trump have become a cottage industry. Beginning with the 81 percent of self-identified white evangelicals who voted for Trump in 2016, the media returns repeatedly to stories about how evangelicals *still* support Trump, in spite of whatever scandalous news has come out about the president.

But I wonder, who are these rank-and-file Trump supporters who tell pollsters that they are "evangelicals"? What do they believe? Do they attend church? Do their lives reflect a transforming experience of grace?

I would suggest that these poll results point to a wholesale watering down and politicization of the term "evangelical." Scholars probably can't do without the term, and historically it was quite a valuable one. But in American pop-culture parlance, "evangelical" now basically means *whites who consider themselves religious and who vote Republican.*

George Whitefield and Jonathan Edwards would be utterly perplexed by this development.[1] These early evangelicals were fighting specifically against cultural Christianity, which was politicized in state churches. In their day, if you lived in Britain or its colonies and had been baptized as an infant, you were regarded as a Christian. No questions asked.

Swimming against the stream of culture, the evangelicals of the Great Awakening preached against nominalism and national faith, declaring that you must be born again. The born-again believer would find a radically different, kingdom-minded way of life in the community of the redeemed.

Much has changed since the 1700s, and the change seems to have accelerated since the 1980s. I would point to three key factors in the corruption of the term "evangelical."

1. *The success of the evangelical movement itself.* From its origins on the fringe of Anglo-American Christianity, evangelicalism in the 1800s turned into the de facto established religion of many parts of the country, especially the South and Midwest. By the mid-twentieth century, many Americans could grow up imagining that they were "evangelicals" because that term seemed, in some quarters, equivalent to Protestant "Christian" or even "American." You were now born an evangelical, not born again as one.

2. *The political alignments of the 1970s and 1980s.* In those decades, many northern and southern white evangelicals started voting in similar ways for the first time since before the Civil War. That became apparent in their support for Nixon and his "Silent Majority" and culminated in the election of Ronald Reagan. Reagan knew many evangelicals but was not one himself, in spite of allusions he made to a born-again experience he had in the 1960s. Reagan mastered the art of evangelical-sounding talk, and he promised progress on issues like school prayer and abortion. But when he got in office, actual progress on those issues was fairly meager, with notable exceptions such as the appointment of Antonin Scalia to the Supreme Court in 1986.

Since that time, self-identifying white evangelicals have often supported GOP candidates who learn evangelical lingo and who promise good Supreme Court appointments, whatever the candidate's other positions and background. This meant that much of the media, puzzled by the concept of evangelicalism

1. Both Whitefield and Edwards had their own forms of politicized, British nationalist Christianity. It came out especially in seasons of war against Catholic powers. See, for example, Thomas S. Kidd, *George Whitefield: America's Spiritual Founding Father* (New Haven: Yale University Press, 2014), 196–97.

anyway, could disassociate evangelicals from theology, or affinity with other evangelicals, and link them inextricably with GOP politics.

3. *Modern political polling.* Political polling is pretty good at predicting electoral outcomes, even when everyone believes the numbers can't possibly be true (see Trump in the 2016 primaries). But pollsters are awful at understanding the people they're polling. The most serious problem with understanding "evangelical" political behavior, then, is letting respondents define their own religious affiliation.

We see this difficulty all over the religious map. For example, there are the much-discussed "nones," or those Americans who have "no religion." Many writers assume that the nones are agnostic or even atheist, and they certainly assume that they are nonpracticing. Baylor research has shown, however, that when you dig deeper with people who say they have "no religion" in polls, you find that a significant fraction of them attend church regularly. (These are the "nones" who say, "I am not religious. I have a relationship with Jesus.")[2]

Likewise, time-strapped pollsters often let people tell them that they are evangelicals, without probing what that means. Indeed, calling oneself an "evangelical" was not that common until the word gained traction in the media in the 1976 presidential election. In the 2016 primaries, some evidence suggested that "evangelicals" who did not attend church were more likely to support Trump. (To be fair, post-2016 election surveys indicated that "churchgoing" evangelicals were more likely to support Trump.) For those who have a deeper understanding of the term's meaning, there can be no such thing as a nonchurchgoing evangelical. But polls typically don't account for these sorts of nuances.

Are many of these "evangelicals" in the polls honest-to-goodness evangelicals? Of course. But I also suspect that, tragically, many others of these supposed American evangelicals have no clear understanding of the term "evangelical," or of the gospel itself. Polling by LifeWay Research has confirmed that many who identify as evangelicals don't actually hold to basic evangelical beliefs, such as Christ's atoning death or Jesus as the unique savior. Meanwhile, African Americans are the ethnic group most likely to hold evangelical beliefs.[3] But African Americans and many other traditionalist Protestant people

2. "Baylor Researcher Refutes Reports of Religion's Decline in America," Baylor University, September 25, 2014, https://www.baylor.edu/mediacommunications/news.php?action=story&story=146819.

3. Bob Smietana, "LifeWay Research: Many Who Call Themselves Evangelical Don't Actually Hold Evangelical Beliefs," LifeWay, December 6, 2017, https://blog.life

of color steer away from the term "evangelical" itself, since it comes with so much ethnic and political baggage. And pollsters often only provide a category, explicitly or implicitly, for white evangelicals anyway.

Why would someone who does not attend church, or who does not hold evangelical beliefs, still call himself or herself an evangelical? We won't know without much more rigorous and expensive polling data. Some nominal white evangelicals presumably figure that "I'm Republican, conservative [another ill-defined term], and a Protestant, therefore I am an evangelical." Or maybe they think, "Well, I watch Fox News, so I must be an evangelical."

These vague associations have turned "evangelical" into a term that luminaries like Jonathan Edwards and George Whitefield would not recognize. And, more problematically, they represent a faux gospel of moralism, nationalism, and politicization. That is a gospel that certainly cannot save.

Historians (including me) will keep on using the term "evangelical" and examining what it has meant in the past. But in public references to ourselves, it is probably time to put "evangelical" on the shelf.

What else will we call ourselves? That may be the biggest problem with not using "evangelical." One option is just to identify with your denomination. (For me, that means Baptist.) Or you can tell people you are a follower of Jesus Christ, or a gospel Christian.

I know there are occasions where you just can't be nuanced. But if a pollster asked me today if I was an evangelical, I couldn't give the pollster a straight answer. I don't want to be lumped in with an amorphous mass of white religious Republicans who share ethnicity and voting behavior but not biblical beliefs or the experience of conversion. If "evangelical" has become fundamentally politicized and divisive, we can get along fine without employing the term.

---

way.com/newsroom/2017/12/06/lifeway-research-many-who-call-themselves-evangel ical-dont-actually-hold-evangelical-beliefs/.

CHAPTER 13

Can Evangelicalism Survive Donald Trump?

Timothy Keller

Timothy Keller is the founder and pastor emeritus of the Redeemer Presbyterian Churches of New York City. Although his ministry and his writing—including *Making Sense of God: Finding God in the Modern World* (Viking, 2016) and *Preaching: Communicating Faith in an Age of Skepticism* (Viking, 2015)—testify to the use he makes of scholarship, he approaches current American debates over the meaning of evangelicalism as an active practitioner.

This article was published in the *New Yorker* on December 19, 2017, under the title "Can Evangelicalism Survive Donald Trump and Roy Moore?" It is used here by the permission of the author.

*   *   *

For centuries, renewal movements have emerged within Christianity and taken on different forms and names. Often, they have invoked the word "evangelical." Followers of Martin Luther, who emphasized the doctrine of salvation by faith alone, described themselves in this way. The Cambridge clergyman Charles Simeon, who led the Low Church renewal movement within the Church of England, adopted the label. The transatlantic eighteenth-century awakenings and revivals led by the Wesleys were also often called "evangelical." In the 1940s and '50s, Billy Graham and others promoted the word to describe themselves and the religious space they were seeking to create between the cultural withdrawal espoused by the fundamentalist movement, on the one hand, and mainline Protestantism's departures from historic Christian doctrine, on the other. In each of these phases, the term has had a somewhat different meaning, and yet it keeps surfacing because it has described a set of basic historic beliefs and impulses.

When I became a Christian in college, in the early 1970s, the word "evangelical" still meant an alternative to the fortress mentality of fundamentalism. Shortly thereafter, I went to Gordon-Conwell Theological Seminary, to prepare for the Presbyterian ministry. It was one of the many institutions that Graham, Harold Ockenga, and J. Howard Pew, and other neo-evangelicals, as they were sometimes called, established. In those years, there was such great energy in the movement that, by the mid-1990s, it had eclipsed mainline Protestantism as the dominant branch of the Christian church in the U.S. When I moved to Manhattan to start a new church, in 1989, most people I met found the church and its ministry to be a curiosity in secular New York but not a threat. And, if they heard the word "evangelical" around the congregation, a name we seldom used, they usually asked what it meant.

Today, while the name is no longer unfamiliar in my city, its meaning has changed drastically. The conservative leaders who have come to be most identified with the movement have largely driven this redefinition. But political pollsters have also helped, as they have sought to highlight a crucial voting bloc. When they survey people, there is no discussion of any theological beliefs, or other criteria. The great majority of them simply ask people, "Would you describe yourself as a born-again or evangelical Christian?" And those who answer yes are counted. More than 80 percent of such people voted for Donald Trump, and in early December 2017, a similar percentage cast their ballots for Roy Moore, in the Alabama Senate race, even after Moore's alleged history of preying on young women came to light. So, in common parlance, evangelicals have become people with two qualities: they are both self-professed Christians and doggedly conservative politically.

The fury and incredulity of many in the larger population at this constituency have mounted. People who once called themselves the "Moral Majority" are now seemingly willing to vote for anyone, however immoral, who supports their political positions. The disgust has come to include people within the movement itself. Earlier this month, Peter Wehner, an op-ed writer for the *Times* who served in the last three Republican administrations, wrote a widely circulated piece entitled "Why I Can No Longer Call Myself an Evangelical Republican." Many younger believers and Christians of color, who had previously identified with evangelicalism, have also declared their abandonment of the label. "Evangelical" used to denote people who claimed the high moral ground; now, in popular usage, the word is nearly synonymous with "hypocrite." When I used the word to describe myself in the 1970s, it meant I was not a fundamentalist. If I use the name today, however, it means to hearers that I *am*.

Understanding the religious landscape, however, requires discerning differences between the smaller, let's call it "big *E* Evangelicalism," which gets much media attention, and a much larger, little *e* evangelicalism, which does not. The larger, lowercase evangelicalism is defined not by a political party, whether conservative, liberal, or populist, but by theological beliefs. This non-political definition of evangelicalism has been presented in many places. The most well known is by the historian David Bebbington, whose *Evangelicalism in Modern Britain: A History from the 1730s to the 1980s* has become standard. He distinguishes evangelicals from other religions and Christians by a core set of beliefs. Evangelicals have generally believed in the authority of the whole Bible, in contrast to mainline Protestants, who regard many parts as obsolete, according to Bebbington. They also see it as the ultimate authority, unlike Catholics, who make church tradition equal to it. In addition, the ancient creedal formulations of the church, such as the Apostles' Creed and the Nicene Creed, as well as others, are taken at face value, without reservation. And, again, unlike many in mainline Protestantism, evangelicals believe that Jesus truly did exist as the divine Son before he was born, that he actually was born of a virgin, and that he really was raised bodily from the dead.

Under Bebbington's formulation, another defining evangelical quality is the belief in the necessity of conversion, the conviction that everyone needs a profound, life-changing encounter with God. This conversion, however, comes not merely through church attendance or general morality, but only through faith in Christ's sacrificial death for sin. A lyric from Charles Wesley's famous hymn captures the evangelical experience of conversion through saving faith in Christ alone: "My chains fell off, my heart was free; I rose, went forth, and followed thee." Finally, contemporary evangelicals feel bound by both desire and duty to share their faith with others in both word and deeds of service. In this, they seek to resemble, as well as to obey, their Lord, Jesus, who is described as mighty in word and deed.

Do the self-identified white "big *E* Evangelicals" of the pollsters hold to these beliefs? Recent studies indicate that many do not. In many parts of the country, Evangelicalism serves as the civil or folk religion accepted by default as part of one's social and political identity. So, in many cases, it means that the political is more defining than theological beliefs, which has not been the case historically. And, because of the enormous amount of attention the media pays to the Evangelical vote, the term now has a decisively political meaning in popular usage.

Yet there exists a far larger evangelicalism, both here and around the world, which is not politically aligned. In the U.S., there are millions of evangelicals spread throughout mainline Protestant congregations, as well as in more theologically conservative denominations like the Assemblies of God, the Southern Baptist Convention, and the Lutheran Church–Missouri Synod. But, most significantly, the vast majority of the fast-growing Protestant churches in Asia, Latin America, and Africa all share these same beliefs. And in the U.S., while white Evangelicalism is aging and declining, evangelicalism overall is not.

The enormous energy of the churches in the global South and East has begun to spill over into the cities of North America, where a new, multiethnic evangelicalism is growing steadily. Non-Western missionaries have started thousands of new urban churches there since the 1970s. Here in New York City, even within Manhattan, I have seen scores of churches begun over the last fifteen years that are fully evangelical by our definition, only a minority of which are white, and which are not aligned with any political party.

In my view, these churches tend to be much more committed to racial justice and care for the poor than is commonly seen in white Evangelicalism. In this way, they might be called liberal. On the other hand, these multicultural churches remain avowedly conservative on issues like sex outside of marriage. They look, to most eyes, like a strange mixture of liberal and conservative viewpoints, although they themselves see a strong inner consistency between these views. They resist the contemporary ethical package deals that today's progressivism and conservatism seek to impose on adherents, insisting that true believers must toe the line on every one of a host of issues. But these younger evangelical churches simply won't play by those rules.

In a book published earlier this year, *In Search of Ancient Roots: The Christian Past and the Evangelical Identity Crisis*, the historian Kenneth J. Stewart makes the case that the evangelical impulse in Christianity has been with us for centuries, taking on many different forms and bearing many different names, while maintaining substantially similar core beliefs. Many have analyzed the weaknesses of the current iteration of this movement. The desire by mid-twentieth-century leaders to foster more widespread cooperation between evangelicals and downplay denominational differences cut believers off from the past, some religion scholars have found. The result was an emphasis on personal experience rather than life in a church with historical memory. This has made present-day evangelicals more vulnerable to political movements that appeal to their self-interest, even in contradiction to biblical teachings, for example, about welcoming the immigrant and lifting up the poor. However, evangelicalism is much more resilient than any one form of itself. The newer forms that are emerging are more concerned with theological and historic roots, and are more resistant to modern individualism than older, white Evangelicalism.

Does the word, then, have an ongoing usefulness? For now, the answer may be no. These new urban churches are certainly not mainline Protestant, yet they don't look at all like what the average person thinks of by the term "Evangelical." Will these younger churches abandon the name or try to redefine it? I don't know, but, as a professional minister, I don't think it is the most important point to make. What is crucial to know is that, even if the name "evangelical" is replaced with something else, it does not mean that the churches will lose their beliefs. Some time ago, the word "liberal" was largely abandoned by Democrats in favor of the word "progressive." In some ways, the Democratic Party is more liberal now than when the older label was set aside, evidence that it is quite possible to change the name but keep the substance.

The same thing may be happening to evangelicalism. The movement may abandon, or at least demote, the prominence of the name, yet be more committed to its theology and historic impulses than ever. Some predict that younger evangelicals will not only reject the name but also become more secular. That is not what I have been seeing here in New York City. And studies by the Pew Research Center and others indicate that religious denominations that have become more friendly to secularism are shrinking precipitously, while the evangelical churches that resist dilution in their theological beliefs and practices are holding their own or growing. And if evangelicals—or whatever they will call themselves—continue to become more multiethnic in leadership and confound the left-right political categories, they may continue to do so.

CHAPTER 14

Idols of the Trump Era

Molly Worthen

The years after Donald Trump's election to the White House presented American evangelicals with many political and moral dilemmas. One such crossroads appeared in the fall of 2017, when Trump's appointment of Jeff Sessions, senator from Alabama, as attorney general triggered a special election to choose his replacement in the Senate. The race pitted Democratic candidate Doug Jones against Roy Moore, a Republican firebrand and Southern Baptist. Moore first came to national attention when, as chief justice of the state's supreme court, he led a campaign to install a large granite monument displaying the Ten Commandments in the rotunda of the state courthouse—and then defied a federal court order to remove it. Moore appealed to many conservative evangelicals as a culture warrior who would go to great lengths to preserve their vision of America as a Christian nation.

Then, in the course of the 2017 campaign, nine women accused Moore of inappropriate sexual conduct. Some said that they had been mere teenagers when Moore assaulted them. As the testimonies against Moore mounted, many conservative white evangelical supporters continued to defend him. One Alabama public official even invoked the Gospels in an attempt to downplay the allegations: "take Joseph and Mary," he said. "Mary was a teenager and Joseph was an adult carpenter. They became the parents of Jesus." Yet this surge of support for Moore prompted other evangelicals to challenge the conservative, mostly white, face of their faith—and to ask whether the culture wars had driven their fellow believers into political idolatry. This essay first appeared in the *New York Times* on November 19, 2017, under the headline "How to Escape from Roy Moore's Evangelicalism."

Molly Worthen, who teaches in the history department at the University of North Carolina, is a widely published historian and essayist on American religious life. She is the author of *Apostles of Reason: The Crisis of Authority in American Evangelicalism* (Oxford University Press, 2013); her journalism appears in many national publications.

*   *   *

Kaitlyn Schiess has a sterling evangelical pedigree. She grew up in evangelical churches in Colorado and Virginia and graduated from Liberty University before entering Dallas Theological Seminary last year to prepare for a career in the church. But lately she has been frustrated by evangelicals' failure to challenge the prejudice and predation in their midst. Over the course of the week, as Roy Moore, the Republican senatorial candidate in Alabama, faced more allegations of inappropriate sexual contact with young women and teenagers, many evangelicals leapt to his defense.

To Ms. Schiess, this is one more sign that a new ritual has superseded Sunday worship and weeknight Bible studies: a profane devotional practice, with immense power to shape evangelicals' beliefs. This "liturgy" is the nightly consumption of conservative cable news. Liberals love to complain about conservatives' steady diet of misinformation through partisan media, but Ms. Schiess's complaint is more profound: Sean Hannity and Tucker Carlson aren't just purveyors of distorted news, but high priests of a false religion.

"The reason Fox News is so formative is that it's this repetitive, almost ritualistic thing that people do every night," Ms. Schiess told me. "It forms in them particular fears and desires, an idea of America. This is convincing on a less than logical level, and the church is not communicating to them in that same way."

It's no secret that humans—religious and secular alike—often act on "less than logical" impulses. Social scientists have documented our tendency to reject reliable evidence if it challenges our beliefs. Hours of tearful victims' testimony will not deter evangelicals who see Roy Moore as the latest Christian martyr persecuted by the liberal establishment. "Their loyalties are much more strongly formed by conservative media than their churches," Ms. Schiess said. "That's the challenge for church leaders today, I think—rediscovering rather ancient ideas about how to form our ultimate loyalty to God and his kingdom."

When I sought out conservative and progressive critics of white evangelical politics and asked them how to best understand it, this was their answer: pay attention to worship, both inside and outside of church, because the church is not doing its job. Humans thrive on ritual and collective acts of devotion. And the way we worship has political consequences. It shapes our response to evil and our reaction to people different from ourselves.

Some evangelicals have grown so frustrated with their tradition's captivity to a particular brand of politics—and the idolatries of white supremacy and the free market—that they have proposed a radical withdrawal from both Moral Majority–style activism and modern consumer culture. Worship, after all, is not just something that happens in church.

The philosopher James K. A. Smith, who teaches at Calvin College in Grand Rapids, Mich., has argued that our lives are shot through with unconscious acts of worship, whether we genuflect at the Apple Store or wake up whispering prayers for our child's admission to the Ivy League. "We are, ultimately, liturgical animals because we are fundamentally desiring creatures," he writes in his book *Desiring the Kingdom*. "We are what we love."

In that case, rooting out idolatries means radical lifestyle change. Some disillusioned conservatives have embraced what the Christian writer Rod Dreher calls the "Benedict Option": a retreat from the world to preserve the values of Christian civilization during these new Dark Ages, in the spirit of St. Benedict.

He argues that Christians should stop trying to "make America great again," abandon the ends-justify-the-means politics that leads them to defend predators and scoundrels like Mr. Moore, and focus instead on nurturing local Christian community. "Hostile secular nihilism has won the day in our nation's government, and the culture has turned powerfully against traditional Christians," Mr. Dreher writes in *The Benedict Option*.

This kind of intense localism may lead one to befriend unfamiliar neighbors, and hospitality is a major theme of Mr. Dreher's book. But at a time when many Americans live in economically and ethnically segregated communities, it seems doubtful that further withdrawal from the world will stimulate radical empathy. The urge to batten down the hatches may actually feed the cultural patterns that enabled the election of Donald Trump: the impulse to associate only with people like ourselves and grow even more certain that evil forces are persecuting us.

Luma Simms likes to say that she tried the Benedict Option before it was trendy. She emigrated to California from Iraq as a young girl. Her father was Syrian Orthodox, her mother a Chaldean Catholic, but the desire to assimilate drove her to convert to evangelical Protestantism. "When I asked myself, what does it mean to become American, part of the answer was espousing an evangelical Protestant worldview," she told me. "I wanted to be on the political side that believed America was good."

After Ms. Simms became a parent, she began to worry about the influence of secular culture on her children as well as the politicization of mainstream evangelicalism. In 2006 her family moved to Arizona to join an insular church that promoted home schooling and strict patriarchal authority. "We were protecting our children, raising them up to be stronger citizens of a rightly understood America, so that when American culture starts collapsing like Dreher keeps telling us it will, they would rise up, having been well disciplined and educated, to become leaders," she said.

The community was so cloistered and dogmatic that it estranged her from her oldest daughter and pushed her to cut off contact with her own parents. The church "made families like us view almost everyone outside that circle as a potential enemy of our thoughts," Ms. Simms told me. After a dispute over the pastor's authority, the church disintegrated in 2010.

Even mainstream churches can inadvertently encourage this kind of cultural quarantine: Most Americans still bow their heads in congregations dominated by a single racial or ethnic group. Although the diversity of congregations is growing nationwide, eight in 10 Americans still attend a house of worship in which one ethnic group makes up at least 80 percent of the congregation, according to the most recent National Congregations Study.

Reformers have long been working to build multiracial bridges in Christian academia and media, but these efforts alone won't desegregate religious fellowship. Ekemini Uwan is a Nigerian-American who has ventured farther than most black Christians into the citadels of white evangelicalism. Last year she graduated from Westminster Theological Seminary in Glenside, Pa. For most of her time there, she was the only black woman in her program, she told me (the school has a sizable Asian student population, but fewer than 6 percent of students identify as black or Latino). She writes for traditionally white evangelical media, like *Christianity Today* magazine. But she has continued to attend "a predominantly black church" in Philadelphia, she said.

Ms. Uwan is used to keeping her guard up in scholarship and journalism, but worship is different: It requires the freedom to be vulnerable. "There's what we theologians call an eschatological intrusion. It's a foretaste of what we're going to experience with God around the throne in the new heavens and new earth. It gets us out of our own world for an hour or two. You're lost in worship, in wonder." In a largely white worship setting, "when you have to prove yourself all the time, when your orthodoxy is always in question due to your blackness, you're not safe to be vulnerable and honest," she said.

When the Rev. Dr. Martin Luther King Jr. observed that 11 o'clock on a Sunday morning is the most segregated hour in America, he was acknowledging the special power that ritual and community have to stoke or weaken both love and hatred. There is no substitute for sharing the bread and wine—the climax of the Christian liturgy—with people unlike yourself, Ms. Schiess said. She called for fighting false idols with right worship: "Fox News forms a fear, a caricature of other people; if communion were done in churches with diverse populations, it would counteract that fear."

A new theology of communion appealed to Ms. Simms, the Christian in Arizona. A few years ago she converted to Catholicism, moved by its balance of otherworldliness and earthly compassion: "The sacraments elevate us," she said. For Catholics, the bread and wine are not metaphors for Jesus' body and blood, but the real thing—a miraculous, fleshly conduit between God and creation. The Vatican has stressed the doctrine of the "mystical body of Christ"—which includes, at least potentially, all human beings—in response to racism, genocide and other atrocities of the 20th century.

Catholic theology is not inherently more moral than Protestantism, and the sacraments have not saved the Catholic Church from its share of hypocrisy and crime over the centuries. But for some evangelicals, a stronger sense of participation in holy mystery offers a metaphysical jolt to the system—at a time when the relationship between evangelical worship and politics seems broken.

Richard Rohr, a Franciscan friar and prolific author who runs the Center for Action and Contemplation in Albuquerque, was surprised when his publisher told him that his books on Christian contemplation and the power of liturgy are most popular with young evangelical men—who see a direct connection between changing worship and changing politics. "So many of the millennial evangelicals I work with, they're so disillusioned with their good parents' inability to deal with racism, sexism and homophobia—the issues tearing our country apart," he told me.

Other young Christians are pursuing new forms of worship outside of traditional churches altogether. If you're wondering what the future of not-so-organized religion looks like, look to the community that has grown up around "The Liturgists," a podcast hosted by Michael Gungor, a musician, and Mike McHargue, a science writer (both are former evangelicals).

When they began the podcast in 2014, "we started it out of a sense of existential loneliness," Mr. Gungor told me. They broadcast liturgical music, meditations and interviews with theologians and activists. The podcast has nurtured a community with a life of its own. Listeners find one another through social media, and the co-hosts travel the country to convene events where fans eat, drink and worship together—groups that often continue meeting after Mr. Gungor and Mr. McHargue leave town.

"As America deinstitutionalizes and moves away from religion, people—especially millennials—have lost something. Their community becomes primarily virtual, they're seeing people through a screen and not flesh and blood, and there's great data that this leads them to loneliness and depression," Mr. McHargue said. "The core of every podcast is, 'you're not alone,' and that draws people in, but we can't stay there. We have to draw them into some kind of communal practice."

One to two million listeners download the podcast each month, and it is surely one of the most theologically diverse subcultures on the internet. The audience includes atheists, evangelicals, mainline liberal Protestants, Catholics and Orthodox Christians, all seeking new spiritual community.

All these people have one thing in common: the instinct that worship should be an act of humility, not hubris. It should be a discomfiting experience, not a doubling down on what's easy and familiar. The battle for the soul of evangelicalism, the struggle to disentangle it from white supremacy, from misogyny—and from the instinct to defend politicians like Roy Moore—demands sound arguments grounded in evidence. But the effort must also advance at the precognitive level, in the habits and relationships of worshiping communities. Fellowship has the power to refashion angry gut feelings and instead form meek hearts and bounden duty.

CHAPTER 15

Are Black Christians Evangelicals?

JEMAR TISBY

Jemar Tisby is president and cofounder of The Witness: A Black Christian Collective. His first book, *The Color of Compromise: The Truth about the American Church's Complicity in Racism*, was published by Zondervan in January 2019. Tisby's essays on race, religion, and contemporary America have appeared in the *New York Times*, *Washington Post*, *Christianity Today*, and elsewhere. He is a graduate of the University of Notre Dame and Reformed Theological Seminary, Jackson, Mississippi; he is now a PhD student studying race and twentieth-century American history at the University of Mississippi. This essay, which visits a subject addressed several times in the preceding pages, was written expressly for this book.

*   *   *

The 2016 US presidential election brought questions of religion and politics surging to the fore of national conversations. Evangelicals, in particular, became the subject of much debate, as observers analyzed and commented on the massive support, 81 percent, that evangelical voters gave to the man who became the forty-fifth president of the United States, Donald J. Trump. These men and women, often labeled "values voters" and the "Religious Right," mobilized their support behind a man notorious for philandering, vulgar language, half-truths, and lies, all while showing only a passing familiarity with the Bible and basic Christian doctrines.

In the wake of the election, the baffled, the curious, and the outraged public started asking a question American religious scholars have debated for decades, "What is an evangelical?"

What goes unstated in most of the contemporary discussions about evangelicals is that the designation refers mainly to white evangelicals. People of color, black people in particular, do not fit many of the descriptions, especially in terms of political patterns, that apply to white evangelicals.[1] To complicate matters further, many black Christians share much in common theologically with white evangelicals. They believe in the bodily resurrection of Jesus Christ, the need for a personal relationship with Christ, and the importance of evangelism to spread the good news. Some black Christians are even members of predominantly white evangelical churches. The question arises, then, "Are black Christians evangelicals?"

This essay addresses that question from an interdisciplinary perspective by means of a theoretical framework and a case study. Borrowing from theologian and philosopher John Frame's tri-perspectival method, we will examine the term "evangelical" from multiple angles to assess whether black Christians are evangelicals. Once the theoretical parameters have been set, an examination of Tom Skinner, a self-described black evangelical, will demonstrate whether black Christians fit within late twentieth-century manifestations of evangelicalism.

This study will show that from a variety of perspectives, black Christians can be considered evangelicals, but to the extent that they assert racial and social justice concerns, their participation in white evangelical circles has been circumscribed. Black Christians in evangelical churches and organizations must always face the issue of limits and control based on how explicitly they address the issues—such as racism, police brutality, economic inequality, and access to quality education—in their ministry and how comfortable the white majority is with their message.

In the end, this study illuminates more than whether black Christians are evangelicals. It also asserts the importance of race in the broader endeavor to define and describe evangelicalism. Race sits at the heart of evangelical theology, church polity, and political outlooks. Any explanation of evangelicalism that treats race as a peripheral matter misses a primary characteristic of the movement. Insisting on the centrality of race to definitions of evangelicalism highlights the ways race informs religion and how religion informs race.

---

1. For example, responses from black Protestant Christians are often separated from white evangelical Christians in surveys and polls.

The Theory: A Tri-Perspectival Approach

Historians have not yet agreed on a definition of evangelicalism. This is partly because it is a dynamic movement constantly shaped by and shaping the context around it. Mark Noll points out that "evangelicalism was and is a set of defining beliefs and practices easier to see as an adjective (e.g., evangelical Anglicans, evangelical missionary efforts, evangelical doctrine) than as a simple noun."[2] Nevertheless, David Bebbington's description of four main evangelical characteristics proves a beneficial starting point. According to this "quadrilateral," evangelicals emphasize "conversionism," an emphasis on a personal decision to follow Jesus Christ; biblicism, an understanding of the Bible that interprets miracles as true and Scripture as divinely inspired; crucicentrism, a focus on the crucifixion of Christ as a sacrifice for his followers; and activism, an engaged faith whose adherents seek to influence the broader culture with their beliefs.

To Bebbington's quadrilateral, other historians have added helpful modifications. For instance, Timothy Gloege emphasizes the individualism present in much of evangelicalism. An individualistic relationship to a personal God coupled with a similarly individualistic interpretation of the Bible that opts for a "plain" reading of sacred text makes evangelicalism distinctive from other Christian traditions that might otherwise fit into Bebbington's quadrilateral.[3] Journalist Kenneth Woodward defines evangelicalism as "essentially an entrepreneurial religion." This tendency to strike out and start new churches and religious organizations captures evangelicalism's distinguishing feature.[4] After a detailed linguistic analysis, Hannah Butler and Kristin Du Mez emphasize the political aspect of modern evangelicalism. They conclude that "it seems reasonable to assume that when Americans self-identify as evangelicals today, many are identifying with the movement as it has taken shape in recent decades—a conservative politicized movement—and not with a static conception rooted in a centuries-old history."[5] The basic theological contours

---

2. Mark A. Noll, *The Rise of Evangelicalism: The Age of Edwards, Whitefield, and the Wesleys* (Downers Grove, IL: IVP Academic, 2003), 21.

3. Lutherans, for example, might fit Bebbington's quadrilateral description, but the ecclesiology of the church precludes the kind of individualistic interpretation of Scripture inherent in large segments of American evangelicalism.

4. Kenneth L. Woodward, *Getting Religion: Faith, Culture, and Politics from the Age of Eisenhower to the Ascent of Trump* (New York: Convergent Books, 2016), 129.

5. Hannah Butler and Kristin Du Mez, "The Reinvention of 'Evangelical' in American History: A Linguistic Analysis," *Anxious Bench*, May 31, 2018.

of evangelicalism can be debated and refined, but there's another approach, actually multiple approaches, to defining evangelicalism.

John Frame served as the chair of systematic theology and philosophy at Reformed Theological Seminary's Orlando campus. He has written multiple lengthy volumes on Christian epistemology and apologetics. He, along with his colleague Vern Poythress, devised a way of understanding theology known as tri-perspectivalism. As the term indicates, it focuses on three perspectives: normative, situational, and existential. Although Frame has extended treatments of each perspective, they broadly correspond to knowledge of God, knowledge of the world, and knowledge of self.[6] In Frame's words, the normative perspective asks, "What do God's norms direct us to believe?" The situational perspective asks, "What are the facts?" The existential perspective asks, "What belief is most satisfying to a believing heart?" Each perspective informs the others, and all are necessary for a more complete understanding of the object under scrutiny. The specific Christian connotations of Frame's framework need not enter into this discussion, but his categorizations prove helpful in defining evangelicalism.

For the purposes of this essay, the normative perspective corresponds to evangelical theology as a standard of religious truth. The situational perspective includes the patterns and events within evangelicalism as they have unfolded throughout American history. Finally, the existential perspective refers to an individual's experience of evangelicalism as well as whether one self-identifies as an evangelical.

Disagreements about the definition of evangelicalism may happen, in part, simply because historians attempt to define it from different, though not necessarily mutually exclusive, perspectives. One historian may point to Bebbington's quadrilateral, which emphasizes the normative-theological aspects of evangelicalism. Another may point to the rise of the Religious Right and the connection between evangelicalism and conservative politics, which places the situational-historical perspective at the fore. Yet others may speak of an existential-individual perspective and point out whether a person self-references as an evangelical, as in the case of Billy Graham.

When applied to the question of whether black Christians are evangelicals, each perspective lends valuable insights. Normative-theologically speak-

---

6. For a detailed explanation, see Frame's *Doctrine of the Knowledge of God: A Theology of Lordship* (Phillipsburg, NJ: P&R, 1987). A short explanation can be found in his essay "A Primer on Perspectivalism," in *John Frame's Selected Shorter Writings*, vol. 1 (Phillipsburg, NJ: P&R, 2014).

ing, can black Christians be considered evangelicals? The answer is yes. Black Christians hold many of the same core beliefs as evangelicals. Referring again to the quadrilateral taxonomy, many black Christians would adhere to biblicism, conversionism, crucicentrism, and activism.

From the situational-historian perspective, black Christians should also be considered evangelicals. White missionaries had little success converting black slaves to Christianity until the Great Awakenings of the eighteenth and nineteenth centuries. Many black people converted to Christianity in the revivals hosted by evangelists such as George Whitefield. Some of these large open-air revivals allowed both black and white participants, although they were still segregated into different areas; so black and white listeners converted under the same preacher and the same preaching. If black Christians and white evangelicals found the same messages convincing, then it would be reasonable to include black believers as evangelicals.

Historically, black Christians even attended the same congregations. As Charles F. Irons writes in his book *The Origins of Proslavery Christianity*, "Sunday morning only became the most segregated time of the week after the Civil War. Before emancipation, black and white evangelicals typically prayed, sang, and worshiped together."[7] This interracial interaction was not the result of egalitarian notions of white Christians but an expression of paternalism and a means to prevent slave insurrection. Nevertheless, black Christians and white evangelicals showed up to the same place on Sunday and often heard the same message. So from the situational-historical perspective, yes, black Christians should be considered evangelicals.

Lastly, from the existential-individual perspective, many black Christians have in fact referred to themselves as evangelicals. The clearest twentieth-century example of this is the organization called the National Black Evangelical Association (NBEA). The reasons for the formation of the NBEA in 1963 out of the National Evangelical Association (NEA) necessitates a separate study, but it is telling that black Christians called themselves "evangelical" in the title of their new organization. Howard O. Jones, a member of the NBEA, served as the first black associate evangelist for Billy Graham, and *Christianity Today* called him "the Jackie Robinson of evangelism."[8] Since using their own

7. Charles F. Irons, *The Origins of Proslavery Christianity: White and Black Evangelicals in Colonial and Antebellum Virginia* (Chapel Hill: University of North Carolina Press, 2008), 1.

8. Edward Gilbreath, "The 'Jackie Robinson' of Evangelism," *Christianity Today*, February 9, 1998.

terms ascribes agency to the subjects under consideration, the fact that black Christians themselves used the term "evangelical" to describe their beliefs and associations is perhaps the most compelling reason to answer the question, "Are black Christians evangelicals?" in the affirmative.

From all three perspectives, black Christians can indeed be called evangelicals. But additional factors complicate this answer. Why are there so few black Christians in white evangelical churches and denominations? Why are black Christians pushing back against the term "evangelical" and refusing to claim the label? Why do black and white evangelicals express their faith so differently? All these questions point to the final salient factor in answering whether black Christians are evangelicals—race.

The Case Study: Tom Skinner at Urbana '70

None of the twelve thousand college students at Urbana '70, the triennial conference on evangelism hosted by the InterVarsity campus ministry, knew what to expect when Tom Skinner took the stage for the keynote address. But they were eager to hear him. The nationally known black evangelist from Harlem had ignited tens of thousands of people with his evangelistic crusades. What they heard that night was no different.

"Any understanding of world evangelism and racism in our country must begin with an understanding of the history of racism," Skinner began.[9] He then went on to trace America's racial history from 1619 to the late twentieth century. Skinner decried the failure of Christian fundamentalists and liberals alike to address the spiritual and physical well-being of inner-city inhabitants.

Skinner then made a rhetorical move that his largely white, evangelical audience probably did not anticipate. He started talking about systems, revolution, and liberation. "I am a militant; make no bones about it," he proclaimed. "Jesus was militant. And there are those of us who will be called to adopt the militant lifestyle." Skinner added an evangelical inflection to his liberationist discourse. In a climactic ending, Skinner shouted, "Proclaim liberation to the captives, preach sight to the blind, set at liberty them that are bruised, go into the world and tell men who are bound mentally, spiritually and physically, 'The liberator has come!'"

9. Tom Skinner, "The U.S. Racial Crisis and World Evangelism," InterVarsity, December 1970, https://urbana.org/message/us-racial-crisis-and-world-evangelism.

Tom Skinner's momentous speech at Urbana '70 illustrates the limits of black Christians within majority white evangelicalism. The backlash he faced in the aftermath of that address related directly to his connections between traditional evangelicalism and the specific applications he made to racial problems and the plight of black Americans. Skinner's story serves as a helpful case study not because everyone experienced exactly what he did, but because his narrative puts in stark relief what many everyday black Christians experienced on a smaller scale when they pushed the boundaries on race and justice.

Born in 1942 to Alester and Georgia Skinner, a couple who had moved to Harlem as part of the great migration of black people out of the South, Thomas Skinner spent some of his teenage years as a gang leader until he underwent a dramatic conversion to Christianity. In 1954, when he was twelve, a couple of neighborhood teens approached Skinner about joining their gang, the Harlem Lords. Having been beat up on the way to the grocery store and accosted by neighborhood teens more than once, Skinner decided to join the Lords. Two years later, he challenged the gang's captain to a duel for control of the group. He won and became a teenage gang leader.

After two years of gang activity, Skinner turned from a life of crime and violence literally overnight. As he recalls in his autobiography published in 1969, Skinner had sat down to map out a strategy for a gang fight the next day. He was listening to a rock-and-roll radio program, but instead of the regularly scheduled station break at 9 p.m., the radio station aired a sermon. As he listened to the radio, all of his objections to Christianity began to fall away. "There was no emotional, traumatic experience that night. I simply accepted God at his word." Skinner bowed his head and prayed for Jesus Christ to enter his life. When he looked up again, he knew something had changed.[10]

Skinner, now an ex–gang leader and a new Christian, could not contain his enthusiasm about his newfound faith. He immediately began talking about religion to any Harlem resident who would listen and telling them to believe his interpretation of the good news. Eventually, he began holding Billy Graham–style crusades in Harlem and other majority black communities. In fact, Skinner's oratorical flair and evangelistic fervor gained him a nickname at the time as "the black Billy Graham."[11]

10. Tom Skinner, *Black and Free*, rev. ed. (Tracys Landing, MD: Skinner Leadership Institute, 2013), location 1090.

11. Randall Balmer, *Encyclopedia of Evangelicalism* (Louisville: Westminster John Knox, 2002), 530.

As the 1960s progressed, comparisons between evangelicals like Graham and Skinner would become increasingly difficult to make. By the time of Skinner's speech at Urbana, he was speaking out against white evangelical apathy in the face of persistent racial discrimination. Skinner's form of evangelicalism consciously drew on elements of the Black Power movement of the late 1960s and 1970s, which emphasized a collective racial identity, an awareness of national black freedom struggles, and a militant style of proclamation. In the process, it provided an ideological challenge to white dominance within evangelicalism and a broader social critique of racial inequality in America. Skinner's words that night at Urbana '70 gave a clear sense of how he redeployed evangelicalism within a black racial framework.

As Skinner brought his exhortation to a close, he explained that the choice between a message of spiritual salvation and social uplift was a false dichotomy. "There is no possible way you can talk about preaching the gospel if you do not want to deal with the issues that bind people. If your gospel is an 'either-or' gospel, I must reject it." Instead of this binary choice, Skinner pointed to an alternative—black power evangelicalism. He spoke of Jesus as a "revolutionary." He described Jesus as a radical concerned with overthrowing an unjust system, but who did not use guns. Instead he healed the sick, spoke words of comfort to prostitutes, and aligned himself with the poor. The most revolutionary act of this religious leader, according to Skinner, was willingly dying for a people who rejected him. "It was more than just a political radical dying. . . . On that cross Christ was bearing in his own body my sin, and he was proclaiming my liberation on that cross." Skinner climaxed his speech with a challenge to be a new kind of Christian. "You will never be radical until you become part of that new order and then go into a world that's enslaved, a world that's filled with hunger and poverty and racism and all those things of the work of the devil."[12] In redefining "radical" in religious terms, Skinner had used the ideology and vocabulary of the Black Power movement and attached it to an evangelical framework.

Although Skinner received a rousing ovation from the students at the end of his talk that night, not everyone received his message at Urbana '70 so positively. Just over a week after the conference ended, Warren B. Appleton, the white father of a student who attended Urbana, typed an angry letter to John Alexander. He objected to Skinner's appropriation of the words "revolution" and "revolutionaries," which he associated with communism. "The net results are that twelve thousand of America's finest

12. Skinner, "The U.S. Racial Crisis and World Evangelism."

young, idealist[ic], Christian intellectuals are mis-lead into giving a standing ovation to a speaker demanding overthrow of the present order he branded as Satanic, while the musicians brandished Communist clenched-fist salutes."[13] Appleton ended with a challenge to Alexander and the other leaders of InterVarsity to explain why they would permit such messages to be part of Urbana.

Skinner might have anticipated such a response, since he had received pushback before. Earlier in 1970, Bob Jones, the founder of the ultraconservative Bob Jones University that would later lose its tax-exempt status for refusing to admit black students who were in interracial relationships, wrote a booklet entitled *Is Jesus a Revolutionary?* He asserted that talk of rebellion contradicted the Bible, which taught that God had set up the government for society's protection. "A popular evangelist [Skinner] echoes this blasphemy in an effort to court the favor of lawless men and make himself acceptable to the Communists," wrote Jones.[14]

Skinner continued to apply evangelical beliefs to the black situation in America, and as he did, others became agitated. Four months after Urbana, the Moody Bible Institute radio station, WMBI, canceled Skinner's thirty-minute weekly program because "the broadcast has been becoming increasing political with less emphasis on God's message to all men."[15] The managers of the station had become concerned that Skinner's insistence on discussing issues of racism and injustice would alienate their white evangelical listeners.

These responses indicate that a message challenging the social, political, and theological categories of white evangelicals could be the source of controversy. White evangelicals favorably received Skinner as an evangelist who talked about soul winning but not as a Christian who taught a race-conscious and socially active faith. Although subsequent correspondence shows that Skinner stayed in touch with the white leaders of InterVarsity, he was never again invited to speak.

13. Appleton to Alexander, January 9, 1971, Wheaton College, Billy Graham Center Archives, InterVarsity Christian Fellowship Records, Collection 300, "Urbana—1961–1974."

14. "Bob Jones: Jesus No Revolutionary," Evangelical Press News Service, September 26, 1970, 5.

15. E. Brandt Gustavson, memo from Moody Broadcasting Department, April 14, 1971, Wheaton College, Billy Graham Center Archives, Papers of Tom Skinner, Collection 430, Box 1, Folder 45—"Correspondence, 1971–1982."

The Limits of Black Christians within White Evangelicalism

Skinner died from an acute and aggressive form of leukemia in 1994. He was fifty-two years old. Although the grave silenced his voice, his speech at Urbana '70 provided part of the motivation for further efforts by black evangelicals and their allies to close the racial gap and focus on issues of social justice. The current CEO of InterVarsity is an Asian American. The organization created a position called Executive Vice President of People and Culture, which is currently occupied by a black woman.[16] The organization also has a department of multiethnic missions that specifically serves African Americans, Asians, Latinos, and Native Americans.[17]

In spite of the shifting demography of organizations such as InterVarsity, black Christians continue to distance themselves from the "evangelical" label. According to the comprehensive Pew Religious Landscape study of 2014, only 6 percent of black Protestant Christians identified themselves as evangelicals.[18] In terms of voting patterns, black Christians exhibit consistently large differences with white evangelicals. Of those who identified themselves as "born-again" Christians in a special election runoff for an Alabama US Senate seat between Democrat Doug Jones and Republican Roy Moore in 2017, 95 percent of black Christians voted for Jones while 80 percent of white evangelicals who voted cast their ballots for Moore.[19] A *New York Times* article labeled the steady departure of black Christians from white evangelical churches a "quiet exodus."[20]

The tri-perspectival method of examining the definition of "evangelical" reveals that in multiple ways, black Christians can be considered evangelicals. Yet the theological, historical, and personal aspects of religion work themselves out in markedly different ways among black Christians and white evangelicals.

16. "Our Ministry," InterVarsity.org, accessed February 14, 2019, https://intervarsity.org/our-ministry.

17. "We Are Multiethnic Ministries!" InterVarsity.org, accessed February 14, 2019, mem.intervarsity.org.

18. "Religious Landscape Study," Pew Research Center, 2014, http://www.pewforum.org/religious-landscape-study/.

19. Michelle Boorstein, "The Stunning Difference between White and Black Evangelical Voters in Alabama," *Washington Post*, December 13, 2017; Sarah Pulliam Bailey, "'A Spiritual Battle': How Roy Moore Tested White Evangelical Allegiance to the Republican Party," *Washington Post*, December 13, 2017.

20. Campbell Robertson, "A Quiet Exodus: Why Black Worshipers Are Leaving White Evangelical Churches," *New York Times*, March 9, 2018.

While the question most often raised is, "Are black Christians evangelicals?" the more salient query is, "What limits do white evangelicals place on black Christians?" or "When do black Christians distance themselves from white evangelicalism based on race and justice concerns?" In other words, can black Christians bring both their race and their religion with them into white evangelical spaces?

Addressing the question, "Are black Christians evangelicals?" is the beginning, not the end, of a discussion. Further research should address how class affects black Christian views and participation in evangelicalism. The role and impact of black Christians within predominantly white churches and parachurch organizations remain only lightly explored. The differences among self-identified black evangelicals in the twentieth century also require detailed examination. Historians must also probe how the intersections of gender and class influenced black Christians in the context of white evangelicalism. Regardless of how one defines "evangelical" or whether black Christians are indeed evangelicals, the answers must include considerations of race as a critical component.

CHAPTER 16

To Be or Not to Be an Evangelical

BRIAN C. STILLER

As Global Ambassador for the World Evangelical Alliance, Brian Stiller reports on his widespread travels in regular essays entitled "Dispatches from the Global Village" (https://dispatchesfrombrian.com). The following dispatch from March 2018 is his response to increased North American concern about the viability of the designation "evangelical" in light of the United States' current political upsets. It explains why he still believes the word and what it stands for have a very bright future indeed, and it appears here with the permission of the author.

Stiller, the former head of the Evangelical Fellowship of Canada and former president of Tyndale University College and Seminary, Toronto, is the author of many books, including *From Jerusalem to Timbuktu: A World Tour of the Spread of Christianity* (InterVarsity Press, 2018). He was also the lead editor of *Evangelicals around the World: A Global Handbook for the 21st Century* (Nelson, 2015), which Mark Noll discusses in the last chapter of this book.

*   *   *

A friend wrote, 'I no longer call myself an Evangelical.' Thoughtful, well informed but now I suspect feeling embarrassed, he has chosen to avoid a term used globally by hundreds of millions of Christians. For many within shouting distance of U.S. media circles and party politics, the word has become a banner of disrepute. 'Evangelical' is now a word disfigured by political pundits, muddied by protestors from the left and right, and brought into dishonor by self-proclaimed spokespeople who excuse inappropriate behavior and language as the necessary price for political power. The center has shifted, and many Evangelicals now wonder where they fit.

I come to this subject as a Canadian, not caught in the political wars of our great neighbor to the south, and with no need to offer opinions on their issues. I am also part of a world association which came into existence in 1846 and is today a global body that numbers some 600 million Christians. Obviously, I have reason to be concerned over the use of the term 'Evangelical' and its meaning to the world. This is a deeply emotional issue, and not just for Americans.

There are three centers around which this conversation revolves. First, there is a community of those who self-describe as 'Evangelical' and who support American conservative politics, leadership and policies. Second, there are self-described 'Evangelicals' who abhor a particular type of politics and populism, currently exemplified by the President, his language, life and social policies. Third, there are those who, like my friend, continue to believe the essential theological affirmations of Evangelicals, but whose commitment to its related mission has led them to forgo using the word and exempt themselves from any associated identity. Does it matter? Is it best (like the 'red letter Christians' or 'followers of the Way') to drop it altogether and find another term or label? Wouldn't just being called 'Christian' or 'a follower of Jesus' work?

To enable a helpful discussion, consider these items to frame our conversation.[1]

It Is Global

While the recent sharp reaction to the use of the label has come about in the U.S., in part because of divisions following the 2016 presidential election, a decision on what name best suits us globally is not a choice we can leave for Americans to decide. The U.S. does not set the agenda for the world, and we should not assume that what matters to them will define what matters globally. As influential as they are, and recognizing that American concerns do affect the world, the real place of evangelical growth is in the global south (Asia, Africa and Latin America). Here is where there has been an explosive growth of Christians. For example, in 1900 in Latin America, there were just 50,000

1. A helpful way to understand 'Evangelical' is to follow David Bebbington's fourfold definition with one addition: 1) the Scriptures as our ultimate authority; 2) the crucifixion as our only means for atonement of sin; 3) the importance of personal conversion; 4) activism—being a witness of Christ to our neighbors and society; 5) trusting in the empowering work of the Holy Spirit.

Evangelicals. Today in that region there are 100 million. Any conversation on this issue needs to take into account how it is seen by Christian colleagues in other parts of the world. At the same time, I would warn that we should beware of a liberal backlash just as much as we need to beware of a conservative 'export of the American gospel.' Both sides end up trying to silence the voices of the majority world, and the indigenous hearts and minds who interpret the Gospel within their worlds.

It Is a Definer

There has developed over the centuries a number of identifiable labels which are helpful in denoting the core beliefs and organization of major Christian traditions: 'Roman Catholics,' 'Eastern Orthodox,' or 'Mainline Protestants,' for instance. The term 'Evangelical' is another helpful identifier for a major, self-conscious stream of Protestantism which has spread around the world since the 1730s. (Pentecostals are usually located in the Evangelical family.) Roman Catholics comprise 1.2 billion. Eastern Orthodox and Mainline Protestants organized around the World Council of Churches are 500 million. Evangelicals make up 600 million. If you pastor a church up the Nile and are accused of being a cult (an accusation which has dire consequences in settings with dominant public religious majorities), identifying with a global body of Christians known by a suitable title—like Evangelical—is of great value. It does not, however, just define one's organizational family. The term 'Evangelical' also locates one's faith. Wycliffe College, an Anglican seminary at the University of Toronto, self-defines as Evangelical. Its choice of identity is historical, theological and contemporary. Its web page in part notes, 'It is affiliated with the Anglican Church of Canada and is evangelical and low church in orientation. On the other hand, the University of Toronto's other Anglican college, the University of Trinity College, is Anglo-Catholic in outlook.' Such identifiers are not separators; they are invitations to dialogue, not exclusion or violence.

Its Roots

The New Testament word *Evangel* comes from the Greek ευαγγέλιο, denoting all that pertains to announcing the *Good News*. That 'good news' is none other than Jesus of Nazareth, not merely information about him, but Jesus himself. Located in the life and witness of Jesus, the richness of early church references to the *Evangel* provides as clear a word as one can find to describe both the nature of the news—it is 'good'—and the embodiment of the news—it is Jesus. Mark launches his Gospel with 'The kingdom of God has come near. Repent and believe the good news' (1:5). The verb *euangelizō* was used in the Greek translation of the Old Testament, the Septuagint; in Isaiah 52:7 the Prophet announced good news to Jews who were in exile.

Its History

Martin Luther, who 500 years ago set loose a reforming of the dominant European church, chose this word—*evangelischel*—to distinguish his movement from the church headquartered in Rome. In time, it became a term synonymous with Lutheranism itself. William Wilberforce, who pressed the British commonwealth to outlaw slave trading, brought the term into English usage in the early 1800s, from the associations of friendship formed from evangelical Protestants who, by then, were moving all over the world. In time, it became associated with Protestants who pressed society to consider human value within a biblical framework. During the early 1900s, as much of mainline Protestantism moved to a more liberal theology, the division within the larger Protestant community led to debates over fundamentalism and modernism, and eventually (in the post-War period) to the term 'Evangelical,' to describe those who were not inwardly turned as sectarians, but who saw the Bible as trustworthy, and Jesus as the Christ of God, resulting in a move outward, into the world.

Today

The storm we are in is not just about a president or a self-enclosed liberal discourse which resonates with the outrageous claims of the new Atheism. It arises from a controversy that has been brewing for some time. Many within the U.S. Evangelical community have been fractured by harsh debates and contrarian views and caught up in matters of culture, the ongoing issue of race, debates over American exceptionalism and concerns over political power. The suburban and rural radical Right sought to tap into a broader sense of populist cultural dispossession, and was convinced that to put in place conservative courts, they needed a leader who would insure its membership. Those in the urbanized radical left have held their ground, and used their cultural power to further inflame the debate. For each side, the others have been repainted as fascists or bolshevists revisited. Even so, this is a skirmish located largely in one country. It is not the world, despite the influence that American media wields in framing globally connected public debates far from their core constituencies. As fierce as it is, the fury of this storm will pass, admittedly leaving stories of destruction in its wake. To impose this first world debate on hundreds of millions of Christians world-wide would be worse than a mistake; it would be a new form of first world intellectual colonialism.

Options

Do we even need a term or label to identify ourselves? Jesus, after all, knows his own. Are we not best to keep our heads down and avoid using the term in certain moments and situations? Yes, I think there are times when that is prudent. Do we look for another, one that has biblical certitude and Christ-honoring resonance? I'm open to suggestions. The problem of terms, of course, is that they all arise in cultural moments. In a world where the very word 'Christian' is a cause for some to turn up their noses, are we not as likely to choose another label which in a few years will be just as polarizing? Roman Catholics didn't debate a name change when reports of pedophilia in the priesthood hit the media. Growing up in Pentecostalism, a group which has often been marginalized, I never felt that it was a matter of concern among our people to find another name for our church.

A Way Forward

What we are experiencing today will not forever define the term to the world. The North American community will move from being seen as controlled by white Evangelicals into a wider and more Christ-honoring witness. Then as Christians migrate into North America, they will bring with them biblical faith. Current battles among American minorities will not be the base on which future witness will depend. Older, white Evangelicals will become less a factor of what defines the Evangelical faith as younger generations take over and as migrants change America's complexion and makeup. The wind of this current controversy will in time lose its fury. Leaders from all sorts of churches, universities, agencies and movements will step up and assert their views. Resilient voices will counter today's negativity that so clouds debates and rules choices.

For myself, I'm sticking with the term. Its biblical message still resonates. Its historical influence reminds me of Christ, the Good News. Its theological emphasis grounds me when all else in my culture is shifting sand. Its message of transformation empowers me in thought and deed. Its prophetic call to be 'salt' and 'light' reminds me of Christ's call to love my neighbor. And for my friends around the world, it helps them in their identity and witness. The really great news is the *Evangel*, a faithful reminder that Jesus is ever present, himself the Good News.

PART IV

Historians Seeking Perspective

The editors return in this last section of the book in an attempt to shed further light on how considering evangelical history might relate to contemporary American debates over the meaning of evangelicalism. George Marsden offers a more extensive explanation for how evangelical cohesion can coexist with evangelical diversity than he provided in his pioneering essay from 1984. David Bebbington examines evangelicals and British politics as a revealing counterpoint to the parallel American story. And Mark Noll explores the relationship of evangelicalism in the United States to the rapid proliferation of evangelical-like movements throughout the rest of the world.

CHAPTER 17

On Not Mistaking One Part for the Whole: The Future of American Evangelicalism in a Global Perspective

GEORGE MARSDEN

Back in the 1980s when "evangelicals" were making the news in some unbecoming ways, my friend and Calvin College colleague Ronald Wells wryly announced that he would like to resign as an "evangelical" but did not know where to send the letter. These days one need not worry about the lack of an evangelical headquarters; one can simply post one's resignation online. The overwhelming support among white American evangelicals for Donald Trump in the presidential election of 2016 sparked a flurry of such postings.

Scot McKnight stated the problem succinctly: "The issue is politics; the present painful reality is Trump. The reality is 81% of evangelicals voted for Trump. The word 'evangelical' now means Trump-voter. The word 'evangelical' is spoiled."[1] One Southern Baptist ethicist went so far as to declare that "evangelicalism has ceased to be a faith perspective rooted on Jesus the Christ and has become a political movement whose beliefs repudiate all Jesus advocated."[2]

While much of such alarm is understandable in the face of an American media that now use "evangelical" just for a certain group of white ethnoreligious voters, I wonder whether it makes sense to give up on the wider use of the term or to renounce the whole multiethnic multinational movement just because of the political behavior of only one of the many ethnic or tribal

---

1. Scot McKnight, "Bury the Word 'Evangelical,'" *Patheos Evangelical*, October 16, 2017, http://www.patheos.com/blogs/jesuscreed/2017/10/16/burying-word-evangelical/.

2. Miguel De La Torre, "The Death of Christianity in the U.S.," *Baptist News Global*, November 13, 2017, https://baptistnews.com/article/death-christianity-u-s/#.WmisXSOZOnf.

subsets of evangelicalism as a whole. If we think, rather, of evangelicalism from a global perspective as a diverse but related set of worldwide religious movements with historical roots going back centuries, then does it not seem sadly American-centered to give up on the term and even the whole movement just because of widespread confusion of religious with political categories in our part of the world? I would argue rather that the term "evangelical" will still be around as a useful designation for a large and varied category of Christians long after Trump is gone, assuming the human race survives that long.

One way to help clarify the relationship between the commonalities found in evangelicals around the globe and the striking diversities among some types of them is to consider that relationship as analogous to that between the biological class of mammals and particular, individual mammalian species. Mammals share a number of essential traits (as a biologist counterpart of David Bebbington might remind us). Yet various species of mammals, such as cats and dogs and giraffes, lions, hippos, humans, and sloths, differ immensely in personality and temperament. So we could hardly generalize about what mammals are like on the basis of the behavior of house cats. Likewise, it should be easy to see that it is a mistake to generalize about evangelicals on the basis of the behavior of white American Trump voters. And for similar reasons, we would not want to attribute to evangelicalism as a whole all the traits of prosperity gospel Pentecostals in Kenya, Presbyterians in South Korea, or participants in the evangelical Christian Union in Oxford.

This worldwide perspective on evangelicalism that reminds us of the diversity among its various subspecies provides an important corrective to the local American usage that turns evangelicalism not only into a political category but also into a racial category. Typically, American pollsters and pundits restrict "evangelical" to mean only *white* voters who, when polled, will select "born again or evangelical Christian" as their religious identity. Yet that usage obscures the ethnic diversity of evangelicalism, even within the United States. As Michael Hamilton's review of the role of evangelicals in the 2016 election points out, many commentators have observed that if one includes as "evangelical" the substantial numbers of Hispanic Americans, Asian Americans, and African Americans, whose faith is evangelical by the usual religious measures, then the percentage voting for Trump is far lower than the 81 percent of white evangelicals.[3]

3. Just one example: Ryan P. Burge, "How Does Being White Shape Evangelicals' Voting Habits?" *Religion in Public*, November 6, 2017, https://religioninpublic.blog/2017/11/06/how-does-being-white-shape-evangelicals-voting-habits/.

Nonetheless, the election of 2016 and the resulting critiques of the 81 percent *do* turn a spotlight on a major flaw that has almost always existed wherever evangelical forms of religion (defined by the four Bebbington characteristics) have flourished. These forms of Christianity have almost always featured popular movements guided by marketing instincts; they have adapted readily to different cultural environments; and they have often carried out those adaptations without a great deal of cultural self-criticism. In this respect, the analogy of biological evolution is once again helpful. Evangelicals come in so many very different subspecies because each species has skillfully adapted to its own environment. That means that many secondary traits of various evangelicals may vary immensely. It also suggests a great strength of the essential gospel message in that it has proven itself adaptable to so many settings around the world. Again, especially from an international perspective, it has been a strength of the movement (or movements) that interevangelical international relationships can be genuinely diverse. One sees that diversity at international gatherings such are those associated with the Lausanne Movement. Despite conspicuous differences, a common core of similar beliefs and practices really does provide a basis for fellowship for people from all over the world.

Yet the downside of evangelical market-driven diversity and adaptability is that, while the gospel message proclaimed by evangelicals has undoubtedly changed lives radically, it also leaves some preexisting cultural assumptions virtually untouched, or even reinforced. That is especially true of deeply ingrained social-cultural loyalties and prejudices. One can think of many examples in American history. The "second great awakening" of the early decades of the nineteenth century brought great evangelical successes in both the North and the South. At one time a significant strain of evangelicalism throughout the United States held that slavery was wrong, but that strain simply died off in the white South. As a consequence, by the 1840s the largest Methodist and Baptist denominations divided over the slavery issue, even though the overall evangelical message remained otherwise identical in all regions of the country. By that time white evangelical religion in the South tended to reinforce African slavery by alleging biblical precedents, while in New England, the same evangelical religion reinforced antislavery.

On the whole, that cultural conformity has marked the history of white evangelicals and racism throughout American history. Attitudes of these evangelicals toward race have varied with region and era, but specifically evangelical emphases have only occasionally made for concrete differences in dealing with the national history of systemic racism.

Throughout American history much evangelical political behavior has fallen into patterns where religion as such does not challenge, or where it simply reinforces, attitudes that are already ingrained in constituencies where evangelicalism spreads. Religious identification has often been strongly correlated with party identification, but once that correlation is in place, then political behavior follows that party identification. Most Americans pull for their political party in much the same way that people in Wisconsin root for the Green Bay Packers. For instance, as Michael Hamilton's essay points out, in the 1930s most white evangelical voters in the South were voting for Franklin Roosevelt, simply out of loyalty to the Democratic Party and despite the New Deal. Sometimes evangelical religion has played a role in creating or altering party loyalties, and sometimes political parties will expand the numbers of their supporters by cultivating such loyalties. But in most cases, specific evangelical teachings have had relatively little to do with specific political loyalties.

White evangelicals did divide in the antebellum decades over slavery, and each side saw the Bible as supporting its views. But once antislave evangelicals became Whigs and proslavery evangelicals aligned with Democrats, they really did not draw on evangelical beliefs to shape their attitudes toward tariffs, the banking system, railroad construction, or internal improvements. Instead, evangelical Whigs supported Whig policies, and evangelical Democrats supported Democratic policies.

Similarly, today most evangelicals (white, black, Hispanic, Asian American) are pro-life to one degree or another. But for almost everything else on the political landscape, they look to their party for guidance, as on whether the government should support universal health care, whether welfare is helpful or harmful, whether the government should do more to protect the environment, whether gun ownership should be more regulated, how welcoming the nation ought to be to immigrants, and whether there should be greater taxes on the wealthy. Most people find themselves simply going along with their party's view, the dominant opinion of their local communities, and perhaps their favored news sources on such issues.

Likewise, attitudes regarding gender roles that are preexisting in local communities have been shaped and reinforced by Christian traditions and, as Kristin Kobes Du Mez shows, have in recent times been strengthened by specifically evangelical teachings and movements. Those movements are reactive against progressive cultural trends and reinforce conservative reactions against such trends. Even though those specific movements do not directly touch a numerical majority of those counted as evangelical, they articulate and reinforce attitudes already characteristic of many white communities where evangelicalism is more or less the default religion.

Even stronger has been the evangelical role in reinforcing American patriotism and militarism, attitudes that have been crucial in shaping the explicitly evangelical political movement that arose after the Vietnam War. Patriotism and militarism have, of course, been prominent parts of American life since well before the American Revolution. And most American subcommunities, Roman Catholic, for instance, have come to share in these traits. Yet, despite some evangelical critiques of mixing religion with nationalism, most evangelical religion has blended with and reinforced American patriotism. American flags are more likely to be displayed than crosses in many worship spaces. It is also often difficult to find any clear line that separates evangelical religion from civil religion. In many communities of the heartland, these two were the default religions for public occasions and national holidays.

That cultural background has made it natural for many white American evangelical Christians simply to take for granted that America used to be an essentially Christian nation. That assumption helps justify militarism as well as their patriotism. It also provides a simple and compelling account of obvious changes in cultural mores, especially regarding gender roles, sexual identities, racial attitudes, acceptance of minorities, and when it is acceptable to say "Merry Christmas." To reuse an old analogy that still seems helpful today,[4] one way of understanding religious-cultural militancy in some older-stock white Protestant communities is to think of their experience as comparable in some ways to that of immigrants. Faced with the new cultural standards of modernity and inclusiveness shaping much of education and the mainstream media, they feel like strangers in their own land. Their taken-for-granted ideals, beliefs, and practices that they grew up with are now often ridiculed and even despised. Unlike actual immigrants, however, they share memories of having been the dominant group in the very national culture in which they are still living. So resisting assimilation to the new ways is not just a matter of separating from the cultural mainstream (although it may involve that), but it also involves a resolve to "take back" their culture.

Such widespread attitudes, resentments, and sense of lost better times help explain the popularity of writings about America's Christian origins such as

---

4. I first used this analogy (which seems just as relevant today) regarding fundamentalists of the 1920s, in "From Fundamentalism to Evangelicalism," in *The Evangelicals: What They Believe, Who They Are, Where They Are Changing*, ed. David F. Wells and John D. Woodbridge (Nashville: Abingdon, 1975).

David Barton has provided. Barton is simply capitalizing on and reinforcing attitudes that are already there, conflating Christianity and patriotism in a nostalgic civil religion. Especially since the Vietnam era, Republicans have cultivated such sensibilities much more than have Democrats. Among old-stock white Protestants in the heartland and the South, these quasi-religious patriotic sentiments and generalized resentments of many recent cultural trends[5] have probably had more to do with locking in at least two-thirds of white evangelicals as Republican loyalists than have specifically evangelical commitments, even if these factors are often intertwined.[6]

So the takeaway regarding the 81 percent is not a demonstration of how much evangelical religion shapes political behavior—but just the opposite. In most cases[7] the specifically religious commitments of evangelicals have lacked the capacity to challenge the cultural-political beliefs that are already working powerfully among the constituencies to which white evangelicals belong.

What we see here, then, is that, as Chris Armstrong has described it, evangelicalism often has a chameleon quality of blending in with its environments.[8] More generally, that feature is likely to be common in almost any Christian group in a country where it is not being oppressed. It is relatively rare for churches to take social-political stances that depart much from the already existing social-political sentiments of their constituencies. But, to the extent

---

5. Cf. the white evangelical "political quadrilateral" that Michael Hamilton describes above in his essay.

6. For instance, one 2016 poll found that only 4 percent of evangelicals named abortion as their number one concern in the presidential race. For a good many others, it would have been among their concerns but not as important as issues relating to a strong economy and national security, which were the dominant concerns. Bob Smietana, "Evangelical Divide Seen in LifeWay Research Survey," *Baptist Press*, October 14, 2016, http://www.bpnews.net/47727/evangelical-divide-seen-in-lifeway-research-survey.

7. Given the many varieties of evangelicals, there of course are some conspicuous exceptions (including on the political left and middle) to this predominant tendency. And there is no denying that the organizations of the Religious Right have played a significant role in shaping and mobilizing quite a few white American evangelicals. But no one speaks for or controls the political behavior of a majority. See also Michael Hamilton's comments on the relationships of evangelical leadership to their constituencies.

8. Chris R. Armstrong, "Heart Religion, Tradition, and the Evangelical Chameleon," *Public Discourse*, May 10, 2018, http://www.thepublicdiscourse.com/2018/05/21373/. Over the years there have been a good many exceptions to this tendency among the more sectarian type of evangelicals who have maintained conspicuously distinctive mores, including styles of dress.

that an inability to challenge many of the prevailing cultural idols, loyalties, and prejudices is a problem, it is probably more often a problem among the more populist groups of evangelicals such as those found in the United States.

*　　　*　　　*

So what are the lessons for self-identified evangelicals who might be theologians, pastors, scholars, or writers and who might read books like this one and agree that blanket support for Trump and the Trump agenda undermines Christian faith itself? How could they push evangelicals toward more thoughtful and well-rounded cultural engagement?

First, such people should not be discouraged by what may look like a huge mind/body problem among American evangelicals. Without question there has been a remarkable renaissance of evangelical and related Christian thought in the past generation.[9] Yet many who have taken part in that renaissance are disheartened, since it seems as though so few other evangelicals have been paying attention. As one thoughtful scholar summarized the concern: "It is simply no longer clear that evangelicalism functions as an expression of Christian faith capable of sponsoring either serious intellectual engagement or genuine cultural renewal."[10]

Yet such judgments, while understandable, depend on thinking of evangelicalism as a whole rather than taking sufficient account of its many separate and often disconnected parts. If there are something like 75 million American evangelicals (some estimates are considerably higher, counting all races and ethnicities),[11] then it may seem discouraging that the nuanced work of evangelical theologians, scholars, and social ethicists seems to have little impact

9. See, for instance, George Marsden, "A Renaissance of Christian Higher Education in the United States," in *Christian Higher Education: A Global Renaissance*, ed. Joel Carpenter, Perry L. Glanzer, and Nicholas S. Lantinga (Grand Rapids: Eerdmans, 2014), 257–76.

10. Jay Green, "Whither the Conference on Faith and History? The Politics of Evangelical Identity and the Spiritual Vision of History," *Fides et Historia* 49 (Winter/ Spring 2017): 1–10 (quotation 10).

11. "Religious Landscape Study," Pew Research Center, 2014, http://www.pewforum .org/religious-landscape-study/, lists 25.4 percent of Americans as evangelicals (counting by denominational affiliation). That would be over 80 million if the US population is over 325 million. The Pew Forum lists an additional 6.5 percent of the population (about 21 million) as "Traditional Black Protestant." Another 14.7 percent are mainline Protestant (which also includes some evangelicals).

on the vast majority of those. Anti-intellectualism and "the scandal of the evangelical mind" still reign in many places.

Yet if we remember the global diversity of evangelicals, and the many subtribes or species among American evangelicals, and also all the denominational and theological divisions among evangelicals, then it should be no surprise that those we might label academic evangelicals are appreciated only within their own and other closely related evangelical species. There are many evangelicals, especially among various folk species, that academic evangelical communities are never likely to touch. Suppose that a particular perspective favored by certain academic evangelicals had the phenomenal success of directly or indirectly helping to shape the lives of 5 million American evangelical Christians. Should they count that as a dismal failure because of the 70 million (more than 90 percent) of all sorts of other American evangelicals whom they have not reached?

It is hard to know how to measure the value or the impact of the renaissance and expansion of evangelical and related Christian scholarship in recent decades, but we can be sure that it is not by looking at the percentages of white American evangelical voters who remain loyally Republican. If we can resist the trap of viewing everything through a political lens, then we should see that many species of American evangelicals are flourishing in ways not recognized by the politically obsessed media. Many evangelical seminaries have truly impressive faculties and are sending out many thoughtful pastors. And these seminaries are also notable centers of international diversity. Quite a few evangelical churches that are not anti-intellectual are flourishing. Some evangelical churches have impressive multicultural urban ministries that demonstrate the fallacy of conflating all evangelicals in the stereotypical "white evangelical" subgroup. Or if one doubts the impact of evangelical scholarship, one might sample the lives and work of the alumni of the more than one hundred institutional members of the Council for Christian Colleges and Universities, let's say, over the past fifty years, to see how these graduates have exerted a positive influence and provided thoughtful Christian perspectives for church parishioners and church leaders. And, for a generation now, talented young "evangelicals" have been crowding into graduate schools, so that there is no lack of scholarship of stellar quality. More significantly, evangelical charities in America and around the world illustrate generous interpretations of the gospel in action. Many of these have been founded and supported by graduates of evangelical schools and seminaries or by protégés of parachurch ministries of the self-consciously evangelical networks and reflect the conviction that Christians need to witness to the gospel in ways that go beyond their local interests and prejudices. Moreover, all these schools, agencies, and movements have connections and counterparts throughout the world. Percentage-wise, these leavening accomplishments may not seem particularly impressive, measured against the huge numbers of those who may be counted as evangelical Christians in the nation and in the world. But by almost any other standard, these are flourishing ongoing movements.

A Postscript in Pursuit of Empathy: Imaging a Democratic Trump

For those who are (as I am) troubled by the seemingly uncritical support for Trump among so many white evangelicals but who are willing to ask difficult questions of ourselves, I suggest the following thought experiment. Suppose Trump, or someone a lot like Trump, had decided he had a better chance playing the role of a populist Democrat and had succeeded in being elected. I am imagining someone with all the character flaws and questionable actions analogous to those that so upset the real Trump's critics. We can suppose that, at first, many principled Democrats would have deeply opposed the nomination of such a person, and some would have remained in the "Never Trump" camp. But the rank and file might have been energized, and many of the working classes might have been brought back to the party. Many Democrats might also say that they voted for Trump largely because they found the Republican candidate even more objectionable.

And then let's say that the Democratic Trump administration succeeded in establishing a single-payer health-care system, significantly tightening environmental regulations, instituting sensibly strict gun-control laws, and appointing several Supreme Court justices who would protect such policies for the next generation. But at the same time, the president would have solidified his populist base by appealing to instincts for sheer partisanship. So imagine for the sake of argument that the Democratic Trump called a "national emergency" regarding the divisiveness spread by the media. He then instituted for all media outlets a regime of federal "fact checkers" whose functions became, in effect, solely to block criticism of himself and his policies. That soon led to the closing of Fox News. And suppose, in the same vein, the Democratic Trump administration removed tax exemptions from certain churches and accreditation from certain schools that were "too engaged in politics," meaning those that criticized administration policies, including the most progressive views of sexuality.[12]

12. Just as the real Trump has mixed policies that appeal to positive conservative

One can imagine, given such a scenario, that among moderate and left-wing evangelicals who normally voted Democratic, a minority (including a good many "thought leaders") would resolutely remain in the "Never Trump" camp. But it is not hard to imagine that a lot more would capitulate to support for the administration. After all, for Christians with deep concerns for social justice and the environment, might not this Democratic Trump seem a Godsend? How else might America ever get good medical treatment even for the poorest among us? How else to take the steps necessary to save us and our children from environmental disaster? And think of all the lives being saved by the new gun laws. And, after all, wasn't it true that Fox News and the like *had* been creating truly dangerous polarization? Certainly we can imagine that some progressive Christians would in their partisan enthusiasm seemingly overlook that the Democratic Trump was a scoundrel and a threat to the republic. And we can imagine that some Christian leaders would take advantage of the popular sentiments to support a winner and get on the uncritical Trump bandwagon. They would gladly accept invitations to the White House and opportunities perhaps to influence him and at least to show their support. Might not even some say that God had raised him up as a sort of Cyrus to save all these lives, to do justice, and possibly even to save the planet?

This thought experiment, as should be apparent, is not intended to justify support for Trump. Rather, it is meant as an exercise in looking for empathy by trying to put those of us who think the real Trump is a disaster in the shoes of fellow believers whose loyalty to the real Trump we find mystifying and reprehensible. If there were a Democratic Trump, lots of Democrats who were Christian would loyally fall into line, often with great enthusiasm. Probably most would do so largely out of partisan loyalties of the sort that blind one equally to the evils on our side and to the convictions of the other side. But others would be supporting Trump not because they lacked principle but rather because of the ironic flaw in human nature that Reinhold Niebuhr identified, that a too confident sense of justice often leads to injustice. In either case, we can see illustrated the dangers of the political temptation that Jesus resisted (Matt. 4:8–10), of allying with the powers of darkness in order to gain political power. In a participatory democracy we should do our parts to see

---

values with attitudes, such as racism and xenophobia, that betray the best conservative moral principles, so in this fantasy the Democratic Trump mixes positive progressive achievements with policies that betray the best progressive moral principles. I realize that there is not an exact moral equivalency in the scenarios, but I'm trying to provide an approximation, however improbable it may seem.

that government is used for the good, to the extent that is possible. Yet we need also to recognize that, especially in an era of media-enhanced intense partisanship, politics often becomes one's religion, or at least our political loyalties overshadow and reshape our religion. Recognizing how this happens among fellow believers with whom we may disagree is a good reminder that the capacity for selective blindness in human nature operates not just on our political opponents but on all of us.

CHAPTER 18

Evangelicals and Recent Politics in Britain

DAVID W. BEBBINGTON

In light of current American controversies over the issues explored in this book, it seems particularly pertinent for a British historian to reflect on the political history of evangelicals in Britain. It is obvious from such a review that both similarities and differences abound in the parallel evangelical histories of the two nations. To set out those differences will be one way to continue the transatlantic discussions that have been so fruitful in recent efforts to record evangelical history.

The Evangelicals of Great Britain were traditionally divided. On the one hand, there were the adherents of the established churches, the Church of England and the Church of Scotland. On the other, there were the members of the Free Churches (also called Nonconformists), chiefly the Congregationalists, Baptists, and Methodists. This rift between Church and Dissent, at least in England and Wales, was commonly associated with politics. The Conservatives, dedicated to the preservation of the institutions of the country, were supported by most Anglicans, so that the Church of England was labeled "the Conservative Party at prayer." The Nonconformists outside the established church, however, were not normally Conservatives. During the nineteenth and early twentieth centuries, they were usually attached to the Liberal Party, which aimed for constitutional reform, and increasingly in the twentieth century, for social reform. From the First World War onward, the Labour Party, a non-Marxist but socialist party representing the working classes, was attractive to many Free Church people, especially those who were Methodists. Evangelical Christians who worshiped in the Anglican parish churches therefore tended to be Conservatives, but Evangelicals who were Nonconformists tended to be supporters of the Liberal or Labour Parties.

The Second World War ushered in an era of consensus politics. The parties continued to compete for power, but they adopted similar policies. The experience of total war had forged common aims, chief among which was the maintenance of high standards of welfare for all the people. Partly inspired by the writings and example of the wartime archbishop of Canterbury, William Temple, the parties set about creating a welfare state. Labour, in government from 1945 to 1951, was its main architect, but the blueprint for the fresh arrangements had been set out in a wartime document framed by William Beveridge, a Liberal, and the Education Act of 1944 had been introduced by R. A. Butler, a Conservative. So the expansion of state powers for the common good was an interparty achievement. The capstone of the new system was the National Health Service, introduced by Labour in 1948, which provided health care at the expense of government for every inhabitant at the point of need. Although the Conservatives objected to other aspects of Labour's program, such as the nationalization of the coal mines, they were in principle content with the health service. Over subsequent generations it remained an institution of which all parties were proud. The British state seemed not a dangerous threat to personal liberty but a benign agent of potential good.

Evangelicals shared that view. They remained comfortable with the tenor of public life during the 1950s, as normality returned after the pressures of war and the benefits of prosperity began to be felt. During the 1960s, however, Evangelicals became troubled by the turn of events. Abortion law became more liberal, censorship of the theater ended, and homosexual acts between consenting adults in private were decriminalized. The first was the result of an initiative by the Liberal Party leader, and the second and third were the work of a Labour government. The moral assumptions of society were diverging from those of Evangelicals, and the more progressive parties seemed responsible for the decadence. Evangelicals mobilized against such changes, launching the Festival of Light in 1971. Asserting that "moral pollution needs a solution," it rallied Christians to the cause of defending the interests of the family. The festival managed to recruit not only Anglicans, who formed 42 percent of attenders at a demonstration in London's Trafalgar Square in 1976, but also Nonconformists, since 24 percent of the attenders were Baptists. Many outside the established church shared the conviction with those within that the priority was resistance to change.

Over subsequent years Evangelicals became more likely to assert traditional values in the public arena. The Evangelical Alliance, representing Evangelicals of all denominations, made regular representations to Parliament against further relaxation of laws such as those restricting the Sunday closing of shops. From 1983 the Festival of Light turned into Christian Action, Research and Education, an organization dedicated to exerting pressure on politicians. One of the key issues was abortion, on which Evangelicals actually strengthened their stance during the 1970s. Instead of supposing that a fetus was only a potential human being, they generally began to hold, with Roman Catholics, that a fetus was already a child. Yet abortion never became a party issue, partly because the Labour Party, which included keen advocates of abortion rights, also contained a large number of members of Parliament who were Roman Catholic. The question remained a matter of conscience for parliamentarians, and so divisions over the question never coincided with the borderline between the parties. For a few Evangelicals, the question was of immense importance, but for most it was a minor factor in determining how to vote. In 2014 only 23 percent of Evangelicals strongly agreed with the idea that abortion can never be justified. So, although most Evangelicals became troubled by the moral trends of the times, even abortion did not turn them into combatants in a culture war.

During the years when Margaret Thatcher was prime minister, from 1979 to 1990, there was considerable Evangelical sympathy for her stance when she took up certain moral issues. In particular, her government, under section 28 of a Local Government Act of 1988, prohibited local authorities from actively promoting a homosexual lifestyle. A few charismatic leaders were prepared to accord Margaret Thatcher the status of a secular prophet, speaking to the needs of the times. Some Evangelicals also supported her championship of capitalism. Brian Griffiths, an academic economist, published *Morality and the Market Place* (1982) as an avowedly Evangelical analysis. He denounced Marxism as wrong and treated capitalism as right but lacking in theological foundations, which he attempted to build. Griffiths was no wild extremist, but preferred quiet influence from behind the front ranks, rising to become head of the prime minister's policy unit. When supporting Margaret Thatcher, Evangelicals were usually restrained in the tone of their endorsement.

A small number, however, did adopt a more strident version of conservative values, especially on moral questions. Christian Voice, Christian Concern, and Action for Biblical Witness to our Nation were three bodies that vigorously opposed continuing liberalization of the statute book, but all were small and marginal. A weightier organization, founded in 1991, was the Christian Institute, based in Jesmond Parish Church in Newcastle-upon-Tyne, a particularly vibrant Anglican congregation under its vicar, David Holloway. Its main concerns, listed on its website in 2018, were the sanctity of life, marriage and the family, Christian freedoms and heritage, together with other matters such as gambling, the homosexual question, and cannabis use. Clearly its weight was thrown behind causes that would have found favor with the conservative Right in America.

The most significant agency for bringing together Evangelicals and the Conservative Party, however, was the Conservative Christian Fellowship. Founded by Tim Montgomerie in 1990, the fellowship existed to provide a congenial setting for Evangelicals within the party. Montgomerie, who had been converted at sixteen, created the fellowship while still a student. His abilities as director drew the attention of his seniors, so that from 1998 he was a speechwriter for two party leaders and briefly in 2003 chief of staff to Iain Duncan Smith, the Conservative Party leader. Montgomerie went on to run an influential website called Conservative Home from 2005 to 2013. He believed in reducing public expenditure and was a skeptic over climate change, so that he fitted aspects of the profile of transatlantic right-wingers of his generation. The Conservative Christian Fellowship was even supported by the Christian Coalition of America. Yet with Duncan Smith he launched a program of "compassionate conservatism," echoing George W. Bush, and set up with him a Centre for Social Justice. Montgomerie was clearly eager to promote some of the causes usually more associated with the Left. He gradually came to regret his earlier opposition to a homosexual lifestyle and in 2013 supported the Conservatives' promotion of a same-sex marriage bill. When in 2010 accused of advocating an extreme American form of Christian conservatism, he declared that the United States had done a lot wrong as well as a lot right and that the identification of the church with opposition to abortion and homosexuality was "a terrible failure."[1] Montgomerie, who left the Conservative Party in 2016 because of its leadership's support for the European Union, had previously developed an influential role within the party, but he was never a champion of exclusively right-wing causes.

If those Evangelicals who were inclined to the Right tended not to be single-minded culture warriors, there were a large number of fellow believers who increasingly inclined to the left. Theological change facilitated the shift. The dispensationalism that fostered pessimism about social engagement and the Keswick spirituality that demanded separation from the world were in decline during the postwar years. Conversely, charismatic renewal and the resurgence of Reformed teaching, both marked features of the period from the 1960s, were equally likely to encourage making contributions to political

1. *New Statesman*, March 12, 2010.

affairs rather than remaining passive and so upholding a tacit conservatism. A milestone in the dropping of inhibitions about participation in public affairs was the National Evangelical Anglican Congress at Keele University in 1967. The paper by Norman Anderson, a scholar of Islamic law who shortly after became the first chair of the House of Laity of the Church of England General Synod, urged "holy worldliness," a willingness to embrace the opportunities for service offered by the arena of the world. Evangelicals were pointed toward involvement rather than withdrawal.

In the wake of Keele, there was a plethora of initiatives. In the following year the Evangelical Alliance Relief Fund, usually called TEAR Fund, was set up to foster Evangelical giving to projects in the two-thirds world. In 1969 the Shaftesbury Project was established to encourage scholarship and activism about social issues. By 1974 it had given birth to an Evangelical Race Relations Group to draw attention to the needs of the growing number of immigrants of color. In the same year, David Sheppard, the bishop of Woolwich but later bishop of Liverpool, published a weighty Evangelical study of the task of the church in late twentieth-century urban society, *Built as a City*. Again in 1974, the Lausanne Congress on World Evangelization was held, giving its international seal of approval to recognizing social action as a Christian responsibility. Afterward it became received opinion that dealing with the ills of society was a crucial component of Christian mission. A majority of a large sample of Evangelicals in 2014 believed that social action was as important as evangelism. Very few would have avowed that conviction before Keele.

The fresh attitude was upheld by the leading figure in late twentieth-century British Evangelicalism, John Stott, rector of All Souls, Langham Place, in the heart of London. Stott was the dominant influence at both Keele and Lausanne. He embodied the new orthodoxy in his extremely influential *Issues Facing Christians Today* (1984), a compendium of material on social responsibility. Stott rejected the rationale given for the social gospel at the start of the century, repudiating the American Walter Rauschenbusch's view that the kingdom of God could be identified with the reconstruction of society, but the English minister elaborated his own biblical basis for social action. The concern of God, he declared, was "not only justification but social justice in every community."[2] He raised his voice on behalf of ecological issues, then an unusual stance, and by the third edition of his work in 1999 was urgently advocating the campaign for the cancellation of world debt. Stott, influenced by contacts with thinkers in the two-thirds world, was taking up some radical

2. John Stott, *Issues Facing Christians Today* (Basingstoke: Marshalls, 1984), 17.

causes. He quoted Brian Griffiths, the capitalist champion, with approval, but he himself stood far to the left of Griffiths. Stott called himself a floating voter, giving his support from time to time to each of the three main parties, but his natural allegiance was illustrated by his being a reader of the *Guardian* newspaper, the choice of middle-class Liberal and Labour voters. Stott consolidated the commitment of the Evangelical community to social action and pushed its center of gravity in a leftward direction.

Stott's stance was shared by others. The director of the Evangelical Alliance from 1983 to 1997 was the energetic Clive Calver, who in his early years had been a Young Liberal when that was a label for radical activism. He brought engagement with social questions to the fore, and his successor, Joel Edwards, carried the emphasis further by inaugurating in 1999 a Movement for Change that was designed to transform the life of Britain. Other bodies reinforced the trend. In the 1990s a Christian Democratic Movement, begun by members of Parliament from all three main parties, was chaired by Alan Storkey, a sociologist who had written *A Christian Social Perspective* (1979). In 1999 it generated a new political party, the Christian People's Alliance, whose first principle was social justice. The party garnered few votes and subsequently veered to the right, but in its early years it was another sign of the Evangelical commitment to addressing the inequalities of modern Britain.

Evangelicals were willing to participate as Christians in the left-of-center parties. A Christian Socialist Movement, though usually supported by broader-minded Christians, attracted more Evangelicals after it turned into Christians on the Left in the wake of Tony Blair's dropping of the socialist label by Labour. By 2018 the publicity of Christians on the Left sounded distinctly Evangelical. "Our primary identity is in Christ, not a political ideology," declared its website, "but our reading of scripture inevitably leads us to 'speak up for those who cannot speak for themselves.'"[3] The Labour Party enjoyed a remarkable degree of backing from the growing community of voters with Caribbean and African ancestry. In 2014 a survey showed that 61 percent of the members of black majority churches supported Labour. Again, there was a Christian Forum for Evangelicals operating within the Liberal Democrats. Although the Liberal Democrats, an enlargement of the Liberals through merger with a secession from Labour, sometimes presented themselves as entirely centrist, they tended to vie with Labour for the progressive vote. From 2015 to 2017 their leader, Tim Farron, was an outspoken Evangelical. Harried by the media about his attitude toward homosexuality, he resigned the party leadership, saying

3. Christians on the Left, http://www.christiansontheleft.org.uk/.

he was "torn between living as a faithful Christian and serving as a political leader."[4] His retirement reveals something of the tension experienced by a progressive politician possessing Evangelical convictions, but it is notable that he was still able to set out his personal Christian beliefs in a forceful public lecture to the Liberal Democrat Christian Forum in the following year. So left-of-center politics remained as much an option as a right-of-center stance.

Recent British politics has been complicated by questions related to national identity. The Welsh and Scottish Nationalists became options for Christian political action. The leader of Plaid Cymru, the Welsh national party, from 2000 to 2012 was Ieuan Wyn Jones, a Baptist deacon. Scottish nationalism came to the boil in 2014 in a referendum on whether Scotland should be an independent nation, separating from the United Kingdom. In that year, however, both nationalist parties enjoyed slightly less support among a sample of Evangelicals than in the population at large. The question of whether the United Kingdom should leave the European Union was at issue in another referendum, this time in 2016. Two years previously it had been found that 12 percent of Evangelicals, more than the proportion leaning to the Liberal Democrats, intended to vote for the United Kingdom Independence Party (UKIP), which was leading the campaign against the European Union. Nevertheless, it is likely that Evangelicals tended to prefer the "Remain" option that was defeated. A prominent Evangelical, Sir Fred Catherwood, had served as a member of the European Parliament and for a while was its vice president, and in general Evangelicals did not sympathize with the most potent reason for voting "Leave"—anxiety about immigration. In 2014 only 6 percent of Evangelicals ranked race/immigration as the key national issue, by contrast with 21 percent of the population at large. Thus the Evangelical community, though undoubtedly divided by identity questions, was more inclined to the existing state of affairs than to taking steps into the unknown.

Underlying all the other factors impinging on the role of Evangelicals in British politics was the size of their constituency. Over the course of the twentieth century, unlike in the United States, their numbers shrank so that they became a tiny section of the population. During the 1980s, when the proportion of Evangelicals in the United States was estimated at around 22 percent, the comparable figure for England was a mere 2.8 percent.[5] Thus it was roughly

---

4. "Tim Farron," *Wikipedia*, last edited February 11, 2019, https://en.wikipedia.org/wiki/Tim_Farron.

5. Figures for Scotland and Wales are not available. The English figure rests on the proportion of congregations that professed to be Evangelical, and so includes individu-

eight times more worthwhile in terms of potential votes for American politicians to court Evangelical support than it was for their English counterparts. The far greater integration of Evangelical Christianity in a political party in America is hardly surprising.

The most important findings of this chapter emerge from British party sympathies in the 2010s. At the 2010 general election, 40 percent of Evangelicals supported Conservatives, 29 percent supported Liberal Democrats, and 22 percent supported Labour. Four years later (no more recent figures are available), for the next general election, excluding undecideds, 28 percent of Evangelicals backed Conservatives, 11 percent backed Liberal Democrats, and 31 percent supported Labour. The sets of statistics together reveal two significant contrasts with the United States. First, the Evangelicals of Britain were much less likely than their American counterparts to identify with the party of the Right. In the 1970s in the United States, there had been extensive support for the Democrat Jimmy Carter in an upsurge of progressive evangelical sentiment. The partisan allegiance was soon to be reversed by the rise of the Moral Majority, which backed Ronald Reagan. What happened in Britain can best be understood as a continuation of a similar progressive trajectory into the twenty-first century. The British groups equivalent to the Moral Majority failed to gain mass traction.

Secondly, the Evangelicals of Britain were more volatile than their American contemporaries. Far from being fixed in their partisan loyalties, they were willing to alter their political commitments in large numbers. That was partly because a three-way choice between major parties, sometimes expanded to four (with UKIP) or five (with the nationalists), encouraged transfers of allegiance, whereas the two main American parties remained solid and dominant. With some exceptions, therefore, British Evangelicals became less entrenched in their political partisanship than Americans. Evangelicals of the Left and Evangelicals changing sides were not unusual. It never became axiomatic in Britain that conservatism in theology dictated conservatism in politics.

---

als who might not uphold Evangelical beliefs and excludes nonchurchgoers professing those beliefs. Nevertheless, it is sufficient to show the great difference in numbers between the two lands.

CHAPTER 19

World Cup or World Series?

MARK A. NOLL

George Marsden has used a taxonomic metaphor to explain how "evangelicalism" can be a legitimate categorizing *class* with any number of different "evangelical" *species*. Analogies from sport are similarly helpful for considering evangelicals in the United States and evangelicals throughout the globe.

As the 2018 World Cup of soccer/football played out in Russia, a few Americans could be heard attempting feeble witticisms. "How can it be the *World* Cup without *us*, the US?" But also in a more deferential mood: "Well, as long as the Toronto Blue Jays are still in the league and Major League Baseball continues to benefit from so many Latin American players, we can still call our annual 'fall classic' the *World* Series of baseball!" For consideration of the history and present situation of "evangelicalism," it is good to be reminded, if only from the world of sport, that the United States is not the world.

As documented in this book, uncertainties about American evangelicalism are obvious. Rehearsing the reasons for those uncertainties can summarize primary conclusions of the book but also prepare a way for considering evangelicals in the world at large. As both our historical and contemporary sections have documented, difficulties of one kind or another beset identification of evangelicals today but also connections of today's evangelicals to main movements stretching back into the past.

Focusing on the emphases, beliefs, and characteristics that came to prominence when evangelical movements arose in Britain and her American colonies during the eighteenth century is a well-established approach for histories of evangelicalism. In the present, it still remains intellectually responsible to identify evangelicalism with those who embrace *evangelical* emphases as defined by David Bebbington, the National Association of Evangelicals, or others.

But we have also observed the difficulty of that procedure. Of the 30 percent or so of Americans who now affirm these beliefs, only a small minority use "evangelical" as the favored word to describe themselves. In addition, although this 30 percent includes numerous individuals whom the political media call "white evangelical Protestants," it also includes black Protestants, Hispanic Protestants, quite a few Protestants from denominations not known as evangelical, many Catholics, and even a few Mormons. No institutions, periodicals, or other observable bonds link those together who share evangelical beliefs or characteristics. They do not constitute a movement. They share common networks only partially. The identification of beliefs or emphases makes for a good conceptual category, but it does not help much for describing any united action, identifying any particular organization, or discerning any particular position on social, cultural, artistic, denominational, or political questions.

A second well-tried way is to focus on churches, groups, and people who are associated with the denominations, organizations, and networks that call themselves "evangelical" (or an equivalent term) and who stand self-consciously in the tradition of the eighteenth-century awakenings, the revivals of the nineteenth century, and the conservative Protestant theology of the neo-evangelicals who emerged after World War II. This organized evangelicalism can be identified with specific organizations like Cru (formerly Campus Crusade for Christ), InterVarsity Christian Fellowship, many colleges in the Coalition of Christian Colleges and Universities, the Billy Graham Evangelistic Organization, *Christianity Today*, the National Association of Evangelicals, and denominations like the Evangelical Free Church, the Evangelical Presbyterian Church, and (with some ambiguity) the Southern Baptist Convention.

Again, however, problems bedevil this approach. For one, a sizable minority in these organizations and denominations do not unambiguously affirm what various arbiters define as crucial evangelical beliefs, emphases, or characteristics. Billy Graham, for instance, repeatedly said he would not speculate on the eternal fate of individuals who had never heard of Christ, yet the National Association of Evangelicals defines as an evangelical someone who believes that "*only* [emphasis added] those who trust in Jesus Christ alone . . . receive . . . eternal salvation."[1] In this same regard, many adherents to recognizable evangelical churches practice only a nominal membership or do not fully embrace all that self-described evangelical institutions affirm.

1. For a perceptive discussion of Graham on this question, see Grant Wacker, *America's Pastor: Billy Graham and the Shaping of a Nation* (Cambridge, MA: Harvard University Press, 2014), 200–202.

A larger problem with this second approach leads directly to the crisis explored in this book. Popular media have extrapolated outward from the self-defined evangelical groups to identify a social and political cohort known as "white evangelical Protestants." But that extrapolation has been haphazard, it runs roughshod over first-order religious commitments, and it features a concentration on political and social questions. Yet this categorization—simply "evangelical" or "white evangelical Protestant"—has become ever more firmly fixed in the public mind.

The result is three overlapping constituencies: first, individuals who affirm the basic evangelical beliefs; second, organizations that affirm the beliefs and are known as evangelical (this second group is mostly, but not entirely, white Protestant, and it is not necessarily a coherent political or social force); and, third, individuals who call themselves (or are known to the media as) "white evangelical Protestants" and who may or may not affirm the basic evangelical beliefs.

"Evangelical" as applied to any of these three could work as a definition, if only observers agreed on what they meant when they used the word. But they don't. And there is no power to compel such a regular, consistent use. As a result, to save "evangelicalism" as a meaningful religious designation in the United States, it may be necessary temporarily to shelve the term.

American concerns, however, are not necessarily the world's concerns. If "evangelicalism" is a problematic category in the United States because of long-standing black-white racial divisions and more recent political polarization, what about the rest of the world where American racial history and contemporary American politics are far less salient or in many cases simply irrelevant? David Bebbington's summary of evangelical politics in Britain shows that even a closely parallel society can experience something very different from main American patterns.

Yet when widening consideration to evangelical-like constituencies throughout the world, a different but equally daunting challenge arises: Do not realities of cultural, ethnic, economic, and national diversity create an even more fragmented picture than racial and political divisions have made for the United States? Three recent historical efforts suggest that the answer may be both yes and no. Each of the three acknowledges ambiguities, difficulties, and complexities in any comprehensive definition but nonetheless holds out the possibility that "evangelicalism" may still be a viable designation for an actually existing reality.

Doubts about that possibility emerge prominently in the later stages of a five-volume history of evangelicalism in the English-speaking world that

David Bebbington and I have been privileged to edit.[2] The series traces evangelicalism in the English-speaking world from the eighteenth-century revivals of George Whitefield, John Wesley, and Jonathan Edwards to the end of the twentieth century.

The first three books treat the two centuries from the early revivals when considerable cohesion marked evangelicalism in Britain, North America, and British settler colonies.[3] Linford Fisher has shown that considerable fluidity attended use of the term "evangelical" during those centuries. But it is also clear that, to borrow a metaphor from Molly Worthen, evangelicalism can be viewed as a "shared conversation" sustained across the entire Atlantic region from the early eighteenth century to about 1900.[4] To be sure, those years did witness many internal disagreements, some concerning theology (especially Calvinism versus Arminianism and then the meaning of baptism), others about church order (especially state-church Anglicans and Scottish Presbyterians versus those who believed in the separation of church and state), and still others contending over politics and social reform (with competition among individualistic, voluntary, paternalistic, and government-directed positions).

The sharpest of the internal divisions involved race. When in 1846 representatives to the first transnational Evangelical Alliance gathered in London, they agreed on the authority of the Bible, the life-changing work of the Holy Spirit, the atonement won by Christ on the cross, and more. Yet because these evangelicals disagreed over whether slaveholders could join the Alliance—and because Americans were offended that this issue sidelined their objection to state churches—the Alliance never became a vigorous international organization. In addition, the American Civil War heightened dilemmas for evangelical history created by racial divisions. Immediately after the abolition of slavery, the freedmen and freedwomen poured out of the white-dominated evangelical churches into denominations under their own control. Most maintained evangelical beliefs, but network ties with white evangelicals suffered a breach

---

2. The books were published by Inter-Varsity Press (London) in the United Kingdom and InterVarsity Press (Downers Grove, IL) in the United States.

3. Mark A. Noll, *The Rise of Evangelicalism: The Age of Edwards, Whitefield, and the Wesleys* (2003); John Wolffe, *The Expansion of Evangelicalism: The Age of Wilberforce, More, Chalmers, and Finney* (2006); and David W. Bebbington, *The Dominance of Evangelicalism: The Age of Spurgeon and Moody* (2005).

4. Molly Worthen, "Three Questions That Open Up Evangelicalism," *Faith & Leadership*, July 1, 2013, https://www.faithandleadership.com/molly-worthen-three -questions-open-evangelicalism.

that has continued to this day. The result is a continuing challenge for historical interpretation: Do groups sharing evangelical beliefs but not religious practices, and with few ongoing connections—agreeing on most doctrines but inhabiting divergent cultures—constitute one historical reality or two?

Nevertheless, within limits, evangelicals throughout the period were easily identified by dense networks of preachers, prayer meetings, publishing efforts, and personal witnessing that reached back to the eighteenth-century revivals. Diversity within these networks—over theology, denomination, education, geography, class, and race—constantly affected how evangelicalism was understood or applied. Yet much clearer was what David Bebbington aptly describes as the widespread "dominance of evangelicalism" at the end of the nineteenth century. By that time, significant forces were working to weaken evangelical cohesion, especially the rise of urban industrialization that was pushing traditional evangelical strongholds to the suburbs as well as the tendency of wealthier urban church leaders to modify doctrine under the influence of elite conceptions of science, the ancient world, and the human personality. Yet even stronger were markers of network cohesion. The weekly sermons of Charles Haddon Spurgeon streamed out of London to eager readers throughout the English-speaking world and beyond. D. L. Moody was every bit as popular in England, Scotland, and Canada as he was in the United States. Even with some ambiguity about what the word denoted, evangelical denominational families made up in informal contact what they lacked in formal international organizations. And forms of spirituality responding to the era's Romantic currents (especially Keswick teaching on the higher spiritual life) attracted adherents worldwide.

The last two books in the series, which treat the twentieth century, describe an evangelicalism with many more challenges to coherence.[5] To be sure, the extensive national and international networks forged in earlier decades remained vigorous. R. A. Torrey, one of D. L. Moody's chief lieutenants, traveled literally around the world to promote "true religion" as depending on the active work of the Holy Spirit. John R. Mott's great ecumenical energy culminated in the Edinburgh World Missionary Conference of 1910 that drew together a wide assembly of European and North American evangelists, church planters, and missionary medical and social workers. Amy Semple McPherson

---

5. Geoffrey R. Treloar (Australian College of Theology and University of New South Wales), *The Disruption of Evangelicalism: The Age of Torrey, Mott, McPherson, and Hammond* (2016), and Brian Stanley (University of Edinburgh), *The Global Diffusion of Evangelicalism: The Age of Billy Graham and John Stott* (2013).

became a widely recognized North American phenomenon as she proclaimed a fourfold gospel of healing and redemption, which translated older evangelical emphases into a new Pentecostal form. During the second half of the century, the energetic activities of John Stott and Billy Graham demonstrated the broad, ongoing attraction of traditional evangelical preaching. The multitude of their international connections and their cooperation as key leaders of the 1974 Lausanne International Congress on World Evangelization illustrated the ongoing reality of international evangelicalism.

Yet throughout the past century diversifying forces also intensified. Lausanne 1974 is a good example. While Graham, Stott, and other Western leaders headlined the event, emerging voices like René Padilla and Samuel Escobar stressed Christian responsibility for social development in Latin America and elsewhere in the emerging Majority World much more strongly than white evangelicals had done in twentieth-century Britain or the United States. Earlier, although fundamentalist-modernist controversies had considerably less impact outside the United States than inside, they did jeopardize bonds within the evangelical world at large. The First World War also strained cohesion by intensifying nationalistic commitments, disrupting international communications, and testing resilience in the face of death and destruction. The Depression that followed—and then the Second World War, the Cold War, decolonization, technological innovation, and global economic expansion—brought even greater challenges to local evangelical movements and to efforts at coordinating international efforts.

The rise of Pentecostalism was most important as a new force in the world at large, but the rapid proliferation of Pentecostal movements worldwide also posed a challenge to historical interpretation. Most Pentecostals looked directly to the New Testament as their model for how to live as believers in the present, with a strong emphasis on "sign gifts" like speaking in tongues. This focus meant that links to previous Protestant movements and to other Protestant groups receded. Yet in most cases Pentecostals embraced traditional evangelical emphases in some form, even as they placed new stress on an active Holy Spirit. With the expansion of Pentecostal movements in the second half of the twentieth century, as well as the evolution of some into promoters of the prosperity gospel, the challenges grew for writing about evangelicalism as a connected and cohesive entity. In other words, evangelicalism as defined by active embrace in some combination of the Bebbington characterization was experiencing both centrifugal and centripetal forces.

More recently, the most important new reality has become what Brian Stanley labels "the explosive popular Christianity of the southern hemisphere."[6] Popular forms of Christianity, which are expanding so rapidly and with so many varieties in Africa and Latin America, but also in China and elsewhere, have been stimulated in many ways by older evangelical forces, but they also differ considerably. Their concerns are not the problems of nominal religion, the threat to Christianity of secular materialism, or the management of economic abundance, but rather poverty, disease, oppression, and demonic forces. The gospel fueling the newer Majority World Christianity resembles the message proclaimed by George Whitefield, Charles Haddon Spurgeon, or Billy Graham. Yet cultural contexts now differ considerably from those in which generations of English-speaking evangelicals proclaimed the gospel message. Those differences have led Brian Stanley to ask whether in these newer movements the balance will be tipped away from historical evangelicalism—"a Bible-centered gospel that, while being properly holistic, still holds to the soteriological centrality and ethical normativity of the cross"—in favor of "a form of religious materialism that subordinates the cross to a crude theology of divine blessing reduced to the promise of unlimited health and wealth here and now."[7]

In these circumstances, it might seem that positing a worldwide "evangelicalism" has become even more problematic than discerning a coherent "evangelicalism" in the United States. But not necessarily. Insights from a second recent publication underscore the challenges but nonetheless rise to meet them. In their 2012 book from Cambridge University Press, *A Short History of Global Evangelicalism*, Mark Hutchinson (an Australian) and John Wolffe (from England) set out a definition of evangelicalism with meticulous care. As I tried to explain in the symposium from *Fides et Historia* on David Bebbington's fourfold definition, nominalist-minded historians like myself have little trouble using "evangelical" as an adjective to describe different parts, people, emphases, and practices in the Christian past. But without a continuous history of interwoven organizations and interconnected personnel such as found in Anglo-American Protestantism of the eighteenth through twentieth centuries, we find it harder to see what "evangelicalism" could designate as a worldwide phenomenon.

Hutchinson and Wolffe acknowledge the weight of such nominalist concerns but also maintain that difficulties of a definition are not the same as impossibilities. Their effort, as Linford Fisher noted, is probably the best-ever attempt to define "evangelicalism" as a flexible but still meaningful category.

---

6. Stanley, *Global Diffusion of Evangelicalism*, 247.
7. Stanley, *Global Diffusion of Evangelicalism*, 247.

It includes attention to many attempts, historical and contemporary, at a definition, but then focuses on three: George Marsden's care in distinguishing among different senses of "evangelicalism"; David Bebbington's well-known fourfold rubric; and Stuart Piggin's explication of Spirit (activity of the Holy Spirit), word (primary attention to Scripture), and world (experiential renovation of self and often of society) in his general history of evangelicalism in Australia.[8] While acknowledging the incompatibility of some elements in these three definitions, Hutchinson and Wolffe shrewdly draw distinctions that are worth quoting at length:

> Intelligent analysis of evangelicalism needs to start from the recognition that it is a fluid and diverse phenomenon, with boundaries that cannot be rigidly defined. It is this fluidity that has given it much of its power, even as it contributes to confusion. . . . Rather than articulate and defend a single definitional model, we shall develop an interpretation that draws on all three approaches . . . , as well as on the longer-term historical self-understanding of evangelicals. . . . Although emphasizing that evangelicalism cannot be intellectually or organizationally pigeonholed and circumscribed, we would still emphatically affirm its existence as a meaningful concept, representing a recognizable, self-aware distinct style of Protestantism undergirded by shared convictions and assumptions.[9]

The success of the authors' book depends on their ability to show the thick interrelationships that have characterized this difficult-to-define something as it swings "between its missional, experiential, and doctrinal self-definitional touchpoints as it encounters new situations, negotiating between effectiveness and self-definition."[10]

The challenges faced by even such far-ranging definitions can be illustrated by reference to evangelical movements in India. Early in the twentieth century, Vedanayagam Samuel Azariah, the first Indian to become an Anglican bishop, combined extensive connections with Western evangelical movements and deliberate indigenization of Christianity in his Indian

---

8. Stuart Piggin, *Evangelical Christianity in Australia: Spirit, Word, and World* (Sydney and New York: Oxford University Press, 1996).

9. Mark Hutchinson and John Wolffe, *A Short History of Global Evangelicalism* (New York: Cambridge University Press, 2012), 18, with the fuller consideration of definitions, 1–24.

10. Hutchinson and Wolffe, *A Short History*, 278.

contexts.[11] Azariah, born in 1874 in far southeastern India, was educated at schools established by the Church of England and the Church of Scotland and spent three years at the Madras Christian College where he was introduced to the YMCA and soon became one of India's first full-time Y workers. Throughout his life he was particularly keen that Christian evangelism, education, and economic development break the iron fetters of caste. His work for the YMCA brought him into contact with John R. Mott and other international leaders; with fellow Y worker Sherwood Eddy he translated Charles Finney's *Lectures on Revival* into Tamil. During the first decade of the twentieth century he was also instrumental in founding the Indian Missionary Society of Tinnevelly and the National Missionary Society, the latter under the motto "Indian money, Indian men, and Indian management." In 1909 he was ordained as an Anglican priest and assigned to work in Telugu-speaking Dornakal (located in what is now Andhra Pradesh), where he began his remarkable work of evangelizing, teaching, educating, and empowering the mostly untouchable (or Dalit) and tribal peoples who made up the bulk of Anglican adherents. He was ordained bishop in 1912 after prejudice was overcome in the British Parliament against the idea of an Indian exercising jurisdiction over Britons. Although Azariah maintained international contacts during his more than three decades as bishop, most of his time was spent in traveling ceaselessly through the towns and villages of his diocese, which was larger than all of England. His steady resolve to replace caste civilization with Christian civilization won him some wider respect, but Azariah was also attacked by ardent nationalists when he tempered his own firm nationalism with discriminating praise for the British Raj. The cathedral he built in Dornakal was a stunning architectural mixture of classical Christian and traditional Indian motifs. He died in harness in 1945. Long after Sherwood Eddy abandoned his youthful evangelical faith, he said of the sturdily evangelical Azariah that "he was the greatest man whose life I was ever privileged to share."

Azariah's biography clearly supports the definition of evangelicalism that Hutchinson and Wolffe lay out with meticulous care. His work as YMCA organizer and Anglican bishop featured conversion above all, but also Bible, activism, and the cross; it blended Spirit, word, and world; and it emphasized the missional but without neglecting the experiential and doctrinal. His de-

---

11. My information on Azariah is from Susan Billington Harper, *In the Shadow of the Mahatma: Bishop V. S. Azariah and the Travails of Christianity in British India* (Grand Rapids: Eerdmans, 2000).

parture from life on New Year's Day 1945 illustrated the nature of that evangelicalism, since he succumbed to illness after traveling by bullock cart to confirm
a number of largely illiterate rural villagers who recited their catechism with
songs that Azariah had himself composed.

But now, in a more recent India, where evangelical-like movements have
become more like those described by Brian Stanley, it is more difficult to perceive evangelical coherence. As many writers in the train of Andrew Walls and
Philip Jenkins have been pointing out, the demographic center of evangelical
Christian movements is no longer Anglo-America, but neither is it in one
other place. To focus on India alone—and not to mention China, where the
most recent edition of the reliable *Operation World* records almost as many
evangelicals as in the United States; or Brazil, with as many evangelicals and
charismatics as in the United States; or Nigeria, with more evangelicals than
in all of Europe—is a mistake. We now confront an evangelical world where
the cultural imperatives of the gospel message have only minimal connections
with the evangelical traditions of the West.[12] India is home to at least three
times as many broadly defined evangelicals as found in Canada, New Zealand,
and Australia combined; its evangelical communities are sponsoring almost
as many cross-cultural missionaries as come from the United States. And its
tens of thousands of denominations and parachurch agencies include a large
number that are virtually unconnected to anything Western.

Moreover, demography may not be as influential as culture. In Azariah's
native Tamil Nadu, 10 million or so evangelicals include an increasing number
of Dalits, who risk loss of civil standing and harsh persecution from militant
Hindu factions for confessing the Christian faith. Fewer evangelicals live in
Andhra Pradesh, the state of Azariah's fruitful episcopate, perhaps 3 to 5 million out of nearly 90 million inhabitants. But this state includes the great city
of Hyderabad, a hub at the forefront of India's economic expansion, but now
also home to nearly two hundred Christian organizations. Outside the main
urban centers of Andhra Pradesh, great numbers of Dalits have been converted
to Christianity, but some of them have been reconverted to Hinduism through
the efforts of Hindutva nationalists. In other regions of India, the challenges
facing evangelicals range from establishing a beachhead for churches (Uttar
Pradesh with over 200 million people, among whom perhaps 0.2 to 0.3 percent
are Christians) to surviving in the face of militant persecution (Orissa, where
in 2008 hundreds of churches were destroyed, over one hundred Christians

---

12. Jason Mandryk, *Operation World: The Definitive Prayer Guide to Every Nation*,
7th ed. (Downers Grove, IL: InterVarsity Press, 2010), with 418–53 on India.

were killed, and more than fifty thousand were displaced from their homes) to exploiting a new kind of non-Western Christendom where church membership is more widely spread than in the United States (Nagaland in northeast India, which has a higher percentage of Baptists than Alabama or Mississippi). And throughout India, almost all the dynamic, expanding evangelical churches or movements are Pentecostal in one form or another.

Azariah's India, with its burgeoning evangelical population, was clearly connected to a history stretching back to John Wesley, the Countess of Huntingdon, and William Carey. Yet for many Indian Protestant Christians today, those ties are much less obvious. In addition, Indian evangelicals have never enjoyed anything like the middle-class agency that British and American evangelicals so long took for granted; many of them suffer a level of persecution unknown among white evangelicals in the Anglo-American world; a majority are Dalits or tribal people who have faced generational marginalization worse even than African Americans long endured in the United States, and the intellectual-spiritual challenges faced by Indian evangelicals have almost nothing to do with Catholic Christendom, Protestant confessionalization, the Enlightenment, scientific modernity, and the Western discovery of the individual that accompanied the rise of evangelicalism. V. S. Azariah was himself a bridge—from the evangelical world described so well in Hutchinson and Wolffe's global history to the evangelical world of today and tomorrow that the authors insightfully label "global pilgrim[age]."[13] For pilgrims from everywhere to everywhere, it will be increasingly difficult to write a coherent history or perceive a common meaning for "evangelicalism."

Brian Stiller and his coeditors of the recently published handbook *Evangelicals around the World* laugh, as it were, at the difficulty. As indicated by his blog post included in this book, Stiller is entirely sanguine about the viability of "evangelicalism" as a meaningful category for people, movements, organizations, and institutions that—though marked by extraordinary diversity—are linked by the basic evangelical characteristics. This *Global Handbook for the 21st Century* is a 2015 publication of the World Evangelical Fellowship brought out by Thomas Nelson in Nashville.[14]

On the perennial conundrum of a definition, the *Handbook* does not obsess. Rather than trying to adjudicate this always tricky problem, the book functions as an equal-opportunity enumerator by using definitions supplied by both Gordon-Conwell's World Christian Database and *Oper-*

13. Hutchinson and Wolffe, *A Short History*, 274.
14. For my longer review of this book, see *Books & Culture*, May/June 2016, 18.

ation World.[15] The former uses a definition similar to those that come up with "white evangelicals" in the United States; it counts adherents of evangelical or partially evangelical denominations, many of which have formal or historical connections to Western organizations. The latter employs the strategy of the National Association of Evangelicals' recent polling, which counts as evangelicals those who believe or embrace traditional markers of evangelicalism. With its approach, the database presents a total of about 300 million, while *Operation World* counts about 550 million. By offering results from both of these valuable, carefully specified enumerations but without trying to adjudicate between them, Stiller's *Global Handbook* simply gets on with its task of providing useful information rather than punching the tar baby of definitional precision.

Most of the time this strategy works very well. In Cambodia, for example, churches begun by Christian and Missionary Alliance missionaries were all but wiped out in the genocide orchestrated by Pol Pot in the late 1970s. Remnants of those churches straggled into Thai refugee camps, where they hung on until allowed to return. Shoots from that metaphorical stump have become more than two hundred thousand evangelical-like Cambodians in flourishing churches that also dispatch their own missionaries into unevangelized villages. Cambodian evangelicals also provide the main support for Ratanak International, an NGO founded by Brian McConaghy, a former member of the Royal Canadian Mounted Police, that combats sex trafficking under the leadership of individuals like Reaksa Himm, whose family was killed by the Khmer Rouge but who obtained training as a psychologist in Canada before returning as a missionary to his own native people.

The combination of links to well-recognized Western evangelicals and rooting in local contexts also describes developments in sub-Saharan Africa, yet with even greater diversity. In East Africa, as an example, fifty-three organizations have joined to create the Tanzania Evangelical Fellowship. In Nairobi the African International University—still, to be sure, with some North American faculty—offers doctoral training (Scripture, theology, missions, and Islamic studies) on a Western model but addressing African questions. In Nigeria, the Evangelical Church Winning All (ECWA), an offshoot of the Sudan Interior Mission, now includes over five thousand congregations with 6 million adherents, while sponsoring two seminaries, eight Bible colleges, fifteen theological training centers, four hospitals, one hundred medical clinics, an

15. Gordon-Conwell Resources, accessed February 15, 2019, http://www.gordon conwell.edu/ockenga/research/index.cfm; Mandryk, *Operation World.*

HIV/AIDS ministry team, and a school for nurses and midwives. Connections to a recognized evangelical heritage are looser for the huge variety of rapidly expanding health-and-wealth, charismatic, and Pentecostal churches, but many of these also have some traditional evangelical links or practice a faith with at least some of the traditional evangelical markers.

The angle of vision from which *Evangelicals around the World* was prepared helps explain why it sidesteps American preoccupations. Two of its four editors are Canadians (Brian Stiller, Global Ambassador for the World Evangelical Alliance, and Karen Stiller, who edits the Evangelical Fellowship of Canada's *Faith Alive* magazine). The two other editors are Australian Mark Hutchinson (now dean of the faculty at Alphacrucis College) and an American who studies the majority Christian world (Todd Johnson, director of the Center for the Study of Global Christianity at Gordon-Conwell Theological Seminary). From these positions the editors offer an understanding of world evangelicalism in which Britain and the United States are only part of the story.

As an instance of the book's perspective, John Stott comes up regularly in its pages, but not for his well-known ministry at All Souls Church in London. Instead, it is Stott's leadership in writing the 1974 Lausanne Covenant, which recognized social service as an essential partner of evangelism, and for the philanthropic foundation he established to provide advanced theological education for students from the Global South. In its early phases this Langham Partnership funded students who came to the West for their study, but now it supports more students who receive their advanced training at institutions in their own, non-Western locations.

The book also does good service in advertising the World Evangelical Alliance (WEA) itself. Although the Alliance coordinates the efforts of 150-member organizations in 129 countries, it remains underappreciated in regions like the United States that luxuriate in countless evangelical, evangelical-like, and evangelical-derived organizations. An insightful essay on the history of the WEA by Ian Randall, who before retirement divided his time between Spurgeon's College in London and the Baptist Theological Seminary in Prague, helpfully describes an organization with roots in nineteenth-century pan-evangelical efforts but with a modern structure that emerged after World War II.[16] In typical evangelical fashion, the WEA is a voluntary organization supported only by the good will of its members and friends. It does not, in other words, represent all who might be considered evangelical in the way

---

16. Ian Randall, *Evangelicals around the World*, ed. Brian Stiller et al. (Nashville: Thomas Nelson for the World Evangelical Alliance, 2015), 210–17.

the Vatican functions as an icon of organization for Roman Catholics. Yet in its efforts to link the often strongly individualistic segments of worldwide evangelicalism, the WEA does represent a meaningful reality.

Two important conclusions arise from taking the perspective of the *Global Handbook* seriously. First, for questions about the meaning of "evangelicalism," it is now imperative to consider the entire world. By either of the enumerating strategies mentioned above, more evangelicals now live in Nigeria and Brazil, when taken together, than in the United States. More evangelicals are now found in each of these two countries—and also in each of China, Kenya, South Korea, India, and Indonesia—than in any of the European homelands from which evangelicalism emerged. And today, the most evangelical nations in the world, when measured by proportions of national population, are not the United States, England, Scotland, or Canada—but Vanuatu, Barbados, the Bahamas, Kenya, the Solomon Islands, South Korea, and the Central African Republic.

Second, if observers can accept a certain sloppiness in boundary marking and if coordinated political activity is not their chief criterion, then conceptual similarities focused on religion and connections that are not political define a worldwide phenomenon. Or at least that is the conclusion of the mostly non-American authors who produced *Evangelicals around the World*. Their book is a way of saying—well, we can't give you a uniform, precise definition of "evangelicalism," but you will know it when you see it.

The five-volume InterVarsity Press history of evangelicalism in the English-speaking world, Hutchinson and Wolffe's *Short History of Global Evangelicalism*, and the World Evangelical Alliance's *Global Handbook* all acknowledge the significant challenges in recording the history of a general "evangelicalism." Yet all consider that task at least an ongoing possibility.

*   *   *

And so we come back to connecting written histories of evangelicalism with the endangered status of evangelicalism in the contemporary United States. For that consideration, the difference between "evangelical" and "evangelicalism" may be crucial. Deep confusion in the United States concerning who counts as an "evangelical" is not necessarily the same as confusion about the reality of "evangelicalism."

From the perspective of the World Evangelical Alliance—or George Marsden's taxonomic analysis—or David Bebbington's outline of British evangelicals and politics—it is easier to contextualize current intense disagreements among Americans who once were content to be known as evangelicals, or content not even to worry about what they were called. In fact, intense political disagreement may coexist with the reality of ongoing webs of connections among groups where the Bebbington characteristics are more or less visible (though with extensive variation) or where meaningful similarities of religious faith and practice exist among groups with no visible connections to each other.

Historically considered, it is all too obvious that the religious-political controversies of the American present are the latest chapter in a long evangelical history that includes at least the following: Bible-believing patriots in violent opposition to Bible-believing Loyalists during the American Revolution, black slaves filled with the Holy Spirit alongside white slave owners affirming their absolute trust in the Trinity, converted Confederate and converted Union soldiers killing each other with abandon, dispensationalists and the Reformed and Pentecostals anathematizing one another, indifference to the New Deal with conceptions of FDR as the antichrist, and active support of integration versus active support of the segregationist status quo. Just as historians of American evangelicalism have explained why evangelicals could divide so passionately in theology, ideology, and politics, so have historians of world evangelicalism explained why a myriad of local particularities do not entirely obscure a shared faith.

In the United States, it may be the case that the "e-words" should be put to rest for a season because of their excessive entanglement with national political controversy. But even where "evangelicals" and "evangelicalism" lose their cogency in one location, it does not mean that the words are irrelevant for those with the world in view. By no account does decentering the United States resolve all problems for conceptualizing evangelicalism in general. It might, however, mean that for both the general history of evangelicalism and assessments of the contemporary American situation it would be easier to follow the lead of George Whitefield—immensely significant for the upsurge of evangelical movements in the eighteenth century but also blithely unconcerned with so many matters about which we academics and our cousins in political punditry obsess.

In September 1740, on one of his first trips to New England, the young itinerant was taken to task by his fellow Anglicans among the Boston clergy. They were concerned about Whitefield's willingness to preach in all sorts of churches and to sustain fellowship with Baptists, Presbyterians, Independents, and others whom these leaders did not consider true followers of Jesus because of their faulty forms of church order. Whitefield in reply disagreed: "I saw regenerate souls among the Baptists, among the Presbyterians, among the Independents, and among the Church [i.e., Anglican] folks,—all children of God, and yet all born again in a different way of worship: and who can tell which is the most evangelical?"[17]

What Whitefield "saw" but could evoke more easily than define has spread throughout the world in variations beyond his imagining. Those countless variations, and not the vagaries of American political history, will determine the boundaries, acceptable ambiguities, evolutionary byways, and, indeed, the survival of evangelicalism in the days and years ahead.

17. *George Whitefield's Journals* (London: Banner of Truth, 1960), 458.

Index

Note: Page numbers with "t" and "n" represent tables and notes, respectively.